SIGNIFYING PAIN

SUNY Series in Psychoanalysis and Culture
Harry Sussman, editor

SIGNIFYING PAIN

Constructing and Healing The Self through Writing

JUDITH HARRIS

STATE UNIVERSITY OF NEW YORK PRESS

Published by
State University of New York Press, Albany

For information, address State University of New York Press,
90 State Street, Suite 700, Albany, NY 12207

Production by Marilyn P. Semerad
Marketing by Patrick Durocher

Library of Congress Cataloging-in-Publication Data

Harris, Judith, 1955-
    Signifying Pain: constructing and healing the self through writing / Judith Harris.
        p.cm. — (SUNY series in psychoanalysis and culture)
    Includes bibliographical references and index.
    ISBN 0-7914-5683-8 (alk. paper) — ISBN 0-7914-5684-6 (pbk. : alk.paper)
    1. Creative writing—Therapeutic use—Congresses. I. Title. II. Series.

RC489.W75 H37 2003
615.8'515—dc21
                                                                2002029234

10   9   8   7   6   5   4   3   2   1

For my mother, Dorothy
(from the Latin, Dorothea, from the Greek doron, meaning gift + theos,
meaning god)

CONTENTS

ACKNOWLEDGMENTS

Some of the chapters/pieces have appeared in different forms in the following periodicals and books: *South Atlantic Quarterly, AWP Chronicle, College English, Journal for the Psychoanalysis of Culture and Society, (JPCS), After Confession: Poetry as Autobiography* (Graywolf Press), *MLA's Approaches to Teaching Series: Charlotte Perkins Gilman's* "The Yellow Wallpaper" and *Herland* (Modern Language Association), and *Bright, Unequivocal Eye: Poems, Papers, and Remembrances from the First Jane Kenyon Conference* (Peter Lang Publishers).

My thanks goes out to the writers and educators who have been the guardians of my words, and have generously and most graciously advised me throughout the writing of this project. Their wisdom has been immeasurable: Jeffrey Berman, Elisabeth Young-Bruehl, Stephen Rosenblum, Donald Hall, Mark Bracher, Marshall Alcorn, Peter Caws, Jeanne Gunner, Jonathan Hunt, Martin Gliserman, Denise Knight, Gregson Davis, Kate Sontag, David Graham, Bert Hornback, Michael S. Harper, Pam Presser, Divya Saksena, Jane Vandenburgh, Judith Plotz, Marilyn Penney, James Peltz, Marilyn Semerad, Carolyn Betensky, Connie Shade, Christopher Sten, and my husband, Walter Kravitz.

PREFACE

This collection is about the writing process and about writers who have used their literary expression as a means of signifying their pain and, through that signification, have found a better way to construct and heal themselves. Some of our greatest literature—from Keats's odes to Charlotte Perkins Gilman's "The Yellow Wallpaper" to Sylvia Plath's confessional poetry—have been, in essence, attempts to use literary expression as a form of self-renovation and therapy. Writing through pain is an exigent process, which more often than not, offers profound relief for the writer as well as the larger community. We share a common bond, whether we call it empathy, or compassion, or simple identification with another's radiant sadness. (This book confirms that literature is not merely a systematic discourse, but involves the underwriting of the whole person in all of his or her emotional complexity.)

These chapters deal not only with literary representations of psychic pain, but also with the pedagogical ramifications of using and teaching personal writing in academic classes. Such a prospectus for writing about pain and its therapeutic effects on both the writer and his or her social world involves turning to authoritative critics who have addressed the mutual dependencies of literature and psychoanalysis. Therefore, the works of Freud and Lacan are indispensable to this book, as are the theoretical perspectives of numerous clinicians, critical readers, and teachers of writing. Although I did not intend to unite these chapters, I have found that the authors themselves are linked by their willingness to expose themselves to the disorder of everyday life to make from it some meaningful order in a calculated art form. (And yet it would be naïve not to acknowledge that writing about painful experiences is at least one way of repairing the self by reconstructing personal traumas or crises to better contend with them.) In a post-Freudian age in which the "talking cure" has begotten a "writing cure," more writers analogize personal pain and political horror in an attempt to record and renovate the self through a shared language of suffering.

In accounts by writers, we learn how arduous a task it is to draw strength from introspection and how one must be willing to admit the dark power within that works for good or for ill. This results in alchemy of the deepest and most intense sort—alchemy achieved by the hammering away of the inmost solid block of soul into an airy thinness, a gold vapor. Writer and psychiatrist Kay Redfield Jamison reflects upon suffering the highs and lows of manic-depression in *An Unquiet Mind:* "Having heard so often, and so believably, John Donne's bell tolling softly that 'Thou must die,' one turns more sharply to life, with an immediacy and appreciation that would not otherwise exist."[1]

Indeed, psychic suffering is a heavy burden because it refuses the future, corresponding with stillness at the center of being, although it is a terrible stillness. The literary work is an anti-burden because it is able to traverse boundaries with a weightlessness of the always forward-looking: the word, the melody, and the ineluctable step into air. Language is a body that mourns and is simultaneously mourned; it is what we trust in most, but never completely. Always approximate, language will never quite burn a hole in the cloth; it is only day-heat as opposed to the conflagration of fire. This is a good thing, although it may occur only sporadically, or briefly, for the writer who tries to induce it.

Because psychic affliction often involves a withdrawal from the objects of the world, a dissatisfaction with ordinary things, writing helps writers pay attention to objects outside of their own suffering. Attention dissolves incertitude. The crucial moment is not the moment of insight that comes from the thinker, but from that which is thought about. Contemplating things that offer themselves up to a certain movement of mind, and incantation, can be therapeutic as well as restorative. We say things more than once when we want to keep them alive. A healing process in which the artist's testimony endeavors to reconnect fragments of a patient's buried history will ultimately help to unify the divergent body of literary expression included in "painful" literature.

How literary artists have used painful material raised by the unconscious for more prudent self-comprehension can be instructive to all writers and teachers of writing. Our students are not strangers to painful experiences. Psychoanalytic composition theorist Marian M. MacCurdy quotes the contemporary poet Lucille Clifton talking to a room full of educators and clinicians: "You need to know that every pair of eyes facing you in the classroom has probably seen something that you could not endure" (Pain is a communal experience. One finds its attributes in the solid forms of nature. Like the wind in winter, it leaves its dents in the snow, redistributing its weight, altering us in ways that are identifiable but ungoverned. What we make of pain through our own signatures is what makes pain useful to others.)

Many more shared precepts seem to link the chapters in this book. Both poets and patients in psychoanalysis construct self-descriptive narratives,

narratives that often originate in childhood. Also, because many of the chapters deal with writers who have been in one way or another traumatized or oppressed, it is reasonable to suggest that an issuing of the poetic self (derived from the social realm) is more difficult for the subjugated or politically disenfranchised. Hence the Nobel Prize–winning poet from the West Indies, Derek Walcott, his African-American contemporary Michael S. Harper, and confessional women poets such as Sexton and McCarriston, have a special problem of indirection and difference; they can express themselves only in opposition to (while being subjected by) the hegemonic culture, father, psychiatrist, authority, whose language they must borrow to make themselves not only visible but also understandable. Sylvia Plath, too, appropriates the authoritative language of patriarchy to transform her domestic realm into mythic allegory, capturing the reality of a woman's "imprisonment" to find the best means of liberating her. In doing so, she creates a world within her poetry in which the condition of female wildness and madness, aloof from male governing, becomes acceptable if not desirable.

The writers included here share the desire within each of us to overcome our isolation and to see and be seen by the other in a relation of authentic connectedness. The desire for mutual recognition, as especially expressed by Walcott in *Another Life* is the foundation of our social being and is as fundamental to our sense of who we are. Writers are not only dependent on personal histories, but also on a specific epoch or moment in social history and the legacies of nation and speech. Without such an accounting of collective suffering and endurance, we lose our moral vision and risk slipping into solopsistic relativism. The best writing begins with an inescapable relationship to the universal and society. There is always an eager exchange between internal comprehension and outer phenomena. Balancing this exchange often involved what Coleridge always contended was the test of the imaginative writer's ability—melding together the divisions of our world and our hearts.

Contemporary poetry, particularly under the influence of the modernist poet Robert Lowell's *Life Studies*, derives much of its power and impetus from psychiatric themes incorporated into personal narratives. As Lowell himself demonstrated, one may write privately and intimately and still give resonance to public concerns. Both literature and psychoanalysis can provide insights into human behavior and what structures it, opening up an awareness of what constructs desire in the psychic and political realms of human experience. Understanding that we are often limited in our ability to control some prejudicial conduct or manner, much less correct it, may be the first step in improving our existing social institutions—as well as refining our definitions of work, friendship, and community.

Postmodern challenges to meaning, self-presence, identity, and congruity have cast a skeptical shadow over the very idea of analysis, whether it is psychodynamic or literary, at its core. Is the signifier a historical, eternal event or is the signifier simply what we will it to be? Are we somehow so narcissistically invested in the text that we are unable to read through our own projections and idealizations that tend to conceal the author's meaning or intention?

These writers seem to go beyond that limitation in two important ways. First, they suggest that poets and creative writers move readers because they share and elaborate on unconscious fantasies that would be difficult or dangerous to act out in reality. Second, they depict the mastery or resolution of their own conflicts by making the writing process itself self-unified: joining aspects of the various self, childhood with adulthood, suppression with mastery, victimization with revenge, cruelty with compassion, love with hatred. Although we may agree that the self, as a concept, is fragmented or dislocated, this does not necessarily exclude the fact that this self can speak through a narrative that is revealing of what is most human, even when what is most human is disheartening or disturbing. Poetic or artistic genesis, when infused with melancholic and mercurial moods, can become a powerful crucible for imagination and experience. The limitation of mortality as a borderline between pain and mercy is not only the raw seamwork of anguished writing, but also its suture.

With its emphasis on the unconscious and on what one does not yet know about one's self until it is uttered or written down, psychoanalysis offers a view of the writing subject in process. Rather than seeing the writer as someone who is chameleonlike and changing with each protean discourse he adopts, the more holistic approach of psychoanalysis enables us to view the individual as a core being whose identity is fluid, mercurial, but self-constant. The writer unravels the mystery of being through the drama of writing whether that writing is overtly "imaginative" or frankly testimonial. This process can be an instructive venture within academic writing praxis.

Still, confessional writing, like the psychoanalytic encounter, is a complicated interplay of subject and object positions. From a Lacanian view, any speech act marks a continual dissociation and disunification of integrated identity.[3] The human subject is always contingent, always ontologically insecure. One alternates between the level of emergent ideas and the stepping back in order to observe those ideas, through and for the Other. For Lacan, the function of self-reflection, which he discusses in relation to childhood, is used to "establish a relation between the organism and its reality." Yet reality is not separable from the illusory identifications we impose upon it to make sense of our world. We are seen as we seek to see others: as whole and representative of an identity that is as elusive as any reflection, such as when we peer closely into another person's eyes and see our convex likenesses imprisoned there)

Identity, Lacan suggests, is an infinitely regressive and self-perpetuating mirage, which we base on how we imagine others see us. Hence, we are often at the mercy of outward representations with which we personally identify, yet we are unconscious of doing that. Personal writing can be a means of creating a stable identity and regaining ego strength lost in crisis or infirmity. In Lowell's poem "Thanksgiving's Over,"[4] the narrator, feeling guilt at having his wife committed, recognizes that he is not only complicit in her imprisonment, but that it is his as well. He cannot escape her purview from which he ultimately judges himself:

> And the bars
> Still caged her window—half a foot from mine,
> It mirrored mine:
> My window's window.[5]

Throughout the discussions of these writers, particularly that of Gilman's and Walcott's works, we find similar expressions of confinement—in which inward reflection is the only view outward, and the window or gaze is an endless, but always enclosed, circuit of receding projections. The window only gains its definition as a window through the consciousness of the artist who designates it a *window*, rather than being merely a cut through the wall. For the writer and for the patient, there is always a question of the view of the viewer: the difference between seeing and looking. Seeing a view is always intentional. Consciousness must pierce through the obdurate surface of things as they are, singular and separate, to begin to integrate those dissimilar parts into a unity that means something both to the writer and to his or her reader. It is then that the act of writing—particularly when writing is about pain—can facilitate a careful process of self-construction and renewal.

INTRODUCTION

More than other kinds of writing, confessional writing can broaden the vernacular of human understanding. Readers are moved by the liberation that touches the lives of those people who have endured painful experiences and then had the courage to revisit these experiences. These are not only the voices of suffering, but they are also voices of resistance, reconciliation, and healing. A personal chronicle of survival in writing often mirrors historical chronicles of survival in war or political oppression. In both cases, the survivor is the one who refuses to go away, but is the irrepressible presence who is compelled to witness and tell the story of martyrdom and shame, guilt, and sometimes forgiveness. Although a common response to personal trauma is to banish it from consciousness, certain violations of the social contract, as Judith Herman shows in *Trauma and Recovery*, simply refuse to be buried.

Yet still other occurrences are found in which personal writing is not only testimonial, but also redemptive, as is true for the writer who is contending with a life-threatening illness, chronic depression, or grief over the loss of a loved one. Writing about painful experiences can sustain a life. Even if a personal story only selectively captures what a life has been about, it will never diminish the worth of human striving and feeling. As Caren Buffum, a Philadelphia woman with advanced breast cancer confided online in 1995, "I think there is a comfort in knowing that as I slip closer to the end of my life, it is not growing smaller like a candle burned to the bottom. Writing is more like a road—though traveled upon—which continues to exist behind me."

Writing about painful experiences defends against world-dissolving powers that often accompany trauma, depression, and mourning. When writing is healing, it can intercede for us by demonstrating our strength to confront our own pain without descending directly into the abyss or retreating into lethargy. Writing one's way out of anguish and isolation is only possible when the spirit can exist at the depths of despair and still shape and articulate the words for what arising out of despair is really

1

about. Words can serve to allay anxiety and dread; they can begin to lift the oppressive weight of dolorous moods and infirmity. On fragile wings the monarch butterfly finds leverage in the midst of its migratory climbs. Like the monarch's, the distressed writer's rise to light and stratosphere is through overcoming (its) inertia and gravity. The writer must be opened to vulnerability, to innerness and permeability, to grasp the edge of words, even when that edge is harrowing in its impermanence: hovering between death and life. Why do writers do this? Why do they continue to examine their pain when they are most at risk for more heartbreak in reminiscence? Why do they admit into their own psyches what Gregory Orr calls "the angels" of their own imagining, strange, even torturous angels that are welcomed, even repined, by the writer who allows them to exist? Writers do this because writing saves life in fact and function.

In the recent *New York Times* article "Sustained by Fiction while Facing Life's Facts,"[1] novelist Alice Hoffman explores the transcendent quality of her writing as well as her own conviction to be true to it, even in circumstances that might silence another writer. Hoffman begins her narrative about her personal tragedy with what is not only concrete but also affective: "I was told I had cancer on a blue day in July . . . it was far too gorgeous a day for a tragedy. Roses in full bloom. Bees rumbled by the windowpanes, lazy with pollen and heat."[2]

Hearing the news from her surgeon leaves her bereft, disoriented: "In a single minute, the world as I knew it dropped away from me, leaving me on a cold and distant planet, one where there was no gravity and no oxygen and nothing made sense anymore." Her shock is characteristic of all shock: the body's natural defense of numbing is a protection against a person's feeling more than he or she can bear in a moment of crisis. Writing through and about distress becomes a kind of moral conduct, a sensibility and approach to literary art. Such writing about personal experience translates the physical world into the world of language where there is interplay between disorder and order, wounding and repair. Gradually, fiction and reality can become tangential realms braided together by the sparest of translucent threads. This brings writer and life into some state of equilibrium in which life, even divested of hope, can be sustained by the art that has always informed, if not consecrated, life.

However, confronting one's mortality threatens sensibility itself, a writer's need for adhesion. Hoffman recalls she had spent years as a caretaker for a failing sister-in-law. When tragedy shifts to herself, she is forced to examine herself at the core: "In my experience, ill people become more themselves, as if once the excess was stripped away only the truest core of themselves remained."[3] Asking herself who she is ("Who was I at the bottom of my soul, beneath blood, skin and bones?"), she can reply only,

"More than anything, I was a writer." As a writer, she can transform the facts of her life into the life of her fiction.

Hence her story of a dismal diagnosis on a gorgeous day becomes a story whose ending is still possible. In fictional stories, gorgeous days in nature often suggest goodness and benevolence—stories rarely take such sudden, oxymoronic turns without reason or motive; but life does. At a time in which everything else seems out of control and fate is especially cruel, Hoffman is beset by a desire to get to the end of something, to find out in fiction how her life turns out.

To face life down, writers in the midst of such a crisis draw on a reservoir of stored imagery, especially of nature's noteworthy particulars. Attention to images and objects for their own sake is a palliative for the withdrawal and debilitation that so often occurs in a person who is ill. Whether remembered images are derived from life or from art, they offer an alternate realm of sensual and aesthetic appreciation, a welcome reprieve. As Hoffman writes: "When I was too ill to sit up, I moved a futon in my office and went from desk to bed, back and forth until the line between dreaming and writing was nothing more than a translucent thread."[4]

A writer's homage to fiction as what sustains life, rather than the other way around, is not new. Readers will recognize John Keats and Henry James in Hoffman's claims for the reality of imaginative truths, which are as powerful, if not more powerful, than ordinary states of consciousness. Only art can transcend life by transforming it into something more palpable, more munificent, than it actually is. People undergoing all sorts of sensory deprivations—prisoners, invalids, exiles—use mental imagery to transform the paucity of their circumstances and find some respite in a diminished world. Even in crisis, Hoffman finds writing to be nurturing and maintaining: "I wrote to find beauty and purpose, to see day lilies and swimming pools. . . ."[5] Writing affirms purpose in the everydayness of living. The natural fact is always the adequate symbol for inner states of mind.

In an essay titled "Self-Pity," Carol Frost, like Hoffman, writes about her struggle to write poetry after a battle with breast cancer. She begins by recording a percipient dream in which a wounded deer is chased by black dogs. She tries to remove the arrow from his shoulder, but he falters and dies. His chest turns to a breastplate. His "one powerful arm is covered with pagan signs."[6] Only weeks later, Frost is diagnosed and begins treatment. Reflecting on the symbols of her dream, Frost recalls, "What suppleness of imagination or intuition made me aware of bodily danger?"[7]

Indeed, signs of bodily danger are indecipherable, even in their most cryptic and heretical form. Language is an armor that guards the body; it is also how the body exhibits its distress. At the core of Frost's prophetic dream is her fear of death. As Mark Bracher states, death does not exist for us as a simple given. Perhaps more than any other phenomenon, death is only revealed as signified by the action of other signifiers. It is marked by its lack of a mark. Although death is classified as a noun, the dictionary defines it as a process: an "act" or "manner" of dying, or a state of being dead. Death must remain an act in progress in order to be consistent with its own definition. Otherwise, we are confronted with the inconceivable: the terminus of terminus, the "death of death." Hence, when we refer to death (or to life, for that matter), we refer to what is becoming but never completing itself. This is also the case with language. Because we, as human beings, are able to symbolize, we are able to reconstitute ourselves as the subjects of death. In Frost's dream, an arrow enters the chest of the deer; this is what happened to it. Thus, we can say, death happens to us; we do not happen *to death*.

As Bracher elaborates, "although we have indirect access to real death through empathy with dead or dying creatures, we never *own* death as real; as long as we are alive and experiencing at all, we can only apprehend our own death as Imaginary or Symbolic phenomenon."[8] Like the verb being, nonbeing is something that occurs solely in the register of speech. Speech makes us aware of what is not graspable even as we reach out to grasp it. Contemplating one's own death results in a sudden shifting of perspectives, a lack of grasping, or support, as Frost reflects, after hearing the diagnosis:

> Who was I then? I, who had always had a physical relationship with the world and built my trust on that bedrock felt the ground shifting. I could neither write nor dream—*my thoughts wore a groove, and if I die, and if I die. . . .*[9]

"And if I die" repeats like a broken record. "If" is used to introduce a subjunctive clause—meaning a possibility, condition, or stipulation. "If" is always contingent on a future state of being, which cannot be verified in one's present state of being. Tossed into self-doubt and self-questioning, Frost can no longer spurn the use of the "I" as a legitimate impetus for poetry, but senses she must write not for language but about her life experience within language. Although she was principally a formalist poet who avoided the first-person pronoun because she did not want to indulge in the sentimentality of self-honoring, her illness causes her to move inward and to search for a model poem that successfully universalizes personal grief.

Frost finds that model in poet Walt Whitman's "Hours continuing long," where Whitman's egocentric speaker regards his pain as something that afflicts "other men" as well. The hours of enduring sorrow form a human face; they are not simply the receptacles of hours passed or passing. Pain is an individual experience, but pain is also what we understand about ourselves and through other people with whom we empathize. Characteristically for Whitman, we are all each other's reflections; and yet suffering, like desire, must be modeled on someone else's suffering: "Is there even one like me. . . . Does he see himself reflected in me? In these hours, does he see the face of his hours reflected?"[10]

Whitman's lines resonate with life regardless of the facts of his situation in life. A poet must bring sadness or lament into the reader's heart. Where else does the meaning and value of poetry, if not of all writing, lie but in the reader's ability to embrace the writer's deepest convictions? The reader of Whitman patterns his own suffering after the poet's and more important, on Whitman's convincing claim that he is able to bear it and to feel empathy for others. Writing can be a means of going beyond the limits of the suffering body; indeed, it can provide a protective cuirass for the wounded. With Whitman's poem in the background, as an example of universalized grief, Frost regains her confidence in expressive writing as a healing force. She says that she is no longer deterred by physical limits such as those of the body's, "as if the imagination trusted or could go on without it."[11]

These are extraordinary claims for the therapeutic effects of writing about pain. Without such a belief in language as something that is inseparable from the body, particularly the suffering body, writing would not have its influence or its effect. As Lacan suggests, death is understood through the imaginary register as bodily fragmentation and disintegration; that prospect is what we find most anxiety producing about mutability. The creative writer contends with various types of fragmentation—temporal, intrapersonal, interpersonal, sensory, ontological—and uses associative language to unify disparate experiences. Frost's trust in the imagination as limitless probing is resounded by the Romantic poets, particularly Keats and Shelley. In his own lifetime, Keats tried to address the problem of why human beings suffer and envisioned a dream of paradise on earth, an entwining of the art of fiction and life. For Keats, pleasures enjoyed on earth would be redoubled in heaven according to a higher aesthetic. Hence he wrote, "what the imagination seizes as Beauty must be truth—whether it existed before or not."[12]

Waking up from the dream of life, to the reality of the spirit, Keats proposes a spirit of terrequeous sensations rather than of thoughts. Keats hypothesizes that our happiness on earth would be repeated in a finer tone not only in the Imagination, but also in the hereafter. During our lives on earth we store up a treasure of sensual experiences that will later be "reflected upon" in graver times when we can no longer look outside, but

only within, for solace. This describes Hoffman's sense of writing as a
resource, an imaginary storehouse of intoxicating sensual images, which
will be shored up against life's negation of itself. As Keats discerns in
"Ode to a Nightingale," the human condition is fraught with anxiety,
where "men sit and hear each other groan; / Where palsy shakes a few,
sad, last gray hairs, where youth grows pale, and spectre-thin, and
dies."[13] Sensory pleasure can be revived in the scene of the mind, and the
mind is its own place. Although stricken in body, Hoffman feels "lucky
all the same. . . . Once I got to my desk, once I started writing, I still
believed anything was possible."[14]

Suchlike possibility reverberates in Keats's insistence on seeing
what cannot be seen with the physical eye, but which is fleetingly flashed
across the inner eye in moments of sorrowful self-derision:

> I cannot see what flowers are at my feet,
> Nor what soft incense hangs upon the boughs,
> But, in embalmed darkness, guess each sweet
> Wherewith the seasonable moth endows
> The grass, the thicket, and the fruit-tree wild;[15]

A writer's imagery burgeons forth in rapid succession, reminding the writer
that he or she is too much of a writer to ever desert or be deserted by the
art that has succored life.

The writers discussed in this book seek to validate the human
condition of pain and to reexamine the entire house of literary discourse—what it is and what it does. (My study draws on the idea that
creative writing and therapy are two forms of a single expression with
similar objectives for healing the suffering psyche. Both are labors of a
signifying language of pain) Throughout the history of written and visual representation, the vast majority of books and paintings (particularly
those involving religious themes) have incorporated images that perform
as representations of something else. All such images serve as signs for
the represented subject matter. But the relationship of the image as a sign
to what it signifies is sometimes overlooked. A square topped by two tri-
angles can suggest to a viewer the head of a cat, although the image itself
is not really a cat. On the other hand, more seemingly naturalistic paintings of cats are simulacrums as well and differ from any actual cat—the
image is flat, the fur is only paint, and so forth. Although one image is
more rudimentary and more removed as a "sign" from what it signifies,
it is still a language *signifying* something that can be referred to only by
a symbol, image, or a word. A writer signifies felt experience through a
functional realm of language, bringing disorder into order, inner turmoil
into inner reserve. His or her ability to connect with the world and to

render mental or physical phenomena in appropriate signs is what makes literary expression valuable to others.

"Always in emergencies we invent narratives," said literary critic Anatole Broyard, suffering from a terminal condition. "We describe what is happening, as if to confine the catastrophe. . . . Stories are antibodies against pain and illness. . . ."[16] Stories exist to make order of chaos, to structure and organize experiences into something separate from the events that first induced painful and chaotic emotions. The writing about the innerness of the self is a fundamental gift of the nearly shattered, even stifled, human voice. We all must make sense of sorrow and loss. The key word here is the verb to make, because sorrow and loss are already beyond creation or remedy. In themselves, they have already vanished; as signs, they are only aftermaths, after traces of what they once were. Writing makes these signs sensible or palpable again and significant to others. As Stanley Kunitz once said, "It is the voice of the solitary that makes others less alone."[17]

Although some critical readers abjure the confessional nature of personal writing's "self consciousness" and "exhibitionism," claiming that these characteristics diminish its artistic worth, I argue the opposite. Writers (as disparate in approach as Derek Walcott and Sylvia Plath) have used language to signify psychic pain and have given public voice to their private selves, politicizing the private world of their experiences. In light of postmodernism's inevitable diminishment of the autobiographical center as generative of any text, I begin this book by arguing that all writing emerges from a *person*, and a person's unique and often painful inscription within what may be an otherwise culturally, socially, or even biologically determined language. Only from this point can we even begin to ask the question of how personal, or even "confessional," writing can be therapeutic or to determine whether its therapeutic function actually enhances or undermines its aesthetic value. What are the linkages between the creative writing process and therapeutic catharsis of pain or suffering? When does writing alleviate pain for the writer or for the reader?

The writer's word not only expresses and regulates subjectivity, but also can translate it into values and principles by which other people can live. These values may differ from the ones offered us by the dominant culture, yet that does not make them invalid. Indeed, the lyric poem is an ancient means, like philosophy and religion, of giving people tools to respond to all kinds of crises. The literary work that delves into human emotions has been addressed by every culture and for a number of reasons. Stories, personal testimonies, and poems can bear more hardship than their authors can bear: the word absorbs them. As Gregory Orr writes, "Poetry offers us story, conflict moving toward some kind of resolution."[18]

(Constructing and healing the self is a matter of *using* our own stories to build a sense of who we are, and then using *who* we are in stories as a means of change and possibility) The confessional quality of telling a story is secondary to the primary act of locating moments in life that perfectly symbolize a state of being in which the self is painfully realized in the world.(Because language is always a sign or representation of what is constructing us as much as we construct it, narrative affords us an appreciable distance through which we can measure and commend the strides we have already taken to communicate human feelings.)

Stories begin with the telling; and in times of personal affliction or suffering, when the individual feels most vulnerable due to feelings of shame or guilt, or justifiable anger, "getting a story out" can be restorative and self-therapeutic. Psychoanalysis is a transforming vehicle, empowering survivors of painful experiences to heal and to rectify the errors of the past. In reading confessional works, readers identify with writers who explore the conditions of their own inner anxiety and remorse. Key to reading the works of writers who write specifically about painful experience is the concept of empathy. Even the most intimate pain, when translated into a language, has the capacity to heal, primarily, the individual, and then, secondarily, the larger groups of family, community, and society. As Jeffrey Berman has vividly demonstrated in his own pedagogy and practice in the classroom, when a reader empathizes with a writer's signification of pain or illness, that reader is already a part of the cure.

Despite the fact that the term *empathy* originally derives from nineteenth-century aesthetics, a field from which Keats borrowed it, empathy or *Einfulhlung* (implying a feeling into an object of beauty) was later elaborated on to include the definition of one person's being "in suffering and passion" with another. Empathy is an imaginative identification with something we intuit in another person's psychological experience. This identification then becomes real to us: we feel for ourselves the gloom, silence, or oppression that another person has experienced. In doing so, we find that everything that is strange to them has now become a strange experience for us as well.

Much can be gleaned about a writer's felt experience through the positioning of his or her speaker in the text. My project focuses on specific conditions that encourage writers to express themselves through introspection and refraction. For example, what did Charlotte Perkins Gilman imagine her reader's response would be to a narrative that dramatizes a nervous breakdown? Would a projection of a reader have altered her story—would she have been more concerned with a reader's judgment of her narrator if she removed herself from the narrator's painful situation? Gilman was forthcoming about the therapeutic effects of her writing

"The Yellow Wallpaper," although she knew the subject was controversial. In fact, she encouraged women to do the same: to write through a treacherous condition such as postpartem depression and if it has literary merit all the better for them. But *not* writing was clearly an agitating factor for Gilman as she struggled to remain sane.

Throughout these chapters, I offer different disciplinary perspectives—as a reader, a literary critic, a creative writing teacher—that will eventually bear on my interpretation of these texts as literary performances that somehow serve to assuage a writer's suffering. Any rhetorical performance has a stage, which is the text itself. The actor, or text, is a silent "voice" that mimes emotions, revealing what is often buried, mute, or repressed.

The focus of this book should help us not only to appreciate but also to gain a real understanding of how writers use painful material to produce compelling narratives about their lives. This is particularly prevalent in the English departments, where teachers and students feel equivocal about the disciplinary boundaries that divide literary and political discourse. To some theorists, composition is a bogus field, an "emperor without clothes" masquerading as a genuine discipline. They would argue that the writing process cannot be taught and that rhetorical strategies originating in Aristotle's *Rhetoric* may be copied but not actually "learned." Changing the subject in the composition class means changing not only the subject of "English," but altering a student's subjective views about what a writing class potentially offers.[19] Many cultural theorists following James Berlin want to help students demystify and critique cultural attitudes that are detrimental to their development as human beings and to the development of society as a whole. However, the postmodernist composition program that these theorists advocate—in which political discourse is the primary means of restructuring the student's ideological subjectivity—is too limited. Political discourse can broaden ideological views and seek to emend them, but personal writing is essential to revealing to the student the preclusive libidinal attachments of unexamined personal or political ideology. Personal writing provides the experiential ground for ideological shifts in subjectivity. When the subject of an English class changes from reading works about painful experiences to writing about painful experiences, students inevitably begin to model their own suffering on those of others and gain insights into commonality, even when they come from diverse backgrounds. Students addressing their own experience in personal essays present writing instructors with new challenges.

However, academic resistance to teaching personal writing—as a field in itself—within English departments has been consistent and is a reflector, perhaps, of broader educational, social, and political beliefs.

Political activists in academia have long been critical of personal writing. They argue that one who is unable to discriminate his or her own emotions from a more objective reality will be less inclined to critique or resist the society that has indoctrinated its citizens into a kind of complacency and an unwillingness to promote social change.

Although Berlin argues that this kind of writing can never succeed in changing or criticizing society, one might take pause to consider how the ideology functions within personal narrative. A subject cannot resist ideology if it is itself to be considered to be merely, and no more than a construct of, multiple ideologies external to it and unrecognized by it. People are attached to language in ways that are not strictly political or lexical, but emotional. Words have histories that precede them, especially in literary discourses. How something is "said" changes the meaning of what is said. A student who tries to appropriate a pastiche of authoritative voices from academic discourses to sound "legitimate" is most likely to end up with an unsatisfactory whole. Berman's approach to personal writing in composition classes—the exercising of a voice that is more genuinely authentic—is perhaps more political than overtly "political approaches" to ideologies in college writing classrooms. The "personal voice" always situates itself in the public sphere.

In such a writing course, the public and the private converge in ways that are often so subtle they go unnoticed. A student who is writing from a perspective of felt experience must exert more pressure on that experience to make it communicate something to the reader. When writing deals with a subject that is controversial, or even taboo, the writer has to contend with prohibitions that would stifle it. The need to express pain is often countered by the fear that one's disclosure of painful feelings will be unabsorbed, rejected, invalidated by a community of readers. No single individual lives in a vacuum, yet pain isolates, separates, and often renders invalid the experiencer when the pain challenges authoritative beliefs that structure society. Personal testimony must confront the censors who would deny its veracity and legitimacy; it must find ways to register meanings that make social change possible. What threatens life is also what makes us realize life is worth living.

Indeed, personal writing goes hand in hand with political identification. It is a democratization of writing, which strives to identify its opponents as much as itself. Women's confessional writing, in particular, and literary works sometimes seen as marginal (postcolonial and African-American writing), emerge from the borderlands of our collective vision to make more visible their private outcry as a variable and provocative public art form. What could be more public than the personal testimony of a victim whose "cultivation of the self" sustains her through cancer treatment? What could be more political than Sylvia Plath's intimate wrath in "Daddy," Ginsberg's rage in "Howl," and Blake's sardonic fury in "The Tyger"?

Responding to psychic pain connects the writer to the work in important, even crucial, ways. Personal writing, which is often dismissed as too self-referential, is not just about language or even the manipulation of language in an aesthetic container; it is about how we find our way to utterance. Although Sylvia Plath and Jane Kenyon (a generation behind Plath) were very different writers on the rhetorical scale, although their biographies point to different trajectories of fulfillment, both poets gave voice to the exigency of their own psychic afflictions; both gave voice to excruciating mental anguish. In view of these two poets, one might well wonder: What else can politics be about but the individual psyche? How else can the writer be linked to the work in a manner that is not only authentic but uniquely restorative, writing about why she suffers or what she protests against that causes her to suffer? Poetry, as Keats wrote, should consent to its wish to be not a tradition but a medium. "Poetry should be great and unobtrusive, a thing that enters into one's soul, and does not startle or amaze it with itself but with its subject."[20]

With Keats, poetry is seen as a natural outgrowth of emotions and sensory impressions. Still complications inevitably arise for readers when we are trying to discern a poet's identity from his or her selective use of language. In chapter 5, I maintain that the poet is altered by the voice of the persona and that the voice of poetry is inseparable from the voice of the poet. There is simply no tacit tradition outside of the personality, as Eliot tries to convince us in his essay "Tradition and the Individual Talent." Just as Keats's poetry was informed by his personal tragedy, Eliot is not immune to emotions that rise simultaneously with poetic utterance. Although confessionalists were quick to subvert Eliot's ethics of impersonalism, deliberately forging the link between writing and psychotherapy or self-analysis, they would have stopped short of arguing that virtually all creative writing (dramatic monologue or personal lyric) is in one form or another a kind of talking cure.

Yet I go further, suggesting that a poet's attachment to language is its own excuse for expression. Literature, equipped with its various imprints, cannot be extracted from a writer's desire to describe or represent a coherent self. Analysis is a tool not only for the clinician, but also for a writer. Unconscious expression in art is always subject to an artist's self-evaluation and lexical control. Psychoanalysis, like the creative process, elucidates covert patterns of human behavior and exposes unconscious structures influencing larger systems of family, culture and society. Confessional writing, particularly confessional poetry, and psychoanalysis share a view of language as a fundamental vehicle for disclosing painful memories that are troubling or shameful. Both confessionalism and psychoanalysis focus on arduous or life-altering moments in the past and certain states in need of human sympathy.

I therefore begin this book with the idea that the conjunction between personal and confessional writing and therapy is a significant area of study—writers seek not only to be heard but also to listen. Various writers have documented the importance of writing as emotional catharsis, but there is a need for more study of why and how this happens. Increasingly more writing groups are being formed that focus exclusively on trauma, or on life-altering events. Survivor groups that form to discuss topics dealing with their illness or calamities seem to find relief and clarity by generating the words that lend substance to their painful emotions.

Two important current texts on writing and healing, Louise DeSalvo's *Writing as a Way of Healing* and Charles Anderson and Marian MacCurdy's *Writing and Healing toward an Informed Practice*, prove how much interest there is in writing and its therapeutic effects. DeSalvo resolves that "by engaging in lament, we care for ourselves."[21] As a writer refines a narrative, she refines her own understanding of what is being portrayed, weaving stressful events into the distinctive fabric of one's personality. Building on the studies of James Pennebaker, DeSalvo stipulates that writers must be able to organize and structure experiences that have provoked troubling emotions, to gain qualitative healing effects. Conversely, inhibiting or suppressing painful events and the emotions they provoke may actually lead to or exacerbate mental illness. The act of translating experiences into words forces some kind of structure onto the experiences themselves. However, in addition to any cathartic outreaching of emotions, a writer must develop a critical process of understanding and synthesis. A writer must write in some depth because the more that writing succeeds as narrative—by being detailed, organized, compelling, vivid, and lucid—the more beneficial the effects.

Hence, key to the healing process is linking memory with emotion, allowing the intensity of feelings to emerge at the time an event is reestablished through writing. In this manner, writers "freeze" or stabilize nonverbal encoded images and emotions into the language of processed understanding. According to DeSalvo, however, not all personal writing is healing or assimilating for the psyche; in fact, a writer's merely reporting the facts surrounding a painful event may be more detrimental than beneficial. Recalling a painful event initiates a new linguistic context or perspective. As DeSalvo quotes Mark Doty on the interchangeability of writing and living, "What is healing but a shift in perspective?"[22] When the past is rewritten, it ceases to be past. Writing can actually diminish painful symptoms by providing a new context in which the writer can see himself exerting control over a fear or threat that once seemed unmanageable. The memory of painful or traumatic events has the power to startle and haunt us. Like a mental drawer we may choose to open or shut, it can sometimes open itself without warning.

For DeSalvo such healing shifts in perspective came only when she could write about her troubled childhood. She felt that when she could adequately restore the "moments of being" she had repressed, she could better cope with their residual affects. Shifting perspective can be especially life preserving for writers who have been assailed by feelings of guilt or low self-esteem. Such writing can actually become a form of self-restitution or the "righting of a wrong" for victims of sexual or physical abuse. Overcoming victimization often depends on making external what had been always internalized: bearing the wounds in words.

Writing and Healing toward an Informed Practice is a compilation of pedagogical chapters aimed at the academic community about the potential value of using a therapeutic approach in the classroom. The authors point out that the concept of *trauma* is not only a private experience, but also a collective one. Surely, global catastrophes have haunted the twentieth century and, in one way or another, have touched all of our lives. Atrocities and disorienting upheavals following the Holocaust and nuclear war have produced universal suffering. As Santayana forewarned and Freud concurred, if we choose to forget the past, we are condemned to repeat it—and this is true for both the individual and collective society. Hence we are bound by an imperative need to express, to witness, to tell the story of what it is like to endure. We speak of traumatic events for the sake of others who are also at risk. Vulnerability is not only the flesh bared suddenly and excruciatingly to the elements, but it is also what causes us to bow and seek protection within our own beings. A critical step toward safety and health is an individual's avowing her experience as something with which others can identify. As the authors state:

> As trauma survivors, we share one very important characteristic: we feel powerless, taken over by alien experiences we could not anticipate and did not choose. Healing depends upon gaining control over that which has engulfed us. We cannot go back and change the past . . . .

> Healing, as we understand it . . . is a change from a singular self, frozen in time by a moment of unspeakable experience, to a more fluid, more narratively able, more socially integrated self.[23]

All writing that deals directly with suffering is already meticulously working through it. Failure to work through grief or pain fully only aggravates traumatic reaction. A healing period helps the bereaved or suffering writer recover from the bleakest times and preserve hope for the future. However, such recovery is often complicated by the fact that our culture tends to provide few opportunities for people to express adequately their emotions, especially when their pain implicates others. To reenter the normal course of their lives, people who are in distress or in crisis need the support of a community that will not shun them for exhibiting their intimate feelings. Without such a community, people are reluctant to bear witness to traumatic events, and the grieving process is halted or forestalled.

(In *The Survivor*, a chronicle of the survivor in fiction and his relation to real political events, Terrence Des Pres explains the hesitation of some readers to absorb the truth of another person's pain or persecution.[24]) Some readers, he contends, may even seek to undermine the survivor by pointing to his complicity in the event. This tendency to transfer guilt to the victim impedes a valuable linkage between writer and reader, because, as Des Pres points out, survivors of atrocities such as the Holocaust speak not only for someone, but also to someone, and the response they evoke is integral to the act they perform in testifying.[25] A witness is both sought and shunned; the desire to hear his truth is countered by the need to ignore him. Insofar as we are compelled to resist hearing what threatens our confidence in the affirmative value of life, we may, deliberately or not deliberately, deny the survivor's voice.

Fearing criticism or ostracization by others who do not wish to hear their story of persecution or turmoil, especially when that story implicates society itself, victims often prefer to stay silent.(However, as both Herman and Des Pres argue in their respective books, if victims are silenced, they might end up unintentionally "honoring" the injunctions posed by their perpetrators to dismiss their pain as trivial or insubstantial. Only by telling their stories will victims overturn feelings of shame and helplessness.) To rescind the past, respondents to political oppression or tyranny must reject the societal demand that they remain servile and mute. They must air their grievances to motivate personal and social change.

Because traumatic events are often repressed, they do not fit into the flow and structure of linear time, but can remain imprisoned within the self, leading to psychic fragmentation and disorientation. These are discrete, often inchoate, moments detached from normal events and memory, and they may reemerge at any juncture into consciousness, bringing the entire force of the traumatic or shocking event with them. To write or transmit a forgotten story, a writer must risk the unraveling of chaotic or suddenly grief-stricken emotions of which he or she may only now be conscious. But pain is always mitigated by the act of writing itself, which melds the nonverbal image into a communicating and, therefore, accessible stream of language. This is a necessary step in recovery: the capacity to reconstitute painful experience for someone else so that it can be subsequently processed or assimilated by the still-suffering psyche.

Writing, then, moves the fixed and the permanent event of the past into the ephemeral flow of talk and redefinition. Indeed, a writer can use writing to change the past. Only through the recursive process can we regulate events we imagine we could never control or entirely contain or comprehend. Any sorrow can be borne if it can be made into a story. Strength becomes fortitude while we begin to face what Hoffman called "life's facts." Only language can contain or restore those events; its substance comes from within.

The universality of mortal predicament is what links the writers in this collection. Yet, pain is not the only subject of these works. Mitigating pain is just as important—as is the benediction that occurs between strangers who have crossed the same path and exchanged some sign of greeting or farewell. A historical overview of the importance of confessional writing, which establishes the importance of pain and its signification through the "talking cure", or literary representation, demonstrates how writers are informed by their personal tragedies and the usefulness of psychoanalysis as a means of understanding and remedying pain.

Chapter 1 is an overview of the historical and literary trends that have paired psychoanalysis and literary efforts together and how the dynamics of a talking cure have been translated into writing. Critical analysis helps us to see that writers have, all along, been using their words to assuage psychic pain. This chapter focuses significantly on the confessional movement of the 1950s as well as the theoretical trends—Freudian and Lacanian—that have influenced our understanding of the literary psyche, especially under solemn duress. Chapter 1, on Charlotte Perkins Gilman, explores the full implications of a psychological approach to reading "The Yellow Wallpaper." Although the story is a realistic documentation of mental illness and subsequent breakdown, it defies the authoritative but often destructive aims of the male psychoanalyst. Gilman arms her narrator with the creative ballast of writing as a better cure for hysteria and depression. With the emphasis on women, pain, and psychiatric treatment, I then turn to a discussion of women's confessional writing and its ideological premises. An analysis of various narratives by women writers who have been traumatized or victimized in some way shows how writing can steal male signifying power as well as protest against its suppressive conditions. Key to this section is the idea that the pain expressed in literary evocation has a social and political dimension and that a tense connection exists between private trauma and trauma caused by widespread political oppression. The violation of the human contract happens not only in war crimes but also in everyday households where power struggles are waged.

Part II, which includes chapters on contemporary poets Robert Lowell, Derek Walcott, Michael S. Harper, and Jane Kenyon (all of whom are not strictly classified as "confessional" poets), fully explores various rhetorical means and strategies in which writing becomes therapeutic. Beginning with Lowell in *Life Studies*, poets have exposed the irrationality and madness of the modern age. In this section, I show how a crafted or aesthetically pleasing use of language and literary tradition can present subtle psychological and historical obstacles for a writer who must contend with psychological, biological, and cultural variables that actually work against the creative process.

Part III is devoted to the pedagogical uses of a healing approach to writing, highlighting strategies for teaching writing (creative or compositional) as a facilitator of personal and social change. I conclude with a personal narrative about how my own writing on traumatic subjects has served as an adjunctive therapy to psychiatric treatment. Like all people struggling with crisis, I have sought refuge in those holding places most apt to provide strength or comfort, and I have tested the waters of what writing means when life is stripped down to the meanest essentials of survival. What I have found is what I hope this book will help its readers to find—that language has its own say always—and that just as one might think that the brink has been reached, another word is always offering itself on the horizon. Language is perpetually availing itself to be used and worked through, often pushing us beyond our own comprehension into new knowledge and insights. It is the word that begets its own meaning but only after drawing more words into fresh context, and context, especially when tragedy and comedy meet, is everything.

Writing about personal hardships, turmoil, or trauma is difficult, but often necessary, for healing. The writer fluctuates between embracing the power of emotions that compel the writing, even as a curse, because it fails to forget, and fending it off as a reminder of painful experience. In narratives about personal affliction, a writer may seek, consciously or unconsciously, a rationale for his travail. He might find fault in his own character: a secret sin to which he might attribute current suffering. The search for repentance, even in a world in which God seems to have withdrawn or disappeared, is a means of repairing a temporary breach with faith. The divine power Western civilization has relied on has become reticent; yet God's silence must still be God. Writing itself can provide leverage in assisting a writer to go past suffering to personal reflection, seeking in crisis what lessons can be learned. Writers can retrieve their confidence through the words that contain painful experiences and are, on some fundamental level, like armors, tougher than we are.

PART I

---·--·---

SPEAKING PAIN

Women, Psychoanalysis, and Writing

1

THE HEALING EFFECTS
OF WRITING ABOUT PAIN
Literature and Psychoanalysis

Recalling periods of inner turbulence, plummeting into black moods can be a disquieting, if not distressing, experience. The mind, as Milton observed, "is its own place." But, if biographer Leon Edel is right, pain can also be a powerful catalyst for art: "Within the harmony and beauty of most transcendent art works, I see a particular sadness . . . but it is a sadness that becomes a generating motor, a link in the chain of power that makes the artist persist, even when he has lived an experience, to transform it within his medium."[1] Writing can perhaps help to transform intense psychological pain into a discursive art form that has significance for others and serves to aid or abet their own emotional trials. In recent years, psychoanalytic pedagogy in writing institutions has furthered the effort to use writing as a means of confronting, as Mark Bracher writes, our "deepest, unconscious desires and gratifications" while cultivating, through self-knowledge, a means of intervening in social problems caused by intolerance and prejudice.[2]

The authors I discuss in this book have used their writing as a therapeutic outlet, although that may not have been their intention. Out of a sense of personal tragedy or conflict, these writers have sought a literary representation that would help them to comprehend better their histories from a present perspective. They share a belief in the therapeutic use of "voice" as a means of confessing and confronting present feelings of shame, guilt, loss, grief, or anger. And they deploy the narrative strategy of voice to use human suffering in the hopes of better comprehending it. Writing is more than a defense—an asylum or refuge into which one can withdraw—it is also an armor one puts on to do battle. Coming to voice is not as simple as it sounds; and it is not the same as using voice, vocalizing, or even signifying. Voice, in both the psychoanalytic and literary encounter, is not only a means of expressing one's pain, but it is also a means of repeating painful experiences that cry out for understanding. Freud's observation, that an individual who cannot remember the whole of what is repressed in him or her is obliged to repeat the ordeal as a contemporary event, rather than remembering it as something that belongs exclusively to

19

the past, helps to explain in part why painful experiences are often dramatized in confessional art.

The struggle to remember in order to alleviate the strain of always
having to forget is toilsome for both the patient and the writer. For each,
language is often a labor of unburying the buried. Equally as powerful as
the desire to deny a traumatic experience is the conviction that the denial
does not work. As Judith Herman writes in *Trauma and Recovery*: "Ghosts
come back to haunt. Murder will out. Remembering and telling the truth
about terrible events are prerequisites for the restoration of social order
and the healing of individual victims."[3] Yet, in the protracted effort to
unearth what is hidden, we often experience our psychic pain as a cry of
protest against what or who violated our sense of safety. An anguished
voice remits from a deep and primary source that is not ours, but is, at the
same time, indistinguishable from our own. How can that be? How does
wood burn without becoming fire? How can the voice within ourselves, the
voice of memory or literary evocation, be different and the same as ourselves? Certainly the emphasis on pain and expressing pain connects the
writer to the work in important ways. For these writers, particularly, signification is not just about manipulating language into a poetic or discursive form; it is about how we suffer and how we seek not to suffer. It is
about mitigating pain that cries out across the years for condolence.

Therefore, when I use the verb *to come to* or *to approach* voice, I
am suggesting that already present within a poem or narrative is a language
to be embodied by the suffering self. I am also suggesting that giving voice
to what is not, or will not be, easily uttered is an arduous and sometimes
agonizing process. Speaking the unspeakable, unlocking the door, and
opening the box are all modes of self-disclosure and self-acceptance, as well
as confession. As Freud knew, confession is not the only rhetorical use of
voice in the clinical situation; it is not the only talking cure. There are also
the voices of outrage, confusion, accusation, mourning, and forgiveness.
These are the emerging voices that make personal and confessional writing
a variable and provocative literary form.

Before Freud's time, Keats was already vigilant about examining his
own emotional states and recording them in a prodigious set of journal letters,
which include startling axioms, insights, and propositions. Keats apparently
understood that writing poetry was a painful mode of literal and rhetorical
exchange between what one is and what one wants to be. The signifying self
speaks of its desire to be heard or seen by the reader in a particular light. Even
the painful aspects of the self must be expressed through the language that formulates an individual into a particular and unique being.

However, what distinguishes confessional writing as a kind of talking cure from other modes of poetic discourse is its insistence on speaking

as a means of clearing away repressed or traumatic material. Suffering is a particular system of discourse; if the word that is embedded in emotional pain can be removed from psychic structure then perhaps pain can be carried around by language and finally unburdened. There is something "unspeakable" about psychological trauma that has found its way, in part, into the symptom of the suffering body. If silence is not liberated to speak it can become its own condemnation. Traumatized people are often caught in the double bind of calling attention to the existence of some secret while simultaneously trying to protect themselves by deflecting attention away from it. What results is an inherent appeal to the reader to listen to the emotional tone of a text and to empathize with a speaker's painful experience firsthand.

Such an appeal makes specific demands on a reader. Mental events, associations, or reflections emerging from the past or from fantasy must be translated into words and images a reader can apprehend. Texts themselves cannot communicate pain. Readers respond to writers' pain when they are able to empathize with a narrative's ethos or character, when they are able to assume that a person is behind the writing. But how does the neutrality of a text and its signifiers take on proportionate suffering to engender responsiveness from a reader who is clearly removed from the writer's plight? How does the writer communicate to a reader painful or shocking experiences that the reader would ordinarily want to resist or censor because it makes him uncomfortable?

Keats understood that dramatizing the suffering self demanded of the speaking self a certain bifurcation and self-distancing. And this kind of self-distancing could be, in both clinical and creative circumstances, therapeutic and healing. In fact, Keats foreshadowed many future things, but Keats's project of "Soul-Making" would find its best coordinate in the idea of psychotherapy. Out of deep suffering, a soul is made. In the chapter on Keats, I explore how Keats strategically brings the lost object of the mother back into present awareness so that he can mourn her loss adequately. Continual displacements of suffering and affect into the language of art and therapy eventually empty the hollowness of pain, filling it with something else—the language of surviving, the language of testimony, and critical focus. Not writing can make one an outcast from one's own sense of location, causing further alienation. In one of her sparest poems, Jane Kenyon reveals the analogue of the mind's disaffection from itself:

> A wasp rises to its papery
> nest under the eaves
> where it daubs
>
> at the gray shape,
> but seems unable
> to enter its own house.[4]

Kenyon admired Keats and the way he pursued resolution through the writing of the poem. Indeed, Keats was a confessional writer, just as Wordsworth was. Both Romantic poets made similar claims about the therapeutic uses of poetry as transforming of the self, as a process that could not help but recover and reenact half remembered, half forgotten psychic material. As "Ode to Psyche" shows, Keats used the power of myth and story as means of dramatizing both personal wish and perpetual fulfillment; he used the magical power of the word to "enter his own house." After Keats and Wordsworth, twentieth-century writers continue to use poetry and confessional writing without apology, as both a psychoanalytic tool and powerful creative inducement.

As examples of what is best and most powerfully achieved through confessionalism, I have selected writers who demonstrate an inversion of what some ordinarily think of as the negativity of confessionalism within a dark penumbra of memory's violence. Instead of ending with the inevitability of death or with the internalization of death, which is also the death of speech or protest(these poets end with a reason to speak, agency)They also implicitly challenge the reader to meet the responsibility demanded of him to bear witness. If the community or reader fails to approach the writing with empathy for human frailty, the poem falters in power.

Louise Bogan avowed that self-detachment was necessary to her craft. Still, she understood that the postmodernist poem could not exist outside of the poet's emotional circumference. The poet had to struggle not only with composition, but also with the elements of her own daily life. In *Journey around My Room,* the memoir that includes her struggle with mental illness and hospitalization, Bogan writes:

> The poet represses the outright narrative of his life. He absorbs it, along with life itself. The repressed becomes the poem. Actually, I have written down my experience in the closest detail. But the rough and vulgar facts are not there.[5]

Herein may lie the divide between the shared territory of psychoanalysis and literary genesis. The narrative must alter itself for the sake of precision and effect; it changes according to the fluctuations of its sounds and its principal relation to sense. "One cannot fib; it shows. One cannot manipulate [the poem]; it spoils."[6] The prospect of finding words to express one's deepest, and often most painful, feelings is always threatening. The poet always hesitates for a moment; the way the patient in therapy may hesitate to claim some painful or traumatic experience. According to Bogan, the poet must have an absolute compulsion to bare something so absolute, or else there will be no resolution, no end to the terror. The poem betrays its own silence and is "always the last resort."[7]

The relationship between the literary artist who searches for some intrinsic truth and the psychoanalyst who searches for the same kind of truth has always been a contentious one. Psychoanalytic theory was conceived at the time in which Freud discovered that the power of merely two literary works, *Oedipus Rex* and *Hamlet*, were sufficient for basing his psychiatric theories on. He named the Oedipus complex after the legendary tragic hero.[8]

Freud believed that artists were investigating the same psychic terrain psychoanalysts were and that they were in some ways more forward-reaching in their grasp of human behavior. Although Freud admired artists, he thought their creative natures, which he believed originated in neurosis, compromised their ability to live normal lives. In Freud's judgment, the artist is responsible for creating the art object, but lacks the rationality to properly understand it. Only the psychoanalyst possessed the rational forethought to be able to analyze its meaning. Even so, Freud conceded that creative writers were presaging much of psychoanalytic theory in their exploratory works and that their themes were expressions of conflicts that cut deep into the strata of the collective and individual psyche.

In the 1950s many poets, influenced by Lowell's provocative autobiographical work in prose and poetry, *Life Studies*, *deliberately* began to introduce psychiatric themes into their works. They sought moments in life that were of pain more than of pleasure and saw such moments as epitomes of the general condition of humanity. But more significantly, these poets turned inward to reflect on their own histories, seeking the origins of their mental afflictions in their memories of being shamed or abused. Writing things out, like talking things out, was an alternative to acting on more symptomatic behavior.

But first the poet or writer must confess. The word *confess* is both a noun and a verb, meaning, (1) to acknowledge or disclose one's guilt; (2) to disclose one's sins in search of absolution; or (3) a place or small stall in which one hears confessions, "a confessional." In fact, the words *confessor* and *confesser* are, by definition, interchangeable for there is a mutual identification between the priest who lifts the burden of the "sins" and the sufferer who expels it through a reciprocal relationship of transference and forgiveness. The confessional poet or writer has acquired the power of articulation to amend or confess the past. But "sin" and suffering also may be accompanied by blame. Where does guilt end and suffering begin? How is the intensification of the memory diluted by a conscious awareness that the past is merely a reflection, not an actuality of the present?

Confessionalism derived much of its power and impetus from psychoanalytic theory, although it was always hoisted on the precept that private pain is not the sole province of the individual; it is more than that; it is symptomatic of a larger society. Assuaging painful symptoms through

talking or writing is the fundamental therapeutic precept behind
Freudian psychoanalysis. The "talking cure," as Bertha Pappenheim
(Anna O.) coined the phrase, presumes language's referential power to
represent and dramatize self-identity.[9] As will be seen, many confessional writers who use the writing process as a form or substitution for therapy were themselves patients in analysis. Both processes, psychoanalytic theory and creative writing, are modes of self-examination and self-
description. Both processes involve a painful excavation into the dramatic center of the psyche, the unconscious signs and symbols that construct a person's libidinal responses to language and experience. As
social and political history become increasingly relative to an artist's
subjective response, history becomes more and more an internal process
of autobiography.

In September, 1950, Lowell was treated for depression at the
Payne Whitney Clinic here he was diagnosed with manic-depression. He
began frequent therapy and by the time he left the clinic he had begun to
ask his parents about "the first six or seven years" of his life. By 1953,
Lowell was reading Freud enthusiastically and wrote in a letter to
Elizabeth Hardwick, "I am a slavish convert. . . . I am a walking gold-
mine."[10] Steven Axelrod points out that Lowell's concern with memory
and time is always referring us to the Freudian theory that "self-examination can yield insight which in turn can yield self-transformation, and that
this self-transformation must begin in the past."[11] Lowell's concern with
his family's history or past in Life Studies points like the compass needle
toward the hope that it will expose some deeper insight into inner chaos
and anguish that informed the violence and beauty of his vision.

Life Studies marked a decisive break with the formal verse patterns
and the lavish rhetoric of the early period that had established Lowell as a
leading poet alongside Eliot in the high Modernist mode. Lowell rejected the
Modernist ideal of the authorial impersonality in favor of what seemed at the
time (1959) to be more private and self-revelatory. Lowell's existential
despair was, therefore, bound up with the anguish of his times, and Life
Studies is generally understood as an odyssey through the author's past and
madness-ridden present. At the end of "Skunk Hour," Lowell confronts his
own preposterous position as a poet who must scrape the garbage for subject matter now that the modern condition has crept into lethargy and has
nothing left but stunned anxiety and fear:

> I stand on top of our back steps and breathe the rich air—
> a mother skunk with her column of kittens swills the garbage pail,
> She jabs her wedge-head in a cup
> of sour cream, drops her ostrich tail,
> and will not scare.[12]

The speaker, in mocking self-parody, looks down from his lofty stance to the scavenger who dives, unheeding, for the remains of an empty cup of sour cream. Romanticism is dead; the external world is no longer responsive to the sympathetic imagination; as Frost had so masterfully articulated in "The Oven Bird," "what to make / of such a diminished thing?"[13] The poet has only the contents of his own mind and buries his head like an "ostrich" in the sand. Art is no longer about subjective reflection or inner illumination in an ongoing dialectic between nature and mind. It is not an outward spiraling movement such as Shelley's west wind or Keats's nightingale; nor is it a mode of synthesis or repetition of the infinite "I am" in the finite mind. For Lowell's speaker art is not progressive but regressive, turned inward and encased within itself as a nut within its shrewd shell. Rather than accepting the model of the poet as exquisitely vulnerable and etherealized—a personified transparent eyeball in Emerson's transcendental vista making, Lowell's speaker is debased by the skunk he expects to scare. The odious skunk rattles the mind with its impervious submission; a degraded symbol of modern times.

What the poet has to say about these lines (that they provoke both amusement and defiance) casts an even darker shadow over their pessimism.[14] Lowell's skunks are quixotic and therefore absurd, hence, the ambiguous tone of the lines. They are less affirmative than they are puzzling.

Like Walcott's and Plath's, Lowell's grasp of civilized history is as ineludible as his grasp of his own family history. In the latter, he saw a degenerative strain of mental and physical disease that sullied the family's health and reputation. Aware of the childhood figure as both available and self-affirming in its continuity, Lowell used the child's imagination to reconcile himself with his arduous personal past. Indeed, as Wordsworth intuited, when the child's imagination has been recovered through the adult's revival of the past,—whether to conceal the harsher aspects of reality or to palliate the threat of derangement and morbidity,—it is beneficial. Childhood memory is auspicious as a "gold mine" because it offers the poet a double consciousness—a capacity for overstepping the limits of time and space to take an implausible yet overwhelmingly satisfying omnipotent position: watching himself watching. The poem as such is always self-contained, even confined within the outer orbit of the mind's observation of itself, continually projected and refracted by the reality of things.

Literary critics associate the confessionalist movement with Robert Lowell and the appearance of *Life Studies*, which was grafted on Lowell's puritanical self-examination. Lowell was seeking a way that would bring the reader into his chaotic world and still allow the reader to escape it, as he did, through the various rhetorical strategies he used—including self-derision,

ironic sets of portraiture, and transcendent parody. Seeking to define the
confessional movement and its goals, M. L. Rosenthal stated in 1967:

> The term "confessional poetry" came naturally to my mind when I
> reviewed *Life Studies*, and perhaps it came to the mind of others just as
> naturally. Whoever invented it, it was a term both helpful and too limit-
> ed, and very possibly the conception of a confessional school has by now
> done a certain amount of damage.[15]

Rosenthal's emphasis on the way the term came to mind, as "natural," is revealing. In reviewing *Life Studies*, the critical reader of the
1950s, confronting something so new, must have been left with an impression, even a question, as to why the speaker of the poem is so intent on confiding his most perverse or self-incriminating thoughts and impulses. One
is reminded here of Hawthorne's unforgettable Dimmsdale, excoriating his
sins on the scaffold, while scanning his own oration for the signs of civil
and moral corruption. Lowell "confesses" what he has not perhaps shared
with anyone else, but what he can now reveal to the anonymous reader.
This is the way in which a patient in therapy confides in his psychiatrist,
intentionally searching, through any disclosure, for the causes and motives
behind his guilt, anger, or depression. Lowell, like Berryman after him,
wants both to evoke the immediacy of experience through a persona or
speaker who is willing to speak extemporaneously, however self-degrading
the truth may be, and at the same time, hear those "ravings" of the ostensible madman with the cool detachment of an analyst.

Lowells *Life Studies* forces both poet and reader to reveal the
"content" of the "self," or personality, through its own alienation, giving
way to private insights about one's own banal and even shocking experience. Lowell did not avoid realistic aspects of human nature, including cruelty and ugliness. Instead, he affirmed their validity, as human qualifiers,
worthy of "study" alongside the more acceptable human emotions of
pleasure, delight, and beauty.

Obviously, confession is not "natural" to speech; it is a sustained
and resisted effort toward self-realization and self-acceptance. Lowell's
confessionalism inspired a movement of writers who were willing to see
what was not easily seen or admitted to. However, as Rosenthal concedes,
the word itself, *confessional*, may have carried overcomplicated connotations. Rosenthal had meant it to be descriptive of the character of this kind
of idiosyncratic, personal writing. He did not intend it to become definitive
about its method or worth. Still, the implied analogy between poetry "confession" and religious confession, as Rosenthal implied, is worth exploring.

What aspect unites confession with contrition, "voice" with dramatic situation? Like the Puritan confessor, the confessional poet has no
assistance in the act of confession but bears, as the psychiatric patient does,

self-consciousness alone. Whether he is writing from a Puritan, Catholic, or even an agnostic perspective, Lowell's vision as a patient's is ultimately tragic. His predilection for turbulence, like Plath's and Sexton's, is an indication of the moral ambiguity of a universe from which God and orderliness have already withdrawn.

Following World War II, the otherwise disenfranchised groups in the United States represented by the confessional poets, found "voice" in the context of social liberation. Confessional poets were considered to be antistructural and antielegant, reflecting the alienation many felt as a result of being radically estranged from the leadership to which they were asked to pledge allegiance.[16] In such a climate, more marginalized ethnic groups became "visible." For Lowell, particularly, the dark side of human nature in this period was marked by its banal or thoughtless capacity for evil, particularly prejudicial evil that is arbitrary and sadistic. In "For the Union Dead" the courageous soldiers who fought for a virtuous cause are monuments relegated to "bubbles" in time's "ever steady servility" to the fixed end, which is death, although the cycle of war refuses to end itself. Flux seemed to trouble Lowell, when life is most radically unstable and unconfirmed. Like the banal and quixotic skunks in Lowell's "Skunk Hour," the poet feels existentially bereft. Although there is striving, such striving is absurdly set against the human lovers who become a parody of Keats's lovers signifying mutability on the urn. For Lowell, beauty and truth are not equitable but in contradiction.

Indeed, Lowell wrote a great deal about his conflicts and anxieties surrounding his relationships to loved ones. But what is interesting about Lowell's confessionalism is that the term is almost never applied pejoratively to him, but only to women poets who use poetry as a therapeutic outlet. For example, in the poem, "To Speak of Woe That Is in Marriage,"[17] Lowell speaks through a soured, termagant wife, who both fears and submits to the man who not only betrays her with prostitutes and alcohol, but also with the "meanness" of his lust. Do we condone Lowell's vision of womanhood as tragic, when his dramatic speaker tells us that "Each night now I tie / ten dollars and his car keys to my thigh" just to keep her husband with her, degrading herself under the weight and representative power of a man she disdains?[18] Her attempt to control him by offering sexual favors is paradoxical and self-defeating, because she confesses to the reader that she feels "gored by the climacteric of his want" as he stalls above her "like an elephant." What if a woman had written that poem, deliberately confiding or confessing her own misery, lust, and loneliness all at once?

If a woman, such as Plath or Sexton, or later Olds or McCarriston, had written this poem, the term *confessional* would most likely connote vulnerability, even weakness, or confusion. The wife is self-destructive; yes, but is the fault hers or marriage's? Should we or can we judge? If we do not subject Lowell to the same "moral" interrogations about what and why he confesses a woman's desperate servitude to a man she would otherwise despise, we are already saying something in favor of the speechlessness of women. A woman might confess her ambivalence in therapy or in the confession box; a woman would then be confessing her victimization and her powerlessness. But if a man confesses for her, we often respond with pity. We do not blame the persecutor for her pain; we are most likely to assume something else and remain more conflicted about who is actually culpable. Lowell, like Browning before him, is most interested in his own cruelty and is willing to explore it. Plath or Olds is interested in the cruelty done *to* her, and therefore Plath's or Olds's tone is more conflated with feelings of deep deprivations, disappointments, and the need for justice to help her break out of the molded "cast" society has put her in.

Lowell's *Life Studies* is a series of frozen studies in life. Ironically, the child is better able to portray the corrupting ascendancy of the Lowell family in which nothing is valued that is not temporary, illusory, or hypercritical. The child, in fact, sees more than the adult poet can and becomes a better judge of the events he witnesses. Even if the speaker is the mature poet reminiscing, one sees the child's visualization, as in the unforgettable close to "Sailing Home from Rapallo":

> In the grandiloquent lettering on Mother's coffin,
> Lowell had been misspelled LOVEL.
> The corpse
> was wrapped like *panetone* in Italian tinfoil.[19]

The witnessing child's tainted participation haunts the adult poet. It may be that personal guilt for Lowell is associated with the child's failure to act heroically because to act, rather than to think about acting, is one way of mitigating later guilt and self-retribution for having been passive and uncommitted when the moment was ripe. Lowell's choice to restrain the speaker, rather than to give way to more assertive soliloquy, results in a mute objectivity and a child's stunned horror watching fraudulent characters such as Uncle Devereax destroy themselves. *Life Studies* is a brilliant repertoire of tragic or comic characterizations in a decadent society. The poet himself acts in the role of both confessor and confesser, both patient and analyst, absorbing his own pain in the child speaker and absolving it through the pensive act of verbalizing suffering.

On the other side of the confessional spectrum, Plath's frequently discussed "Daddy" is also a degraded icon in a world that has lost both order and rationality. Another one of the poems collected in *Ariel*, "Mary's Song," seems far removed from the realism of domestic life.[20] Yet with all of its allusionary majesty, this poem suggests that nothing is more universal than the home and family and that a housewife's private experience is the essential foundation for more public structures that tend to confine or minimize women in the household. In religious enactment, Plath attempts to transcend her own circumstances and provide an allegorical or mythic context for human suffering, guilt, and sacrificial hope. Whereas self-victimization and tenuous identification with the exterminated Jews are the ostensible themes of the poem, it is also about the inexorable hardship of mental illness, which Plath struggled with each and every day. The poem begins as an ordinary domestic ritual, which is characteristically punned with double meaning:

> The Sunday lamb cracks in its fat.
> The fat
> Sacrifices its opacity . . .
>
> A window, holy gold.
> The fire makes it precious,
> The same fire
>
> Melting the tallow heretics,
> Ousting the Jews. . . .
> Their thick palls float. . .
>
> Gray birds obsess my heart,
> Mouth-ash, ash of eye.
> They settle. On the high
>
> Precipice
> That emptied one man into space
> The ovens glowed like heavens, incandescent.
>
> It is a heart,
> This holocaust I walk in,
> O golden child the world will kill and eat.[21]

In an astonishingly brief number of strokes, Plath is able to resurrect the martyr, who is not only the lamb, Christ, but also more significantly, the mother, Mary. In an ironic, if not strategic subversion of Lowell's practice of using the private to invoke the public and political implications of suffering, Plath immediately invests the mythic with the personal. We suffer individually, and we suffer in imitation of Christ's martyrdom (or "mar[t]yrdom"). The frying of the Sunday lamb is a primitive symbol of the passive slaughter of the purely good and innocent—the soul that escapes the putrid body that, as Plath writes, "cracks in its fat" and "sacrifices its opacity." From the sacrificial and domestic, Plath deepens her vision toward the demonic: "The burning of the sun" is immediately linked with the burning of heretics on the cross and with the "ousting of the Jews."

The sun (or son's) burning is synonymous and simultaneous with the martyrdom of other tortured souls who represent the lamb, the child, and the innocent all merging within one "vaporous cloud" the steam or essence of the body that will not expire. The tortured soul will not die, but only land on the precipice as far as man has ventured into space. The man-made modern "ovens" that cremated the Jews "glowed like heavens," a harsh betrayal and deception on God's part for initially letting loose evil in the world. Civilization has not spared the lamb, but invented a savage evil to destroy it, as a carnivorous fire burns the meat. The speaker is then haunted by the ashes that seem to fly like gray birds unable to pass into paradise, becoming old tokens of the light of belief that was doused and charred within the Jewish souls that were incinerated. Hence, what is left to this woman is a vision of a universe of torrid destruction equitable with her own mental anguish. She confesses to a heart that is equally cruel, suffering and dangerous because it is a heart that torments her. This is the poet's most difficult part of confession: showing her human guilt for the genocide of the innocent, "the golden child" that the world (not she) kills and eats.

From a Christian standpoint, humanity has destroyed its own opportunity for salvation, and the poem suggests that this is already determined by the inevitability of an evil predicated on the vulnerability of the "meek and the mild," the victim, the subjugated. Plath's horror eats at the heart, as the fire consumes its victims. In the final lines, Plath clearly hurls blame at the world for her own suffering. The heart, turned against itself as an agent of blame rather than forgiveness, may itself be cruel and self-destroying as a holocaust. The indeterminacy of where blame ends, where self-pity begins, and where expiation or forgiveness is asked for is the crux of "Mary's Song." Self-pity is not to be confused with self-indulgence here, but is part and parcel with the divided self who both confesses and then forgives and embraces; it too can be seen as a personal process that has its correlative in the outer world.

All poetry, whether confessional, lyric, or narrative, is a mode of self-dramatization or the talking of a self into being. Psychoanalysis and confessional writing are unique in that both practices deliberately and self-consciously involve the surfacing of painful or traumatic memories. In fact, poetry pedagogy has followed the techniques and strategies of psycho-analysis in an effort to locate what is arguably the most powerful locus of the psyche—the unconscious. But there is always resistance to the unbar-ring of unconscious memories because this is why memories are repressed in the first place. Freud's intuition told him quite early in his career that the conscious mind seeks to deny the unbearable wound that cannot be admit-ted into consciousness. It splits off into a bodily sign, a physical symptom, a hemorrhaging, what might be said to be a "scarlet" letter of the text. The poetic text is comparable to various metaphorical substitutions: Gilman's wallpaper, Browning's lover's mask, St. John's yellow gloves, Plath's plaster cast—each one the outer wrapping or container of inner psychic space.

Psychoanalysis, like poetry, breaks through this resistance through dramatic language. Freudian analysis, too, encourages a patient to reexperience some portion of the forgotten life, and, at the same time, to retain a present perspective. He must realize that "in spite of everything", anxiety is often a reflection of a forgotten past. In both cases, the patient, or author, simply by virtue of having to use language, is often split between being a participant and an observer. But once the trauma is reenacted, it must be displaced, dispensed, or put away into a pattern such as language, or put back into the larger pattern of an identity theme. Like the narrator in "The Yellow Wallpaper," the patient/poet continually has to look backward to make sense of the entire pattern; therefore she is never where her subjectivity is centered, but always at one remove.

Over the years, I have been writing about poets and writers who have deliberately used psychoanalytic processes to mine the unconscious and disclose certain truths about the psyche. I would predict, as most readers would, that these writers' accounts of traumatic experiences have also been therapeutic. Victims and survivors of political oppression or domestic abuse exorcise their pain through art, confession, or testimony. Because art demands a certain amount of detachment (even if this detachment is subordinated to the exigency of communicating something meaningful in the rendering of qualitative elements), artistic activity perhaps accelerates the therapeutic process. A painter or poet understands that a "disinterestedness" weighs on the principles and determinants of her art. Materials of expression must be molded to achieve a particular effect. This investment in the larger principles of the art, as a product as well as a process enables the writer or artist to step back from the traumatic event before being able to depict it. Indeed, a relief exists concomitant with unburdening one's self to an/other, even when that process is seemingly outside conscious apprehension. Transferring pain, with the belief that an objective observer, analyst, or reader can shoulder pain, seems very much at the heart of these writings.

Both psychoanalysis and literature are interested in the therapeutic process of bringing disorder into order, the chaos of the inner self into control and coherence. Language is the medium that mirrors the struggle, and the interplay between subjectivity and objectivity. In language and articulation, the introspective writer explores the complex relation of knowing and not knowing, the point in perception in which sometimes, tragically, knowing and not knowing meet. Trauma, unlike anxiety, presupposes that the psychic wounding happened unexpectedly, by surprise, that the threat to one's existence was so overwhelming that it could not be fully absorbed by consciousness. Therefore actual experience associated with pain enters a liminal realm in which it is both acknowledged and unacknowledged. (Like the word itself, the representation, or signification of pain, is always beckoning toward what is inexpressible, except through the body.) Some people are compelled to repeat what is most painful, and, yet, what is not remembered.

This conflict between the will to deny what has happened and the will to speak it aloud is the central dialectic of trauma. Victims who speak about trauma often do so in a fragmented, emotionalized discourse, which may seem to undermine their credibility; they may seem contradictorily dispassionate or even numbed. But victims who do *not* speak, who repress the trauma to protect themselves, the perpetrator, or both, may often suffer somatic symptoms in which the verbal narrative is displaced to the suffering of the body. This was the phenomenon that so baffled and compelled early psychoanalysts such as Charcot and Freud to decipher the body's language of pain from the signifying symptom of hysteria in women patients.

Although a patient's or writer's trauma may be forgotten, recurring patterns of behavior suggest that catastrophic events seem to repeat themselves for those who have passed through them. But why does this happen? Perhaps the pattern is perpetuated because the afflicted psyche does not remember the pain and can only reproduce it as something seemingly disconnected but, as we shall soon see, actually deeply connected with the early event. The cry is always only on the verge of speaking, because it is not the wounding but the reply to shock. Hence trauma is always belated rather than immediate: one feels the shock of pain after the delivery of the blow. It is in that moment, between the impact and the response, that Freud imagines a body is able to defend itself by forgetting, by denying what has come to pass. As Freud writes in his early *Preliminary Communication* with Breuer :

> But the causal relation between the determining psychical trauma and the hysterical phenomenon is not of a kind implying that the trauma merely acts like an agent provocateur in releasing the symptom, which leads to an independent existence. We must presume that the psychical trauma—or more precisely the memory of the trauma—acts like a foreign body which long after its entry must continue to be regarded as an agent still at work. . . .[22]

What cannot be remembered will be repeated in various ways through different reissues of associated thoughts, actions, and inclinations. The memory of trauma is something ingrained in the psyche and can be brought to the surface only through abreaction of that trauma in which painful affect is "put into words."

When regarding trauma, Freud finds the universal in the idiosyncratic, the mythic in the mortal. In his reading of *Gerusalemme Liberata*, which Caruth cites so artfully in *Unclaimed Territory*, Freud explains that the hero, Tancred, unwittingly slays his beloved (who had been disguised in the armor of an enemy knight).[23] After her burial, he finds himself in a strange forest where he slashes his sword at a tree, but blood streams from the cut. Then, the voice of his beloved, her soul imprisoned in the tree, is heard complaining that he has wounded her yet again.

Freud calls this "moving" and symbolic. He intuited that Tancred's trauma repeats itself through the unknowing acts of this survivor and against his very will. The trauma, however horrible, cannot be left behind because consciousness would not allow it. A voice is released through the wound, and this voice witnesses a truth it would rather resist. Hence as both patient and creative writer turn back to memory to hear the unbearable voice of the past, they are compelled to tell the story of what happened. This story can be told only from the perspective of the one who has already survived the wound, but it will have meaning for others. In trauma, the ego is breached; and this piercing of the stimulus barrier is also a sudden separation from relatedness, a frightening and isolating experience.

Critics, literary and psychoanalytic, including Judith Herman, Shoshana Felman, Jeffrey Berman, and Cathy Caruth, have explored the linkages between literary expression and psychoanalytic theory. These critics have demonstrated the therapeutic advantages of giving testimony to personal and often painful experience, and they have not avoided the controversies surrounding private and political testimonies that have found their most powerful expression in literature. Elisabeth Young-Bruehl and Faith Bethelard have offered a new way of thinking about familiar concepts such as love and attachment, showing us how cherishment (amae) is really the emotional bedrock of adult relationships, formed in childhood, and without which individuals are susceptible to profound feelings of deprivation, anger, and a lack of relation to others.[24]

Postmodernism invites us to deconstruct the idea of a unified, emergent self, not so much because the poet's self is conceived of as a mosaic of fragmented signifiers, but because the subjectivity of the poet is always darting out and into the position of the Other. The writer's self-description cannot stay impervious to outside influences. A writer, like a patient in psychoanalysis, who is aware of exposing raw material in the form of dreams, associations, or even confessions, knows that whatever she has to say, however upsetting or shocking, is always dependent on a listener's readiness to hear it.

Too close a knowledge of vulnerability, of human insufficiency, is thought to be ruinous.[25] Silence may seem an appropriate response to the "unspeakable," but when it deliberately censors or prohibits expression, it can only be detrimental to well being. A text is always its own silence, which is its world, until the spell is broken by the literal sound of the turning page. The writer, like the patient, must speak through the text not only to summon pain, but also to grant it absolution. Writing about suffering is a complex private and social act. For when testimony enters public consciousness, seeking to modify the moral order to which it appeals, it has implicit value. Confessional poets such as Lowell and Plath felt the urgency to record their personal anguish, not to perpetuate self-pity, but to bring pity into human consciousness, eliciting in the reader deep and comprehensive emotions that could be brought about only through human identifications. Writing also assuages grief by giving the writer a reprieve from inexorable suffering in isolation or silence. In his book-length elegy for his wife, Jane Kenyon, American poet and critic Donald Hall recalls his years of matrimony: "Remembered happiness is agony; so is remembered agony."[26]

Although sadness, characterized by flatness of mood and decreased energy, is a normal response to certain events or crises in life (such as the death of a loved one), depression is unrelenting in its misery; it is an illness. Mania and melancholia have often haunted the artist, subjecting him or her to exhilarating highs and, then, catastrophic depression. In Dürer's *Melencholia*, the angel, in buckling gown, broods under the blazing dark star of Saturn, while a tiny Eros sleeps. Her tools are scattered everywhere in disarray, disuse.[27] In melancholy, faith is broken, the spirit dejected. Depression compels us to view a more fleeting reality, nature at its decaying core, the diminishment of energy to alter things. (As Jamison reveals in her stunning memoir, depression turns us inward, decelerates us; pleasure is scorched and all but annulled. And yet, self-absorption can work to a patient's benefit, leading him or her to tap into emotional tarn and find access to the unconscious.)

A life subject to erratic mood swings is, no doubt, a difficult life. Many acclaimed artists and writers have been diagnosed with manic-depressive illness, or bipolar disorder, a subject literary critics have only recently addressed. They have been reluctant to comment on the significant role mental illness and its various clinical and chemical treatments has played in writers' lives and careers. Jamison, who has written on the biochemical data supporting a causal link between manic-depression and creativity, has described the alternation of dark and light moods as the "dangerous crackling together of black moods and high passions."[28]

Kenyon's poetry deals starkly and directly with the subject of mental illness, perhaps more directly than any poet after Lowell, Sexton, and Plath. She was widely acclaimed as one of the finest poets writing in the United States. In the years between 1978 and her death from leukemia at forty-seven in 1995, she published four books of poetry including *Otherwise: New and Selected Poems*. Her death is one of greatest tragedies in American letters, and her central importance to the twentieth canon is undisputed among critics. An avid reader of Keats's, Kenyon saw nature through his tragic vision—although she was realist at heart and did not reach beyond what would in its economy and precision offer itself to the poem. In moments of unmovable despair and anguish, Kenyon grasped for the smallest solaces in life. After great struggle, there are always sacramental moments in her poetry unlike any other poet's, in which mercy is fierce, but bitterness is undone. When silence comes at the end of a Kenyon poem, there is no other sound but the poem still breathing.

In "Having It Out with Melancholy," (an obvious allusion to Keats's "Ode to Melancholy") Kenyon reaches down into the origins of her invisible incubus, Melancholy, who holds her captive in darkness. She has known her torturer since birth: "the anti-urge," the "mutilator of souls," "bile of desolation," the one who crucifies her, and chars her from within like "a piece of burned meat."[29] At the same time, she is resigned to the fact that Melancholy has given her added precipitance: a more profound appreciation for a world as savagely divided, and as indeterminate as the mind is, when it is tormented by periods of morbidity and welcome hiatus. When antidepressive medications set in, "stopping the pain abruptly," the poet is astonished by the fact she has forgotten what the hurt was, because she no longer hurts, and pain is not memorable. Stepping out of herself, she is graced with a renewed interest in objects and notes a bird "with its small, swiftly beating heart, singing in the great maples, with its bright, unequivocal eye."[30] The bird's eye is not mercurial, but absolute. Unclouded by bias, untouched by tremor of mania, or terror of depression, the bird sings in its strange certitude, an emblem of equanimity. Its redemptive power is in the affirmative, restoring and recreating hope out of an inherent sadness that is suddenly, and inexplicably, made bearable.

In a like manner, Jamison, coming to terms with a suicidal depression, finds a sanctuary from the mental sea, a breakwater wall filtering in just enough light and vitality to balance perilously dark, stagnant periods:

> We all build internal sea walls to keep at bay the sadnesses of life and the often overwhelming forces within our minds. . . . One of the most difficult problems is to construct these barriers of such a height and strength that one has a true harbor, a sanctuary away from crippling turmoil and pain, yet low enough, and permeable enough, to let in fresh seawater that will fend off the inevitable inclination towards brackishness.[31]

The belief that art helps to heal the artist and subsequently helps heal others is an ancient one—and in many instances writers and artists have found salvation and sanctuary in writing. Sexton declared, "Poetry led me by the hand out of madness," suggesting that pain, if not elided, is a curse, an original sin, but it is also an innocent's punishment, and therefore worthy of study. Sexton described, however ambivalently, the importance of using pain in her work: "I, myself, alternate between hiding behind my own hands, protecting myself any way possible, and this other this seeing ouching other. I guess I mean that creative people must not avoid the pain they get dealt with. . . . Hurt must be examined like a plague. . . . "[32]

Writers who write about states of mind, as well as being, do not avoid their own pain, but seek to signify it for others, as they do for themselves, and survive it. Inspired by saturnine states, these writers cast their shadows over the images of things and form a kind of dark tide. In that "awful rowing towards God," Sexton speaks as a woman who has had to come to terms with desperate hopelessness and death, even finding a tremendous resource in them: "Depression is boring, I think / and I would do better to make / some soup and light up the cave."[33]

2

VIOLATING THE SANCTUARY/ASYLUM

Freudian Treatment of Hysteria in "Dora" and "The Yellow Wallpaper"

In her chapter "Writing the Wounded Psyche," Louise DeSalvo cites several female writers who offer testimony how writing about their emotional problems became for them a vital form of self-nurturing. Healing through writing is a matter of *using* anguish and hardship to augment one's understanding. The willingness to examine and to dramatize the dismal periods of one's life can be "terrifically humanizing." If female writers fail to possess the restorative power of narrative, they may be forever trapped in bodies that remain signifiers of subjection and despair.

In 1913, Charlotte Perkins Gilman published an article in *The Forerunner* about why she had written "The Yellow Wallpaper." She attributed it to her own "severe and continuous nervous breakdown tending to melancholia—and beyond." After three years she consulted Dr. S. Weir Mitchell, a Philadelphia neurologist, who advocated an outpatient remedy for neurasthenic women that included isolation, bed rest, force-feeding, and massage, plus the injunction to "live as domestic a life as possible and never to touch pen, brush, or pencil as long as you live."[1] Mitchell's rest cure was a method of enforced inactivity, a bitter medicine of boredom and lethargy, one from which a woman would be grateful to be released once the doctor issued the proper mandate. The regimen was designed to mollify the patient to bring about a physical and emotional regression to infancy.

In her article, Gilman recalls that she returned home and followed Mitchell's directions faithfully, but in doing so, "nearly lost [her] mind."[2] "The Yellow Wallpaper" is a description of the nervous breakdown, which begins as Gilman's did but ends with the result of progressive insanity. Confined to a nursery in a country estate where her husband, John, a physician, tends to her, the narrator's perception of the nursery slowly changes. Through an optical illusion, the narrator invents a frightening phantasm of a woman moving behind the wallpaper. This self-projection, a personification of the narrator's rage and vexation, simultaneously trying to force its way *out* of the paper and *into* the child's room, finally enlists the aid of the narrator, who attempts to peel back the wallpaper in a frantic, but literal, attempt to unfetter it.

Gilman's "The Yellow Wallpaper" is on one level a defiant response to Mitchell's rest cure and what it meant for women of her social background and education. But the narrative is on another level Gilman's resistive response to the psychiatrist's violations of her personal boundaries as a woman and as a writer. Years after her unsuccessful analysis, Gilman indicted Freud for a number of offenses ranging from the violation of the human spirit to an unnatural emphasis on sex.[3] Gilman's debilitated narrator in "The Yellow Wallpaper," already on the verge of helpless resignation to Mitchell's unrestful rest cure, asks, "And what can one do?" The condition itself was so enervating, so lacerating, that the hysterical patient had no option but to rely on the care of those people she feared or distrusted.

After three months of being forbidden to write, Gilman came "so near to the borderline of mental ruin that [she] could not see over."[3] Going against Mitchell's regimen, she decided to write again. "Work, the normal life of every human being; work, which is joy and growth and service without which one is a parasite" rewarded her with sanity and equilibrium. Through introspection she learned that her mental illness was caused in part by her childhood and in part by her miscarriage. She believed she was temperamentally ill suited for the monotony of marriage and motherhood.

Through writing, Gilman's spirits revived. Writing became for her a means of repairing early damage to the self and mastering trauma without requiring a psychiatrist's intervention or treatment. Contrary to Mitchell's belief, Gilman proposed that depression and hysteria were not caused by writing, but by not writing. Writing offered an outlet for feelings she could not express in the real world, but feelings, nevertheless, that she felt had to be vented to promote healing. Gilman believed that other women had much to learn from her experience. She stated that she wrote her story about "going crazy" to save other people from being driven crazy (by their doctors), and it worked. Ann Lane, Gilman's biographer, argues that Gilman wrote not only to rescue her own sanity, but also to find in writing a creative release for her unconscious motivations and feelings. In doing so, she was able to purge the demons that terrified her and to achieve some control over her illness.

Freudian psychoanalysis provides a crucial framework for understanding the narrator's plight in "The Yellow Wallpaper." Mitchell's rest cure obviously worked on the symptoms of mental illness, but it could lead only to a patient's temporary improvement. It was not psychotherapy. No effort was made to probe the dynamics of mental illness or its causes. Although Mitchell's rest cure coincided exactly with Anna O.'s talking cure, Freud's major discoveries were still several years away. According to Berman, Mitchell's views on women were always objectionable. The psychiatrist considered women to be patently inferior, objects to be coddled and condescended to. In fact, Mitchell took serious umbrage with his female patients' intellectual curiosity about their own histories in his treatise *Doctor and Patient*: "The wisest ask the fewest questions. The terrible patients are nervous women with long memories, who question much where answers are difficult. . . ."[4] Gilman, we may assume, had a long memory. Although Freudian psychoanalysis improved on Mitchell's limited view, expanding the meaning and function of psychotherapy, Gilman continued to blame Freud and his followers for the moral and ethical error of violating a patient's privacy, a violation that may well have reminded her of her unfortunate experience with Mitchell and the notorious rest cure.

At roughly the same time Mitchell was practicing in the United States, Freud, in Vienna, was deeply immersed in psychoanalysis. He wanted to alleviate the distress and suffering of his patients who were experiencing symptoms that made it impossible for them to live their lives pleasurably or productively. However, we must recognize that psychoanalysis itself, even as Freud practiced it, as a beneficial cure for psychological conditions, is an abreaction of trauma in the interest of undoing trauma itself. The process of recovering a patient's trauma uses several known methods including hypnosis, free association, and the flooding of memories. Gilman's "The Yellow Wallpaper" is an extraordinary document that wrests power from trauma and from the trauma of psychoanalytic treatment.

Psychotherapy began with Freud's treatment of Anna O., a twenty-one-year-old patient of Josef Breuer's who presented a veritable museum of symptoms: paralysis, hallucinations, a second personality that lived exactly one year in the past, nervous coughing, sleepwalking, and speech disorders. Breuer had Anna O. relive each previous occurrence of a symptom in reverse chronological order through hypnosis, which enabled her to release negative emotions that she had not expressed at the time and helped in the catharsis and relief of her symptoms. Unfortunately, Breuer's absorption in Anna O. caused his wife to become jealous, and he was forced to drop the case to avoid embarrassment. Still, he had successfully proven through the case study that the forces behind psychogenic symptoms were largely unconscious and could be brought to light in words and ideas alone.

Freud was impressed by Breuer's findings and moved to help liberate unconscious material to consciousness through a talking method that would enable the patient to achieve an intellectual and emotional understanding about such unresolved issues. Because Freud believed that the origin of neurosis was rooted in childhood, he sought to bring about psychic regression. Such therapeutic regression is affected by carefully applied frustration with the psychoanalyst remaining silent for considerable periods of time. By remaining silent (presenting a blank wall to the patient), the therapist avoids excessive empathy, which Freud reasoned would add to the secondary gains of neurosis and make it harder for the patient to get well.

Indeed, any textbook on psychotherapy will offer a picture of the Freudian encounter as one in which the patient reclines on a couch and says whatever comes to mind through free association. The process was meant to render the patient most vulnerable and self-exhibitionistic. As Freud instructed his patients:

> Your talk with me must differ in one respect from ordinary conversation. Whereas usually you try to keep the threads of your story together and to exclude all intruding association, here you proceed differently. You will notice that as you relate things various ideas will come . . . and you feel inclined to put aside certain criticisms and objections. You will be tempted to say to yourself: "This or that has no connection here, or is unimportant, or nonsensical, so it cannot be necessary to mention it, but mention it nonetheless, even if you feel a disinclination against it, or indeed just because of this.[5]

The goal of analysis was to minimize the effects of conscious intentions and to emphasize material that was related to intrapsychic conflict. During periods when free association was not impeded, the patient was to relive childhood experience, guided by the therapist. Yet interpretation was to be withheld until the patient was close to insight and ego defenses were worn down. Gradually, the patient learned about the truth of unconscious material. Whatever the form, neurotic symptoms can be remarkably resistant to the psychoanalyst's prodding or directives.

The relationship between psychoanalytic procedure and a patient's uneasy sense that her personal boundaries have been violated, raises troubling and provocative questions. Troubling as they are, these questions need to be addressed, even retrospectively in light of Freud and his ethics. Through a reading of Freud's *Fragment of an Analysis of a Case of Hysteria*, "Dora," it is clear that Freud was aware of the violations peculiar to the practice of psychoanalysis as well as its beneficial effects. In 1893, for example, Freud (in collaboration with Breuer) wrote a paper on the psychical mechanism of hysterical phenomena.[6] In it, Freud states that to discover the precipitating cause of hysterical symptoms, a patient must often be hypnotized to arouse memories of the time from which psychopathogenic symptoms first occurred. Freud posited that simply recollecting trauma is not sufficient for the patient to; he must re-enact it with original, anguishing "affect." Without such revivifying affect, inducement "almost invariably produces no result."[7] Therefore, as Freud himself recognized, psychoanalysis as a course of treatment, whether through hypnosis or free association, is at least as painful as the symptoms it tries to assuage. Freud used the analogy of the embedded fishhook that must be pushed in and the barb cut off before it can be extracted.

Freud conjectured that Dora's unresolved Oedipal conflicts were due to an overindulgent father who tried to compensate for an unhappy marriage by asking Dora to be his confidante at an early age. Aided by two detailed dreams, Freud soon concluded that Dora's symptoms had multiple meanings. They reflected a conflict between an impulse for oral sex and the repulsion of such an act with coughing being the symptom that provided some fulfillment in the appropriate erogenous zone. Freud attributed her vocal difficulties to her father's absence and that they expressed a concealed wish to remain silent unless she could speak to him.

With Freudian psychoanalysis as a background, I hope to show the parallels between Dora's resistance to the violations inherent in analysis and the resistance of Gilman, as reflected in her story "The Yellow Wallpaper." But before turning to Gilman's story, one should note that "Dora" was a groundbreaking exposition of a case study that failed because, among other reasons, the patient deflected the aims of analysis. The "Dora" case is also important in revealing Freud's not entirely un–self-critical ambivalence about having to force his way into his young patient's unconscious to discover the source of her troubles. Psychoanalysts and scholars as wide ranging as Lacan, Jeffrey Masson, Janet Malcolm, and Phyllis Chesler have commented on the case at length.

Both Dora and Gilman were diagnosed as hysterics: Dora by Freud in 1895; Gilman by Mitchell in 1888. Hysteric, in the nineteenth century, was a term given to women's emotional disturbances, anxiety, or excitability. It was thought to originate in the uterus and became a metaphor for everything men found mysterious and unmanageable in the opposite sex.[8] Jean Martin Charcot pioneered the first scientific studies of hysteria at the Salpêtrière—an ancient, extensive hospital complex that had long been an insane asylum— where patients (often comprising the most wretched of the Parisian proletariat) were treated very badly. Chains bound the hands and feet of the most disturbed patients, their bodies encased in large iron rings, which were riveted to the walls.[9] Underfed and neglected, they received no medical care. Charcot improved conditions for the patients and transformed the neglected facility into a haven for neurological research, attracting distinguished physicians from all over Europe, including Freud and Janet.

With his flair for classification, Charcot distinguished *hysteria* from other neurological disorders, chiefly epilepsy. Prior to Charcot's time, hysterical women were considered malingerers whose symptoms were delusional, created by a kind of autosuggestion. Charcot proved that hysteria was not the product of deception or exaggerated bids for attention, but a real affliction affecting the nervous system. Although fascinated by the symptoms of hysteria (ranging from partial paralysis and catatonia to convulsive and hallucinatory states), Charcot viewed his patients' volatile emotions as outer

symptoms to be catalogued, their speech as "vocalization" rather than sub-
stantial disclosures.[10] He was less concerned with the etiological causes of
their disturbances.

    At the Salpetrière, Charcot's celebrated "Tuesday Lectures" on hys-
teria gave forth a resounding echo; students packed the amphitheater to hear
him; classic illustrators such as Brouillet were commissioned to capture on
canvas the spectacle of hysteric patients going into uncontrollable fits or
trances. One student, J. Babinski, recalls the way Charcot outlined a remarkable description of the paralyses that he called "hystero-tramatiques" and
then demonstrated how it was possible to reproduce by means of suggestion
paralyses having exactly the same characteristics, distinguishing the disorder
from other "organic coxalgia."[11] Notes from another lecture show verbatim
Charcot's chilling stance towards his patients' suffering. Judith Herman cites
this demonstration on a young woman in a hypnotic trance:

> CHARCOT: Let us press again on the hysterogenic point. (A male intern
> touches the patient in the ovarian region). Here we go again. Occasionally
> subjects even bite their tongues, but this would be rare. Look at the arched
> back, which is so well described in the textbooks.
>
> PATIENT: Mother, I am frightened.
>
> CHARCOT: Note the emotional outburst. If we let things go unabated we
> will soon return to the epileptoid behavior. . . . (The patient cries again:
> "Oh! Mother.")
>
> CHARCOT: Again, note these screams. You could say it is a lot of noise
> over nothing.[12]

    Through hypnosis, Charcot was able to better demonstrate that his
already highly suggestible female subjects could be induced to perform
posthypnotically more or less "reasonable" acts. He also believed that hypnosis could help cure certain abnormal clinical manifestations of the disease. Contrary to popular belief that the hypnotized individual, obedient to
the will of the hypnotist, was impelled posthypnotically to follow the com-
mands the hypnotist suggested, Charcot claimed that the integrity of his
patients' psyches were never compromised by being put in a trance. He
stated that, in fact, a patient would resist any behavior that she found
morally offensive. Hypnosis, Charcot stated quite clearly, "is not an excuse
for rape." "Hypnosis does not paralyze the will nor does it bestow on the
hypnotizer a power to violate it."[13] Here, Charcot protests too much, and
we are left to wonder how many unscrupulous professionals were, in fact,
taking advantage of their patients and engaging in questionable practices.

    Feminists and the medical establishment are still debating the
extent to which Charcot exploited his patients, having them perform in an

exaggerated way that people came to expect as the antics of hysterical behavior. Followers of Charcot, including Janet and Freud, praised him for recognizing the roles of conscious and unconscious memories associated with trauma in the etiology of neurosis and hysteria. Freud credited Charcot for being the first to take hysterical phenomena seriously, restoring "dignity" to patients who were often scorned or laughed at and whose bizarre symptoms were, more often than not, treated as curiosities.[14] But Freud understood that taxonomy was not sufficient for understanding the inner causes of hysteria, especially in its severest forms. Freud then resolved that to understand what was at the bottom of his patients' troubles, he would have to delve into their inner lives; he would have to listen to them. As Freud listened, he became convinced that hysteria was caused by psychological trauma, and that emotional reactions to psychological trauma produced an altered state of consciousness, that in turn, induced hysterical symptoms.

By the mid-1890s, these investigations led Freud further to the startling hypothesis that hysteria could be attributed to painful memories of premature sexual experiences. He disclosed his troublesome conclusions in *The Aetiology of Hysteria* (1880): "I therefore put forward the thesis that at the bottom of every case of hysteria there are one or more occurrences of premature sexual experience, experiences which belong to the earliest years of childhood, but which can be reproduced through the work of psycho-analysis despite the intervening decades."[15] But after publishing *The Aetiology of Hysteria*, Freud apparently changed his mind and stated those scenes of seduction had never taken place and were fabricated. This conclusion led him to the famous Oedipal theory, in which he proposed that all children entertain sexual fantasies about their parents. Hence, a patient's confession about a sexual encounter with a parent or a parental figure might be as much wishful fantasy as actual event.

Freud's conflict concerning his patients' credibility, particularly when they claimed they had been sexually abused or molested by a parent or relative reached its height in the "Dora" case. Eighteen-year-old Dora (her real name was Ida Bauer) sought treatment from Freud in October 1900, but abruptly terminated her analysis only eleven weeks later. Freud wrote up the case in 1901, but did not publish it until 1905. In his introduction, Freud explains that his intention in the fragment was to give a concrete example of how dream interpretation can be used in treating female hysteria. But more consequential for Freud and for the entire history of psychoanalysis, was what Freud learned about the girl's transference of amorous and enraged feelings onto him. Unwilling or unable to exploit his patient's transference as a productive means of furthering her progress, Freud failed to win Dora's trust and cooperation. And in return, Freud's lack of empathy for Dora created a cold, if not hostile, environment for doctor and patient, a virtual tug-of-war.

Dora's resistance and hostility toward Freud, as well as her attempts to conceal her aggressive and sadistic feelings, undermined his attempts to cure her. Janet Malcolm argues persuasively that Freud's study of Dora is as fraught with his paternalism as it is with his rage and frustration over her defection. By putting forth the transference theory, Freud hoped to explain the erotic importunities of women patients as a universal phenomenon, rather than a reaction he provoked.[16] One may also charge that Freud, from the outset, was already critical of the sexually initiated girl who confided in him a story of exploitation, molestation, and betrayal by the adults around her. So extensive was her sexual knowledge that Freud felt he had to defend himself against the allegation that he himself must have planted sexual fantasies in the girl's mind because no "decent" girl of eighteen would be able to speak so frankly about sexual matters:

> I am aware that—in this city, at least—there are many physicians who (revolting though it may seem) choose to read a case history of this kind not as a contribution to the psychopathology of neurosis, but as a roman à clef designed for their private delectation.
>
> Now in this case history—. . . sexual questions will be discussed with possible frankness, the organs and functions of sexual life will be called by their proper names, and the pure-minded reader can convince himself from my descriptions that I have not hesitated to converse upon such subjects in such language even with a young woman. Am I then to defend myself upon this score as well?[17]

Dora's symptoms included severe abdominal pain, morbidity (although her father did not think she was suicidal), and depression. To discover the etiology of Dora's hysteria, Freud had to work swiftly toward extracting the cause· of her repression. Although Freud initiated the "attack" against the girl's defensive repression, he found that he had to fend off Dora's retaliatory attacks at the same time that he absorbed them. As Malcolm observes, Freud's treatment of Dora was adversarial: "He sparred with her, laid traps for her, pushed her into corners, bombarded her with interpretations, gave no quarter, was as unspeakable, in his way, as many of the people in her sinister family circle, went too far, and finally drove her away."[18] Instinctually, Dora refused to surrender her secrets to the psychoanalyst, and her profound opposition to therapy is well documented throughout the study.

From its origins in treating hysteria with hypnosis, psychoanalysis, as has been stated, consisted mainly of encouraging the patient to recall the past to isolate traumatic events of childhood. In the clinical view, trauma is always related to neurosis. Freud then isolated trauma as part of the larger pattern of repression and defense anxiety, postulating that the nature of symptoms could be seen as compromises or "somatic compliances"[19] within the psyche, allowing the scenic aspects of the trauma to be forgotten, while the wounding in/on the body remained. The discourse of the symptom is also the discourse of the illness because as the traumatic incident is converted into somas, a physical (but not unrelated) sign of the body, it is also trying to protest against the original threat that caused the symptom to be split off in the first place. In hysterical patients especially, the symptom serves as a means of ridding trauma from memory by acting it out covertly.

Mitchell, more punctilious than Freud, and more clinically based, apparently adopted some of Charcot's moralistic recommendations for treating the symptoms of hysteria, as this quote shows:

> I remind you gentlemen, that there are two parts in the treatment of hysteria, two distinct elements: 1. The psychic element that entails a change in the moral environment, the separation of patients who are too weak or too complacent, the separation of patients from other patients with hysteria, and the promotion of discipline, and of moral and intellectual hygiene; 2. The physical element, which consists of the use of general reconditions, hydrotherapy, gymnastics, balneotherapy, tonics, and restorants. . . .[20]

The noun *hysteric* is a derivative from the Latin *husterikos*, or afflictions of the womb, because hysteria was thought to be due to womb/uterine disturbances. Through a careful analysis of Freud's metaphorical tropes, one can see that he did, in fact, consciously or unconsciously conflate the idea of the unconscious (and its secrets) and the womb (and its disturbances). Both are sites of incubation and delivery. Freud's reintroducing trauma as part of the therapeutic process results, through difficult labor, in a secret that is ultimately surrendered to the therapist. In his case studies, Freud took great pains to describe how he overcame a patient's resistance to imparting his or her secrets. In fact, one of the aims of this chapter is to catch Freud in the act of carrying out his own fantasy of mastery or dominance and to account for patients' suffering as a result of being in therapy.

Consistent with his idea that "the course taken by illness . . . always go[es] back to traumatic sexual experiences,"[21] Freud speculated that Dora's later anxieties were awakened as a signal of an earlier situation: hence, the weight given to her childhood past. However, in the broader sense, Freud knew that trauma is always associated with some kind of injury to the psyche in which a wounding results. Freud referred to Dora's lapses into illness as her "attacks," suggesting that something outside of her control kept persecuting her from within. When Dora seemed to "cloak" self-reproaches by antagonistically projecting them onto her analyst, Freud observed that "the analysis cannot attack such ideas because they are only too anxious to escape from criticism and consciousness."[22] Why did Freud refer to his own technique as an "attack," which was identical to how he describes the onset of physical symptoms?

In the Freudian psychoanalytic encounter, words alone can define the pain of the body, and the body itself becomes a submerged language of the psyche. In *Preliminary Communications* Freud wrote: "At first it seems extraordinary that events experienced so long ago should continue to operate so intensely—that their recollection should not be liable to the wearing away process to which, after all, we see all of our memories succumb."[23] For Freud, the wearing away of a memory depended on various factors. If a patient could adequately and "energetically" react to a present injury, then that experience would probably fade along with the affects that accompanied it. Linguistic usage bears witness to the fact that human beings have always tried to exorcise themselves of harrowing emotional demons in the moment: "one cries oneself out," "blows off steam," or "rages one's self out."[24] If, however, the reaction to immediate danger has been suppressed, or fails to be discharged, Freud reasoned that the affect remained painfully attached to the memory.

Moreover, Freud understood that a psychic injury addressed in words or action was to be recollected quite differently from one that has had to be accepted or silently endured. Trauma that was stifled or maintained in secrecy built tension. Language itself recognizes the distinction between an injury that has been "repaid" and one that has been suffered in silence.[25] This is why for Freud and his immediate followers the patient's giving voice to what has been submerged or stifled is so crucial. As Freud explained, in the psychoanalytic situation, language acts as a substitution for action: "by its [language's] help, an affect can be 'abreacted' effectively."[26] In other cases, speaking is itself therapeutic, especially when speaking is, as Freud specified, in the form of a lamentation or a tormenting confession. Giving up such secrets can be excruciating for the patient, although in Freud's view it was a necessary infliction of pain that would subsequently prove cathartic.

But how was this to be accomplished? Purging, in nineteenth-century medical as well as psychiatric practice, was a means of eliminating infectious material from the body. To assuage the painful secret of the symptom, Freud insisted that the layers of the unconscious must be peeled back to uncover the source, which he believed to be rooted in some kind of sexual guilt or trauma. But Freud knew there was resistance to this kind of penetration, especially when the walls of the unconscious exist as barriers against such external threats. In this tension between a patient's resistance and the therapist's need to enter the site of trauma, there exists, not only pain but also real violation. Indeed, if Freud thought trauma always originated in the radical crisis of birth, of being "torn away,"[27] then his image of "tearing" away the original secret of the trauma from the walls of the psyche, through the surfacing of repressed material, was another kind of evisceration of the unconscious.

We can then consider the unconscious as a place of refuge, a kind of "asylum" into which the trauma has temporarily concealed itself to protect itself against further wounding. In fact, the noun asylum means "a place offering safety, without the right of seizure." But to shed the secrets of the psyche, the psychoanalyst must first encounter the "walls" that structure and protect it. If the unconscious were to give its consent to such intrusion, then it would not require concealment. One could then compare the psyche to an inner but not impenetrable space, that exists, at least in Freud's imagination, only insofar as its defenses are relinquished to the analysis.

How did Freud enter an asylum, or the contents of the unconscious, as his right? Perhaps there were less invasive routes to therapy, although less satisfactory to the voyeuristic desires of mastery on the part of the doctor. In "Dora," Freud discussed how mental events, especially dreams, can be seen as a "chain" successive in time and development. He observed that "in the long thread of connections [of mental experiences], which spun itself out between a symptom of the disease and a pathogenic idea," a dream is yet another link or stitch in the larger design, or pattern, of the signifying unconscious that repeats itself. The dreamer, by permitting the mind to wander freely in connection with various parts of the dream, is guided to the meaning of the dream, to the wish at its center."[28] As Freud stated: "one of the roads along which consciousness can be reached . . . has been cut off by consciousness and repressed."[29] Indeed Freud's metaphor of a "road to the unconscious" conjures up for the reader Medieval images of knights and crusaders, especially when reminded of the fact that this road is a means to his female patient's secret citadel: the unconscious. Freud's tone while describing this necessary transgression is notably cold, intellectual, detectivelike, and sexually Victorian.[30]

Hypnosis was perhaps a more direct means of embarking on that road and gaining access to unconscious secrets. By limiting a patient's resistance to suggestion, Freud broke down at least one barrier to analysis, a patient's "dislike" (Freud's word) for discussing memories that somehow might be linked to psychopathogenic symptoms.[31] Freud claimed that the original trauma "must be brought back to its status nascendi,"[32] where it is then to be converted into the language of confession. He then challenged himself to break down the barriers of his patient's secrecy. Because he viewed women's symptoms as neurotic productions stemming from intractable female stubbornness, it is easy to imagine that he felt force and mastery on the part of the analyst were necessary for overcoming female will.

Even so, the desire to bring Dora's secrets to light presents an interesting problem for Freud with regard to publishing his study. He becomes apologetic while explaining why he must adopt a pseudonym, *Dora*, to protect the girl's true identity. Here, Freud reveals his own desire to shield the girl from dubious notoriety and to cover up the indecency of her past. Freud's choice of the name, *Dora*, out of all other possible names, can be traced to his associations with his sister Rosa's nursemaid, whose name was also Rosa, but who took the name Dora to avoid confusion with her mistress.[33] *Dora*, then, as a substitute for his sister Rosa, is an appellation that carries unmistakable incestuous connotations for Freud, who was the first to introduce into theory the sexual dynamics of the family. Moreover, the name *Dora* is resonant with the mythical Pandora, who opens the box to her own seductiveness and destructiveness.[34] In fact, Freud goes to some lengths to display his Victorian distaste for the sexual origins of Dora's hysteria, and as a result, he admonishes his clinical audience for possessing any prurient interest in reading the case, forewarning them that the origins of Dora's illness, "in all of its psychosexual . . . secrets" should be kept strictly confidential.

> If it is true that the causes of hysterical disorders are to be found in the intimacies of the patient's psychosexual life, and that hysterical symptoms are the expression of their most secret and repressed wishes, then the complete elucidation of a case of hysteria is bound to involve the revelation of those intimacies and the betrayal of those secrets.[35]

At this point, we can draw parallels between Freud's condescending attitude toward Dora and the narrator's husband, John in "The Yellow Wallpaper" (who represents the medical profession). Although "The Yellow Wallpaper" predates Freud as well as Gilman's subsequent condemnation of psychoanalysis, the story is startlingly modern in its depiction of mental illness. Anticipating Freudian discoveries, the story situates the patient in a childhood space in which she continues to regress. Mitchell himself noted that "the cause of breakdowns and nervous disasters and consequential emotional disturbances and their bitter fruit are often to be sought in the remote past. [The doctor] may dislike the quest, but he cannot avoid it."[36] Both Mitchell's and Freud's remedies forced the female patient to regress to an infantile state and to relinquish her will to male inquisition and authority.

In the interest of propriety, John maintains his privacy, not allowing his wife's illness to be exposed (or published). While holding her captive at the country estate and in the nursery, under strict dosage and control, John exploits his wife's illness as a course of scientific study, just as Freud exploits Dora's case for the edification of his fellow physicians. By prohibiting her to write, John hopes to cut off his wife's ability to nurture her creative "infant" so that she might more readily nurture her biological one. Literary production, like childbearing, is a means of bearing and baring one's being in a substitute form.

Like the narrator in "The Yellow Wallpaper," a patient undergoing psychoanalysis is encouraged to free associate. What results is a stream of consciousness, a meandering design of interlining, but seemingly unrelated, thoughts and memories. In "The Yellow Wallpaper," the narrator lets her mind wander aimlessly over the wallpaper pattern. However, she becomes noticeably irritated and frustrated by its lack of consistency, its artistic "sins" of style:

> It is dull enough to confuse the eye in following, pronounced enough to constantly irritate and provoke study, and when you follow the lame uncertain curves . . . they suddenly commit suicide—destroy themselves in unheard of contradictions.[37]

Forced then into seclusion, in which she can do nothing but think aloud, the narrator in "The Yellow Wallpaper" can be seen voicing one side of the psychoanalytic encounter. In such a manner, she attempts to follow the meandering pattern of the wallpaper, ultimately submitting to a monstrous self-projection. Like any patient in analysis, Gilman and her narrator are vulnerable to the blockages, inconsistencies, or "talking" suicides incurred when something crucial to expression refuses to give itself up to consciousness. A writer, like a patient, often encounters a psychic block or barrier that halts the flow of images and words.

Although a patient may consciously or unconsciously resist full disclosure in the analytic session, Freud insisted in the "Dora" case that he could decode a patient's secrets. He states that he can interpret the girl's involuntary gestures, especially those surrounding the act of masturbation. Dora's body language is a code Freud is able to decipher and control in his own authoritative discourse: "a small reticule of a shape which had come into fashion; and as she lay on the sofa and talked, she kept playing with it—opening it, putting a finger into it, shutting it again, and so on. I looked on . . . then explained to her the nature of a symptomatic act."[38]

Accordingly, Freud comments on how clinical observation can perforate the outer surfaces of what is most hidden:

> There is a great deal of symbolism of this kind in life, but as a rule we pass it by without heeding it. When I set myself the task of bringing to light what human beings keep hidden within them, not by the compelling power of hypnosis, but by observing what they say and what they show, I thought the task was a harder one than it really is. He who has eyes to see and ears to hear may convince himself that no mortal can keep a secret. . . . And thus the task of making conscious the most hidden recesses of the mind is one which is quite possible to accomplish.[39]

Indeed, Freud was convinced Dora intended to "play secrets" with him, that she withheld the narratives that, once exposed, would best help to cure her, and that she was on the verge of having her secret violently "torn" (his word) from her by "the doctor."[40] The word *torn* will become increasingly significant as we begin to analyze the narrator's compulsion to strip back the floral pattern in "The Yellow Wallpaper" to release the entrapped secret phantasm. John, too, demands that his wife relinquish her imaginative fantasizing by suspending all creative writing. If she is no longer able to hide her inner thoughts in writing, he is at liberty to examine them. Stressing the physical dimension of Dora's psyche as a kind of interior space, a space within the body, that could be entered like a room or a house and in which the analyst is at liberty to look about, Freud wrote:

> The experience of Herr K—his making love to her and the insult to her honor which was involved—seems to provide in Dora's case the psychical trauma which Breuer and I declared long ago to be the indispensable prerequisite for the production of a hysterical disorder . . . as so often happens in histories of cases of hysteria, the trauma that we know of as having occurred in the patient's past is insufficient to explain the particular character of the symptoms. If the trauma theory is not to be abandoned we must go back to her childhood and *look about there* for any influences or impressions which might have had an effect analogous to that of a trauma. [Emphasis added.][41]

Freud clearly pursued his trauma theory in a manner that was voyeuristic and detectivelike. Once he resurfaces Dora's childhood through the analytic process, he is free to look for parental influences or impressions that might have contributed to traumatic effects. This resurfaced childhood space, as Freud described it, is exemplified by the "nursery," in Gilman's story, a room that is covered by layers of yellow wallpaper. As Gilman's narrator surveys her surroundings: "It is a big, airy room, the whole floor nearly, with windows that look all ways, and air and sunshine galore. It was nursery first and then playroom and gymnasium, I should judge; for the windows are barred for little children, and there are rings and things in the walls."[42]

The narrator's syntax reveals that she is increasingly susceptible to paranoiac distortions. She reports that "the windows look all ways," implying that although they may look out to the exterior world, they also stare, guilelessly, in on her. Moreover, when one thinks of how this narrator suffers from a chronic sense of being espied by "absurd, unblinking eyes," her description of the botanical shapes of the wallpaper, it seems more than coincidental that Freud emphasizes the importance of "sight" as an accessory to analysis. We may assume that Freud's histrionic patients ventilated intolerable emotions in the analytic session, rendering them "in the *mildest* cases in tears."[43] However, Freud himself would have had to remain detached from his patient's suffering to observe it. Not surprisingly, then,

Gilman's narrator, as revealed by her "nursery," views herself as a kind of spectacle where even the walls are endowed with the power to scrutinize her.

Additionally, we learn that the nursery "floor is gouged and splintered, the plaster itself dug out, and this great heavy bed looks like it has been through wars." Ravaged by the marks (the signs) of "children," the nursery (like the psyche) is both aged and yellowed. Not unexpectedly, then, we find much of Gilman's discourse emanating from a psychiatric patient's reclining position, "following pattern about by the hour," just as Dora painfully "labors" (as a mother gives birth) to remember trauma to please the expectant father Freud.

In the story, the narrator spins out her anxieties and fears (hour by hour), punctuated by condescending visits by her husband (as doctor): "I lie here on this great immovable bed—it is nailed down, I believe—and follow that pattern about by the hour."[44] Language in such a situation becomes a mechanism of repetition, a proliferating circuitous discourse. Caught in a web of her own exacting but dispiriting complaints, the narrator's speech refuses to end while unceasingly trying to mean something. Likewise, in the clinical session, a patient free associates, forming through language an effluent, orbicular pattern. The key to successful analysis is the doctor's ability to decipher the meaning of the patient's unconscious by determining what these repetitions mean.

Let us pause to consider, yet again, the similarities between the narrator's insistent talk of the wallpaper—which she continues to focus on—and the patient's insistent talk deriving from the unconscious. In the analytic session, the analyst does not resolve the open-endedness of the patient's associations. Rather, the repetitions and elisions in a patient's monologue are goals in themselves; they are, in a sense, "devices" for the analyst. As a pattern is gradually established, the analyst works toward discerning its operative elements. The wallpaper pattern, too, like the associations produced in the pattern of a patient's talk in analysis, is always one sequence ahead of itself. Each identical, successive image in the wallpaper motif must refer backward to the previous image (which it has already preempted), giving the impression of simultaneous progression and regression. In psychoanalysis, too, the patient speaks now and into the future but only with the aim of revealing the far past.

John's disposition, like the analyst's, causes him to be "practical in the extreme" and to restrict his wife to a room ordinarily reserved for dependent children. Barred windows confine the narrator as well as protect her from herself. Living within a daily schedule prepared by John (the hourly sessions), the narrator finds herself high above the rose-"infested" gardens and velvet meadows. Feeling both dejected and agitated, the narrator views the "real" garden (outside the artificial garden of the wallpaper walls) as similarly overproductive and "sickened" by neglect. Suspending her connection with external reality, she displaces her attention to an inner replica of the outside world: the wallpaper. Through her eyes, however, the scheme is repellent, almost revolting. The color has yellowed and begun to peel off due to old age; and the rotating moonlight casts grim, tumultuous shadows on the walls that support it. Moreover, the pattern comprises an intricate, branchlike design. Like the associative speech of the patient, it ambles into whatever angle it pleases (ugly or grotesque), growing wherever it "feels necessary" to expand or to digress.

Apparently, long before writing "The Yellow Wallpaper," Gilman had studied the edges between fantasy and reality, the borderlines between sanity and insanity. In *The Living*, she recollects that as a child she was such an avid daydreamer that her mother had to impose on her fantasy world, insisting she put such idle pleasures away: "My dream world was no secret. I was but too ready to share it, but there were no sympathetic listeners. It was my life, but lived entirely alone."[45] Gilman's mother seized her "inner fortress" (her words) of happiness by simply detecting its existence "behind closed doors." Eventually, Gilman chose to comply with her mother's wishes, severing herself from the fantasy that "pushed hard" to be let back in.

Years later, and after her nervous breakdown, Gilman equated her mother's intrusion into her dream world to Freud's objectives in analysis. She accused Freud and his disciples of "violating" the "human spirit," which she equated with her creativity. Freud should not have been shocked at such a characterization by a literary woman. As Berman notes (while discussing the rift between Breuer and Freud over Anna O.), "From Freud's point of view, Breuer failed because he was not intellectually audacious enough, not a *conquistador*, as Freud viewed himself."[46]

One of Gilman's earliest rescue fantasies apparently served to compensate for a lack of maternal affection. Gilman's fantasy illustrates the way in which children, once discarded by their egotistical parents, eventually find their way to ideal surrogates:

> In this fantasy world lived a Prince and Princess of magical powers, who went about the world collecting unhappy children and taking them to a guarded Paradise in the South Seas. I had a boundless sympathy for children, feeling them to be suppressed, misunderstood.[47]

In this early Freudian family romance, at least two features are unique. First, Paradise is situated in the "South Seas", a place associated with primitive rather than civilized impulses. Gilman's eroticized, but moral, Paradise is at odds with her mother's Victorian restraint. The children, like Gilman herself, are fortunate enough to be "collected" by the

Prince and Princess, implying that they have not only been gathered, but also accumulated. This verb indicates that the fantasy has been revisited habitually, accumulating a store of "saved children."

Indeed, Gilman's early fantasy world was a world of preverbalization, in which language is not yet separate from affect. Happy or unhappy, the children symbolized, in turn, satisfied or unsatisfied desire. Paradise alone can transform once unhappy or deficient children into euphoric, well ones. But the children can only qualify for Paradise on the basis of being dejected or depressed. If these children are misunderstood in their own households, they can find in their magical parents the gratification of desires without the usual postponements.

Gilman seemed to resort to her fantasy world as a refuge where she was free to act out, and, at the same time, to control her anxieties. The same impulses, although in an inverted, demonic form, may well be at work in "The Yellow Wallpaper", where the narrator is also "misunderstood" by more than one severe parental figure in her household. When Gilman's mother insists that she forfeit her "guarded" secrets, she is quite literally intruding on her daughter's mind, just as, in Gilman's later view, psychiatrists meddle with their patients' minds, which Gilman considered to be unethical if not immoral. All of her writings about Freud are pejorative. In her lecture "The Falsity of Freud," Gilman compares the psychoanalyst with evil and oppression, and in "Parasitism and Civilised Vice," she argues convincingly that an obstacle to the progress of women's rights is the "resurgence of phallic worship set before us by psychoanalysis."[48] She wondered how "intelligent persons would permit these mind-meddlers, having no claims to fitness except having read utterly unproved books, to paddle among their thoughts and feelings, and exact confessions of the last intimacy."[49]

Gilman's mother feared that her daughter's daydreaming would result in her becoming "uncontrollable" and unsuitable for society. Similarly, in the story, John enforces all measures of restraint against his wife's fantasizing in the hopes of bringing her back to the domicile, yet he only aggravates her nervous condition. He even seems to suspect that his wife's mental state has deteriorated to a delusional state and that her hallucinations are actually aiding her in denying deeper, negative feelings about maternity that would otherwise impact on her "real life." "[John] says that my imaginative power and habit of story making is sure to lead to all manner of excited fancies, and that I ought to use my will to check the tendency."[50]

In conventional psychotherapy, a patient would be *encouraged* to explore all types of fantasies, good and bad. But Gilman's narrator was repeatedly denied an outlet for her "excited fancies." In fact, the story begins with the narrator's being stultified, because John uses his dominant roles as husband and doctor to keep her imagination in check. Redolent with Freudian discoveries about the unconscious, the story's depiction of the otherwise suppressed monological center of the text (the narrator) is released only by free association or stream of consciousness. Increasingly, the woman in the wallpaper is struggling to get out from within the interior of the nursery, indicating that something that was once held back or too appalling to admit to consciousness is now emerging from the deepest recesses of the narrator's unconscious. The narrator's delusions become more and more alarming, suggesting she has lapsed into a psychotic state. Freud discerns psychosis in a patient when repressed material becomes so powerful that it overwhelms the ego and reality proves so traumatic that the ego surrenders and throws itself into a fantasy world. As the hallucinatory woman asserts herself, emotions become more strenuously vocalized. This emergence is a ripe but often agonizing moment in analysis, but it may leave a patient more vulnerable to shock and dissociation. As Freud first claimed, *the traumatic experience is reproduced in the patient even with the intervention of decades*, leading to a splitting of consciousness. If the mind is like the womb, then the birthing of one's former being results in an infantile, but often monstrous, form.

With the birth of an infant daughter, followed by a postpartum depression, a correlation occurs between Gilman's literary creation (the narrator's monologue) and her biological creation (her infant daughter). Both "creations" result in potentially dangerous, autonomous "offspring" who are so demanding of the mother-author that they threaten to suffocate her. Both infants are querulous, excitable, and when denied gratification, mute, or enraged. The woman behind the wallpaper "skulks" about in a prehensile, even savage form. In response, the narrator is torn between a mother's diligence, her obsessional involvement with the wallpaper, and repulsion at the infant's devouring claim on her attention.

The scene of "The Yellow Wallpaper," like the sanctuary/asylum, is a place of secrecy and a place of labor and delivery. The wallpapered room in which the narrator is confined, like the womb itself in its torn condition, signifies both bodily and emotional grief. With the infant safely "emptied out" of the mother's body, the womb must gradually repair its wounding from within. The narrator is only too aware of being enclosed in a space as repellent as the relic of the empty womb:

> The color is repellent, almost revolting; a smoldering unclean yellow strangely faded by the slow turning sunlight. It is a dull yet lurid orange in some places, a sickly sulfur. . . . No wonder the children hated it! I should hate it myself if I had to live in this room long.[51]

John's "rest cure" secures his patient in the nursery, as a patient in therapy is regressed to infancy, for the purposes of her incubation and restraint. But in such a subservient position, the patient is always subject to John's (or the analyst's) "attacks." It is not insignificant that infants and children in the midst of paroxysms and tantrums have occupied this space, which is the territory of the postpartum womb: "How those children did tear about here! I have locked the door and thrown the key down into the front path."[52]

As the narrator grows more agitated, John insists that she lie down for "an hour" after meals. Ironically, only the aberrant pattern of the wall-paper keeps her quiet, again "by the hour." In such a passive state, the patient is also susceptible to analytic suggestion. Whether by Freud's voyeurism or Mitchell's injunctions against female "will-lessness," the male analyst counters a patient's resistance by demanding something concrete: a confession, a pen, a secret in the midst of being torn away. The patient often convinced that such seizure is necessary for recovery, submits to the desire of the analyst. But if a patient resists, progress in therapy is halted. In "Dora" and "The Yellow Wallpaper," boxes (Dora's jewelry box, the nursery "box"), which Freud believed represented the womb or uncon-scious, remain locked to the analyst.[53]

If it is true that the unconscious, like the womb, is protected as a "locked box" suggesting impenetrability, then an opening of that box (like Pandora's box) is managed with a key. The irony, of course, is that the key is always, at least for the patient, a violation, a symbolic "rape" of the self, and Gilman's resistance to the analyst's violation cannot be dismissed. In the story, John alone holds the master's "key" to the narrator's sanctu-ary/asylum where she is being reproved for her conduct. If we substitute Freud for John, then it follows that the analyst must violate the inner space of the patient (just as Freud violated Dora's psychic space) to coax the secret out. Indeed, Malcolm argues that the Pandora myth that haunts the Dora case is actually a myth about defloration.[54]

But in this story and in the "Dora" case as well, the secret is indis-tinguishable from the symptom, and both are locked within the same con-flated space, the "psychic" womb. Nineteenth-century physicians, anxious to explain women's symptoms, had already conflated the mind of the hys-terical patient with the womb by blaming women's psychological maladies on malfunctioning reproductive organs. Uncannily, Gilman, while dis-cussing the wallpaper, refers to the nursery's "hymenium" or spore-bearing fungus which is growing just beneath it: "all those strangled heads and bul-bous eyes and waddling fungus growths just shriek with derision." Violation of the psyche/womb suggests by analogy the tearing of the "hymen," a kind of protective wall or barrier. The now-damaged psyche, which has been overexposed to light and insemination, must be peeled away ("Then I peeled off all the paper I could reach"). The phantasm—

ugly, terrified, and outwardly suppressed— starkly represents the difficulty of bringing repressed material or trauma to necessary catharsis.

Appropriately, the narrator describes the woman in the wallpaper as a wordless, sulky creature, who epitomizes this archaic pattern of infantile dependency and rage underlying the vileness of the paper. The fact that the figure goes awry, stalking about in anger or uproar, may confirm what Freud suspected was at the bottom of hysterical symptoms: a trauma tied to childhood or infancy. Only by excising the ancient injury is recovery possible. Hence the woman is described as "ancient" and crawling, suggesting how the past, particularly when revisited in the psychoanalytic self-encounter, is old, ancient.

"The Yellow Wallpaper" is in many ways a case study just like "Dora." Gilman depicts the reality of the patient's "unreal" anguish, and how therapists who seek to cure mental illness respond to that unbearable anguish. Both Dora and Gilman were required to submit to the incursions endemic to psychoanalytic treatment, which proved ineffective for various reasons. Both Dora and Gilman apparently viewed the cure as an assault on their very essence, not just their illness, and as such, an invasion to be guarded against.

Gilman's mistrust of psychoanalysis was an appropriate reaction to the patriarchal biases of early psychoanalytic practice. She was perhaps one of the first women writers to consider her writing as therapy and to reject psychoanalysis as a solution. Through writing, Gilman could express deeply felt emotions and finally put them outside of herself. Although self-analysis occurs in writing, writing is not the same as therapy. Writing has a different resonance than other forms of confession, such as talk therapy or even confiding in a friend. Writing permits the careful construction of a cohesive narrative in a way that simply talking about experiences does not. Whether the writing is ultimately shared with a reader or an audience, it tends to be more inward and reflective, uncontaminated by the expectations and responses of others. Moreover, writing can transmute personal suffering into an art form that has moral and ethical implications. This is what Gilman accomplishes in creating a narrator who loses her sanity as a result of incompetent and unethical treatment. She challenges us to reexamine our cultural and societal definitions of sanity and insanity. Which frame of reference is more sane: the narrator's (exemplifying creativity and expression) or John's (exemplifying regulation and suppression)?

As Anderson and MacCurdy suggest, by choosing to treat trauma as a problem only of the individual sufferer rather than as a site of individual and collective interaction, an opportunity for significant social change, some psychoanalytic approaches to trauma have intensified the feelings of individual powerlessness and a sense of isolation arising from traumatic experience. For women, especially, psychoanalysis was yet another hurdle to overcome in order to gain personal and public credibility. Both Gilman and "Dora" pose a reality that is not in keeping with the hegemonic views of the patriarchal culture that is dismissive of women. Victorian paternalism could only consider hysterical women to be a threat to the normative values pertaining to gender roles and would logically seek to suppress their narratives.

Although psychoanalysis need not constitute a transgression or a subjection of the patient, in its assumptions or methodology, Freud apparently saw psychoanalysis as a process of exposing the source of a patient's suffering to assuage it. Seen in this way, the wallpaper becomes almost moment by moment symbolic of a patient stripping away at her own psychic being to reach the core of her suffering. Ideally, the surfacing of a trauma, what Freud called "the half-tamed demons released by the work of analysis," should result in relief. But for Gilman, analysis felt more like an exorcism than therapy. Her narrator, equally skeptical, fears the possibility of future treatment: "John says if I don't pick up faster he shall send me to Weir Mitchell in the fall."[55]

3

BREAKING THE CODE OF SILENCE
Ideology and Women's Confessional Poetry

Author's Note: *when I first wrote this piece in 1991, I had not read Judith Herman's book* Trauma and Recovery, *a landmark study of the posttraumatic stress syndrome, and one that takes the necessary, but then daring, step of connecting the testimony of trauma survivors who have suffered from political oppression and terror with those who have suffered from domestic violence and sexual abuse. The coordinates between these two groups of victims are well supported by clinical studies. Herman's study documents the symptoms and stages of recovery that survivors must undergo to reconnect fragments, reconstruct histories, and make meaning of current suffering in light of past events. Integrating clinical and social perspectives on trauma has given Herman pause to address readers who are skeptical about equating the complexity of individual experiences with those that are political and collective: "I have tried to unify an apparently divergent body of knowledge and to develop concepts that apply equally to the experiences of domestic and sexual life, the traditional sphere of women, and to the experiences of war and political life, the traditional sphere of men."*[1]

Now, more than ten years later, Herman's clinical findings are even more crucial to our understanding the therapeutic benefits of confessional writing because they implicitly point to the shift in contemporary poetry when the poet's desire for the unmitigated truth of his or her early past, however violent or shocking, became one with his or her desire to create an aesthetic object that would reverberate for the reader. Psychic content became, however reluctantly, discursive form: a revelatory and an ongoing process of examining and reconstructing conscious and unconscious thought.

But something else brought confessional poets of the 1950s together—the aftershocks of World War II and the discovery of the concentration camps, their heroic attempts to confront and conquer the chronic losses of the body, tormented by manic episodes, or scarred by suicide attempts preceded and followed by long periods of depression. The early confessional poets understood that they were explorers of the psychic terrain and that they were at risk. They showed that the family not only is its own battle-ground, but it is also a Pandora's box, the forbidden story we beg to hear about ourselves. And as Herman writes, "The tyrannies and servilities of the public and private spheres are inseparably connected. It is now appar-ent that the traumas of one are the traumas of the other. The hysteria of women and combat neurosis of men are one."[2]

In the twenty-first century, the survivors of the Holocaust are dying out like distant stars, and the Vietnam War is a dim memory. The tes-timony of those who have undergone psychological trauma is essential not only to comprehend the full magnitude of evil, but also to preserve the innocence of those who were wronged, violated. The victim never deserves the perpetrator's crime; he or she is rendered powerless by an overwhelm-ing force, an atrocity. It is only the survivor who can tell a story of his or her own victimhood; some victims do not survive. It is the responsibility of the living to make certain that their outrage is not only justified, but also the only appropriate response to the extremities of helplessness and terror and to confront the past as past.

David Aberbach has suggested that the impulse to create usually happens as the result of some early damage to the self.[3] Reviving painful events can be cathartic for people who must reconcile themselves with painful episodes in the past. Freud saw in the creative writer a capacity for launch-ing fantasy as a means of protecting the already vulnerable and often wounded psyche. Charlotte Perkins Gilman's creation of an imaginary fortress helped her to deflect her hostility toward her mother. Fantasy served Gilman well as a way to shield the injured ego, sending up "papered" (as in textual) walls. And fantasy, even nightmarish fantasy, became Gilman's earliest strategy for distancing herself from realities she considered intolerable and too limiting.

While confessional writing precipitated grave and painful discov-eries about the unconscious, such writing also enabled writers to better comprehend and survive their pasts. Writing is a significant way to master trauma and complete the work of mourning. For Gilman, the process of healing required her reentry into the chaos of the wallpaper, which offers both escape and the safety of containment. As Gilman writes her narrative, the woman in the wallpaper increases its ferocity as if to remind her that she would suffer the consequences for such outrageous and insubordinate behavior. Among other things, the woman who emerges from the pattern of the wallpaper reflects not only Gilman's conflicts about being a writer, but also about being the object of her own representation, which tends to mutate the self and to proliferate it outside of conscious control. The writer is never extractable from her writing, any more than the patient is extractable from the sickness that defines her. However, the fictional device of a narrator helps Gilman to camouflage the autobiographical nature of her text, allowing it to speak for her, just as the woman in the wallpaper "speaks for" the narrator who must maintain "good conduct" in the society she keeps.

In many ways, Gilman provides an apt model for both male and female poets who use their own mental distress as a subject for writing. Poetry known as "confessional" holds an important place in the development of twentieth-century American poetry. Confessional poetry is a poetry of suffering; however, it is also a poetry that seeks validation of the personal condition of pain.

In recent years, however, critics have given the term *confessionalism* negative connotations. Poets who have found their way by the constellation of Plath, Sexton, Berryman, and Lowell, to name but a few of the original members of the confessional school, have been belittled and even demeaned for writing poems deemed as exhibitionistic, self-indulgent, narcissistic, or melodramatic.

In a recent book review titled "The Forbidden," in *The Three Penny Review,* Louise Gluck applies the descriptive tags of "narcissistic," "constricted," and "tedious" to confessional works by Sharon Olds and Linda McCarriston.[4] Her complaints are representative of many criticisms of confessional poetry. Glück is a percipient critic, but many of her assumptions are troublesome. To examine how confessionalism seeks to break the silences that encode, censure, and censor private and public truths, we can open the discussion by responding to Glück's provocative points.

Glück finds fault with the means through which Olds and McCarriston arrive at the thresholds of speech. She suggests that a personal and political agenda overdetermines these poems in a way that is "mechanistic," which weighs down the creative process and hinders discovery. Glück believes the poems strain "to give encouraging voice to the life force" and to demonstrate personal triumph over adversities."[5] She questions the immediate conjunction of private "guilt" and the outside world's acknowledgment of what guilt is and how to receive it. Although she would concede that these works commit themselves to social responsibility, she seems to dismiss the significance of these goals and how Olds's and McCarriston's energies embrace a whole spectrum of religious and political problems that bear down on the individual and connect him or her to the collective. Olds and McCarriston achieve their powerful artistry through dissenting voice and agency rather than silence or passive resignation. Is this a realm of art or politics? Is it beauty or truth? I would argue that, not unlike Keats's "still unravished bride," the silent urn, this type of confessional is an art vessel that confronts the reader with one's own capacity to retell the story in his or her own terms and to identify the human truths and values it puts into motion.

Although the urn is also constricted by time, it is compelled to tell the same human tragedy again and again until it exhausts itself as a principle of mere narration and self-transcends as an object of aesthetic truth and paradoxical wisdom. Beauty pertains to both the temporal and the eternal; this is also characteristic of the beauty of the earth-trodden poems of Olds and McCarriston. The transcendence of the flesh to spirit, confusion to logic, horror to realization, mortal to divine is less fluid than in Glück's own work. But it is there, and perhaps more accessible to more readers. Olds and McCarriston present voices of suffering, but they are also voices of survival: naming the oppression that their resistance addresses. If these poems struggle to affirm the life force, they do so because it is the survivor's arduous task: to persevere rather than surrender. Conservation, concentration of will, self-reflection, consideration of the divisions of good and evil comprise directions of a compass for those who must daily explore new ways to live. The poets' turn toward social responsibility is far more complex than Glück's critique suggests, because only through the personal experience of pain does pain becomes "disinterested" and indicative of a universal context. Confessionalism presses toward outrage and accountability, *not guilt*, and this is the first integral sign of social responsibility and moral maturity.

Confessionalism often draws an important distinction between *guilt* and *shame*. According to McCarriston, *guilt* is a misnomer for what many victims feel, because guilt suggests that a person is wrong, has done wrong, and has accepted the condemnation for hurting others. She would ask: what is the guilt of the beaten child, or the neglected, or the ignored? The victim of unjustified cruelty is innocent. If we assume she is complicit in the perpetrator's will against her, then she has already taken on his face instead of her own. The victim should feel not guilt, but shame. Shame is the painful feeling of embarrassment or disgrace, a feeling that something unfortunate or regrettable has happened; but unlike *guilt, shame* does not blame and condemn its own heart, although shame, like innocence, is still in darkness. Shame repeats the question "why?"—and unfortunately, guilt is all too anxious to provide the answers.

For McCarriston especially, guilt deceives the victim into believing she was responsible for transgressions she did not commit. Faced with morality that is more comfortable with guilt and with concessions that obscure the revolting truth, the victim of shame is particularly pressed to find an ear that will believe her. Without such an ear, the world is not of her own making and its illusions make her own existence a hall of vacant mirrors in which self hides behind self like so many cards in a pack. Beginning with the idea of the Catholic "confessional" itself, guilt is often a means of institutional indoctrination, which mandates and sanctions the power of the righteous to maintain dominance. Guilt is always accommodated by one's traditional faith because guilt always places the blame on the individual rather than the institution, which protects its power by shielding itself from suspicions and blame. Shame is the victim's self-awareness of being the target of undeserved cruelty, and insofar as shame feels like guilt, orthodox religion may only subvert shame to guilt, self-accusation, and self-hatred, rather than allow shame to become outrage or dissent. Outrage and dissent pose troublesome questions, which institutions and the status quo would rather avoid. Such shame is a species of horrified awe or wonder, like Job's shame over God's arbitrary punishments, mixed with a faith in good, liberation, and love. That is Job's ultimate salvation: not guilt, but the love and the courage to live and love with unanswered questions.

The victim may wrestle over her undeserved shame through saying the unspeakable, turning to judge, doctor, psychiatrist, and priest. However, these channels may support the hegemony of perpetrator over victim by trying to project guilt onto the innocent. The victim stays penitential and self-blaming. Only through writing can the poet address the collective human order by submerging the individual's evil in the deeper more impermeable causes of universal evil and its implication. In her ideological view, the "crime" was not individual but collective—with roots in power structures that so often invert good to evil in its own name. The past or former self (so often a child) cannot do this and that is why the child is so often the ironical speaker within the confessional poems. The child points out the corruption of the adult world in contrast to the child's own naiveté. The child can be a savior if the mature poet can reconjure him and begin the testimony of horror that was suppressed in the past. By revivifying the child, the confessional poet may rescue the afflicted adult. And like Wordsworth's benign child—within, the child continues to accumulate associations—former self, former heart, former soul. In *The Prelude*, Wordsworth confesses that in later years he lacked the spiritual confidence that the inner child naturally possessed. The restoration of the child as the inner morality and truth not yet spoken may be analogous to the confessional process because the child within the poet is permitted to resurface. The poem is an opportunity for the child to reveal and counter the tyranny she lived under when she was unable to "speak" or disobey.

The mature poet summons the child in a variety of ways to witness, to demonstrate the reality of victimization, to enforce justice in response to abuse, and to liberate the adult poet from pain. This displacement of adult perception into the child, who can feel but only partially comprehend the events that surround him or her, is a strategy for endowing the child with conscious reflection. Contrition is available only to the mature poet, for not acting now to forestall the evil she recognizes through the past, within the family or within the broader social world. Here is the power of the expansive processes of Olds's and McCarriston's so-called "giving encouraging voice to the life force." They may present a pattern, but they are hardly "mechanistic." The poems are imperatives for rising from the depths, like Lazarus's need to warn and disclose, to use the incendiary coal of language to speak, and to illuminate the broken innocence of children and their shame.

Glück's assumptions that Olds and McCarriston remodel poetry into a mechanistic poetry that avoids discovery seem to premeditate Gluck's own obligations as both an agent of hurt and the one who gets hurt in *Ararat*. Glück's singular brilliance grows out of the image and into the quick volt of elliptical wisdom that often lulls the poem back into a like frieze of the Keatsian urn. The private sphere of the child/daughter in *Ararat*, and her pain, is weighed by the adult's reflection and finally judged and settled. In Glück's "myth" of the nuclear family, the poems draw us toward the already vanished, like the mother's heart drawn to her dead infant's "like a magnet."[6] The contexts of the poems are within the daughter's response to the mother, to the sister, to the markers of time and memory. But they stay locked there, riveted on the self-reflexive retrievals that offer up the daughter's own face within the poet like the veins of a translucent leaf. Syntactically and tonally, they float back to their deepest origins—which is silence itself. Glück's visionary imagination harkens back to the romantic's conviction that imagination is a prefiguration of the life hereafter, that what it reveals is a transcendent and universal destiny that is its own fulfillment. That tendency to restrain speech from becoming a tenor agency rather than vehicle is Gluck's way, but not Olds's or McCarriston's.

In Olds's and McCarriston's best poems, private suffering is connected with collective suffering, and the poems relate our contemporary concerns more profoundly than the poems of some reactionary movements that subordinate content to the execution of form. Plath, Olds, and McCarriston grapple with the issues of the morality, cruelty, and virtues of the human spirit faced with the "unbearable." In doing so, they adopt a victim's vocabulary and bring the reader into events by the beauty of the poem and then, ironically, confront us with hideous truth. This confrontation links personal confessions of survival in art with historical chronicles of survival in extreme circumstances of deprivation or atrocity. In both cases, the survivor is the one who refuses to go away. The survivor's irreducible presence compels us all to be witnesses, to hear the story of martyrdom and shame and sometimes forgiveness. Confessionalism contains the positive belief in expression as liberation from the powers that would disarm the truth.

The concentration camps provide many witnesses and confessions. In a television interview, Elie Wiesel narrates his experience of liberation from a concentration camp where he was a child. He recalls that children in the camps already had the wisdom of old people because they had been exposed to the polar extremes of human savagery. When the liberation came, Wiesel recalls, an African-American sergeant was confronted with the stench, the corpses, and emaciated forms of what were once living men and women. The sergeant cursed and cursed. He screamed and cursed all of humanity, as well as the perpetrators, for tolerating the savagery there. Wiesel said that the children wanted to thank the sergeant, to lift the man up on their shoulders in a hero's fashion, but they were far too weak and kept falling back to the ground. The sergeant did not give up, however, and tossed himself in their arms, *trying to be light*. Wiesel recalls the man's frolic in the midst of the tumbling children; he wanted to levitate himself for them, he wanted to do what a savior would do: to fly. Wiesel's testimony is beautifully symbolic: the liberating angel opens and attempts to revitalize the children again, both physically and spiritually to restore their strength.

Burdened by the gravity of history and its succession of endless atrocities, it is inevitable that the female confessional poet, seeking a symbol to express the deepest tragedy of her own sense of victimization, would choose a constructed identity of the political martyr, the victim those in power must censor or silence for her views, beliefs, or genetic origins, which can only be extinguished along with personhood. Olds and McCarriston include in their books historical and political victims because they engage the "literary" reader. At the same time, these poets deconstruct the very idea of confessionals by restoring voices to the survivors, who testify that their supposed guilt was innocence and that the judges of old are really to blame. Like the Holocaust survivor, the female confessional poet who has endured a traumatic experience is not untouched by shame for having been there to witness, present to terrible acts. The female confessional poet must break the code of silence and overturn the imbalance of power relations.

McCarriston's poem "Le Coursier de Jeanne D'Arc," demonstrates how martyrdom can represent the human dilemma of how to "speak" truthfully even when violence and pain seem to distort everything.[7] In the poem, Jeanne D'Arc is not the central victim, at least not yet. Instead, her dramatic demise is displaced by the horse they burned in front of her eyes—both as a foreshadowing of the punishment she was about to receive and as an impetus for her to repent. The horse is a substitute for the children Jeanne never had: "she had no sons to burn" in a "world not of her making." Of course, mothers populate the world but have no power to provide their children with a safe world in which they might thrive.

The victims here are both the saint and her horse, whose slow agony accompanies a submerged yet articulate "voice":

> the long mad godlike trumpet of his terror,
> his crashing in the wood, the groan of stakes that held,
> the liverblack hide, the pricked ears catching first
> like dryest bark, and the eyes.[8]

First "the pricked ears" and then the recording "eyes" burn at the decrees of "Men of God" who are more interested in the spectacle of a burning animal or woman than in demands of justice and truth. Jeanne D'Arc's voice and vision are threatened by their corruption, by

> the cruelty that can make
> . . . of what a woman hears a *silence*,
> that can make of what a woman sees
> *a lie*.[9]

They pressure her to "confess" that what she sees and hears are not what she saw and not what she heard, that she is deluded by evil and blinded to good. And yet, what she confronts in the poem is tantamount to the Devil's Hell. Like Hester Prynne, Jeanne is threatening to the "Wise Men" because of self-dependence—her capacity to find God without their aid or control and without their lies.

What McCarriston emphasizes in the poem is not the victimization of woman at the stake, or the "ecstasy of her agony" ("This is yet one of their lies"), but the flesh-and-blood figure martyr forced to watch her masculine double similarly sacrificed to the fire of purification. The horse's "chest with perfect plates of muscle," her mate, perishes before her as if it might be the last shred of her will to resist or rebel. She wrestles with the possibility of recanting, to avoid "the narrow corral that would not / burn until flesh had . . . " but then realizes to do so would be to surrender not only her religious beliefs, but also her morality. She will not "put on their truth," their mendacity, at whatever cost because it would sacrifice her own spirit that only God, not she, can do. Deadly fires transform hue from "yellow-green" to" blackening red" as they are fed animal or human flesh; and in the same way, McCarriston suggests that the perpetrators are tainted by their own sins, forever guilty as the blaze itself becomes the color of the charred body. Thus this is not simply about the martyrdom of one woman, but the ideology of the truth: what is human and what is not, and what is bestial and what is not. The body of the horse is allowed to burn "untended" as if it were game—and here, "game" is intended to carry its cavalier meaning. This is a savage, criminal game of torture and power and affliction. It has its historical linkage to other forms of mass persecution and atrocity, such as the Holocaust.

In strong poets such as McCarriston and Olds, confession is a personal outcry that seeks to address a community's consciousness. By conflating the inner domestic realm of the woman with the broader, historical realities, a woman can curse the evil of the perpetrator rather than confess to her own guilt. Olds may do so by trying to transcend her own—or the family's pain—through a knowledge of the suffering all around her. On the other hand, McCarriston refutes the derogation of the term *confessional* by insisting on her work's cool logic and therefore by ironically maintaining the traditional expectations of masculine discourse while telling stories that reveal their deceptions. Both poets wish to call our attention to how injustices imprison victims in visible or invisible cells; yet it is the "cells" that unite us in one living world. Such poetry finds its analogy in religious poetry, demonstrating how the shocking truth of human suffering can reveal the need for a community to support the private pains and the healing of others. Writing about victims and survivors of the Holocaust, Des Pres states :

> But as a man or woman is unjustly condemned he is connected to others, first to the Jews and then to humanity who like himself are the victims and scapegoats of power. At first, he insists that he is not a political person. But gradually his suffering brings home to him the pain of all people in extremity and that when the exercise of power includes the death of innocent people, there is no such thing as an unpolitical man.[10]

But what does the private anguish of some literary confessionals have to do with the Inquisition or the Holocaust? One linkage is that poets such as Plath and Sexton, and even Olds, have appropriated the symbol of the Jewish survivor as an analogy through which they can make publicly understood the private anguish of being oppressed, victimized, or extinguished. Another linkage is that the historical survivor's stages of psychological experience often parallel the poet's. According to Des Pres and Wiesel, the survivor possesses a need to testify and make the truth known: to break the silence (although silence is an appropriate response to the darkness of civilization), to judge that silence on the part of the outsider is conspiratorial, to insist that silence must be broken through the witness who is most often a child who logically connects past with present.

As a Jew myself whose parents lost most of their families in concentration camps in Poland, I am not bothered by the "proportional discrepancy" between linking a non-Jewish poet's literary confessional of survival and the testimony of a survivor of Auschwitz, although one is assumably "art" and the other is "history." I think that both can be grave and difficult, although the latter more lacerating for what it says about the madness of civilization's so-called progress, but the former is still authentic and unignorable. For the survivors of political oppression and for the confessional "survivors" of poetry, the problem is how to preserve their own souls in predicaments that are seemingly soul-*less*.

Still, readers may question the relevance (if not the morality) of a poetry that is seemingly so private and resistant to temperance and unapologetic about making anguish (personal or historically dramatic) the centripetal force of the poem. But these suspicions may arise from traditional and stifling poetics; a poem should not be grim or offend our sense of "good taste"; it should not be self-indulgent; it should please rather than threaten, shock, or disgust. Yet, the poem cannot be severed from its maker: it is asking too much from the poet to permit the reader to exclude certain material on the basis of its taboo or shocking subjects. When we begin to do that, we join the "conspiracy of silence." The poems of Olds and McCarriston are admittedly a "victim's vocabulary" but with self-awareness and purpose. Both poets successfully absorb the reader through the textual reenactment of horror and beauty.

Given these pressures and ironies within the female confessionalist poet's psyche, how do we come to define *confessionalism* as Olds, McCarriston, and Plath practice it? What are we to make of detractors who dismiss this type of poetry as "self-indulgent," "self-righteous," or "narcissistic"? Confessionalism denotes "speaker," or as Olds defines it, "personalism" is a mode of expression within the traditional lineage of poetry, beginning with Sappho, and including intellectual and social voices in poetry after World War II. Confessionalism goes hand in hand with the politicism of poetry. This type of poetry is exceptional for its characteristic themes of self-interrogation, expiation, and blame. As examples of the most powerfully achieved poetry in the lineage of "confessionalism," the works of Olds and McCarriston do not end with passive submission, with the acceptance of inevitable atrocities, or with the internalization of death, which is also the death of speech, but with a reason to speak and hope and with the power to change.

Through confession, there exists a mutual identification between the priest who lifts the burden of the "sins" of the sufferer and then expels it through transposition and forgiveness. Unlike the child, the mature poet has acquired the power of articulation to amend or confess the past. But blame may also accompany "sin" and suffering. Where does guilt end and suffering begin? And how does the innocent, the textual child, born out of recollection as a poet's progeny (to borrow a descriptive phrase of Mary Shelley's as she conceived of *Frankenstein*), come to separate the two?

The poems of Olds and McCarriston confront this very difficult moral and psychological problem. When the child is the confesser of a sin in which she was forced to participate, the problem is how to speak about shameful experience in the face of "propriety" and censorship. When the reader rejects possibilities of where art can take a reader, the reader breaks an implicit bond of human trust that, in this context, is analogous to the priest's role as listener.

Confessional poets must search for symbols to represent maturation, filtered through the many layers of self-objectification and self-supervision because they failed to address or refute the event when it happened. However, the disruption of the integration process is one of the central features of the psychology behind confessionalism. That is not to say that it destroys the process; rather, it fuels it. When the individuation process is fraught with anxiety and pain, the passage toward the exterior is thwarted, mental stress may result in a contained paroxysm of costumed surrogates for the "truer" personality. This is certainly true of Plath who masquerades as Lady Lazarus, Nick and the Candlestick, Ariel, and perhaps, most memorably, as the tortured Jew in Dachau accusing her "Nazi" father of sadism.[9] '"The "Jew" is used here impressionistically, not allegorically. In reality, the Jew, of course, is not a masochist, but a nonparticipating victim—there is no complicity between torturer and tortured. Plath takes poetic license to show complicity, particularly between father and daughter in questionable, intimate relations of punishment and submission, of the seductive child who racks blame on the father who either assaulted her or ignored her as if she were nothing. The idea tended to blend the edges between infantile wish and reality, making the child an unconscious agent of seduction or aggression within the family. The fact that the confessional writers *seek out* key moments of heightened anxiety and pain suggests that Freudianism gave confessional poetry its reputation as the talking cure or self-therapy.

The background of confessionalism is one of a convergence of anxieties shared by the post–World War II generation and by the individual's dissociation from some of the values—religious, social, and moral— she once relied on for personal stability. Civilization itself was suffering a nervous "breakdown" as intellectuals examined the problem of evil in its grossest form, a systematic destruction of European Jewry and the world-wide destruction to which all warring nations contributed. In the Nuremberg trials, the war criminals were interrogated to force them to disclose that each one was aware of the aberrant crimes he had committed against humanity. Without awareness, there can be no logical accountability. Awareness was proved through action, and deliberate evil was shown by deed, cover-up and secrecy.[12] The Gestapo went to great lengths to disguise, bury, and conceal what they had done; demonstrating their understanding of what they had done and how the world would judge it. Had they not known the difference between right and wrong, there would be no reason to hide it. Hence, some acts of cruelty are unforgivable and human goodness and evil are not relative, but fixed states of human action and culpability. Although we may consider the concept of genocide as insane, the Nazis had to be, ironically, considered sane to prove their guilt. Those who knew what was happening to the Jews, but did not raise their voice to halt it, whose civility would not permit the possibility much less the fact of human brutality—they were in some ways as guilty as the Nazis themselves.

Like the revelations of history, confession serves as an antidote to the extreme harm that civilized silence can do. The female poet working through the complexity of her own victimization may arrive at a symbology of action and submission, silence and speech, to overturn the scales of power and powerlessness. Thus, Plath, for example, takes on herself the roles of the Jew and biblical or mythological figures who have suffered and survived to express her own sense of degradation and justifiable outrage at her "torturers." Identification with the Jew in "Daddy" expresses a deep sense of being despised and powerless to fight the forces of brutality. Plath's appropriation of the suffering and martyrdom of the Jew is both a sign of victimization and rebuttal. Yet "Daddy" is sometimes faulted for being an artful but self-exhibitionist work of indulgent rage and bitterness directed at a neglectful and verbally abusive father. His abandonment of her to death and silence may have influenced her idiosyncratic "art of dying" in which art itself became the intangible but seductive realm into which dying seemed pleasurable. She "did it again and again" trying to perfect her art and her own death simultaneously. In her work, pain and anguish serve to bind reader and poet together as the one confessing and the one hearing the confession are bound by mutual recognition.

In "Daddy," the child's shame is supplanted by the power of her utterance when she can speak against those forces that censor her: the father, female propriety, the world of oppositions such as hate and love, torturer and tortured. We are moved by the nakedness of the confession as a testimony of the underprotected child who is violated until the perpetrator is himself silenced by death or absence. "Daddy" is about learning to speak: and this is evident by the child's primitive babbling and by the many references to silence or the failure to articulate:

> I never could talk to you.
> The tongue stuck in my jaw.
> It stuck in a barb wire snare . . .

Ich, ich, ich, I could hardly speak . . .
the black telephone's off at the root,
the voices just can't worm through . . .[13]

At the end of "Daddy" the reader knows that the shame of the confessor is bound up with her utterance, which is a belated response to her silent victimization. Her identification with the Jew persecuted by the Nazi is an allusion (and also an evasion) of the conflictual terms of the poem. The Jew's "guilt" is untenable because the Jew is absolute victim, despised not for his or her self, but for what is less tangible, his or her genus. The Nazis willed the destruction of the Jews not only from one country to another, but also from the existence of the world itself. If they had succeeded, the descendants of those who survived the Holocaust would not be. In "Daddy," the role of the Nazi torturer is not simply predicated on hurting the child but in willing her out of existence. Hence, there is a half-hidden wish to extirpate her father and herself to regain some primal level of communication with him in a realm beyond death. Her father's unwillingness to see her as a person, rather than being a specimen in a collective genus (that is, female), accompanies her worst fear that, so classified, she is an abomination to him. Her femaleness brings on more self-destruction through masochistic relationships with men. But the masochist is only the flip side of the sadist, and, in some ways, needs him to perpetuate her agony and wrath.

Plath's duality resembles the duplicity of humanity in general, which is to itself both the victim and victimizer. Plath further dramatizes this rift in the poems of *Ariel*, the collection published after her suicide. The poems insist that nothing is more universal than the home and the family, and that private experience is the essential foundation for more public and universal structures that continue to confine or minimize women. The indeterminacy of blame and guilt is understandably disturbing for some readers of Plath. Irving Howe wrote about "Daddy" that there was, in fact, something "monstrous" and utterly disproportionate about entangling one's emotions about one's father with the fate of European Jews in the Holocaust.[14] But Plath is writing from the standpoint of not only the victims, but also from the center of Nazi barbarianism. Her choice is to plunge willingly into the dark abyss of modern madness to reach the bottom of degradation and sorrow.

While exploring the extremity of human virtue and human depravity, both Olds and McCarriston illustrate the divisions of human good and human evil. The comprehensibility of hurt and blame may divert itself back to the mature and analytical poet or back again to the incarnation of the poet within the child. But the harboring of the child within the protection of the mature consciousness may not be, as some have charged, outright displays of narcissism, but moments of needed self-awareness.

Olds and McCarriston do not squelch rage and human terror by answering to a dubious "aesthetics" or by keeping a polite distance from their subjects. Rather, they use language as an ally, an acquired means for fighting back against those who stripped them of defenses early on. Implicitly, the poet understands that indirection and neutrality are stances that only serve to weaken the metaphysical armor of the poem. Olds and McCarriston find routes through confrontation as well as confession. As women, they refuse to mitigate the literal fact of the body and what happens to the psyche when the body is abused. Therefore the language of confession is torrid, descriptive, and often brutal. The child does not lie; not in art, for art lives and breathes in the conditional, not in the verifiable. Silence only sustains suffering, but the artist breaks the silence by giving up suffering to speech and writing.

Women's confessional poetry offers, in place of the traditional Catholic acknowledgment of sins, the possibility of empowerment through language as a spiritual and therapeutic process of exoneration. Olds does not abdicate her responsibility as the speaker who is contaminated by the sins of others who are in control, but tries to reveal aspects of consciousness that we all possess but do not like to acknowledge. Does Olds want us to see that we are no different than the victim, the perpetrator, or the damned? Can we not both tell what happened (as witness) and still love (as child)? Does she want us to eye the face of humanity when all its masks of acceptability are lifted? "Satan Says":

> I am locked in a little box cedar box
> with a picture of shepherds pasted onto
> the central panel between carvings.
> The box stands on curved legs.
> It has a gold, heart shaped lock
> and no key. I am trying to write my
> way out of the closed box
> redolent of cedar. Satan
> comes to me in the locked box a
> and says, *I'll get you out. Say*
> *My father is a shit.* I say
> my father is a shit and Satan
> laughs and says, *It's opening.*
> *Say your mother is a pimp.*
> My mother is a pimp. Something
> opens and breaks when I say that.[15]

The poem follows the child's attempt to get out of the "confession box" by testing God through Satan. She allows Satan to rescue her from the stultifying silence of supposed guilt and by repeating his blasphemous profanities, by sacrilege. The box then becomes a jewelry box on a child's bureau (like Pandora's box or Gilman's wallpapered room), making a smooth transition from the authority of the church to the home; both places have "locked her up," first in sin, then in childhood, and finally in gender. Once situated at home, Satan continues to taunt her with her own wish to punish her father and mother as one supposes they have punished or tortured the child. But in doing so, the child begins to feel, for the first time, guilty. In damning her mother and father, she realizes what that might really mean to her. In her collusion with the devil, she has sentenced her parents to death. For a moment, she reneges: "Oh no, I loved them too" and realizes that in taking side with the devil, she has damned herself because she has answered violence with violence, disregard with disregard, in spite of her love. Justice and love fall at odds with one another. If her parents are bad and she says so, then has she really elevated herself into the realm of the good—the "ballerina's" realm? Or if she is bad, cursing them as Satan says to do, does her incrimination restore them as principles of goodness that are justified in punishing her? But here, her own sentence has merged with that of her parents. In surrendering them to the devil to be tortured, she sees the evil within herself, "the red eye" of the ballerina; but in her own "fire" or wrath, she has "suddenly discovered knowledge of love."

Metaphorically, the poem suggests that language will unlock her from the confines of her silence. The subversion of the priest's ear or God's ear to Satan's voice, from acceptance to dissent, mirrors the child's change from powerless, silent victim to angry, wrathful poet who can use speech to confess and presumably escape guilt and suffering. However, the twist in this poem is the poet's admission that she is implicated by sacrificing "loved ones" to evil, and that her own perpetual damnation is bound up with theirs.

In another early poem, "That Year," Olds, like Plath before her, compares herself with the Jewish captives in Auschwitz, the fate of whom she recalls having learned about in social studies class "that year." The poem begins with this initial idea, "that was the year I started to bleed / crossing over the border in the night. . . ."[16] Her associations finally lead her to an identification with the "six million Jews." That year she discovered brutality in her own private sphere: a girl discovered murdered, her father's abuse of the family, and other, more obtuse events such as getting her period, "the mask of blood" that she was unprepared for and that she interpreted as a sign of the pain already inflicted on her. She recognized the cause of that pain

> like my father's face, the face of the guard
> turning away or worse yet
> turning towards me.[17]

The mature poet remembers her own sense of guilt as a child, as victim of her father's abuse, an abuse that perversely fosters within the child identical shame for being that which is reprehensible to the parent and therefore deserving of punishment. But what if the punishment is undeserved? Undeserved punishment is the underlying linkage between private confession and symbolic representation of the Jew in Auschwitz. And that is also the definition of parental force or abuse. And the association of menstruation adds to the idea that she may be rejected or hated for her difference as a female, leading to more masochistic assaults on herself (that bring "blood").

Yet the speaker then realizes that she is not to be counted among the Jews ("a word for us"), but that she was a survivor:

> there was another word for me
> and for many others
> I was: a survivor.

The survivor rises above the shame and rebels by sustaining her own humanity—her ideological defense. Although she was not the cause of the cruelty inflicted on her by others, she cannot extricate herself from its happening; it happened to her and not because of her. The father begets in his daughter the image of his self-repulsion. That is how he wins over her. But even the child realizes, through the confession, that she may not be a victim, but a survivor, because she has survived the father's threat to her autonomy and not relinquished the process of her own individuation. Even so, she knows that survivors never do forget or escape their personal guilt for surviving when others did not.

And in surviving, there is testimony to give the past meaning, even if meaning is the conflation of many emotions. In Olds's poem "Tricks," redemption comes through confession, speech, or writing. The inscrutability of the mother is dramatized in how she uses her body and not her speech to make things happen, or conversely, to make nothing happen:

> She pulls scarves out of her ears . . .
> My mother the naked magician
> stands on the white stage
> and pulls her tricks.[18]

The mother is deceptive and powerless in her disappearance and reappearance, in her magician's guise. She is depriving her daughter of what she seemingly offers: "She closes her hand / and when she opens it, nothing." The only continuity between daughter and mother is the act of biological procreation, yet the mother abrasively takes back the life she gives, through the fact of her silence, which is an emotional starvation. The daughter can counter with her visibility and voice, now redirecting it to her own status as magician for the reader, a poet-performer: "All this / I have pulled out of my mouth / right in front of your eyes." The mouth is a substitute for the mother's sexual parts from which the infant was "pulled out" like another prop in an intangible magic show. There is nothing reassuring about the mother's presence or that she values one prop (her jewels) any more than her daughter. But the daughter can seek reprisal against the mother by magically, if not improbably, giving birth to herself through speech itself. The guilt of the mother is sealed by the daughter's accusation through "the mouth" (the witness) and beseeching the reader's "eyes" as judge.

In an article, "The Refrain of the Repressed: Incest Poetry in a Culture of Victimization," Allison M. Cummings argues that a popular influx of "incest poetry" has served only to perpetuate rather than to abate women's sense of their own victimhood by adopting a stance of passive resignation.[19] Citing the inadequacy of several techniques, including leaving the point "implicit" in the imagery and metaphors, Cummings "prefers" poetry about incest in the form of a "social critique" to personal, evidentiary testimonies that emphasize psychic damage stemming from the traumas that have silenced victims for years. According to Cummings, victimhood can be overcome only by a victim's adopting a more active image of agency and speech founded on intellectual and creative agency. As Cummings declares, "Despite locating the blame without, incest poetry is rarely angry."[20]

Cummings's contention that survivors of sexual abuse should respond to their traumas with bare outrage is refuted by clinical evidence. In fact, as Herman points out, victims of childhood sexual abuse will often react in a state of detached calm, or "constriction," in which they experience the events as if they were happening to someone else.[21] This is the body's natural defense against acknowledging what is actually happening. Moreover, clinical studies have shown that in treatment, patients who have suffered childhood abuse may not exhibit symptoms for years after episodes of abuse, but are susceptible to feelings of worthlessness, bewilderment, and promiscuous behavior.[22] The tendency toward masochism as a means of turning parental sadism against the self in an effort to identify with the abusive parent rather than risk being abandoned by that parent is frequently observed. Cummings's attempt to stifle or condemn the victim's response, any response, will only serve to discourage the anger she feels is the more appropriate feminist response. Silence and denial are always a means of aiding the perpetrator rather than protecting the victim. As Herman argues:

> Denial has always been the incestuous father's first line of defense. For a long time it has served him well. The belief that incest is extremely uncommon, and the tendency to discredit children's reports of sexual encounters with adults, have until recently remained entrenched in public consciousness. With the collusion of the larger society, the incestuous father has been largely successful in keeping his secret.[23]

McCarriston, like Olds, pushes past the limits of the silence that was once imposed on her, and she does judge, blame, and try to forgive. Both poets write about unnatural things that happen in the private contexts of the family, but the terror of the underprotected child is not easily recalled or refined into such a lucid art of reconstruction, recollection, and tonal irony. The violent acts of the parent become poignant as they are resurrected in the self-witnessing representations of the victim herself, who cannot call herself a victim until she recognizes what the victor took from her. Initially the survivor stays frozen in the past and only later fights the impositions of her own shame, her silence, not wanting to bring the inside out. The deepest truth is the confessor's confrontation: "*Here I am, you can't wish me away.*" McCarriston shows admirable discipline in maintaining a fixed eye on the brutality and does not seek a higher authority to reason with it. In her work, the child within is a spectral figure, a beacon or lighthouse, whose beam of light is so direct and concentrated that it may cause the reader to want to blink or look away.

What is exceptional about McCarriston is how confession becomes a trope that is deliberately inverted to show its signifying "difference" from itself. This poetry dramatizes innocence that is corrupted by the parent, along with conflicted feelings of love and hatred, anger and penance, blaming and punishment. Hence, confession is the refusal to be guilty under the pressures of the other who hopes to contain the victim within that guilt. The flawed representation of the betraying parent *within* must itself be banished, expunged, amputated from the daughter's psyche for her to use language as a belated weapon against a mother's neglect and denial or a father's sadism. Power generates from the extremity of a child's release into the fluid authority of language that will, due to its own limits, never tell the whole story, but can partially expel the isolation of a child taught not only to take what is handed to her, but also to privatize her pain.

Shame, horror, and self-disfigurement are compelling effects of the psychically bruised child who has accepted the bad and evil and ugly as her own flesh. Although she was innocent, the fall into corruption is not so much a complicity with the arbiter of the transgression or their mutual punishment, but a solitary drop into groundlessness.

In McCarriston's poem "Billy," the poet recovers a scene of horror as the abusive father is seen beating her brother:

> and even our father,
> who stood beating you with his fists
> where he'd stuck you into
> a barrel, as a mountaineer might plant
> a banner in a peak to keep your
> skinny thirteen-year-old body erect
> till he was finished . . . the whole

rest emanates and fades.
It was winter. . . . You had driven
your homemade go-cart into a door
that he was saving for something. . . .
I see his upper body
plunging up and down like one
of those wind-driven lawn ornaments. . . .
The barrel reaches your bottom.
Your body sounds different than
a mattress. The noises he makes
are the noises of a man trying
to lift a Buick off the body
of a loved child, whose face he can
see, upturned just above the wheel
that rests on her chest, her eyes right
on his eyes, as yours were on mine.[24]

The father has raped her mother or even her. That fact is revealed through the metaphor of a man "trying to lift a Buick off the body of a loved child." The sister has associated the beating with the act of rape, and they are one. The "eyes" are autonomous, as the "eyes" of God's judgment watching the father's beating, then his raping, watching the victims look at him with deathly horror and then to witness with the same look, that is not guilt but the knowledge of who is to blame. The victims are speechless, but the poet recounts the experience with extraordinary objectivity. This is by no means "a narcissistic indulgence" or "manipulation" of a reader's readiness to be shocked. This poem terrifies because it goes beyond the horror of the act but seizes us with the truth of our own capacity to look on and do nothing while people commit heinous crimes. The particular complication within the poem is the mirroring of brother and sister who corroborate for one another the event. Because they are figuratively "one flesh" they serve as priests for one another and their unspoken confessions. Because they are assailed by feelings of their own incipient evil or worthlessness derived from the father's sins, they are also somehow implicated in his guilt. Do the eyes connote helplessness, guilt, or shame? What is the poet "confessing" if not the complexity of all three? And yet there is also anger and blame in which the reader participates, conceding that this is humanity in its most complex, incestuous light: love and hatred, abuser and abused, suffering and transcendence. If the poem has no room for forgiveness, it has room for understanding. A violent tableau, the memory of the terror of the child who is already locked in the "confessional/coffin" springs forth through the savagery of what it has occupied and finds its justification in articulation.

In "To Judge Faolain, Dead Long Enough: A Summons" the mature poet blames, without reservation and without ambiguity, the judge who allowed her abusive father proximity to the wife and children. The judge's reliance on "justice" and "law" is in ironic juxtaposition to the reality of what is actually happening in the family. The judge's failure was in his incapacity to identify with the people he stood above as a "symbol" of authoritative justice. "Let your name be Eva Mary. Let your birth be dawn. / Let your life be long and common, and your flesh endure."[25] The bitter and satiric irony of the last line emphasizes that the flesh, like the outer shell of beaten daughter and mother is only temporary; what does endure is the evocation of the experience and the poet's right not only to talk back, to refute and correct the error of judgment, but also to blame the perpetrator of that error, the judge.

The child speaks for the injustice done against her mother and turns the poem from the private confessional into an allegory about the subjugation of all dependent women who are vulnerable to the physical, spiritual, or judicial authority of men who regard women as inferior, as body rather than "light." The mother's flesh will not endure; ultimately, it is the book her father has already effaced, an accounting of his sins on which the writer has now left her own voice, her own text of liberation. Here, womanhood, Eva Mary, combines with the social class she represents in the courtroom. Both woman and the poor signify powerlessness before the judge's bench, a powerlessness that is childlike because it must go without appeal and cannot find reality in the judge's official but artificial rhetoric. Indeed, there is someone to blame here. My point is that the fact of blaming does not minimize the power of the confession as a moment of vital communion and identification of writer and reader.

The poet stands here as both witness and defense for her mother against all of violence and "unforgivable ignorance" of the men who did not see her for what she was. The title "Eva Mary" is in itself a suggestion that poetry (Mother, Eve) in this mode seeks to resurrect the past, to mother again, and to bear the child as a deliverer of language that seeks not to mollify, but opens the possibilities of saying what is most difficult to confess. In another poem, "Hotel Nights With My Mother," McCarriston demonstrates without self-pity or excuse the difficulty of accommodating a class-conscious world that critically appraises her as inferior due to her outer trappings:

> I scanned the row of faces
> their cumulative skill in the
> brilliant adolescent dances
> of self-presentation, of hiding. . . .
> I was watching them all
>
> for the dark-circled eyes,
> yesterday's crumpled costume, the marks
> the sorrowful coloring of marks
> the cuticles flaming and torn.

I made of myself each day a chink
a few might pass through unscathed.[26]

The poignant aspect of the class conflict is not in the society that condemns her but within the self-consciousness of the child who feels she is nothing. The authorities, however, are sympathetically depicted; the girl's undeserving "contamination" is synonymous with our specious condemnation of them. McCarriston is not after such a facile opposition; rather she exposes the resentment the child feels when trying to measure up to the standards of her "superiors." She cannot see herself in them, and therefore she is extinguished, unable to join their circle; and they cannot see themselves in her so that they seem to walk through her, as if she were invisible. Invisibility in the class context has its own definition since Ellison, a theme that is by now familiar yet not correctable in the social sphere. The subject of the poem is not the poor child, but what she signifies about misinterpretation and apprehension in people faced with "difference."

Works of the confessional mode, or the "personal," offsprings of introspection and dissidence, often provoke the question among readers: Why should we care? Why should we care about the private suffering of others? To that position I would respond, Why should we not? We read them not because they are brave, or scandalous, or masochistically enthralling. We read them not because we are, or they are, voyeurs or missionaries. We read them because they impart truth about cruelty, about the need to unify aspects of the self, and because they show the inscriptions of collective pain as a language that can be uttered, received, and transcended. We read them because they plummet through the surface, break the code of silence, and yield wisdom. These poets touch irresistible pain, pain that unites us or tears us apart. They recognize the gravity of human history that is a succession of atrocities as well as a progress of accomplishments. And we should come to recognize ourselves in them, our own vulnerabilities, in the human truth they speak, or even, as the African-American sergeant did—curse, liberate, and fly.

4

FATHERING DAUGHTERS

Oedipal Rage and Aggression in Women's Writing

The desire for male recognition is often at odds with a female writer's desire for literary primacy. Indeed, a female writer need not capitulate to the patriarchal demand that she stay subordinate. When permitted access to the imagery of the unconscious, a writer may well surface with demons instead of angels. When female writers find a vehicle for expressing their long withheld anger and rage at the Oedipal father in literary fantasy, the effect is both cathartic and therapeutic.

Lacan has stated that the goal of psychoanalysis is to allow the patient to come to terms with the inner dead, especially the dead father. The dead need not be really dead; rather, they are the ones who left deposits of affect-laden signifiers in the unconscious and then went away. A dead father may do no visible harm, although he can be destructive. And a daughter can fantasize about harming a father, whether he is alive or dead. A father who has not been adequately mourned may, in all likelihood, refuse to stay dead, posing even more problems for a female writer in forming social attachments.

In the following pages, I reveal how female writers deliver themselves to a canon from which they have often been excluded. Detailed recollections and narratives in which the damaged or weakened self is mobilized by expression, seek not only therapeutic outlets but also social accountability. This chapter will expand on the previous chapter by focusing on how psychoanalytic criticism can identify specific textual strategies female writers have adopted to dismantle patriarchal structures that have obstructed their writing. Due to the encouragement of critical readers who have deemed self-analysis a respectable goal for literary inquiry, women are remaking literary history by rewriting it.

By acting out fantasies of revenge or aggression against the Oedipal father, female writers seek to imaginatively sever the social "contract" that they comply with a standard of man's control, man as "law," whether that man be judge, father, psychiatrist, or rejecting love object. Positioning themselves as victims of misogyny, these female poets transgress boundaries and venture into enclosed circles of supercharged images and symbols not yet authorized by men. They understand their rage at the Oedipal father as a species of love, as well as the result of not being adequately loved. An early fixation with the father and what he signifies may well keep these literary daughters emotionally bound to the original object of their cathexis and exclusively identified with him. Although there is obvious indebtedness to the paternal figure, these "fathering daughters" have adopted various discursive maneuvers for recouping the father's authorial post and reinventing his language.

In her well-known essay "When We Dead Awaken: Writing as Revision,"[1] Adrienne Rich elaborates on the problem female writers have in speaking within the rhetorical codes and structures of patriarchal culture. Rich calls for the reawakening of sleeping or "core" consciousness as a means of transforming political realities inside and outside the home. Until, she argues, we can understand the patriarchal assumptions (and images) to which women have always been subjected, women can have no real knowledge of themselves. For Rich, the drive toward self-knowledge is both personal and cultural, the two being enmeshed.

Freudian psychoanalysis consists mainly of encouraging the patient to recall the past to isolate traumatic events of childhood. Believing that anxieties in the here and now are repetitions of ancient childhood injuries, analysts have tried to retrieve memories to delve deeper into this "core" consciousness.[2] Analysis leads a patient back to repressed Oedipal and pre-Oedipal material. Just as one memory is retrieved, another floats intriguingly past her, encouraging more pursuit of, and probing into, the past. Only by finding the essential quality of representation of a woman's symptoms can she be awakened from the darkness that Rich maintains has crippled her life and her art.

Although Freud's theories of individual development helped people better comprehend their personal histories from the perspective of their present suffering, psychoanalysis itself has been under direct attack by critics who have challenged the notion of a causative relationship between developmental stages in the individual to the present psychopathological phenomena.[3] Without a direct linkage between childhood experiences that have been repressed and adult psychopathology, Freudian theory loses much of its efficacy and power. If memory cannot be trusted to construct an accurate description of the self, then of what use is memory in awakening the "dead of the unconscious," as Rich has called for?

The politics of memory, particularly "recovered memory," has been the topic of much controversy and has permeated the boundaries of women's poetry and letters. Allison Cummings, for example, finds fault with women's poetry that encourages a "glorification of victimhood" rather than expressing genuine anger at male authority. As belated daughters to the signifying codes of language always identified with "Man" or judge, whether in or out of professional institutions such as the courts or the academy, women have used their writing to deflect their rage and resentment. Even as the voice of the speaker obliquely struggles against it, one detects the iconic father's presence. The father's presence, like the Freudian concept of the superego, is internalized and may well be censoring of a female descendant's spontaneous expostulation.

Rich's metaphor of the reawakening of the "dead" is an apt description of her generation of women coming to terms with their indoctrination by a patriarchal system. Breaking with the rules of conduct or, in more extreme cases, fighting against what has been psychically deforming, women must be called on to look not only backwards but also inward, to register their revisionary claims. Hence Rich refuses to compromise what in her work may be, as Ted Hughes in his forward to Plath's *Collected Poems*, remarked about Plath's more bellicose poetry, "too hard for the reader to take." On the refusal of the poet to conceal the intensity of her emotions, Kinnell comments: "The crying of a baby is the tuning fork for a poet. The baby does not hide what it feels and what it feels has not yet found a reason to hide."[4] Poets are burdened with the responsibility of being true to their personal and political experience, however difficult it is to bear.

Since the publication of Mary Wollstonecraft's *Vindication of the Rights of Women* (1792), female authors have continued to challenge gender ideologies, arguing that a woman's education should include philosophy, politics, and the sciences. Whereas women's nature may differ from men's, women have a greater capacity for expressing emotions and are therefore better orators against slavery and other forms of social injustice. In the 1970s and 1980s, feminist critics such as Sandra Gilbert and Susan Gubar, Margaret Homans, Mary Poovey, Elaine Showalter, and Nancy Chodorow expertly argued that imaginative writing presented problems unique to gender and classification. Female writers, affirming the domestic sphere as a worthy topic for poetry, had to use their ingenuity to raise the mundane matters of household management to the level of masculine achievement in the social and political world.

More recently, feminist literary criticism has shown that gender may well determine writing style and sensibility. Critics now assume what they would not dare to hypothesize fifty years ago: that women are biologically and cognitively predisposed to certain codes of writing that actually simulate aspects of their natures. Increasingly, writing specialists are pointing out women's predilection for certain rhetorical strategies: literal figuration over abstraction, orbicular or circularity of thought over linear or teleological progression. From the perspective of psycholinguistic criticism, gender and socialization determine to some degree the use of syntax, grammar, and sequencing. Although female writers desire a literacy that is more fully descriptive of female identity and its representations, women have been less eager to formulate a language that would strictly exclude men or their patronage.

As Rich maintains, a female writer, sensitive to her own literary legacy, must possess a double vision. Although she must exercise her prerogative to reimagine herself, she must also remold male stereotypes that have served to control her. Rich also insists that the language (or self-images) that men have "trapped" along with her has to be liberated as well. Where appropriate, women invert the roles that gender plays in traditional poetry, treating the male figure as an object, as male poets have treated the female figure for generations. If the language, form, and syntax of a masculine tradition in poetry, as well as its depiction of Woman as a bewitcher or seductress, a la "La Belle Dame sans Merci," are somehow unraveled, as a web is "undone," it will eventually extinguish itself. Women must find a way to articulate the Male body in poetry that upsets, if not overturns, the balance of power by reinventing the male's body as "muse." As Rich quotes Jane Harrison in her essay: "By and by, about women, it has always bothered me why women never want to write poetry about Man as a sex, why is woman a dream and a terror to man and not the other way around?"[5]

Harrison's quote cuts deep into the myth-making tradition, deep into how women have been ritualistically imaged and signed by men. In Plath's and Sexton's literary depictions, the image of man is often seen as an enticement and a terror, and is inevitably associated with the paternal image. As Gilbert and Gubar[6] pointed out some decades ago, women's representations of men in poetry as torpid or appalling visages is actually an inversion, and subversion, of the male poet's tribute and veneration of the submissive female muse. Such reversals of power in women's fantasies become a decisive substitute for more assertive action in the political world, where women have withstood a hailstorm of psychological and physical attacks by men with little arsenal for refutation or counterattack.

Indeed, women will get even; "murder will out." What is remarkable about the works under consideration is their consistency because each presents a fantasy about revenge or anger toward the father, or father image, which is rendered both dead and alive through symbolic strategies of rerepresentation. The male body returns, whether impersonated, incorporated, or inseminated, but will not stay dead in each writer's fantasy. At each step, the writer, or poet, particularly, is convinced that the body of father or lover will survive any outright rage or aggression, but he will be far more subdued by the end.

Plath's and Sexton's angriest poems directed to the father might better reveal a self-destructive desire to be fused with him. Such expressions of rage directed at the paternal object are often more dangerous to the daughter than the external threat of the father himself. Although a daughter might feel an overpowering impulse to defend herself against the male figure, there is perhaps a deeper fear and anxiety that by destroying the father, one will be left abandoned, defenseless, and hopelessly alone. Fusing with the simultaneously loved and hated object through a fantasy about his revival in the creative work may also be a means of preserving the abusive or destructive relationship without having to cope with the reality of the object itself.

Anger at fathers (and sometimes mothers) inflates these poets' vernacular power, raising or intensifying the "volume" of their voices. Deflecting parental chastisement, the tones of these kinds of poems tend to be sarcastic or reproaching; a means, perhaps, of equalizing the powerful advantage a father has in physical size or strength. The daughters' "bad tempers" imitate male stridency. Often, a confessional poem opens with a daughter's anger predicated on a crime, which predates the origin of the poem, and therefore serves as its history, a history not yet remembered or explained. A poem's history is then synonymous with the writer's psychological history as she comes to recount it in narrative or in therapeutic sessions.

The publication of *The Journals of Sylvia Plath* offers insights into her psychiatric treatment and the relationship between the creative and therapeutic process.[7] Suffering from acute depression, Plath sought treatment just before her suicide attempt in 1953 and then secretly reentered therapy after her marriage to Ted Hughes in 1959. As Berman writes in his definitive chapter on Plath, some of Plath's best poems reflect the image of the artist as a "bad" daughter who expresses her rage toward mother and father.[8] "The Colossus," "The Beekeeper's Daughter," and "Electra in Black" exemplify the anguished familial themes that she was laboring through in both her writing and psychotherapy. Apparently, she used her art to extricate herself from the dilemmas that were causing her writers' block, especially in the years of married life. Plath's productive use of analysis, as recorded in her journals, documents her feelings toward her family and herself. Working with Dr. Ruth Beuscher, "an extraordinary therapist," she was determined to mine the quarry of her unconscious and get to the root of her anguish. Going to therapy once a week was a small price to pay for some peace of mind: "If I am going to pay money for her time & brain. . . I am going to work like hell, question, probe sludge & crap & allow myself to get the most out of it."[9]

To illustrate the residual tensions between daughter and father as Plath remembered them, we can begin with a discussion of Plath's "The

Colossus." During the period in which the poem was written, Plath was exploring, both in her art and in her psychotherapy, her disappointing relationships with men. In pursuit of the origins of her depressed condition, she visited her father's grave (presumably for the first time) and confides in her journals that she felt tempted "to dig him up." The archeological metaphor is unmistakably linked to the task of excavation in front of her, exhuming the fragments of the dead father while considering the negative effects he had on her life. Viewing her father's burial site helped Plath to prove he existed and really was dead. While psychotherapy insisted on her dredging up the memory of a mythic father to contend with his persistent threat to her happiness, Plath's father would simply not stay dead. In fact, Plath's writing is everywhere animated by this ubiquitous figure that will not be considered as anything other than someone very much alive.

In Freud's study "Delusions and Dreams in Jensen's *Gradiva*,"[10] a study Plath would have been familiar with because it is one of the first times Freud examines the relationship between literature and psychoanalysis, he offers us the essential relation between the fetish and arrested movement. In Freud's preliminary notion of the fetish in "Three Essays on the Theory of Sexuality," he discusses the issue of overvaluation and substitution of the fetish for the original or normal sexual object. However, ten years later in "Repression," Freud introduces the idea of the splitting of the instinctual representative, which in "Fetishism" is more fully developed and is shown to relate to the element of ambivalence operational in the fetish. In this later discussion, Freud explains that the fetishist's relation to his (or her) prized object not only simulates pleasure but also can generate a certain amount of displeasure, a radical shifting from adoration to abuse of the object both as a poet and as a patient in psychoanalysis. Freud states that what is substituted for the original sexual object is a part of the body (such as the foot or the hair) that is in general inappropriate for sexual purposes, or some inanimate object that bears an assignable relation to the person it replaces. These substitutes become like the fetishes in which primitive deities are said to be embodied.

In Jensen's novel, an ancient Roman bas-relief, which captures the suspended gesture of a young woman walking, overpowers the imagination of a young archeologist, Norbert Hanold. He becomes fixated with the image of the girl's feet and has a plaster replica made, but the central conflict in Jensen's novel arises with the Hanold's search for a live "Gradiva." However, once he discovers an animate "Gradiva" (Freulein Zoe), the girl provokes profound ambivalence rather than pleasure. Although Hanold has the urge to touch his live "Gradiva" to ensure that she was not simply a delusion, there is an equally strong hesitancy that holds him back even from the idea. Although Freud suggests that the archeologist was reluctant due to the fact that he suffered delusions, it may well be that the live replica was all too real. When threatened with the reanimation of the frozen figure, the archeologist asks her to lie down and assume the frozen pose of a relief, looking "as peaceful and beautiful as marble." Immobile and asleep, without the possibility of an exchange or reprisal for being so disturbed in the grave, Hanold would prefer the living counterpart be restored to a fetish, something he could alternately adore and abuse, worship and desecrate. As both a patient and an archeologist, Hanold makes his own childhood coincide with the classical past so that there was a perfect similarity between the burial of Pompeii—the disappearance of the past combined with its preservation—and repression of the fact that Hanold had met Zoe before. "You mean," said the girl, "the fact of someone having to die so as to come alive; but no doubt that must be so for archeologists."[11]

Unable to renounce or relinquish his omnipotence in her psychic life, in "The Colossus" Plath identifies her father as "some god or other," a Roman statue who refuses to speak; yet he is clearly the oracle in whom she seeks guidance and prediction—he is an intermediary between the mysterious heavens and the callow civilization of her past. Like Jensen's *Gradiva*, Plath's poem takes place at the ruins of the Coliseum where both protagonists are intent on digging up a phantom figure whose history will serve as some kind of explanation for the fall of civilization.

One discerns in the background of Plath's poem Freud's *Civilization and Its Discontents*, a late essay in which Freud sums up his long-held theories of culture by demonstrating that a study of human institutions must begin with a study of human nature. From a psychoanalytic perspective, the text draws on Freud's theories of aggression and the super-ego and leads to a structural theory of the mind:

> Perhaps we ought to content ourselves with asserting that what is past in mental life may be preserved and is not necessarily destroyed. It is always possible that even in the mind some of what is old is effaced or absorbed whether in the normal course of things or as an exception—to such an extent that it cannot be restored or revivified by any means; or that preservation in general is dependent on certain favorable conditions. We can only hold fast to the fact that it is rather the rule than the exception for the past to be preserved in mental life.[12]

A psychoanalytic reading of "The Colossus" thus reveals a deeply flawed relationship between father and daughter, a relationship that once explored renders the body of the father as not only dead, but *petrified*. And yet, the poem revolves around the speaker's prodding and testing the colossus as if to make certain it is in fact dead enough to be properly dissected to be analyzed and eventually restored. For "thirty years," the speaker confides to the reader that she has been trying to fit together the puzzle of her father. Otto Plath, a professor of entomology at Boston University, was a remote, enigmatic figure, some twenty years older (more "ancient") than his wife was. His death was particularly traumatic due to the fact that it was avoidable. He had been ill for years before he was diagnosed with diabetes. The tragedy was that his condition could have been controlled if treated promptly. However, out of fear or denial of morbidity, he refused to consult a physician until it was too late. After his leg had turned gangrenous, necessitating amputation, a surgeon remarked to Mrs. Plath: "How could such a brilliant man be so stupid."[13] Plath apparently absorbed her father's death as a kind of bungled suicidal act, which nevertheless ended with his abandonment of her. Had Otto Plath loved her more, Sylvia would have reasoned, he would have done more to preserve his own health.

Otto Plath's death left Sylvia wondering if he had not been at the root of her mental illness, all along, because as we have seen, Freudian theory attributed a patient's suffering to early psychological trauma and its damage. She might well have suspected sexual abuse in her childhood although those scenes were not fully brought to recollection; at the very least, there were signs of a flirtation between father and daughter. In any case, she had justification for her rage at him for ignoring the signs of a serious complication in his illness and hence, allowing himself to be buried under. In "The Colossus," Plath assumes that she will have to resurrect him before she can put the puzzle together or herself back together after her mental breakdown. Unable to crawl out from his shadow, out of his predominance, "like an ant in mourning," Plath's speaker clings even more desperately to her Electra complex, imagining herself to be a tragic figure, sacrificed by her father and in homage to him. While she "dredges" his throat to clear it of silt, she is still left with an enigma:

> I shall never get you put together entirely,
> Pieced, glued, and properly jointed.
> Mule-bray, pig-grime and bawdy cackles
> Proceed from your great lips
> It's worse than a barnyard.
>
> Perhaps you consider yourself an oracle,
> Mouthpiece of the dead, or some god or other.
> Thirty years now I have labored
> To dredge the silt from your throat.
> I am none the wiser.[14]

The daughter's dilemma is how to decrypt the father's meaning, even as she tries to recall him from ancient memory. As an archaeologist of her own mind, she is left to chip away at the surface to locate the precious bedrock of psychic strata: a cacophony of cackles, "worse" than a barnyard's. The allusion to psychotherapy is clear: the speaker is absorbed in her work of excavating the past, convinced that the father holds the crucial key to unlocking her secrets, but sadistically refuses to do so, sending her battling against a stone wall. Her anger at his persistent rejection provokes her undercutting and derision: instead of worship, she is there to "disinfect him," instead of bringing him gifts of homage, she condescendingly picnics on him: "I open my lunch on a hill of black cypress." The only way through the analytic process is through the sometimes excruciatingly slow sifting of things piece by piece, fragment by fragment, image by image. Lost to a Roman graveyard and multiamputated ruin, she can neither mourn her father nor give him up for dead.

Whereas grief was the crucible of Plath's existence, she was more than willing to be widowed by it: "Nights, I squat in the cornucopia / of your left ear / out of the wind. . . . My hours are married to shadow."[15] It may be no coincidence that Plath's response to the news of her father's death was to present to her mother, Mrs. Plath, a paper on which was written in capital letters: "I promise never to marry again. Signed: _____." The mother signed the note immediately and never did marry again. What is obvious here is that the note was intended not only for Aurelia but also for herself. Plath never would marry "again" in the sense that when she did marry it would be to a man like Ted Hughes who was a replica of her father; perhaps, even through Plath's acerbic humor, what might be termed "a chip off the old block."

During the time she was writing this poem, Plath's therapy had brought her to precisely this conclusion: that she had a severe case of an Electra complex. Although she may not have fully convinced herself of the veracity of Freudian application, she nevertheless began to consider the meaning of her "often-seductive" behavior toward men, tracing it back to her wish to regain her lost father. Associating women with a defective lack and incompleteness, she apparently strove for masculinity so that she could merge her ambitions with its apparent strength and freedom. Her dreams, however, were often preoccupied with images of deformity and mutilation, reflective of her fear of fragmentation. Hence, her poems are often occasions for her to fantasize about male power and scorning the threat of being punished for her transgression. As she later reflected on her own tendency to engage in sadomasochistic behaviors in and out of her fictions: "If I really think I killed and castrated my father may all my dreams of deformed and tortured people be my guilty visions of him or fears of punishment for me? And how to lay them? To stop them operating through the rest of my life?"[16] Indeed, at the end of the poem "Daddy," Plath gives her father permission to halt his phantom stalking of her, causing her to want to torture him "back": "Daddy, you can lie back, now."

Castration fear—the fear that her father will avenge himself and symbolically castrate her as a punishment for her killing or castrating him—is a particularly strong motif in her writing and may derive from biological, psychological, and cultural forces. She uses the chastising voice of her poem to silence her adversarial father before he can manage to deprive her of a verbal outlet through which she can air her complaints. Psychotherapy demands that a patient's unconscious associations from the past or childhood must be raised without fear of parental recriminations. When Plath does that in writing, she is discharging the same kind of anxieties and accusations as she would in therapy in an effort to put them to rest. In the 1950s, male domination in the social and political spheres made achieving self-fulfillment and wholeness more difficult for women. Otto Plath himself embodied the belief in male supremacy and his own disfigurement and ultimate silencing may have seemed a fitting end to some of his more authoritative ideas.

As a direct consequence of Plath's castration anxiety (that she did it and it would be done to her in return), she envisions her father's body through piecemeal imagery that itself signifies the piecemeal fracturing of language, brought back together again in the fixing together or composing of the fractured text. Her first image is appropriately of a mouthpiece, pertaining to both father and daughter, a detachable symbol of the power to speak and create simultaneously: "A blue sky out of the Oresteia / Arches above us. O father, all by yourself / You are pithy and historical as the Roman Forum."[17] So immense is her father's corpus that the speaker loses her bearings as she attends to her mundane, and rather degrading task of restoring the ruin with a daily routine of maintenance:

> Scaling little ladders with gluepots and pails of Lysol
> I crawl like an ant in mourning
> Over the weedy acres of your brow
> To mend the immense skull-plates and clear
> The bald white tumuli of your eyes.[18]

Of course, such work is as futile as it is exhausting. Next, comparing her father to the coliseum, a site where spectators gathered to watch gruesome scenes of Christian martyrs being thrown to lions or gladiators slowly and excruciatingly skivered to death, Plath makes his sadism (as well as hers) abundantly clear. His punishment is to be nonresponsive, to refuse to answer her. Instead, he is a "noisy" architecture in stone, overrun by "mule-bray" and "pig-grime" and a daughter's trespasses.[19] Not only does the colossus stand for the ogre of the biological father, but also the superego of the literary father. In either case, intimidation and an anxiousness to please stall the speaker. Susceptible to feelings of inferiority, the speaker manages to make a few cosmetic improvements to the structure, but seems unsuccessful at the bulk of her task: "I shall never get you put together entirely / Pieced, glued, and properly jointed. . . . / I am none the wiser."[20]

As critics have long recognized, Plath's technical achievements were unsurpassed, and she was well trained in classical form. She derived her sprung rhythms, lush alliteration, and mathematical intensity in the pattern and sound of her lines[21] from male precursors such as Donne and Hopkins. As a female poet vying for the prize of recognition, Plath most likely resented, as much as she adored, the male canonical poem that was epitomized by modern epics such as "The Wasteland" or "The Cantos" (which take place in similarly arid landscapes as "The Colossus"). Her husband's reputation had eclipsed her potential stature, and she would not have welcomed the idea of being merely a footnote to his work. Indeed, the footnote has immediate associations with Plath's sense of being an appendage to men, as well as her fascination with her father's missing limb, which was apparently at the root, or the cause, of her morbidity and depression. *Footnote* is defined as an afterthought, something that comes after the more important work has been done. In the shadow of the patriarch (which both her husband and father represented), a colossal relic made of stone, she is merely a toe or "an ant," servile and directionless, squandering away her intellect and originality in deference to him for whom history is analogous to a birthright. For her own survival, the speaker suggests that the colossus must be left behind; she can no longer be a caretaker. Still, she is reluctant to leave it, because it comprises all she knows and all she relates to.

As the poem proceeds, the speaker, stranded for some unspecified time, spurns the idea of rescue, further strengthening her resolve to stay faithful to death, which results in her own exile. She prefers to remain a caretaker to a myth rather than a participant in life: "No longer do I listen for the scrape of a keel, on the blank stones of the landing."[22] She concludes her speech with a listening for what will come next. Both elegiac and contemptuous in tone, the poem hovers between anger and mourning, between an insatiable need and a casual dismissal of the object of her affection. Thus she listens for the sound that will not come, closing the poem with its own frustration and desire for self-extinction.

Nursing her sadness and dejection, Plath takes unmistakable pleasure in indulging a negative state that can only be characterized as agonizing. Elisabeth Young-Bruehl's description of what makes people attach to their "negative states" is as good as any analysis of why Plath chose to be a caretaker to her misery: "Nursing a negative state, for lack of a love object, for lack of relatedness isn't that masochism? And sadism when the nursing one lashes out, attacks. . . . This kind of relationship to yourself—to your negative state—keeps you from being related to any person. You are split internally, loving your hate; that is your ambivalence. It has become familiar. . . ."[23]

While one could well read "The Colossus" as being about the anxiety of literary influence, Young-Bruehl's reflection on why people persist in being wed to their misery is closer to the poem's exigency. Anger at the father is an attack on the self—because the poet is so intensely identified with him. But her choice to stay there, affixed to the painful icon is best explained by Young-Bruehl: "It's not an instinct for death but a self-preservative ego-instinct that has gotten turned in on itself and fixed on growth stoppage."[24]

What do we make of a poem that listens while it is trying to speak? This is like a dancer in motion trying to be still, as if to alert herself to the fact that she is not being still, but in constant movement. Listening to one's self is key to the psychoanalytic process, as it is to the confessional process of creating a poem. A patient begins by talking, as Plath herself alludes to in her "Poem for a Birthday": "I am all mouth."[25] The mouth and the foot are often referenced in Plath's poetry and can be combined as an unconscious reference to her fears of inadequacy—as a poet and as a woman. She fears she will blunder or stumble in the forming of her poetic craft: she will put her foot in her mouth—which is of course yet another pun on the Freudian slip. One slips when the foot is out of line, when there is a misstep, possibly yet another signal of her insecurity about her form, in body or poetry. From the Freudian view of the Electra complex, a woman is always assailed by her lack of a penis, her condition of being incomplete. The same can be said about the metrical laws surrounding poetic craft—Hughes being an impeccably skilled craftsman and manipulator of the iambic or trochaic foot. Absorbed in the silent labor of writing a poem, the poet sounds out words for their syllabic effects, their "kick," as well as their meaning.

One could go on finding more clever word play in Plath's Freudian slips in this poem and in others. Perhaps, nowhere but in psychoanalysis and in the poetry that partakes from its theory, would a writer's uninhibited surges of revelation appear. Beneath her conscious protest against the father's hold over her adult life, was Plath's unconscious need to humble herself to a man. In "Daddy," she makes it plain that she attributes her unhealthy relationships with men to her masochistic fixation with the father figure. Her father's emotional absence from her life, as well as his early betrayal of affection, left her yearning for male recognition and drove her to even more intense pleas for attention and on to anger, despair, and finally, suicide.

In "Daddy," Plath recalls her reticence as a girl (she must say Ich, Ich, Ich, three times to try and assert "I") trying to break out of speechlessness and assert herself:

> I never could talk to you.
> The tongue stuck in my jaw
> I have always been scared of you,
> With your Luftwaffe, your gobbledygoo
> So daddy, I'm finally through.
> The black telephone's off at the root,
> the voices just can't worm through."[26]

If her father refuses to allow her to be verbally or emotionally "connected" to him, the speaker retaliates by insisting, at least within the context of the fantasy, on severing ties with her him ("the voices can't worm through"). Asserting her power to silence him, she now dismisses the intimidating figure that once kept his daughter tongue-tied.

Confessing that she is responsible for selecting the men who will mistreat or desert her, just as her father did, with a 'Meinkampf' look / a love of the rack and screw," Plath takes on the challenge of understanding why she does it or what pleasure she receives, unconsciously, from such ostensible torture. By substituting other men for her father, Plath understands that she is trying to keep her father alive. Getting back to the original father figure would demand a patient's regression back to the artifacts of childhood: "At twenty I tried to die / And get back, back, back to you. / I thought even the bones would do." Through regressive techniques, such as hypnosis, an analyst helps a patient to surface the ancient wounds within the unconscious as part of the arduous process of healing. Clearly, Plath is adopting those principles in her effort to use the poem as adjunctive therapy that would support her psychoanalysis.

"Daddy" is a sardonic elegy in which the speaker attacks the father's character. Plath's desire to "get back" at her father by orally castrating or vilifying him, reflects, perhaps, a childlike belief in the magical power of words. When spells are cast, they are always reversible with other counterspells, other words. A malevolent thought is eradicated by a child's verbal pronouncement: "I take it back" and, with that, all will be forgiven. Caught in a double bind of being angry at parental neglect at the same time she is narcissistically wounded by it, she is pressed to acknowledge anger alongside of need. Plath's hostility is directed not only to the father but also to the surrogate she has replaced him with: "If I've killed one man, I've killed two—."

But Plath's speaker is also hoping to get back what she has lost by demanding a substitute (a father figure), just as all signifiers demand their own replacements, or substitute for the objects they come to stand for. From this idea, it follows that Plath would turn to the repetition of a single word: "*back, back, back.*" Steps backward signal a retreat, the way players are moved back in a board game. On multiple levels, Plath's poem simulates a patient's talk in psychotherapy.

In fact, Plath parades Freudian clichés and references in front of the reader, particularly ones pertaining to phallic imagery and fantasies about castration. Indeed, in a self-satire of severing the father's "voices" (which she blatantly compares to "worms"), the speaker imagines she is able to orally castrate her father. Then, she puts him back in the grave, as a baby may be put back in a womb, indicating a reversal of gender roles, which is consistent with Freudian theory about the Electra complex as it correlates with his theory about psychosexual development in the analogous Oedipal complex. Freud's idea of "penis envy" in the Electra complex is highly suggestive in the instance of the poem: having her father's baby would compensate a daughter for her lacking a penis. In Plath's case, the baby is the autonomous poem, which she takes out and puts back into the earth's belly or grave, making certain to sever thoroughly her father's voice to make certain he is really dead. By doing that, Plath's speaker fuses with the father's identity and assumes a voice that is autonomous rather than inferior or dependent. She has successfully recaptured the power she had lost to her father's language by gaining a solo voice in the poem, as a substitute for both a baby and a phallus.

Plath's famous chastisement, "Daddy, daddy, you bastard, I'm through" is an abrupt ending that resists its own closure. Using a double entendre, Plath plays on the word "through" as both an adjective and a verb. Is she "through" with trying to raise her father from the dead so that she can try yet again to elicit his love and affection? Is she "through" with men such as Ted Hughes who remind her of Otto Plath, who are so sadistic and perverted as to be labeled "bastards" and "Nazis"? Or is she "through" in the sense of "finished," sensing the danger of her suicidal impulses as a consequence of her father's revival in the unconscious? The poem, as a therapeutic outlet, has served its purpose by bringing the father back to life and then putting him back to death, as if he were a child being put to bed: "Daddy, you can lie back now."

In the poem's fantasy of reversals, Plath desecrates the father's burial ground with impunity, by "*dancing and stamping*" over his grave, a mood that sharply contrasts with the one dominating "The Colossus." Celebrating her control over the dictatorial figure, Plath holds that both the father and daughter are bound together in a domestic cycle of malevolence and self-destruction and that the cycle is unavoidable and inevitable. Paradoxically, she may believe she has taken control over her father, but she does not believe she can rewrite the myth adequately; hence, the poem ends with a line that is self-defeating and curses both her father and herself: "Daddy, daddy, you bastard, I'm through." One year later in 1963, Plath, overwhelmed by the various crises in her personal life and assailed by feelings of incomparable loss and inadequacy, committed suicide.

As Freud believed, verbalizing anger helps a patient liberate himself from otherwise paralyzing symptoms. The fantasy of controlling a male figure as a means of liberating one's self is also central to any reading of "The Yellow Wallpaper." In Gilman's fantasy, John collapses from the shock of seeing his wife behaving like a madwoman. With John subdued, or "stifled" from speech, the narrator has triumphed. Having imaginatively fled John's flat world (the nursery and its paper walls), the narrator has ample room to broaden her fantasy and to traverse the three-dimensional realm of her own speculative fiction (the borderless realm of daydream and imagination). John, as patriarch, can no longer hold her hostage to indoctrination because he is less of an obstacle, something the narrator has the liberty to put aside:

> "I've got out at last," said I, "in spite of you and Jane. And I've pulled off most of the paper, so you can't put me back!
>
> "Now why should that man have fainted? But he did, and right across my path by the wall, so that I had to creep over him every time!" [27]

Gilman's narrator and Plath's speaker both emancipate themselves from an oppressive pattern that has held them captives. Perhaps it is no coincidence that Gilman spent time as a decorator of greeting cards, inventing patterns and borders to complement manifold sentiments, sentiments that were systematically reproduced. In both Gilman's and Plath's middle-class society, talented women could be ambivalent only about fitting into an inferior standard that belied their linguistic powers and creativity. As feminist critics have long observed, women must break out of this pattern of submission even when they can barely distinguish themselves from the fiction that denotes them.

Although the kinds of fantasies and daydreams Plath and Gilman exhibit in their works are violent and often sadomasochistic, they are, nevertheless, expressive of feelings and impulses readers share but may not as readily admit to consciousness. As Freud wrote, "the aesthetic pleasure which a creative writer affords us has the character of a fore-pleasure [arising from deeper psychical sources] . . . and our actual enjoyment of an imaginative work proceeds from a liberation of tensions in our minds." [28]

Freud believed that such images associated with primitive emotions float to the surface, but, as is typical of dreams, this material may be disguised or concealed through symbols that may appear to be conflicted with what they are meant to represent. The mechanisms of substitution and displacement that operate in dreamwork can be applied to the writing process that, at least in the confessional mode, may rely solely on the unconscious or free association. In Lacan's axiom, "the unconscious is structured radically like a language." Lacan adopts Freud's notion of the unconscious as that region of the psyche that is submerged and unreachable. Yet he also maintains that what emerges from the unconscious is outside the control of the individual because language and its structure exist prior to the moment at which each person at a certain stage of mental development makes his or her entry into it.

Lacan's psychoanalytic theory can help to elucidate the unconscious patterns that are so pervasive in women's expressive writing. In Lacan's view, one person's reality is always contingent on being recognized by another person—without such a recognition, whether in language or gesture, a person is faced with psychic instability and fragmentation. Language itself symbolically represents the lack of connection to as well as the forbidden root of reconnection with the mother's body. Lacan then proposes that infants are forced to use language as a substitute for the objects they lack, such as an integrated self-image, and to recognize desire through the other that speaks of it. Henceforth, desire finds its meaning in the desire of another person (mother or father), not so much because another person holds the key to the object desired but because the infant's first object of desire is to be seen or recognized by the other as an object of desire. To love, according to Lacan, is a narcissistic expression of the desire to be loved.

Positive mirroring is essential to ego development and self-esteem. A child must first be seen as an adequate and integrated being before she can see herself as one. Without such mirroring, a child may lack a stable model on which she can build her own social self-definition and self-referencing. If parents or caretakers are neglectful of their children, children may well turn inward and become anxious or depressed. Loss and separation in the early stages of growth add to the human sense of the perishable nature of all individual things. But in normal formation of the autonomous self, such senses of lost objects are socially ritualized and substituted by new object relations. When the pain of a parent's loss or abrupt separation is fixated in the ego (as in "Daddy"), social relationships can be negative or disappointing for the individual.

The failure to bond adequately with a parent and the inability to move beyond narcissistic wounding and disappointment is perhaps nowhere more apparent than in Mary Shelley's *Frankenstein*. Like "Daddy" and "The Yellow Wallpaper," the novel is essentially a clinical picture of a daughter's self-destructiveness surrounding her rage at the Oedipal father.

Mary Shelley's strained relationship with her father began with the inauspicious circumstances of her birth. Her mother, Mary Wollstonecraft, died a few days after her labor with Mary from a postpartum infection. Her father, William Godwin, a widower, much aggrieved, was slow to warm up to his daughter. For years, Mary Shelley felt bereft of not only a mother, but also a father. When her father remarried, she was further displaced by the inhabitance of stepmother and stepsiblings. As the novelty of the new occupants wore off, she found herself competing even harder for parental attention. "I was benevolent and good; misery made me a fiend," Victor Frankenstein's monster reproaches his creator. "Make me happy, and I shall again be virtuous." Are monsters born or created by circumstances? That is, are irrational and even violent behaviors by certain groups who have been deprived essential rights or equal privileges the result of their imperfect nature or a product of social injustice? Although the novel does not answer it definitively, *Frankenstein* thoroughly engages the question.

From a psychoanalytic perspective, *Frankenstein* is less about unreal monsters than it is about real and neglected children. Neglected children create in themselves emotions and images in their phantasmagoric quests for parental affection; feelings, both positive and negative, become magnified. In *Frankenstein*, the monster endures a series of exasperating attempts to gain a father's attention—indeed, to persuade his father to gaze on him without overt horror or repulsion. When this fails, the monster develops homicidal impulses, disguising his more genuine wish to punish himself first by provoking Victor's contempt. Although he has been repeatedly rejected, the monster continues to relive the primary scene of trauma by pursuing Victor even after Victor has shunned him again and again.

In Lacanian terms, if the father-creator refuses to glance on his own infant, the monster has lost his only means of capturing the gaze of the *other* on whom he must model his desire. Hence, if the mirror (as embodied by Victor) that will secure or sustain his existence successfully eludes him, the monster is threatened with both external and internal extirpation. How does consciousness become aware of itself without an image or letter of a text that will not only signify but also testify to that awareness? Without external ratification of the fact that he exists, the monster, so contingent on others, is doomed to extinction. This is especially true when Victor refuses to create for the monster a wife. The missing but longed-for wife (who would also be the father's daughter) is an effigy of Mary Shelley's search for her own image. She discerned her identity in the reflecting pool of her mother's literary legacy and in her father's memory of her mother preserved through his writing about her in his collection of her letters and journals.

And yet for Mary Shelley, producing her own fiction is not only presumptuous, but also borders on the taboo. As the offspring of two celebrated authors, her entry into the realm of authorship is tantamount to her intruding on her parents' private literary legacy. She is thus reluctant to assume her right to be there, just as she would be to open the door to the primal scene where she was, in fact, conceived, and to look into it guiltily. There was something hideous in Mary Shelley's conception that caused the death of her mother, just as there was something hideous in the monster's conception that will ultimately cause the utter demise of the father. Both conceptions cause multiple casualties within the family and among loved ones. Early in the introduction to *Frankenstein*, Shelley makes reference to her tangled history:

> It is true that I am very averse to bringing myself forward in print; but as my account will only appear as an appendage to a former production, and as it will be confined to such topics as have connection with my authorship alone, I can scarcely accuse myself of a personal intrusion.
>
> It is not singular that, as the daughter of two persons of distinguished literary celebrity, I should very early in life have thought of writing. As a child, I scribbled. . . . Still I had a dearer pleasure than this, which was the formation of castles in the air—the indulging in waking dreams . . . the formation of a succession of imaginary incidents. . . .[29]

Mary Shelley would prefer to attribute *Frankenstein* to the phenomenon of daydream and fantasy rather than to any subsequent or delayed "scribbling" in words. The verb *scribbling* denotes careless, hurried, or meaningless marks or an author's failure to heed grammatical rules or structure. Mary Shelley's self-characterization as a "scribbler" is not only self-effacing, but also revealing of a childlike wish to imitate the writing of adults without having to comprehend the meaning of words. Because a child has not yet entered the symbolic and socialized realm of language, the prospect of imagining is more pleasurable in its boundlessness and predistinction than the labor of writing something. Language is always at least once removed from immaculate vision, always approximate, and therefore always inferior, or after the fact.

But the deeper tensions within *Frankenstein* reside in the relationship between Mary and her father, William Godwin. Many critics have read Shelley's novel as a self-analysis of her tempestuous relationship with her father and, then, his famous protégé, Percy Shelley, with whom she eloped at age seventeen. Similar to the monster's plight, Mary Shelley was deprived of her bereaved father's affection. Moreover, she could not share his grief, having never known a mother to love or to grieve, except as a phantom. Shelley compensated for her sense of deprivation by consuming a library of books. Included in those books was Godwin's *Enquiry Concerning Political Justice* in which he maintained that a corrupt society debased and perverted its subjects, while only just and benevolent social institutions could ensure a virtuous and contented populace. Wollstonecraft's *Vindication* argues that faulty education and social indoctrination contributed to the narrow-mindedness and avarice of middle-class women. *Origin and Progress* acknowledges the excesses of the French Revolution. The monster, too, learns how to experience emotions by reading three books, *Paradise Lost*, a volume of *Plutarch's Lives*, and *Sorrows of Werter*. Shelley acknowledges through the monster, the influence these books had on her, and how she identified with the outcast or rejected lover :

> I can hardly describe . . . the effect of these books. They produced in me an infinity of images and feelings, that sometimes raised me to ecstasy, but more frequently sunk me into the lowest dejection. As I read, however, I applied much personally to my own feelings and condition.[30]

Comparing and contrasting himself to the De Lacys, Mary Shelley's lovesick monster as self-surrogate refers to others' command over language as a "godlike science." He is impressed by the power of words:

> By degrees I made a discovery of still greater moment. I found that these people possessed a method of communicating their experience and feelings to one another in articulate sounds. I perceived that the words they spoke sometimes, produced pleasure or pain, smiles or sadness, in the minds and countenances of the hearers. This was indeed a godlike science, and I ardently desired to become acquainted with it. But I was baffled by every attempt I made for this purpose. Their pronunciation was quick, and the words they uttered, not having any apparent connection with visible objects, I was unable to . . . unravel the mystery of their reference.[31]

Like the monster, the author must learn how to discern a clear relationship between the sign (the word) and its arbitrary relation to an object (person or feeling). This is not an easy task, especially for Shelley, whose very identity was contingent on names that defined and limited her. Whereas her first name, Mary, was identical to her birth mother's, the family name, Godwin, distinguished her from her mother, because Wollstonecraft never took Godwin's name in marriage. Yet, once married, Mary "Shelley," as author, risked being confused with her husband who had handed her a name. To write, Mary Shelley had to overcome her feelings of belatedness and inferiority as daughter and wife. She also had to conquer her reticence among a company of men of considerable literary reputation and fame. In fact, Shelley conceived of *Frankenstein* in the midst of a literary contest with men, Byron and Percy Shelley among them.[32] Rising to the challenge to conceive a ghost story, she chose to draw on Coleridge's "Christabel" as an influence. Coincidentally, in Coleridge's poem, the witch, Geraldine, places Christabel under a spell that leaves her oppressively tongue-tied as someone with stage-fright. The inability to speak in the presence of the father characterizes the pattern of female suppression, which we have already seen stalking the texts of "Daddy" and "The Yellow Wallpaper."

The monster only gradually acquires the skill to recognize words (*fire, milk, bread, wood*) and to link nouns (*father, brother son, sister*) with characteristic adjectives (*good, dearest, unhappy*). He is then delighted to learn the ideas "appropriated to each of these sounds" and to join, rather than intrude, on the family by using words, of a domestic nature, to describe them. Indeed, a signifying language becomes a force of adhesion in which the monster, as an "outsider" imagines himself an "insider," and is finally able to conjecture his place among this family with whom he desperately wishes to bond.

A daughter's wish to recover the pain of loss is in the interest of overcoming it, as she moves from an attack on the defective parent to a bid for reparations. One is tempted to say that Mary Shelley's own ambivalence is on display in the novel as she presents two sides of the monster: a benign creature demanding justice for his misfortune and heartbreak and a creature prone to murderous rages. Although the monster is associated with the disenfranchised woman or *sansculotte*, the monster is first introduced to the reader in politicized terms, as a slave, or a subaltern creature inspiring both fear and disgust. In contrast to the obviously Europeanized Victor, the monster is an exotic, to be identified with the nineteenth-century woman, the register of reproduction and childbirth and the abject materiality of the body.

The primary trauma and narcissistic wounding caused by a parent's betrayal sets the monster on a path of moral disintegration, exacerbated by Felix De Lacy's beating him and a verbal thrashing by old man De Lacy. Self-obsessed and beleaguered by loneliness, the monster destroys his own beloved and tormentor, and the novel concludes, just as Plath's poem "Daddy" did, with mutual heresy—in acts of patricide and suicide.

Significantly, psychiatric literature suggests that patients with histories of parental neglect or abuse exhibit symptoms including a sense of social isolation, pervasive depressive moods, and dissociative states. The tendency toward "defensive splitting," that is, preserving the tie to the "good-enough parent and at the same time defending against the abusive aspect," is frequent, as is "identification with the aggressor," where the patient fantasizes that she herself is the abuser. Masochistic behavior and need for punishment result from incorporating the abusive parent in the superego. A patient who has had a troubled childhood often fluctuates between narcissistic identification with the abusive parent and self-injury, between guilt-ridden love and self-punishment. In "Daddy" Plath boldly confesses her masochism: "Every woman adores a Fascist."[33] However in *Frankenstein* the monster successfully usurps the father's authority in claiming, "Slave, I have reasoned with you, but you have proved yourself unworthy of my condescension. Remember that I have power. You are my creator, but I am your master."[34]

Shelley's rage over patriarchal abandonment is resounded by her literary descendants. In 1973, Ann Sexton wrote that Ai's book *Cruelty* was

"alive with the arteries of life." It was a woman's work that defied the stereotypes men have always assigned to women and directly held men accountable
for their cruelty. Ai's poetic courtroom afforded abused women, both legally
and morally, a forum to defend themselves. For example, in the poem
"Prostitute," the speaker's acidic rage has driven her to a shocking course of
retribution. After shooting her husband, she scavenges his body for the objects
that have sanctioned his dominance and that she now seizes for herself:

> Husband, for a while after I shoot you,
> I don't touch your body,
> I just cool it with my paper fan,
> the way I used to on hot nights,
> as the moon rises, chip of avocado . . .
>
> and finally, too bored to stay any longer,
> I search your pockets, finding a few coins. . . .
> I stick the gun in my waistband,
> two beaded combs in my hair.
> I never cost much,
> but tonight, with a gun, your boots . . . [35]

Here is the scale of women's justice balanced against male advantage. Stealing her husband's money, "gun," and "boots," the prostitute
enjoys a temporary rise in status, but fails to realize that she is already
articulated with the capitalist system she is trying to bring down, adopting
the code of masculine ascendancy that culture rewards. Although she has
taken his goods for profit, she concedes he is the one who is always
"worth" more: "I never cost much / but tonight, with a gun, *your* boots . . .
[Emphasis added.]" Having no other viable access to male capital, the
prostitute must be content with the emblems of male status that seem, at
least for the moment, to compensate for her personal contingency and
"lack." Borrowing her self-image from her husband only leads her to a
bogus and bankrupt language, where speech refuses to resolve itself and
ends in a lacuna. The prostitute, having denuded her husband as men treat
her—through exploiting her body and consuming its worth, comes to share
his fate, being cut off, nullified, and in a state of unrelieved abjection.

It is significant that the prostitute comes to " voice" only *after*
silencing her husband (by shooting him with his own gun), indicating that
she has no ontological status outside of his existence, living or dead. Voice
is appropriation of male power, whether it be in the form of a weapon or
the phallus, and thus will end the speaker's subjection to the consecution of
male power. Like Adam's rib, her belated being is created out of his pre-
eminence. Even after she shoots him, she is forced to consort with a hegemony that privileges the male sign over the female's. Her only leverage is in
what she has acquired from his *body*, emphasizing the secondariness of her

being an offspring, a daughter. If, however, this prostitute, as daughter fails
to liberate herself, the poet succeeds in legitimizing a woman's power to
duly express her discontent, even if she must "dress" in a dead male's clothing to accomplish the task.

Coming to terms with the dead father in Ai's amoral, irreverent
universe is not easy. Women who have been subjected to obscene forms of
abuse fantasize about getting revenge. In *Cruelty* hurting the one who
hurts, defiling the one who defiles, is a remedy for the pain, but it also
serves as justice. *The punishment fits the crime.* "Everything, Eloy,
Arizona, 1956," for example, draws on the prostitute's last words: "he can
only hurt me a piece at a time." When abject terror becomes vocal, a
woman fights back, her body *becomes* her voice. Blood has always been a
woman's curse, the unstoppable cry that runs from the wound of her body;
but a man's blood is different. It flows from being hunted, executed, or
butchered by women seeking requital. Men's blood in *Cruelty* already runs
cold and his voice is omitted.

In "The Country Midwife: A Day" the speaker has pulled out "a
scraggy red child" after a grueling, animal labor, causing a woman to hem-
orrhage as if in a grotesque parody of castration: "It's done, the stink of
birth. . . . I let her bleed, Lord, I let her bleed." In "Child Beater" the scene
opens on a man's sadistic abuse of his daughter who, from an early age, is
treated like a dog and learns to eat like one:

> I grab the belt and beat her across the back
> until her tears, beads of salt-filled glass, falling,
> shatter on the floor.
>
> I move off. I let her eat
> while I get my dog's chain leash from the closet. . . . [36]

In such brutal circumstances, when all one can do is endure, and
take it, *seeing* the body of the victimizer is essential for the victim to verify
the fact he is no longer a threat. Confronting the body is also a means of
trying to work out conflicting feelings of love and hatred—as much as men
die in these poems, they are not totally relinquished. The desecrated or castrated body of ambiguous gender suggests that both men and women will
suffer for violent acts and that wrongs of the fathers will be rectified. In
Cruelty, women do not have the luxury of showing mercy any more than
men do; neither is above their animal natures. In "One Man Down," for
instance, the wife of the dead man submits to the sexual demands of her
brother-in-law, but finds obvious sadistic pleasure in watching the carcass
of her husband slip from the horse's saddle as it rears it off its back. One
man is now off "her back" and we assume the next man down will be his
brother. Betrayal is a bonus to watching the husband's corpse impassively

bucked off like an ordinary "thing," a "bedroll." Again, the punishment
fits the crime. In the speaker's mind, the corpse must be alive enough to
witness what is happening; he must be able to participate in the spectacle
to receive the full impact of this woman's revenge. As the woman watches
the corpse demeaned as a servile object, "bucked off" by a horse (a pun on
the noun *buck*), she redoubles her pleasure in thinking that he can *see* her
similarly demeaned as she sexually submits to his brother. Her presence is
predicated on his gaze, as she relaxes into her own kind of cruelty:

> Your brother brings you home from hunting
> slung over your horse, dead,
> with the wild boar tied down beside you . . .
>
> He throws the boar at my feet . . .
> I unbutton my skirt . . .
> while he loosens his belt. . .
> The hound's paws bloody the tiles
> lining the flower bed.
> The bitch walks behind him, licking his tracks . . .
> The horse rears,
> your body slides from the black saddle,
> like a bedroll of fine velvet.
> I laugh, close my eyes, and relax.[37]

Profane acts against the male's body are dramatized in yet another poem—where a woman has slaughtered and disemboweled a black goat
to achieve a remedy for what ails her:

> So I have killed my black goat.
> His kidney floats in a bowl,
> a beige, flat fish, around whom parasites . . .
> break through the surface of hot broth . . .
> I hear this will cure anything.
>
> When I am finished, I walk up to him.
> He hangs from a short wooden post,
> tongue stuck out of his mouth . . .
> and further down, where he is open
> and bare of all his organs,
> I put my hand in, stroke him once . . .
>
> It is hard to remember if he suffered much.[38]

Although we don't learn what the kidney of the goat can cure, we learn
much about dismembering the organ. The act of touching the carcass is
taboo, but sexually arousing, offering a substitute for the phallus and its
magical potency. The title "I Have Got to Stop Loving You" suggests
that the sickness for which killing the goat was necessary is heartache,
abandonment. When she strokes the entrails of the martyred, eviscerated

goat, the reader detects the speaker's tendency toward tenderness and absolution. At such a moment, the Christian symbolism of the last few lines
intensifies the physical identification between woman and sacrifice,
although this is not a lamb, but her "black goat." It is only through fury
and, later, "getting even" through the substitution of abominable goat for
rejecting lover, that healing begins. Drinking the goat's blood simulates a
communion, a way of relieving and absolving bodily pain in the act of love.
Similarly, it provides an exorcism against the affliction that love has
brought. Significantly, only in the confessing of what she has done, including the impulse to stroke the intestines, the gory remains, can the psychic
wound begins to close and the painful memory be "forgotten." The blood
of the goat mixed with the blood of her own body proves be purgative,
causing the woman to remark with unmistakable Christian overtones, "It
is hard to remember if he suffered much."

In a poem by Olds, "History 13," the poet surveys her own history through a sadistic fantasy of seeing her father's body hung upside down,
gutted like the corpse of Mussolini. Here, the dictator has been brutally
murdered and displayed for the crowd:

> strung and mottled, mauled as if taken and
> raked by a crowd, and I of the crowd
> over his body. . . .[39]

Although she is freed of his oppressive "regime," the effigy of "the
Fascist"[35] provokes her remorse, her realization that hatred and revenge are
equally eviscerating and that cruelty does not put an end to love. Guilt over
her own fantasies of torturing her father gives way to unrelenting mourning, as if at the magic age of "13" he no longer poses a threat to her:

> that night, the blood
> smeared on his head and face, I did not know who had
> done it. I had loved his body
> whole, his head, his face, untouched. . . .[40]

The father's desecrated body, which the daughter "had loved," is now a
mockery of his once-omniscient power. Faced with the dilemma of enjoy-
ing revenge and fearing the anarchy that takes its place, the speaker is confronted with a deep and human truth—that one can forgive even the most
abominable of crimes; that hatred can convert into sympathy. At "13," the
girl enters into a realm of Oedipal male substitutes, perpetuating a pattern
of abuse: "I turned my back / on happiness, at 13 I entered / a life of
mourning, of mourning for the Fascist."

In Anne Sexton's sequence of "Fury" poems in *The Death
Notebooks*, the roles of Man, God, and Father-torturer are combined into

one. This is yet another mythic father figure who becomes the object of a poet's fervency and rage. In "The Fury of Cocks"[41] the reader is quick to realize that the "fury" does not belong to the cocks, as much as it does to the speaker:

> There they are
> drooping over the breakfast plates,
> angel like,
> folding in their sad wing
> animal sad . . . Whereas last night
> the cock knew its way home,
> as stiff as a hammer, battering in with all
> its awful power.

The male is a batterer. He "flies the coop, and abandons," and yet he is also a parasite insofar as he is nothing without the female, whose "sweet blood" makes the seed bloom. With lacerating humor, Sexton has set the scene of her fury at breakfast, where she, who lays the egg, will eventually feed it to him for breakfast: "In the morning they butter their toast."

Sexton succeeds in inverting sexual power relations, by demonstrating, through the derisive logic of the poem, male ineffectuality. Part of her strategy is to mock, through ventriloquism, the preposterous claims men "crow about":

> When they fuck they are God.
> When they break away they are God.
> When they snore they are God.[42]

More intriguing is the reference to God, the divine patriarch, who inseminated Mary, and from her "sweet blood" Christ was conceived, "the son" of the Father, a castrated phallus. The castration is punned in the central section of the poem in which daylight delivers "mother trucks" (again vehicles for transport) and "engines of amputation" (that which gives fuel to the trucks) and proceeds through the repeating sexual imagery: "She is the house / He is the steeple." The male is what is consumed by and in the woman's body. If the poem is the castrated body of the female body, then the overpowering figure of God is subject to the poet's giving "birth" to Him.

> All the cocks of the world are God,
> blooming, blooming, blooming
> into the sweet blood of woman.[43]

A daughter's rage will come out; it will seek to disrupt the very discourse that either served to protect the father-abuser, or it will attempt to reenact the primal scene of seduction and vilification. Rich's interdiction to women is "to awake" from the slumber "Man" or "Law" has cast her into and to become his equal or even more powerful. Women have used poetry to act out hostile and aggressive fantasies directed at men; they have sought to use their words as cynical weapons for revenge. Resurfacing old wounds scorches the effigy of the father, but helps to reduce her anxiety and helplessness.

By turning the tables on masculine authority by means of registering voice through, to quote Ostriker, "stealing the language,"[44] women gain equilibrium and strength. In McCarriston's work, reprisal often comes in the form of a verdict. Judgment comes when, and only when, the punishment fits the crime. Lashing out at the judge who refused the domestic "plea" of her mother, she offers evidence of the battered body: "the black eye ice, the maw, the mako/that circles the kitchen table nightly."

Many more examples of women's appropriations of strength from men can be found, such as the biblical Salome or Delilah, acting out fantasies of revenge and punishment, demanding their share of political power. Poetry is force, it is the "green fuse that drives the flower," as it is an agency of retribution, a fantasy space where such violent images can surface, acted out in ways that, although not substituting for psychoanalysis, may be just as healing.

PART II

———·•·———

SOUL-MAKING

Conflict and the Construction of Identity

5

CARVING THE MASK OF LANGUAGE
Self and Otherness in Dramatic Monologues

Adopting a mask, or inventing a speaker through language, is often a helpful device for poets who wish to explore the conflicted aspects of their own personalities. The dramatic persona covertly expresses something the poet could not express from within his or her own consistent identity. As the monologue emerges, the poet immerses himself or herself into the flow of speech uttered by a speaker who is, in some fashion, differentiated from the writer's own self. This fictional speaker expresses emotions that are not directly attributable to the author himself or herself. Such dramatization, or "play," can be a therapeutic aid to self-understanding and self-reconciliation. Freud, for example, in discussing creative writers and daydreaming, used the term *Spiel* or *play* to describe the forms of imaginative writing that actually carry out the unrealized wishes of the players or writers themselves and provide a necessary outlet for bearing such wishes. Hence, a dramatic persona is as much of an invention that facilitates a writer's need to act out a certain role in life, because it is a rhetorical genre. Creating a persona and using it as a vehicle for airing volatile or disturbing emotions can also remedy the kinds of repression that researchers have attributed to illness. As Freud suggests:

> the unreality of the writer's imaginative world . . . has important consequences for the technique of his art; for many things which, if they were real, could give no enjoyment, can do so in the play of phantasy, and [sic] many excitements which, in themselves are actually distressing, can become a source of pleasure for the hearers and spectators at the performance of a writer's work.[1]

Indeed, the "unreality" of the writer's imaginative world may include the creation of a persona or self-surrogate who evinces a character through a style of unfamiliar speech. The writer feels as if this creation of character is an "other" separable from the self. However, this character may actually be closer to the core identity of the writer than the writer himself or herself realizes. Like the apparent inchoate nature of the unconscious and its manifest symbols, the dramatic monologue may be an insistent vernacular of the buried self trying to emerge through symbolization and self-extravagation, much like a dream.

Such poems often cost their writers an extravagant effort. Indeed, writers may displace emotional conflict to fictional characters to put them safely outside the mind. But the convenient distinction between inside and out is always collapsing. And frightening or not, the collapse responds to a need. We need to acknowledge the old splits and their latest reiterations; using such divisions, even creating with them is possible. Yet such complexities are not what we want, not at all. As Wallace Stevens wrote: "He had to choose. But it was not a choice / between excluding things. It was not a choice / Between, but of."[2]

Perhaps it is right to say that the dramatic monologue allows the poet to keep the safety of a distance, however illusory or fatuous that distinction is, in check at the same time the poet can bear the slippage of things from inside to outside without acknowledging that these things were always kept within. Attributing our negative feelings to an invented self, a play-actor, can help to both to acknowledge and to refute the difficult conflicts that bear directly on being. Allowing the awful words to rise from within takes courage, perhaps even a mordant humor to express what is most painful within. Some narratives fade slowly or fly away at the close, some are varied and unpredictable, and bear many readings.

Let us begin with a definition. What is the dramatic monologue? As Browning used it, the form shifts the usual positions of poet, speaker, and reader by situating the poet at a distance from the speaker. The reader is then invited to work through the rhetorical "mask" of the poem toward the inferences of the poet who stands behind the speaker's mask. In discussing the relation between poet and speaker, David St. John observes that every poem is, in a sense, a dramatic monologue. The "voice" we attribute to the poet's "persona" is yet another created mask "carved of language."[3]

If every poem is a dramatic monologue, and every dramatic monologue is a "mask carved out of language," then every text is both a self-concealment and a self-disclosure. This essay explores some of the psychological and poststructural issues surrounding the dramatic monologue's speaking "other" and how that other is related back to the poet. The poet's splitting off into a mask, especially within the confessional mode, results in the kind of dramatization that not only gives vent to various impulses, but also helps to master them. The dramatic monologue can be viewed as both a dramatization of the poet as well as a dramatization of what the poet does not yet know about himself or herself. Although confessional poetry and dramatic monologue have been classified in two very different categories, I propose that these are arbitrary distinctions. In contemporary poetry, poets have found the form to be therapeutic just as Browning did.

Historically, the dramatic monologue emerged in the nineteenth century when Tennyson and Browning recognized the possibilities of using it as a literary genre. As a stepsister of the lyric, the dramatic monologue involves a speaker's expression in the presence of a "hearer" who interprets and absorbs the spectacle of this type of self-encounter. In defining the genre, critics, even at this early stage, tried to state the relationship between the speaker (of the monologue) and an audience whom the speaker addresses in the event or situation of the poem. Although some critics saw an audience as necessary to the understanding of the monologue, in some of Browning's poems, for instance, the speaker soliloquizes alone without any apparent listener. According to a strict definition, however, a dramatic monologue can not exist without an audience already present in the poem. The monological center requires the presence, real or imagined, explicit or implied, of an other to make itself intelligible.

Yet, in the early part of the twentieth century, dramatic monologues appeared without any "hearer" or "listener" embodied in the situation of the poem. In Masters's *Spoon River Anthology*, for example, spirits talk and have little interest whether anyone is listening. There is merely an intimation of a townspeople available to hear them.[4] The speaker in "Cooney Potter," for instance, reveals that he inherited some land from his father and has mistreated his family by working them too hard in the fields. Masters confesses Potter's "sin" to the listener, and Potter judges himself from the position of the townspeople, from without. But if no embodied audience is present in the text, it still does not qualify as a dramatic monologue.

The dialogue more closely resembles the dramatic monologue because it proceeds through conversation. If the conversation were to be monopolized by one person, a dramatic monologue would result, including the possibility of a listener who reinforces the speaker if there is no reason to contradict or interrupt him or her. In a dialogue, one speaker's responses are incorporated into the other's. For example, one character responds to another character who says he hears noises in the house by saying, "I hear nothing." In the dramatic monologue, the speaker reveals his fear of noises by asking the implied listener, "You hear nothing?" The result has the effect of a split consciousness. The speaker seems to be speaking both to an Other and to himself at the same time. This is crucial to David St. John's observation of the plasticity of the poetic intelligence as it, too, is transformed by the presence of the imagined other through whom the poet speaks and is spoken to. By confronting the other, the speaking self is assured of its own self-certainty.

But from its nineteenth-century origins, the once-embodied listener has dropped out of the twentieth-century poem. Speakers in contemporary monologues turn outside to the reader rather than to an implied auditor situated in the scene. This suggests an interesting recalculation of the poet and reader interaction, a calculation that invites comparison with the psychoanalytic model. We might ask ourselves what occurs within the poet's mind as he or she constructs a monologue as someone different from the "true" interior being she has always assumed to be? What light can psychoanalysis shed on this kind of self-presentation?

From the beginning of Freud's practice, patients told their stories, in running monologues, unraveling the mysteries of their mental anguish. The analyst held the key to unlocking these mysteries through interpretation and decoding of unconscious material. Although the Freudian analyst tried to maintain clinical detachment, Freud himself became increasingly aware of the existence of a countertransference. *Transference* is the shifting of unresolved issues and primitive conflicts onto the analyst by the patient, a critical juncture in which the analyst can now bring to the light what is really troubling the patient. *Countertransference* is what the analyst transfers of his own issues to the patient. Freud then theorized that both participants in therapy, the patient and the analyst, influence what is observed and felt.

As Norman Holland's work with reader-response theory ultimately argues, the interactional nature of the patient-analyst relationship invites comparison with the reader's reconstruction of a literary text as it fits in with her particular identity theme.[5] The dramatic monologue is a particularly good model for the "talking cure" especially in contemporary poetry, because it tends to appeal to the reader to listen, empathize, or react to a speaker's self-exhibition. Through the otherness of the persona, a poet can reveal personal matter without having to rely on any obvious confessional outpouring. Bertha Pappenheim made the link between confession and therapy, comparing the psychoanalyst to the Catholic priest. An urbane Freud made the same comparison, but observed that "in confession the sinner tells what he knows; in analysis the neurotic has to tell more."[6]

A natural place to begin tracing the convergence of psychoanalysis and dramatic monologue is in Browning's work. With psychoanalysis so pervasive in our culture (from talk shows to therapy), the poet's carving of the mask will be very different than it was for Browning. The Victorian poet conceived the mask as a means of separating interior and often problematic emotions from the outward role-playing respectable society demanded of him. Browning's persona was also a theatrical mask, which the speaker of the monologue lifted and lowered to expose societal hypocrisy. Poems as disparate in tone as "Meeting at Night," "In a Gondola," and "My Last Duchess," demonstrate how

Browning's speakers present opposing but complementary points of view on the subject of romantic love. They either overvalue love, attempting to summon up through romantic attachment the infinite potential of human souls, or they materialize love as an object that belongs to them exclusively. In both cases, the desired object of a speaker's love must be possessed at all costs, even if the lover resorts to murder to keep her with him. Love can be transcendent or it can be relegated to an inert and passive object over which the lover must achieve absolute control to stop himself from going insane.

Throughout Browning's works, lovers are depicted meeting in clandestine places or drifting blissfully in boats, locking out the harsher realities of the world. Romantic love is infused with the power to "charge" seemingly trivial experience with fresh significance. But in poems such as "My Last Duchess" or "Porphyria's Lover," a darker, more pessimistic vision of love emerges in which jealousy, hatred, and sexual obsession haunt the speakers. In "Love among the Ruins," for example, all things "melt away" while a "girl with eager eyes and yellow hair" vigorously awaits the speaker.[7] Civilizations may fall into ruins, but the speaker's own desire redeems and validates his existence, proving that "love is best." As a variant of this theme, a Browning lover (as "In a Gondola") might be a play-actor in the "art" of love. Ironically, Browning admonishes his masked persona for even wearing a mask, for playing at being someone other than he actually is.

But Browning can only allude to this discrepancy because he, too, is subject to the perspective of the "other." In fact, our self-representations emerge through a perspective of the world in which we recognize others as others and see ourselves according to others. As Merleau-Ponty observed, "the ego cannot emerge at the age of three years without doubling itself as an ego in the eyes of the other."[8] As self-identity evolves from childhood to adulthood, there are successive reintegrations of temporarily confused "selves" appear in an ensemble of roles that also receive social recognition. However, if having a self depends on being defined as an object that is given over to a system of cultural signs, preeminently language, then we may not be who we think we are, or at least we are limited by what we can say or "sign," or what those around us can say or "sign" about ourselves.[9] The self we present to the "madding crowd" may not always be recognized as we wish, and we may even deceive ourselves about how we wish to be recognized by the world. The individual maintains, at its core, a *self*-identity, by developing a central power of self-reflection and synthesis.[10] Browning must come out of "himself", to dramatize the other, but this "other" casts new light on *who Browning is*. In this way Browning recognizes himself, a dialectical process that links the talk of poetry with the talk of psychotherapy.

Browning's dramatic monologues show how lovers not only love, but also hate. As Pippa in "Pippa's Passes" observes, love and hate are "the very warders / Each of the other's borders."[11] In both "Porphyria's Lover" and "My Last Duchess," Browning's murderers try to make believe that their victims are still alive by "propping" them up or replicating them on canvas, forcing the beloved object into submission. Their confessions give them away to the reader, who, not unlike the psychoanalyst, is able to decode and interpret the speaker's clues, inferences, slips of the tongue, paroxysms, and puns. The murderous lover's anxious need for reassurance, his possessive nature, and "taste" as a collector all invite comparison with Browning himself. For is the poet not yet another role-player "at love" through artfulness, another version of his dramatic lover who fixes the transient moment of heightened passion into a cold, immobile verse? Like James, Browning's themes put forth the need to love passionately, but not destructively, because those who fail to live and love, like the Duke, are dead to experience.

Typically engaged in confession in the guise of self-justification, Browning's speakers were apparently interested in analyzing and exorcising their personal demons, especially pertaining to the subject of courtship and romantic love. Yet, there is no evidence of Browning's intentionally including the type of confessional material that one might confide to an analyst into the various speeches and postures of his personas as a means of working through personal traumas as a form of catharsis. The same cannot be said about some contemporary poets, such as Plath.

In Plath's "Lady Lazarus," the speaker's situation enabled the poet to construct a drama out of her own recurrent suicidal urges and deflect it through her monologue: "I have done it again / One year and in every ten."[12] Lady Lazarus's ritual of destruction is a religious self-sacrifice that is specifically tied to Plath's lacerating statement that occurs late in the poem: "Dying is an art, like everything else. / I do it exceptionally well."[13] For Plath, the logical disguise for the victim and martyr, foredoomed sufferer, was the mask of the innocent Jew and his or her persecution at the hands of twentieth-century Nazi barbarianism. When she peels off the sheer mask of passive suffering like a napkin, and asks, "O my enemy. Do I terrify?" she sees no end to the agonies of her resurrections, as if Lady Lazarus was called on not once, but multiple times, to testify to the horrors of her annihilation.

Integral to the drama of the poem is Lady Lazarus's mocking of the "peanut-munching crowd," benumbed spectators who witness and listen to the miracle of one woman's reluctant survival. Here, the audience is less appealed to than invited to participate in the speaker's victimization, put in the position of one who "Shoves in to see / Them unwrap me hand and foot— / the big strip tease."[14] Here, the stripping of the flesh, like the bearing of the "soul," is in the pursuit of hard evidence of Lady Lazarus's survival. The flesh "stands in" for the soul; and this is paradoxical, because the soul, not the flesh, signifies the miracle of eternal life. Lady Lazarus, like some of Plath's other personas, is wrapped in an outer casing, or plaster cast, which is itself a camouflage or a mask. Unwrapping the flesh allows Lady Lazarus to speak, but her speech is predatory, turned viciously against herself. Like Lady Lazarus, Plath was "raised from the dead" three days after her first suicide attempt, but her embodied presence was no proof of her having actually survived the ordeal.

Through the mask, Plath is able to reconstruct her tortured history as a psychiatric patient. Gilman had already written a cautionary tale about the practice and its cures; and Plath after her first suicide attempt was entangled in the system, undergoing various regimens (insulin therapy, lithium, electroshock therapy) in addition to her individual psychotherapy. Her mask of Lazarus is, for all ostensible purposes, the "resuscitated" symbol of what can be *saved* by psychiatric practice. But from the point of view of a confused patient, like Esther Greenwood in Plath's *The Bell Jar*, psychiatry's cold clinical approach to the soul's agonies only adds to her aberrant distortions and her sense of being specified as something "abnormal." To the intermeddling "crowd" (which probably included Plath's psychiatrists and family members), Lady Lazarus's survival testifies to the miracle they have performed. Sardonically, she realizes that, as a patient, she is theirs to manipulate, an attraction, "a show." Ultimately, she becomes inseparable from the death she signifies, disintegrating into the air that will eventually and inconspicuously "eat men" alive, starving for true affection.

Tragically, salvation was not offered to Lady Lazarus or to Plath. The dramatic persona's self-diffusion is an ominous foreshadowing of Plath's discouragement about life. Although "Lady Lazarus" is a dramatic monologue, it shows that no strict divisions are found between a confessional voice (ostensibly representative of the "real" poet) and dramatic monologue (an invention or surrogate for the poet). All poems dramatize experience, and all poems transform the "self" into something that seems to belong to the "other" the moment that language is issued through the poem. Plath herself candidly stressed the allegorical intention behind her poem's inception, distancing herself from the theatrics of the poem and referring to "Lady Lazarus" as "light verse": "I believe that one should be able to control and manipulate experiences, even the most terrifying . . . with an informed and intelligent mind."[15]

Repeatedly, Plath has been mythologized as a suicidal temptress who somehow cultivated her madness to create her dark art. But, as was seen in the last chapter, she also struggled to get better and to work through her demons, viewing her work as a therapeutic outlet. She made particular use of her dramatic personae as a means of extricating herself from her pain, just as the patient in analysis surfaces traumatic material to distance herself from it.

Confessional poets made no secret of their reliance on psychotherapy as a practice that could be transferred into poetry. Fatigued by the neo-Symbolist and neo-Metaphysical style that followed Eliot, poets such as W. D. Snodgrass turned back to raw emotion, noting that even Eliot was "disguising" the confessional aspect of his work. The dramatic monologue "The Love Song of J. Alfred Prufrock," is, for example, a personal poem.[16] As Snodgrass also recalls, "'The Wasteland' is a very autobiographic poem. Not only does it have Eliot's mental breakdown in it, it also has his wife's nymphomania, his own sterility and barrenness . . . but we didn't know that his poems were about his personal life."[17]

Snodgrass's insights are supported by even a superficial reading of Eliot's 1919 "Tradition and the Individual Talent," where Eliot argues that poets can develop or procure the consciousness of the past by dissociating poetry from their own emotions.[18] Through such "depersonalization" the poet achieves a mask, or an otherness, who speaks for a literary tradition. This ambition, Eliot concedes, forces the individual artist to sacrifice his or her ego to the authority of tradition. There occurs a continual surrender of the poet as he is "at the moment" to something more refined or valuable. Eliot's idea of a divided consciousness is a division that assumes a poet can divorce his or her personal emotions from the tradition that does not belong to the individual. Eliot pursues this argument to its logical end; that is, poetry is not an emotional outlet but an escape from emotion. Poetry is not, as Plath subsequently viewed it, the expression of personality, but *an escape* from personality.[19]

But how does the poet escape from one part of the personality to another? In "The Love Song of J. Alfred Prufrock" the speaker is so overburdened by his own failure to live up to the literary tradition Eliot venerates in "Tradition," that he figuratively "drowns" or suffocates in his own personal emotions. In fact, emotions ultimately stifle Prufrock's talent and his voice. Instead of being able to linger with the collective voices of "sea-girls wreathed with sea weed [*sic*] red and brown," Prufrock "drowns" at sea bottom when "human" voices alert him to the nature of his own stultifying delusions. Prufrock's delusions are to some extent due to the fact that Prufrock's ego is not strong enough to maintain its boundaries. Prufrock's existence is always subject to the spectator's scrutiny of him, that which "fixes" him in the contingency of a gaze, supported by lines such as these: "There will be time . . . / To prepare a face to meet the faces that you meet" or "And I have known the eyes already, known them all—

the eyes that fix you in a formulated phrase. . . . "[20] Hence Eliot's persona sees himself not as a coherent and recognizable identity (as Browning's dramatic speakers did), but as something that is already precipitated through the phrasing of the one who formulates him. Is this a reference to the poet? How does one come into existence without the speculation and monitoring of the other?

Remarkably, acute self-objectification surfaces in both "Prufrock" and "Lady Lazarus." Both speakers feel inferior to others who assess them negatively. On the other hand, only in the presence of the normalized "other" can they see themselves ultimately "resurrected" or saved. In Eliot's poem, for example, Prufrock compares himself to the biblical Lazarus who is unable to "tell" what he knows about the underworld just as Plath's Lady Lazarus is appalled by the crowd's refusal to hear what it feels like to be dead. The dramatic persona *requires the presence of the other* to hear what he has to say and demands that the other empathize with his pain. Because the reader represents in the poet's mind a neutral, but empathetic "other," the reader, essentially an abstract notion, may very well take on the role of psychotherapist as a witness to pain. As seen in the poem "Revision," explicated in chapter 11, Rewriting the Subject, the constructed role of the reader as a conjectured listener is often necessary to psychic healing. Still, language has its limitations even in psychotherapy. Language is the only available medium for self-expression, but it too is always elusive or based on implicit difference. The speaker registers frustration in trying to talk through and about its own existence.

Indeed, language poses another kind of problem in distinguishing the dramatic monologue from the confessional lyric or, for that matter, from any poetic convention. In postmodernist terms, the poet always finds herself caught up in language that distances the poet from an immediately lived truth. Although language makes us present to ourselves and others in the world, language also opens the gap between essence and the manifestation of that essence in spoken words. Because the dramatic monologue is, in fact, the spoken discourse of the masked other, it expresses perhaps more poignantly the poet's temporary dislocation from his lived experience as he immerses himself in the signifying chain of language. Like our imaginary conceptions of ourselves, the dramatic monologue is another verbal form of dramatization that appears to be whole and intact but actually comprises incremental speech parts, lacking actual integration and self-unity.

From a postmodernist perspective, then, discussing the dramatic monologue as a representation of a fictional self, is much more difficult because postmodernism views any self as illusory or fictional, including the poet's. As signifiers of language are stripped of their transcendent status, so is the unified subject of the poet. The poet is now seen as constituted by the process of language formation rather than the other way around. And because language is always slippery, always pointing to, or becoming, something other than itself, the poet is no longer a self-contained individual who can create objects through language. Rather, language creates its objects. The persona, too, is carved out of language because it is the medium through which the poet's subjectivity speaks, often of the pains of coming to be.

Postmodernism's emphasis on language as constructive of the self, or subjectivity, helps us to better understand St. John's claim that the poetic ego is formed as a result of its inventing a persona and that language is what changes the subject, as much as the subject changes language to strike a particular pose in life. Hence, the poet's writing may be compared to a mirror that, conversely, captures the imagined totality of the fictive self. When the poet transfers his voice, he or she has altered what he or she now knows about his or her own thoughts. The "other," the one who speaks the poem, resides somewhere in the life of the mind and erupts with a strange consistency of its own.

Seen in such a way, the dramatic monologue forces poets simultaneously to withhold and project their fantasies of being onto the other and to dislocate themselves during the process. When St. John advocates the dramatic monologue as a good learning exercise for students, he suggests that the dramatized other is often better drawn than the poet's own enumeration of "self." There is clearly a point at which the "speaker takes over" and, as St. John suggests, the achievement of making a voice can lead to the poet's finding his own reality through the transference. In Browning, the reader detects slippages that undermine a speaker's particular statement. Browning's distance from the speaker allows for a more fluid discourse in which social norms are overreached, leading the reader to question the ethos of a given speaker without judging the poet on the same grounds.

In St. John's own dramatic monologue, "The Man in the Yellow Gloves," the narrative unravels through the discourse of the persona, whose verbal "fit" into the incongruous "lemon silk" gloves enables him to dramatize events.[21] We hear, through the speaker, of the yellow gloves, found in a box "fluted with ivory," once belonging to a grandfather who, "dressed to the teeth," arrived at a cocktail party by "stepping right into water." It was the miracle of the gloves held up, and entirely dry, that strikes the speaker as startling as an apparition:

> two gloves
> . . . their transparence
> a glow
> like the wings of a flying fish
> As it clears the sea's surface . . .[22]

As the poem continues, however, the speaker tells the story of his being caught in a fire while camping on a lake, when his hands were horribly burned:

> . . . my fingers
> Up past both wrists and blazing
> In a sudden and brilliant gasp of flame
> I held up my burning hands. . . .
> Candle boned with five wicks.[23]

His recovery was painful and long. At last he could look at the scars, the "gnarled and shrunken hands" that were continually grafted "in a patchwork until they began to resemble hands again, "you might hold in your own." In an effort to conceal his disfigurement, and in honor of his grandfather, the speaker orders each year from London another ordinary pair of kid gloves, dyed lemon yellow, to wear over his disfigured hands. These gloves are of the type a "dandy" might wear, and the speaker does not want to take one off and "startle or shame everybody into silence," but makes sure each glove is properly secure, "snugly choked in its taut loop / Its minute noose of leather."[24]

The gloves form a correlative for both the speaker's self-fascination and his self-disgust, both spiritual grace and bodily decay. The gloves also suggest the form of the dramatic monologue itself, a mask that is either put on or taken off, exposing of the many roles or "selves" underneath. The persona emerges out of the arbitrary signifiers within the poet's unconscious, which is a container for what is repressed (that is why it is unconscious) and what will be revealed through "talking" things out. The hands are "buried" just as the face is behind the mask. Hands, perhaps, suggest more about the act of writing poetry, because hands are less identifying than the representation of a face, or a photograph, and more versatile.

When the speaker dresses his wounds in the flamboyant yellow gloves he may be addressing a number of ambiguities and resistances about self-disclosure in both poetic and therapeutic processes. The anachronistic formality of the gloves suggests the formality of poetry itself, an attractive covering that not only masks but protects the self from being detected. Again, (as in "Prufrock") the gaze of the other as a poet, reader, or spectator determines a speaker's intense self-preoccupation and self-appraisal. The gaze can either mortify or liberate the speaker as it speaks of the pains of coming to be. Moreover, St. John's earlier figure of speech of the "mask carved out of language" bears immediate relation to the symbolic yellow gloves, a riddle about what defines identity as something unique among other identities. The hands become Christian, pagan, and quotidian emblems "out of date, well mannered," presented to the visitor who is insulated from the horror underneath. Perhaps this is but one indication of the dramatic monologue as an attempt to disguise the poet and, at the same time, to help the poet uncover material she would not want to acknowledge or accept.

In this chapter, I have drawn parallels between the dramatic monologue and the confessional poem to show that both are expressive of the poet's personality, and both seek to raise to the surface psychological material that might not ordinarily be revealed. Through adopting a mask, poets find a representation for volatile emotions in order to master them.

6

---·-·---

GIOTTO'S INVISIBLE SHEEP

Lacanian Mirroring and Modeling in Walcott's *Another Life*

Emerging as a poet whose West Indian cultural identity is frozen within the ontological riddle of the landscape, Walcott acknowledges in an autobiographical preface, "What the Twilight Says," that the New World poet must start from scratch:

> In that simple schizophrenic boyhood one could lead two lives: the interior life of poetry, the outward life of action and dialect. Yet the writers of my generation were natural assimilators. We knew the literature of Empires, Greek, Roman, British, through their essential classics; and both the patois of the street and the language of the classroom hid the elation of discovery. If there was nothing, there was everything to be made. With this prodigious ambition one began.[1]

This ambition is problematic, given the indirection of a language that can only come into being through the presence of an other—*through an other*. As the Lacanian model suggests, subjectivity arises with the child's entry into the symbolic order when he acquires language, a name, and social prohibitions. Subject formation is therefore based on assimilating a variety of elements within one's social context including the crucial element of difference. During Walcott's earliest apprentice years, he speculated about the confrontation of two contrasting worlds, Europe and its former colonies, and how to integrate the Western literary tradition into his provincialism, without destroying his childlike sense of awe:[2]

> Provincialism loves the pseudo-epic
> so if these heroes have been given a stature
> disproportionate to their cramped lives
> remember that I beheld them at knee-height
> and that their thunderous exchanges
> rumbled like gods about another life.[3]

From a psychoanalytic perspective, subject formation is a universal condition of mitigating the profound and frustrating processes involved in forming an identity. For Walcott, the notion of self-alienation is compounded by

121

an adopted culture's language that subjects him as it constructs him. In phenomenological terms, the locus of identity revolves around the Other, that central presence, real or conceived, through which we become self-aware by regarding ourselves as another would. For Lacan, the subject is constantly having to remake itself in encounters with the speech that presupposes an addressee. Lacan's Other is closely associated with language itself, or at least with the *place of otherness* to which language is directed.

Walcott opens "The Divided Child," part I of *Another Life,* with an epigraph from Malraux's *Psychology of Art* in which Vasari's account of the lives of Cimabue and Giotto is rendered. The epigraph's obvious message is that the true artist, accepting his master's tutelage, learns to love works of art over the things they portray. Less obvious is the way in which the apprentice renders the landscape through the master's mediation, hoping to capture an art language that can mediate the world of objects. A Lacanian scheme is especially appropriate as a mode for understanding the process of artistic apprenticeship because it suggests that all language presupposes the absence of the object it signifies; hence a painting or poem refers not to the object from which it was derived (as a series of marks or articulations) but to a prior learned and assimilated object of art. This bears crucially on Walcott's view of every language as owing something to others, with obvious implications for art. As Walcott argues, "There is no distinction between the derivative, which has 'originat[ed]' from 'something,' and the 'original,' from which subsequent forms derive."[4] Even the inimitable is an attempted copy that will itself be copied.

Rei Terada has demonstrated in *Derek Walcott's Poetry: American Mimicry* that Walcott's view of mimicry is an inescapable condition of all art, but one that the artist must use to his or her advantage. In the Cimabue and Giotto paradigm, the master is "struck" by the way in which his pupil has appropriated his own representation of the landscape. Unlike "mimesis," a representation of reality, mimicry is a "representation of a representation," something that the gifted student instinctively knows.[5] Walcott's use of the story of Cimabue and Giotto, then, suggests a paradigm (for "The Divided Child," at least) of a hidden reciprocal relationship between master and apprentice, who mirror one another and influence each other's art. But it also suggests a parallel binary opposition in which the master/apprentice relationship is subverted to disrupt the hegemonic fixity of the colonizer/colonized relationship. This twofold paradigm serves as a reminder of how the West Indian apprentice in *Another Life* transcends the European master's legacy to begin over, subordinating the old to the tabula rasa of the new. A psychoanalytic study of racial identity in "The Divided Child" section of *Another Life* reveals Walcott's rhetorical strategy for undermining the master's vision of reality to interrupt and subvert that racist discourse.

If the New World black is to be liberated from cultural servitude, Walcott suggests, it will be due to nothing less than the spawning of a new language, the reinvention of names for New World things. Growing up in the St. Lucian capital of Castries, he was steeped in classical and canonical (British) literature as well as in the indigenous folktales still popular on the island. Seeking an "electric fusion of the old and the new," Walcott opens part I of *Another Life* with the Vasari/Malraux epigraph just described:

> An old story goes that Cimabue was struck with admiration when he saw the shepherd boy, Giotto, sketching sheep. But, according to the true biographies, it is never the sheep that inspire a Giotto with the love of painting, but rather, his first sight of the paintings of such a man as Cimabue. What makes the artist is the circumstance that in his youth he was more deeply moved by the sight of works of art than by that of the things which they portray.[6]

Cimabue was not aware that the boy was sketching from his own compositions when he was "struck with admiration" for Giotto, although he should not have been surprised, having once been an apprentice himself. But there was something embedded in the drawing of the sheep that went beyond their literal representation. Cimabue, as a boy in the fourteenth century, had been sent to the monastery to study letters, but he spent most of his time drawing imaginary horses, men, and houses in his books. Later, apprenticing himself to professional painters, Cimabue modeled his style on the Greeks, but developed his own idiom. An Italian master by the time he met Giotto, Cimabue then became the subject of what he saw in Giotto's *seeing* him.

The language of painting precedes and preempts the particular subject matter it represents, blinding painter and viewer alike to what is real and what is illusion. Lacan's theories of the Imaginary and of the alienation that underlies human identity postulate a similar misrecognition when the infant takes a mirror image (Giotto's sheep) as the model for self-identity, casting aside the actual conditions of an untotalized, fragmentary being (for example the markings of sheep). The infant's designation of the mirror image as "me" (or *moi*) comes at a developmental point when children are still incapable of controlling the actions of their bodies, and it marks a radical transformation, because the infant is basically treating an imaginary self (that is the imaged self, which is nonself) as one with which it must identify. Therein lies the source of alienation in the infant at the mirror stage.[7] The discordance between the inner, unintegrated experience and the external image opens a gap for a whole sequence of illusionary images that attempt to overcome self-division. Underneath the sense of spatial identity acquired by the infant who sees himself reflected in the mirror, there is the haunting recognition of a more fragmentary being. Although Giotto's sheep might have seemed beautiful to Cimabue, what he appreciated more were their artistic forms.

Without a prior visual language in which to record his own reading of "sheepness," the beauty of this form would not have been perceptible to Giotto's eye. He needed a starting point, a reference for symbolization as well as a desire to articulate a particular aesthetic, for both of which he was indebted to Cimabue.

Similarly, our own form is hidden from us (as the form of a drawing is concealed by its subject, for example, sheep), and it takes others to make one's form evident. It is in the space of the Other that the subject comes to see himself, a psychological and perceptual dynamic that informs Walcott's thinking about the simulations involved in constructing West Indian identity. The mimic needs a mirror in which to see himself in relation to the one he aims to imitate. Cimabue's admiration for what he saw through Giotto enabled him to see a reflection of his own painterly signature. Although he probably did not realize it, Cimabue invested narcissistic libido in his reading of Giotto's work. Narcissism is not solipsistic but has a social dimension, needing an other to model itself on, to impress, or respond to.[8] Alternative versions of the Cimabue/Giotto meeting might mislead us into believing that the beauty of Giotto's sheep entranced Cimabue; more remarkable is the fact that we conceal from ourselves what is an artifice and what is real.

Giotto's rendering of sheep was of what Cimabue saw: *invisible* objects that provide the ground for the Imaginary. Perhaps Cimabue did not even know he desired that appreciation for beauty until he saw it revived through his most gifted student. In *Another Life*, Walcott tried to touch the essence of his native island, as Giotto was trying to touch sheep, but reality is always mediated by language, and as Lacan suggests, no autonomous self can transcend it. Although memory cannot (and should not) erase the past, the shackles of mastery can be broken only by a revelation of the future grasped through the language that claims it. Out of an indigenous idiom, Walcott has crafted a new culture and language for the islands, eliciting what Emerson called Naming in the highest sense.[9] Or, as Walcott quotes Alejo Carpentier as saying in *The Lost Steps*, "The only task appropriate to the milieu that was slowly revealing to me the nature of its values [was] Adam's task of giving things their names."[10]

In "Homage to Gregorias" (part 2 of *Another Life*), Walcott distinguishes his evolving art or aesthetic from that of a painter he calls Gregorias, contrasting his own classicism to the painter's romanticism:

> While Gregorias would draw
> with the linear elation of an eel
> one muscle in one thought,
> my hand was crabbed by that style. . .
>
> it was the classic versus romantic
> perhaps, it was water and fire.[11]

When Walcott tried to "render the visible world" in brushstrokes, he was prone to see the world through subtle metaphors and paradoxes that more properly belonged to a literary tradition. Due to his mixed heritage, the island was "a crystal of ambiguities," including translations from the colonizer's language. Although Gregorias's style was marked by an "aboriginal force" that, inborn, burst through "as the carver comes out of the wood," Walcott's poetry was servile, subdued by a classical training that he likens to the crab's "side-wise crawling."[12] Walcott's self-deprecatory "crabness" suggests a nebulous mixture of influences as well as a myopic, defensive stance. But what made Gregorias so admirable was his courage in discarding traditional Western aesthetics and making "grotesque" images to forge an art that was wholly his own. Walcott, on the other hand, modeled his aesthetic on the one found in his "father's small blue library / of reproductions . . . / and in another / sky blue book / the shepherdesses of Boucher and Fragonard."[13] Seduced by the dazzling splendors of Western masters, especially their radiant depictions of shepherdesses, as "if they were [his] golden Muse," Walcott interpreted his world through them, whereas Gregorias "bent to his handful of earth, / his black nudes gleaming sweat, / in the tiger shade of the fronds."[14] In response to his friend's love of Western art, Gregorias observes: "The thing is you love death and I love life / Your poetry too full of spiders, / bones, worms, ants, things eating up each other."[15]

Yet Walcott's definition of *apprenticeship*, which Gregorias "abandoned . . . / to the errors of his soul,"[16] must account for, rather than eschew, the very same complexities that he has detected in the scene of Cimabue's instruction of Giotto (which was actually Giotto's instruction of Cimabue). Walcott knows that Giotto was concerned not with painting "real" sheep but with capturing painterly images of "sheepness." Mimicry is unavoidable for the West Indian artist, among others, because no true origination exists; only simulation. Gregorias's attempt to discard tradition by embracing a primitivist aesthetic does not make him immune to European influence. Walcott implies that even his landscapes and "black nudes" are derivative, reverential toward Italian painting, with "every brushstroke a prayer / to Giotto, to Masaccio / his primitive, companionable saints."[17] Gregorias's struggle is no different from that of previous Western artists, who also strove to repossess the world in terms of their own earth, their own heaven. Such is Gregorias's victory, however, that "now every landscape we entered / was already signed with his name."[18] But perhaps Gregorias's derision of the formalism that Walcott attempted to *master* became a kind of contamination: "Never such faith again, never such innocence!"[19] As foil to Gregorias, Walcott comes to see himself as a Promethean firebrand who steals from the Western gods, or classics,[20] to

provide for his own native tradition. As a result, he synthesizes both aspects
of his heritage, combining high eloquence with touches of vernacular, stripping away glazed layers of the past to regain that "virginal, unpainted world"
of the islands.[21] Although Walcott envisions a return to origins, ontological
instability divides the self. As Helen Vendler noted in "Poet of Two Worlds":[22]

> Walcott's agenda gradually shaped itself. He would not give up the pater-
> nal patois; he would not give up his patois to write only in formal English.
> He would not give up his topic—his geographical place, his historical
> time, and his mixed blood; neither would he give up aesthetic balance. He
> was in all things "a divided child" loyal to "the stuffed dark nightingale
> of Keats" and "the virginal unpainted world" of the islands.

Walcott is alert to the otherness within, but also to the other *as
other*, consistent with Lacanian subject formation's being based on the
recognition of difference as determinative of personal identity. Moreover, this
is consistent with Frantz Fanon's demonstration of how race fundamentally
constructs and divides black identity as well. Just as a child's visual perception structures sexual difference, forcing a recognition of a lack that is then
internalized, "not only must the black man be black but he must be black in
relation to the white man."[23] Seeing himself fixed through the gaze of the
Other, Fanon suggests that the self-divided black child deflects what whiteness has projected on him, but the internalized complex of racial inferiority
must be exposed for what it is so that the individual can be put in position
to choose action with respect to the actual cause of the conflict, the social
structure. The white man's gaze constructs and subjugates the Other.
Walcott's "Divided Child" is a rare exemplar of how subjectivity is permeated by the social discourse that has preceded and constructed it to such an
extent that the child acquires a "double" image of the self. Desire is poignantly expressed as the need to be recognized by an/Other, even if that otherness
is seemingly self-embodied. When the colonial sees his own disfigured child,
it is an abomination he rejects, forgetting that it was he who created him in
the first place and in his own image: "The dream / of reason had produced
its monster: / a prodigy of the wrong age and colour."[24] To speak is "to exist
absolutely for the other,"[25] suggests Fanon. Indeed, Walcott's mixed racial
origins divide his loyalties, a theme taken up as early as 1962 in "A Far Cry
from Africa." The last, and frequently quoted, stanza of this poem foregrounds not only race but also language, setting the physical beauty of the
landscape against the authoritative "tongue" the speaker loves:

> I who am poisoned with the blood of both,
> Where shall I turn, divided to the vein?
> I who have cursed
> The drunken officer of British rule, how choose
> Between this Africa and English tongue I love?[26]

Postcolonial history still belongs to conquerors who imposed their languages on other peoples and who continue to dominate their writing. Walcott "entered the house of literature as a houseboy,"[27] doting on a reliquary of Victorian heirlooms. But his love for the English tongue did not preclude his expressing moral outrage over the crimes of the epoch, reminding us that "death rattles in every room" of the English mansion and that the muteness of the colonized is a silent scream.[28] In "Gros-Ilet," Walcott describes a "village soaked like a grey rag in salt water," from which

> a language came, garnished with conch-shells,
> with a suspicion of berries in its armpits
> and elbows like flexible oars
>
> There are different candles and customs here, the dead
> are different. Different shells guard their graves.
> There are distinctions even beyond the paradise
> of the horizon. This is not the grape-purple Aegean.
> There is no wine here, no cheese, the almonds are green,
> the sea-grapes bitter, the language is that of slaves.[29]

Civilization has substituted heaven for a primitive horizon; it has framed the New World in what the boy of *Another Life* attributes to "other men's voices / other men's lives and lines." The natives now sleep as if dead, giving up their dreams to a nostalgic idea of Western paradise. The language they have mastered now enslaves them. Western art is coveted and collected by the boy's father: "that fine drawn hare of Dürer's, clenched and quivering / to leap across my wrist . . . / Peter de Wint, Paul Sandby, Cotman."[30] But if the colonizer has imposed his history on the unpainted landscape, Walcott subverts this schema by turning the apprentice into the master, the beauty of his speech transfiguring the local people, making them heroes from the Old World and its myths: "These dead, these derelicts, / that alphabet of the emaciated, / they were the stars of my mythology."[31] Now the master must read his art through the student's inspired reading of him. Hence Walcott's Castries becomes Troy; his city, the New Jerusalem; his drunken painter friend Dunstan St. Omer, a Gregorias elevated to a civilizing papal figure.

"The Divided Child" begins with the boy finishing a sketch of the harbor for a critique by his art teacher (Harry Simmons). The point of view is the boy's, which lends a sense of immediacy, but this perspective is also enriched by the more pervasive reflections of the older narrator's longer view.[32] Here, a narcissistic gaze mirrors the Self through an Other, as Cimabue saw himself through Giotto, birthing a double consciousness:

> Verandahs, where the pages of the sea
> are a book left open by an absent master
> in the middle of another life—
> I begin here again,
> begin until this ocean's
> a shut book, and like a bulb
> the white moon's filaments wane.
>
> Begin with twilight, when a glare
> which held a cry of bugles lowered
> the coconut lances of the inlet,
> as a sun, tired of empire, declined . . .
>   There
> was your heaven! The clear
> glaze of another life,
> a landscape locked in amber, the rare
> gleam.[33]

In "the clear / glaze of another life," a tribal order is frozen in amber, and in the English word *amber*. But "the rare / gleam" shoots through, prefiguring Walcott's mature vision of Genesis, a regenerative motif that, in the title poem of *The Star-Apple Kingdom*, roots the history of the Caribbean in one black woman who sees "the creak of light" that divided the world suddenly dissolve into "the white, silent roar / of the old water wheel in the star-apple kingdom."[34]

As the boy of "The Divided Child" looks out over the harbor, he is eager to finish the sketch before natural light fades. Light, its intensities and shadows, glazes the scene as it "completes itself" in the darkness, becoming what it is even as it becomes invisible. The apprentice must navigate around the obstacles that intrude on the scene, his mind reeling with images of latter day legions and the colonial empire: "the gables of the Saint Antoine Hotel / aspiring from jungle, the flag / at Government House melting its pole."[35] In fact, the vision cannot be sustained *without* the boy's integrating the imperialist apparatus into the familiar scene, with "the last shacks" "transfigured" as "a cinquencento fragment in gilt frame."[36]

Poets are natural assimilators, but, unlike artists, they are removed from the triggering subject by a preposition: one writes of or paints about something. The poet's challenge is to link himself with his subject.[37] In the opening lines of "The Divided Child," we are told that a book is "left open by an absent master / in the middle of another life" and that the apprentice must "begin here again."[38] Whether the master be Our-Father-Who-Art-in-Heaven or "Our Father, / who floated in the vaults of Michelangelo,"[39] or the dead father who is the absent presence in the childhood house, the master artist has become distracted, leaving an opening for the apprentice, who will adapt the master's vision of reality in the interest of his own tutelage.

Each master's "reading" of the world is supplemented by an another's, which is destabilizing of the fixity of hierarchical positions.

As twilight settles on the landscape, the fledgling artist sees the hills "simplified" and turned to "hunks of coal." But the painter's task is to see things beyond use or even colonial exploitation, to retain an aesthetic distance, however self/betraying and self/divisive. As "the moon maintain[s] her station," shipwrecked relics—"antique furniture"—and cheap reproductions of European art are exposed in all their decadence:

> the mantel
> with its plaster-of-Paris Venus, which
> his yearning had made marble, half-cracked
> unsilvering mirror of black servants,
> like the painter's kerchiefed, ear-ringed portrait, Albertina.[40]

Pastoral munificence squandered by European landlords is now evident in the lunar reflections of a servile and "barefooted town." The moon's "sign" is "a dry park of disconsolate palms, like brooms, / planted by the Seventh Edward, Prince of Wales, / with drooping ostrich crests, ICH DIEN, I SERVE."[41]

Framed within the Westerner's primitive picturesque, culture gives birth to its reader. The mind of the painting teacher is haloed, a tonsure encircled by light, "crouched / in its pale tissue like an embryo." As the sketch is finally offered for critique and the teacher modifies the student's strokes according to his own reason and reference, the student becomes aware of yet another interloper: the secondhand nature of an already limited visual language: "In its dimension the drawing could not trace / the sociological contours of the promontory." Art can only allude to political realities:

> the groves were sawn . . .
> down the arched barrack balconies
> where colonels in the whisky-colored light
> had watched the green flash, like a lizard's tongue
> catch the last sail.[42]

More significant here is the disoriented white moon, a symbol of third-person consciousness. Feminized, she is the light that brings objects to the surface, but although she dominates the black sky, the boy, "her subject," desires to be the object of her desire, which is to be white: "from childhood he'd considered palms / ignobler than imagined elms," and "he had prayed / nightly for his flesh to change, / his flesh peeled white by her lighting strokes!" Here, the boy's image is self-rejected, "whitewashed" by a love for another life: "a moon ballooned. . . . O / mirror, where a generation *yearned / for whiteness*, for candour, unreturned. / The moon . . . / . . . whitewashed the shells."[43] The boy's desire is unconscious, for the child's desire is *to be* the desire of the

m(Other). To be desired is to be precipitated forward by language, which
stands for a lack of being that desired object. Lacan suggests that we seek in
the Other (an/other) some recognition of ourselves as desiring subjects outside language, of our identities as not entirely awash in the constructions of
our fantasies.[44] Hence the boy's language expresses his town's futile wish to
be seen positively through the counterfeit gaze of the white moon, to which
these townspeople have no "ontological resistance"[45] (as Fanon would say)
and without which they would seem not to exist: "Well, everything whitens,
/ all that town's characters, its cast of thousands," for "their flesh [is] like
flaking stone, / poor negatives!"[46]

        The moon's "white face" also invites associations with the vari-
ously masked ventriloquist, mime, and satirical minstrel. Through his ven-
triloquistic and satiric deployment of European influences (which, he contends, cannot be extracted from his native tradition), Walcott aesthetically
destabilizes political categories without having to acknowledge history's
molding of poetic form or content. Even for "the divided child," who has
not yet been initiated into the complexities of racial identity, the white
moon is an illusion, "her" light deceptive, a mocking night sun at the stu-
dio window. "She" reads the world below from her privileged position, but
is farsighted, seeing what is close as distant, mirroring the unbridgeable
chasm between the boy's myopic identifications, as "her slow disc magnified / the life beneath her like a reading-glass." The "master's" book that
opened the poem is echoed by the painter's "green book, laid / face downward. Moon, / and sea. He read / the spine. FIRST POEMS: / CAMP-
BELL." Reading, "the painter / almost absently / reversed it," as all things
seem reversed by dialectical relations:[47]

> Holy be
> the white head of a Negro,
> sacred be
> the black flax of a black child.[48]

The white-haired black master is patronized; the apprentice must assume
position in a certain line, but, by accepting one tradition, he betrays the
other. The Scottish poet's book that elicits such enthusiasm from the boy is
"bound in sea-green linen" by a colonized people and from their natural
resources. The boy's self-estrangement seems permanent: "the white face /
of a dead child stared from its window-frame."[49] Here the child reveals a
primal fear of what has been repressed all this time: death, like the Real, is
the "impossible" core of human identity. (As Jonathan Lee notes, Lacan
characterizes the Real as "the mystery of the speaking body," or the unconscious; it is what stands behind the reality constituted in and by our use of
language, only hinting at its presence through the failures and ruptures that

mark this symbolic system.)[50] Walcott's embrace of cultural amnesia may be a gesture toward this mystery of an unconscious that is continually in motion, continually reborn.

The European literary model is indispensable to Walcott's poetry, but so is his native heritage. Out of both his childhood memories and his racial memory comes an imaginative drive "to praise lovelong, the living and the brown dead" of his island, to interpret what that society sees. Walcott's intent in *Another Life* is to *reverse* the perceptual order, to rein-terpret the history of the islands by painting over (whiting out) received narratives with fresh discursive colors and glazes. Although he has been criticized for not taking an explicitly revolutionary stance within the Caribbean culture wars, one can argue that he is effectively doing so by consciously or unconsciously depicting himself as the revolutionary apprentice who rebels against—and surpasses—the colonial master's style and determinative influence. Reacting in 1971 to the charges that he has mimicked the masters' language and literature, Walcott said:

> A great amount of the Third World literature is a literature of revenge written by the descendents of slaves bent on exorcising this demon [histo-ry] through the word. Or a literature of remorse written by the descen-dents of masters obsessed by guilt. . . . The truly classic—written by those who practice the tough aesthetic of the New World—neither explains nor forgives history because it refuses to recognize it as a creative force. . . . The old style Revolutionary Writer sees Caliban as an enraged pupil. He can't separate the rage of Caliban from the beauty of his speech. . . . The language of the torturer has been mastered by the victim. Yet this is viewed as servitude, not as irony or victory![51]

Walcott's appropriation of "heiratic objects" of European art in *Another Life* reveals his love for Caliban's eloquence, however "classical" a charac-ter he may be. While the goal of a back-to-Africa movement is to purge the colonial influence, the movement according to Walcott, is mimicking some-thing that does not exist except in the white colonialist's imagination, a les-son he learned early on, like the boy in *Another Life* who spurns his dead father's artwork, "venerable objects / borne by . . . black hands," and yearns for an ancestry of the "deep country," or the bush.[52] However, he discovers there that this "natural man" for whom he is searching is mere-ly an illusion, one of colonialism's constructs.

Mimicry is therefore an aesthetic concept for Walcott, one that he appropriates and cultivates in positive terms. As Terada aptly demon-strates, mimicry is the very ground for Walcott's creative revolution: "Mimicry, with all its ambivalent freight, replaces mimesis as the ground of representation and culture."[53] Mimicry redefines itself through the lens of postmodernism, which has also questioned the idea of originality, or the

existence of a starting point, and has emphasized the secondariness of a signifying chain. In "The Caribbean: Culture or Mimicry?" Walcott asserts
that once "the meridian of European civilization has been crossed," there
is no longer any point of origination, because "the cord is cut by that
meridian."[54] Lacan makes the same assertion with regard to language:
entering the Symbolic means being severed (or cut off) from the Imaginary,
or body of origination, which can be recaptured only through the substitute of a transitory utterance.

Gregorias's return to aboriginal roots, then, is impossible: "We
cannot return to what we have never been."[55] With nothing more than the
earth to believe in, the boy in *Another Life* is brought back to the soil as
an end point and a starting point. Walcott insists that the West Indian must
have a vision of himself that more closely corresponds to what he is now
rather than where he came from.[56] With nothing to begin with, there is
"everything to be made," as Walcott says. This is an affirming gesture, better and deeper than one of despair.

The act of beginning is always language's beginning, because language fails to end itself. "There is no beginning but no end," as Walcott
states in "The Muse of History": "The new poet enters a flux and with-
draws, as the weaver continues the pattern, hand to hand."[57] What Giotto
saw as great in Cimabue was both the past and the future, and what
Cimabue saw in Giotto was what he did not think he would see in himself—the dawning of the Renaissance. Significantly, *Another Life* concludes
with the poet's declaration of art's power to rename the postcolonial world.
Returning to the image of the painter Gregorias, Walcott shows him
sketching "the smooth white walls of clouds and villages" *over an under-
painting* by the master. In Gregorias's "impossible" yet "inexhaustible"
Renaissance, "brown cherubs of Giotto and Masaccio" mingle with an
incongruous "salt wind . . . / smelling of turpentine, with nothing so old /
it could not be invented."[58] By the end, the sleep of history must be wiped
away, the eyes of the dead master's unfinished portraits "blown out." The
artist, liberated, can begin to construct a new sequence.

The polarizations of the self-divided child are rooted in discourse
and, here, complicated by racial difference. Memory is as fixed as any
object, and as easily lost. Although the object may be gone, however, it will
not be abandoned: language is wrought by shaping words, as an object is
shaped by the hand that it hollows. The poet, like the still-life painter, persists in finding "the rightness of placed things."[59] For Walcott, this prior
positioning depends on the effort to recreate it, although there is always
that misalignment between reality and reflection. In painting, lines delineate the edges between things, edges that in reality do not exist, as Walcott
himself observes: "There are already, invisible on canvas, / lines locking

into outlines. The visible dissolves / in a benign acid."[60] A line in painting has extension but no dimension. No such lines exist in nature. Cimabue, the master, read Giotto's line in the mirror of his own reference, one that Giotto *mastered* in order to copy Cimabue. Walcott's poetic line likewise mirrors his own models, both dividing and connecting his two worlds.

7

RESCUING PSYCHE

Keats' Containment of the Beloved
but Fading Woman in the "Ode to Psyche"

Because myths are populated by figures who are always larger and wiser than mere mortals, yet still embody human foibles, Keats could restore through myth what he could never wholly accept as irrevocably lost: a mother waning away from consumption, a brother afflicted with the same disease—both of whom he had failed to rescue from premature deaths. Freud and Bruno Bettleheim have shown the importance of myth and fairy tales as discursive forms of wish fulfillment, attended by the determination to defer denouement and to make less final the final act of separation. Aileen Ward's definitive psychoanalytic biography is suggestive about Keats's fixation with the maternal object of desire and his inability to be dispossessed of his relationship to her, even in his subsequent attachment to his fiancée, Fanny Brawne.[1] Unlike Wordsworth, Keats never did compose a deliberately autobiographical or confessional work like *The Prelude*, yet his work, as well as the work of other romantic poets, clearly demonstrates that poetry is informed by personal tragedy and that writing can be useful as a form of self-containment and therapy.

Indeed, Keats's unrelenting search for a maternal object that he could ultimately internalize and permanently reinstate in nature had both outward and inward manifestations and found an apt correlative in the ancient myth of Cupid and Psyche. Adapting the myth allowed Keats to simultaneously express and withhold volatile emotions that nurtured his own writing. He sympathized with Psyche's plight and refuge in a fairyland palace, a hiding place of voices and gods, where she is wed to a mysterious phantom who visits her nightly. Certainly, Keats's poetic excursions into dark, luxurious abodes of a sensual nature in which dreamlike imagery was not only accessible, but also gratifying, are similar to Psyche's being infatuated with an invisible and divine Cupid who abandons her at the moment she lifts her lamp and a few drops of oil spill on his back. Psyche learns that inward illumination can be as scorching as it is enlightening. Blind faith in a fathomless sensual darkness is better than knowing what the light of reason tells us we can never fully possess.

My reading of Keats began when I was writing my dissertation on the Greek myth of Cupid and Psyche. I had planned to include a close reading of Keats's "Ode to Psyche," one of the earlier odes and less well known than "Ode to a Nightingale" or "Ode on a Grecian Urn." I had just given birth to my daughter and was absorbed in my prospectus, cobbling together hours to visit the archives of the Library of Congress. I was failing miserably and messily at my maternal duties, my daughter being a colicky baby, and I was certain I never would really complete my Ph.D., that it would be infinitely deferred into senility. At dawn, I was still pacing back and forth trying to calm a crying baby. But I also found unusual solace in recalling fragments of Keats's moonlit and slumbering poems about winged horses and charioteers. I began to look forward to trading my long nights for my afternoons at the stately library.

So that spring, I would walk the ten blocks to the brainy gold dome of the nation's library, and enter through the library's tall wooden doors. The inspecting guard fiddled through my purse and notebooks and passed me along toward the elevator. Cutting diagonally across the marble blocked tiles of the sumptuous pink-marbled atrium, I could hear the echoes of my own heels along with those of the other visitors, dutifully lugging in their book bags to research one thing or another. Every second or another, one of us paused to look up at the frescoes swirling above with the rapt, robust angels and heavenly clouds. I wondered just how many scaffolds it must take to lift an Italian painter so high.

The Rare Books room was on the third floor and even quieter than the main reading room where monklike scholars were deeply engrossed in their esoteric research. The librarian, in rolled sleeves and suede, greeted me with a hush. Allowed only a pencil and a pad, I signed cards for borrowing the thick volume of Keats's letters, or alternately, the early poems, dated March 1817, when the poet was only twenty-two.

Then, I took take my place to wait at the wide oak table. I sat there idly as if I were sitting down to lunch. Outside the window, sunflowers were big as showerheads, and a few marble birds strolled the veranda. Then, the librarian, wearing fastidious gloves, reemerged from the refrigerated vaults. He was holding the book of letters. Handling the cover, I remember thinking, *I could be touching Keats's own flesh and bone*, while handling the ancient paper. But I kept vigilance, as a surgeon does, careful not to crease any more of the fragile pages as I turned them over and over again. Keats's own handwriting had faded to the color of a rusty nail.

Because the figure of Psyche is a recurrent symbol that appears early in Keats's readings and writings, the mythological Psyche was not a casual or unrelated source for the ode. Rather, "Ode to Psyche" was a poetic and public articulation of Keats's most profound thinking about the themes of love, death, and transcendence. Keats's "Ode to Psyche" emerges from this figure of the beloved and fading woman, a multivalent figure who bears the weight of Keats's remembered hopes as well as his fears and disappointments. This beloved but fading woman whom Keats must rescue and preserve from the threat of mutability may have emerged from Keats's reading of the myth because the myth evoked in him powerful feelings of love and attachment. Psyche provides an important paradigm for Keats, a corrective fantasy of restoration. Sometimes a type of one's own soul, or of transcendent knowledge, or of Imagination, this figure assumes human and fictional incarnations in Keats's life and poetry. She returns as Fanny Brawne, Frances Keats, Eve, Francesca de Rimini, and Melancholy, but she is always Psyche. On a conscious and unconscious level, Keats worked and reworked the myth playing all the parts.

Keats's early references to Psyche show he was psychologically predisposed to the emotional qualities and rewards implicit in the myth, the most important being his attraction to dream and dream-life in which sensual satisfaction is granted in the darkness without fear. A pleasurable realm sealed off from the actualities of everyday reality gave Keats a sense of security. Here Keats could find an architectural metaphor for psychic places in which the self is removed and embowered in unconscious delight. Additionally, because Cupid's palace (complete with a hall of mirrors) is the realm most associated with infancy and the reciprocity of love between mother and child, no self-object differentiation is recognized by the infant; Freud calls this the neotic "oceanic feeling," and Lacan refers to a similar disposition in the mirror stage.

Keats's views of the poetic psyche, contained in the letters, are variations on the autobiographical psyche I have just introduced and are inevitably predicated on his childhood as well and may provide useful clues to interpretation of the poetry. Hence, a reading of the myth through Keats is also a reading of Keats through myth. His unique capacities for self-revelation, and his use of myth as a resource for that kind of discovery, is an indication that he was breaking new psychological ground for the poet—drawing his own associations for pain and pleasure as the immediate subject for poetry.

He was born on October 31, 1795, the first child of Thomas and Frances (Jennings) Keats, in the northern part of London. Keats's father worked in the stables of the prosperous John Jennings, Keats's grandfather, a provider of horses for coaches that ran from London to the northern parts of England. When he was eight years old, Keats was sent to a small school in the village of Enfield. Shortly afterward Keats's father was killed in a riding accident. His mother, a vivacious and spontaneous woman, brought Keats and his siblings back to the Jennings household, but soon after that, she abandoned her children for an affair with a roving actor of dubious character with whom she traveled for a number of years. When the relationship ended, a despondent Frances Keats returned home. Unknown to her and her family, she was already infected with tuberculosis. By the time Keats turned fourteen, she was dead. Keats and his three younger siblings were then left with their elderly grandmother Jennings.

At the school in Enfield, Keats had begun reading books. He was an avid reader and apparently, his interest in literature became even more avid after his mother's death. Charles Clarke Cooke, an instructor at the school, recalled that Keats developed a fondness for the classics and the myths. When reading Spencer's *Faerie Queen*, Keats went through it as "a young horse would through a spring meadow—romping."[2] In his eagerness, Keats showed a remarkable gift of empathy and when, as Cooke recorded, Keats came across a phrase in the *Faerie Queen*, "*sea-shouldering whales*," he "hoisted himself up" and looking quite burly and formidable, said, "What an image that is—*sea-shouldering whales*."[3] The capacity for being in a state of uncertainty about ego identity, and to sustain imaginative belief rather than reaching after reason or fact, was a Keatsian trademark that he made famous in his axiom about a poet's gift for negative capability. Sympathetic identification was, for Keats, the vehicle for his migratory flights from imagination to reality and back again—a spinning dialect of the mind in constant interaction with itself.

From his boyhood to the end of his life, Keats suffered shocks and crises, which caused him great emotional distress. His letters suggest that he vacillated between high and low moods. After an arduous courtship, he won the hand of Fanny Brawne. But shortly after that, he realized he had contracted tuberculosis, probably as a result of tending to his brother Tom. Keats broke off the engagement and died a short time afterward in Rome in 1832.

The labor of love and mourning, how to grieve love and how to make grief more manageable, was perhaps, Keats's greatest theme. Drawn to the Greek myths from the time he could read, Keats evidently found myth congenial to his nature. Like many Englishmen of his time, Keats possessed a minute recollection of biblical and mythological texts, and traditional symbols and allusions came adventitiously and plentifully to him. Keats's mythology was not allegorical per se; rather, it was a medium through which the poet spoke and thought—a universal language of the human imagination. Whereas allegory implies doctrines or propositions translated with a one-to-one parallelism into characters or events, to be believed or disbelieved, myths, as Freud later observed, were far more connotative and self-disclosing.

Of those mythic gods and goddesses to whom Keats paid homage, none was more favored than Psyche, and Keats canonized her in 1819 in a springtime epistle to George and Georgiana Keats. It would be to Psyche that Keats would enact his own mystery rite, turning inward to the early incarnation of the goddess Psyche. In a stunning piece of self-analysis, Keats selects for his ode a symbol that has both personal and public resonance. Through Psyche he reflects his hopes for a love that can be memorialized, outlasting the effects of mutability. In this spirit of looking inward, secrecy, and worship of the earth mother, Keats begins writing the "Ode to Psyche" with "moderate pains:"[4]

> O goddess! Hear these tuneless numbers, wrung
> by sweet enforcements and remembrance dear,
> And pardon that thy secrets should be sung
> Even into thine own soft-conched ear:
> Surely I dreamt today, or did I see
> The winged Psyche with awak'ed eyes?

Psyche is a maiden who is so lovely that men worship her instead of Aphrodite. The goddess orders Cupid to punish Psyche by causing her to fall in love with a monster, but Cupid secretly falls in love with her. Psyche is wafted away to an enchanted palace, where Cupid visits her at night and makes her vow never to look at him. But Psyche's sisters convince her to light a lamp and reveal her husband's identity. When Cupid realizes what she has done, he deserts her. Psyche must accomplish a series of tasks to win Cupid back. Finally, she descends to the underworld to obtain Prosperina's beauty box and, unable to resist temptation, falls into a death-like sleep. Cupid rescues Psyche, and she is granted immortality.

Indeed, Psyche bears the weight of Keats's remembered hopes as well as his fears and disappointments. This is the beloved and fading woman, once mortal and now divine, whom Keats must rescue and preserve from the threat of mutability although, according to Keats's interpretation of the myth in the ode, she is already "immortalized." Significantly, as Keats neared the end of his life, he began to view the world rather than himself as something that was beginning to dim and vanish. It was the living, rather than the dying, whom Keats considered in peril of disappearing from view. Hence he came to think of his leaving (as in departing from) the world "unseen" as a luxury that would help him to avoid the heartbreak of separation from loved ones. In September 1820 he wrote to his friend Charles Brown, "I wish for death every day and night to deliver me from these pains, and then I wish death away, for death would destroy even these pains which are better than nothing."[5] And with poignant regret, he adds with regard to his fiancée, Fanny Brawne: "The thought of leaving Miss Brawne is beyond everything horrible—I see her figure eternally vanishing."[6] Although the fading figure never vanishes completely, the slow progress toward absolute diminishment is a means of keeping the end safely at bay. Here, nothing lasts, yet nothing ends, either. Keats is able to welcome the possibility of a death that would fulfill his wish for a perpetual union with the beloved, but fading, woman beyond the grave.

Nearing the end of his life, Keats encapsulates this very idea of a conjectured synthesis of body and soul, and heaven and earth in a fantasy he conveys to Fanny Brawne.[7] Speaking of the "Oriental richness" of a tale that haunts his mind, he says he "sees melancholy men [like himself] dying." Through a series of adventures, "each turns to some reach of heaven, where they meet an Enchanted Lady." Keats then recalls that just as they are about to embrace this vanishing phantom woman, she bids them to shut their eyes. Opening their eyes again, the men find that they have "descended to earth in a magic basket." The basket is another containing vessel—bearing the weight of what its contents are, not unlike a womblike enclosure. The Enchanted Lady is, like Psyche, a mother-image, a means of conveyance from one world to the next. In this fantasy, heaven constitutes a rebirth into life without the sadness of natural process and leave-taking simultaneous with death. The richness of sensual pleasure in a reflective state is the content of Keats's conceptualized heaven. Yet again, this story reveals Keats's awareness of the irony of any expectation. When the men are filled with just enough desire to embrace the heavenly (the impossible mother who has already eluded their reach), the beloved object fades and dissolves. Like Psyche's vision of Cupid, as she sees her own love infinitely fading from her, Keats is moved to relate the sense of his dying as a fear that he will never find relation, that love, even if it is perpetuated into the afterlife, is always tantalizing him at one remove.

The Enchanted Lady represents, as many of Keats's women do, the imaginary oneness that, like Lacan's mirror, allows him to deny his own lack of completion and to believe in the absolute integrity of his own selfhood. This is also what would have appealed to Keats about the Psyche and Cupid myth. Here, in Cupid's palace, Psyche can merge into the totality of one, instating the lost paradise of an earlier undifferentiated wholeness with the maternal image (she calls Cupid her "own soul)". Although Cupid is present, she is not allowed to "see" him; thus he is a phantom presence who grants accessibility to the unreal world that harbors the maternal image. Indeed, the palace is a peculiarly infantine place, where all wishes are granted before Psyche can even think to ask for them. The sensuality associated with the erotic palace is gratifying of the infant's most essential desires: feasts (taste); baths (touch); music (hearing); jewels (sight). The beloved Cupid is yet another "vanishing beloved," and maintains for Keats, through Psyche, a fantasy of unbroken connection with the mother even in the afterlife. Any thought that she is not, in fact, present in the mind or the soul of the Psyche that represents Keats's longing for reunion with the lapsed mother is immediately repelled by wish and fantasy, and reconstituted in the myth.

Although the object of the quest is unattainable, Keats's surrendering the hope of regaining it would constitute an abrupt negation of everything, a theme richly drawn out in the subsequent "Ode to a Nightingale." Keats expresses his ineluctable desire for the object that eludes him through the receding vision of a powerfully attractive love object (such as the nightingale). Although Psyche is already immortal and therefore assumably immune to death and dying, she was once mortal and subject to human frailness. Psyche, as a substitute for the mother whose death Keats could not accept as a finality, is then a safe subject for Keats to project his fears on. Because she is already immortal, her reincarnation in a mortal form in Keats's imagination is without risk. She can never actually succumb to extinction.

The myth of Psyche and Cupid originates in Apuleius's second-century work, *The Golden Ass*.[8] Keats had most likely read the epic as a schoolboy but apparently reread it just prior to composing the "Ode to Psyche." Moreover, he alludes to Psyche in the apprentice poems "I stood tip-toe" and *Sleep and Poetry* and in the way he envisions his own "chameleon-like" identity in terms that are derived from the Greek meaning of psyche, as a butterfly or soul. Discussing his wish to enter into other worlds rather than to stay isolated within his own "ego," Keats repeats lines from Troilos, which sound ethereal and suggest an association with the butterfly as well: "I wander like a lost soul upon the Stygian banks staying for waftage . . . I melt into the air with voluptuousness so delicate that I am content to be alone."[9] In July 1819 Keats wrote to J. H. Reynolds that "I have been late moulting; not for fresh feathers or wings; they are gone and in their stead I hope to have a pair of sublunary legs. . . . I have altered not from a Chrysalis to a butterfly, but the Contrary. . . ."[10] Psyche will also have to experience human servitude before she can return to that initial innocence; this time on a more secure level.

A response to the world as empathetic as Keats's was would necessarily have to elude boundaries; reaching into his own capacity for giving another entity new life and meaning within his own being. His most famous statement of this dark intuition of the other, or Negative Capability, comes through the following example included in the famous letter to Bailey, November 22, 1817: "if a Sparrow comes before my window I take part in its existence and pick among the gravel." As the psychoanalyst James Hillman writes, "the soul becomes operative in converting it into a Thou—making soul of objects, personifying, anthropomorphosing, turning into a partner the object with which it is engaged and in which it has implanted soul."[11]

Increasingly, Keats turns from his enthusiasm for becoming other identities in the cosmic and human world to a quiet seclusion in which identity comes to be an *achievement*, a favorable term for *individuation*. Similarly, Psyche is also a pilgrim, a signifier for development and progress in love and wisdom, through the circumstantial pains of the world as exemplified in Keats's allegorical conception of the "Vale of Soul-Making." Writing about soul-making in the same period as the "Ode to Psyche," Keats forms an analogy between the human heart and the painful lessons of the world imprinted on the heart: "A Place where the heart must feel and suffer in a thousand diverse ways!"[12]

The subject of "melancholy" of soul or spirit reveals the outcast and orphaned Psyche in search of an identity. Her story parallels Keats's own: dejection as a result of his parents' abandonment, desire to see his siblings again, and passion that cannot be consummated in this life (Fanny Brawne). In his absorption of the myth, the adult Keats does something similar to what Bettleheim claims children do in *The Uses of Enchantment*, cutting conflicts by identifying with fairy tale figures. In March 1818, for example while Keats was tending to his brother Tom, Keats wrote to his friend J. H. Reynolds, who was ill. He hoped to cheer him with a distracting poem about the imagination. While he was helping Reynolds to pass the time with his own reverie, the shadow of illness begins to connect with Tom's failing health, and the cheering mood of the epistle letter becomes an anxious one. What is intriguing about the letter is that Keats selected what he called the "unconnected subject" of Claude's *The Enchanted Castle* for the occasion. The painting foregrounds the seated figure of Psyche pondering "fairy lands forlorn."[13]

The Enchanted Castle depicts a muted landscape shadowed by dusk and a medieval castle, which dominates the small figure of Psyche, seated in the foreground. A pale light emerges from behind the furthest corner of the horizon, so that the castle is seen against a mysterious light whose source is unknown. A shimmering light isolates Psyche. There is no hint of the immortal goddess here that Keats will eventually bring to life. The landscape is not fanciful but realistic. The castle is not jeweled and resplendent but fortresslike. Psyche herself is drawn to classical perfection, seeming more muscular than an ordinary woman does. Her meditative pose seems to echo the artist's thought. She is not etherealized but positioned very close to the ground. Hence, if Keats was to make any identification with the figure in his poem about enchantment, it is one of contemplation. There is a distance between what the castle holds and what involves the subject's consciousness. The "outsideness" of Psyche may bear an anticipatory note of Keats's own voyeuristic exclusion in the opening scene of "Ode to Psyche."

Psyche's diminutive figure is brooding over beauty against a vast landscape, which is borrowed from the "wafts of Arcadian scenes"—peaceful, happy scenes. This is an image of Psyche before her troubled awakening and the toll of human loss. However, as is characteristic of Keats, the advent of happiness and innocence is immediately blighted by the foreshadowing of sorrow. The ostensibly peaceful scene will be read by Keats in a way that permits inclusion of its opposite—melancholy and tribulation.

The loss of innocence and the burden of consciousness are themes in the Psyche myth which are explored by both Apuleius and Keats. Forbidden knowledge disrupts Psyche's initial union with Cupid. Her fall is simultaneous with the light of comprehension, causing her pain and chaos, until Cupid, who reawakens her to immortality, revives her. In the "Ode to Psyche" Keats also revives the dormant Psyche, saving the "immortal" figure from death and obscurity.[14] The myth continued to express the tensions of Keats's personality. Perhaps most poignantly we recall that Psyche, like the young Keats, was orphaned by her parents, and her psychic experience in which she is united with Cupid, is permeated by her search to regain the lost object of the mother.

As John Bowlby has shown in his groundbreaking study of children *(Attachment and Loss)*, a child's separation from her mother may lead to adult depression and anxiety.[15] A child who remains fixated at the infantile stage of dependency on a parent who is absent or unresponsive, can easily withdraw narcissistic libido back to the ego in substitution for extending libido toward the external object of attachment. The infantile ego is essentially narcissistic when expressing its demands and desires, but becomes even more desperately so when seeking to pull back into its orbit the idealized object of the mother with whom the infant seeks to identify and bond.

Keats apparently remained preoccupied with such a desired fusion with his mother who constitutes part of the appeal and wonder of the invisible world he explored in poetic reverie. In *Sleep and Poetry* Keats turns inward and identifies with his phantom charioteer who eventually vanishes into "the clear space of ether." Employing the central metaphor of flight to simulate the spatial glide of the psyche drawn into a pleasurable state, Keats reaches an invisible range of dream and fancy which is erotic and delightful. His preference for a diffuse, imaginary world in which things are not anchored to earth is in keeping with his desire to go beyond it and, as stated in "Ode to a Nightingale" "leave the world unseen." On the one hand, Keats's vanishing is to be seen as its *own* fulfillment, because to be free of the body, as a weightless charioteer of winged horses, was a goal in concert with the impetus for self-dissolution and eventual remerging with the mist of the maternal figure—a "dusky space." This is how Keats introduces the poet-charioteer of *Sleep and Poetry*:

> The charioteer with wond'rous gesture talks
> To the trees and mountains; and there soon appear
> shapes of delight, of mystery, and fear,
> Passing along before a dusky space
> Made by some mighty oaks . . .

The platonic element surfaces in the poem (lines 140–160), when Keats envisions a charioteer "with wond'rous gesture" who can "listen" and converse with the chimerical objects of nature in the dream state. The charioteer, an alter ego for Keats, has the capacity "to write with a hurrying glow" before he and his "steeds" disappear into "the light of heaven" and in their stead Keats is left with a sense of "real things" coming on doubly strong. As Keats observes, "the visions are all fled / the car is fled / into the light of heaven" and in their place Keats is aware of "real" or differentiated "things." The dark ideal of sleep departs, fading away. The speaker is left with feelings of dejection and abandonment of love and fulfillment derived from dream. In tandem with Keats's preference for mystery and "half-knowledge," is his advocacy of intuition, a dark and probing concentration associated with flights from reason and fact. Psyche's happiness with a love she could not see, but could find pleasure in, echoes the Keatsian psyche's suspicion of the visible world and his privileging of the invisible or the phantoms of dream.

This invisible object of desire is a motif that runs throughout Keats's poems, especially in the middle period, and may well be yet another incarnation of the lost mother, Frances Keats. Like the Mystery Lady in "La Belle Dame sans Merci," the vanished beloved is usually the immortal of the pair. In Keats' long work *Lamia*, for example, the figure, Lamia, "melts" into the air just as Psyche's Cupid flies off after Psyche's transgression of lighting the lamp. The two immortal characters in the two works, Cupid and Lamia, create palaces for their mortal spouses, palaces bedecked with impressive portals. Mysterious music fills the rooms from an invisible source, and every wish is granted. Madeline, of *The Eve of St. Agnes*, also hears a strange unearthly melody through the halls of her mansion. Keats apparently had an interest in architecture and used spatial metaphors to introduce key ideas about the way in which the psyche (or human mind) moves through the experience of dreams and life. For example, in *Lamia* and *The Eve of St. Agnes* mortal and immortal connect in a momentary fantasy of unity in the "maiden chamber" of dream-delights. But this of course does not last. The mortal is tempted to display to the world his or her divine partner and in doing so, destroys his own happiness. To become conscious of the dream is to chase away the most beautiful of illusions. For Keats this is the true fall—awakening to daylight—where there is sorrow and parting. As he puts it in *Sleep and Poetry*:

> Most awfully intent
> The driver of those steeds is forward bent,
> And seems to listen: O that I might know
> 'all that he writes with such a hurrying glow.
> The visions all fled—the car is fled
> Into the light of heaven, and in their stead
> A sense of real things comes doubly strong,
> And like a muddy stream, would bear along
> My soul to nothingness; but will I strive
> Against all doubtings, and will keep alive
> the thoughts of that same chariot, and the strange
> Journey it went

The car, or chariot, is a conveyer of the Keatsian ego, which vanishes into "the light of heaven," which is a nondisappearing light. Keats's strivings to keep it lit is a burden as well as a delight as writing becomes a simulation of the mourning process—in which the dead person is continually resurrected in the imagination to be mourned. Indeed, although we may be consciously aware of our need to recognize the reality of loss, we often unconsciously maintain the fantasy of the object as present and alive. For Keats, loss was modified by the recuperative power of a language of melody and imagery, and through its substitutions and patterns. The otherwise fragmented self can find jubilant unity through a fixing of word-images that appear to be utterly coherent and intact. This is an ambiguous and ineffable stage that Keats restitutes, fluctuating between union with the mother and the pain of separation from her, just as he does between feeling himself in the luxuriant realm of imaginary flight and feeling himself as an outsider, an onlooker. If the mother is soundless, only the sound of poetry can reconstitute her.

The Psyche myth also appears to be paradigmatic for Keats's personal development in the letters. Psyche, another name for the soul, approximates the responsive principle of Keats's Negative Capability, and arguably, one that is feminine. The poetic psyche represents part of our being that is in touch with the divine, and one discovers her by looking within.[16] Psyche is also an emblem of the wandering and volatile "orphaned" psyche who grieves —as Keats grieved for his mother—a psyche in search of the vanishing beloved in need of rescue whom Keats must somehow enshrine.

As we know, Keats took an interest in books early on and was absorbed in Greek texts such as Tooke's *Pantheon*, Spence's *Polymetis*, and Lemprière's *Classical Dictionary*.[17] So animated by the Greek gods and god-

desses, Keats recorded to Reynolds, "when I was a schoolboy, I thought a
fair woman a pure goddess and my mind was a soft nest in which some one
of them slept though she knew not."[18] Such an early enthusiasm for the
mythic was to be transported to another sphere—and could cause an
observer to swoon. In "Ode to Psyche", included in a letter-manuscript to
his brother, George, Keats describes "fainting with surprise" at seeing the
figures of Psyche and Cupid embracing.

> I wander'd in a forest thoughtlessly,
> And on the sudden, fainting with surprise
> Saw two fair Creatures couched side by side
> in deepest grass beneath the whispering fan
> Of leaves and trembled blossoms, where there ran
> A Brooklet scarce espied
> 'Mid hushed, cool-rooted flowers, fragrant eyed
> Blue, freckle-pink, and budded syrian
> They lay, calm breathing on the bedded grass.
> Their arms embraced and their pinions too. . .

As an extended image, Psyche is wedded not only to her immortal
husband but also to the natural bower in which she and her lover seem, by
contrast, unnaturally still, as if caught only momentarily between the flut-
tering motions that surround them. "Fainting," "trembling," and "calm
breathing" apply to the swooning action of the butterfly. That the lovers
lay side by side gives a symmetrical shape to their two figures perceived
identically as one, visibly imitating a butterfly's quartered wings. In such a
still moment of equipoise, any disturbance would seem to have the effect
of chasing away the fleeting vision. The patterns on the butterfly's wings
are most often concentric, having a common center. This also applies to the
overall shape of the ode, which continues to accumulate a number of natural and sacred objects but returns to the origin, the center, and source,
which is the mother-psyche who gives birth to "Bliss."

Keats presents the goddess as catalyst for his own birth as a mature
poet; and yet at the same time, Psyche is a production (or an offspring) of
Keats's own laboring and life-giving capacities. Maternity, in fact, seems to
be a central trope in Keats's formulation of the inner woman. Spawned
from "the body" of Keats's poem as an autonomous emblem of the imagination, she is made out of corporeal breath: part mortal, part immortal.
The creative act is then synonymous with a rebirth of the goddess who is
nurtured and protected as both mother and offspring.

In Plato, the psyche is a term for the soul; and Beauty, for Love,
"the most memorable of the Forms," which leads the psyche up the ladder
of love and causes its wings to grow.[19] Keats was undoubtedly aware of the
platonic associations for "psyche" and "soul" as revealed in his letters by

his many references to the Greek philosophers. To this end his preamble on the "Ode to Psyche" mentions both Augustus and "the platonist" Apuleius who saw Psyche as the soul represented with the wings of a butterfly rising from the mouth of the deceased.

Keats composed the "Ode to Psyche" in April, the same month that his mother had finally succumbed to tuberculosis years before. The circumstances of his mother's Frances Keats' death were perhaps made more bitter by the fact that she had just returned home to Edmonton after an unhappy second marriage to an emotionally unstable actor when she came down with consumption, the disease that would afflict Keats as well. The young Keats decided to nurse her, cooking her food, administering her medicine, and reading by her bedside. Once, it is recorded, Keats's mother became very ill and the house was ordered to absolute quiet. Keats found an old sword and kept protective watch out-side her door, allowing no one to disturb her.[19] Consumption, or tuber-culosis, no doubt kept her confined to her bed and the door was closed behind her, leaving her children to speculate and worry about her disap-pearing yet again. The disease was insidious, accompanied by lassitude and the worsening wasting of the body.

The painful watching of his mother's "loveliness fade" would most likely result in the wish for reparation of a primary bond, the outgrowth of knowing that pleasure cannot last. His childhood separations from his mother comingled with foreboding of privation. "Ode to Psyche" is rare instance in which Keats is able to assure, for himself, her protection from death by raising his own altar of permanent homage.

From a psychoanalytic view, Keats's history of idealizing his absent mother may have resulted in the attempt to compensate for what is lack-ing, providing a symbolic replacement for that original bond. The fading but beloved figure in the "Ode to Psyche" reenacts, and dramatizes, the loss of the mother in symbolic language itself. Keats then seeks to recover her by deferring the actual event of separation in the poem. Pain becomes signification, and language ensures that there will never be an ending to the son's quest for the fading mother, because there will never be an ending to language, only reiteration, and continual referral to the beginning. Hence, Psyche, as mother figure, is revivified by the son's assent to worshipful mourning after the fact of her death.

By early April 1819, a few weeks before writing "Ode to Psyche," Keats had settled in Wentworth Place with Charles Brown. The winter before, at Well Walk, Tom (Keats's brother) had died. Seeing Keats's evident grief, Brown promptly urged Keats to "have nothing more to do with those lodgings" and to live with him. The house was divided into two adjacent residences, formerly owned by Brown and

Keats's other friend, Charles Dilke. Dilke had rented it out to a Mrs. Brawne and her two daughters, whom Keats met the year before. He soon became infatuated with the eldest, Fanny, and his admiration was too warm to "worship" as their love strengthened. Thus, in that spring, Keats was living in adjoining houses with his "enchantress" and sharing the same garden.

At Wentworth Place, Keats's sitting room, shuttered by French windows, looked out to a grassy plot before the windows. The garden itself extended to the side of the house with plum, pear and mulberry trees, a setting reminiscent of the "Ode to Psyche." There were laurelstine hedges and china roses and a tally of finches and brown chickadees. The sitting room contained two chairs, perpendicular to one another—one for looking out the window on the garden; the other for reading. Keats would rest his arm on the observer chair as he read. In this manner Keats spent most of his time watching through the window, often while he was sick. He watched the building work in the grove and would observe Fanny walking through the garden. Keats begins the epistle ode in this voyeuristic mood of the one who is "unseen":

> I wander'd in a forest thoughtlessly,
> And on the sudden, fainting with surprise. . .
> Their lips touched not but had not bid adiew,
> As if disjoined by soft-handed slumber,
> And ready still past kisses to outnumber,
> At tender eye dawn of aurorian love.
> The winged boy I knew:
> But who was thou O happy dove?
> His Psyche true?

Keats's voyeurism is a redoubled usurping of the Cupid role, as Cupid watched and loved Psyche in the palace, yet went unseen. The woodland setting contrasts with the original myth's setting in the palace or "on the ground" where Cupid discovers the lapsed Psyche. In placing Psyche in a garden bower, Keats has appropriated her good fortune in being awakened to love as his own: "did I see . . . with awak'ed eyes?" There is a momentary identification of the poet (subject) and its object (Psyche) through a characteristic act of Keatsian "sympathy."

The Psyche "bower" is the place of Keats's inner vision and reveals a debt to Milton's lush Edenic bower, an enclosure full of vegetation and self-circling blossom and fruit trees, trees such as those that thrived in the Wentworth garden. When, in Book IV, Satan enters the garden, he spies on Adam and Eve as Keats observed Cupid and Psyche "couched side by side." Satan goes on to predict the fate of the couple's awakening to both love and death. Psyche is the natural equation for this axiom of tragic consciousness because she must suffer first to regain her union with the love that is divinely within. If, as of yet, her humanity had not been fully honored, the poet finds a surplus of devotional offerings including his own belated love:

> O latest born and loveliest vision far
> Of all Olympus faded Hierarchy
> Fairer than Phoebe's sapphire-region'd star,
> Or Vesper amorous glow worm of the sky;
> Fairer than these though Temple thou hadst none,
> Nor Altar heaped with flowers;
> Nor virgin choir to make delicious moan . . .
> O Bloomiest! though too late for antique vows;
> Too, too late for the fond believing Lyre
> when holy were the haunted forest boughs,[21]

Keats bemoans the loss of a numinous nature recalled by myth, because if he is to melt away into obscurity, his love for a mortal woman is also belated. Although the poem includes the sensuality of the physical world in all its ripeness, Keats defends against what will "wither and die" by offering the eternality of mind and spirit in its place. Into the new sanctuary of the mind comes this powerful incarnation of Psyche.

But who is this final and most powerful rendition of Psyche? Keats's conferring of a divine origin to Psyche provides clues for solving the mystery. Milton's Eve (also the recipient of forbidden knowledge) is the archetypal maternal figure from whom all other mothers are born. Keats's entreaty to Psyche shows that he already bears an intimate relation to her, evidenced by the fact that he "will sing thy own secrets into thine own . . . ear" and implying that the Psyche figure is a mother image formed by a son; that she was born to mother, as was Eve. What Keats is attempting to avoid is Psyche's lapse into neglect and obscurity, to defend against her loss or replacement by other surrogate goddesses. As her champion, he will revive her memory as the true origin of all others. Hence, Keats, in his rescue activity, may be attempting to reserve his mother's place in his own heart, after feeling the longing (and subsequent force of betrayal) for her replacement: Fanny Brawne. In any case, through the ode Keats will defend against mutability, on the most difficult of the mind's chambers, "to ponder" by restoring a fading immortal goddess and offering her an eternal place in poetry.

The Psyche myth itself frames a similar dynamic: Cupid is the idealized object from which Psyche was initially separated, and as a result, became aware of her own "lack."[22] Eros, another name for Cupid, actually translates from Greek to "lack" or "zero." Psyche's search for "her other half" simulates the infantile search for reappropriation of the regained Eden of the mother/infant dyad, a magical "reawakening" and reabsorption into the producer of life. Having recognized the object of desire (as Psyche first recognizes Cupid), Keats is at first assailed by the awareness of what is missing—a "lack"—and this is uncovered by the language of negation itself. Keats recounts what is missing from Psyche's devotional attributes; she has no temple,

> Nor altar heap'd with flowers;
> Nor virgin choir . . .
> No voice, no lute, no pipe, no incense sweet
> No shrine, no grove, no oracle, no heat. . .

All of these lacks will subsequently be corrected through the affirmative language of replacement:

> So let me be thy choir, . . .
> Thy voice, thy lute, thy pipe, thy incense sweet . . .
> Thy shrine, thy grove, thy oracle, thy heat . . .

Psyche is belated; she is "too late for antique vows / Too, too late for the fond believing lyre." She has come after the optimum time and lacks contiguity and wholeness. Instead she is seen in fragments, or partial images, as if drawn from cryptic pieces of memory. This may recall once more Keats's early experience with Frances Keats, who returned too late to mother him, because consumption had already claimed her, and death was now the young Keats's most potent rival. Death is apprehended through the imaginary register as bodily fragmentation and disintegration; that prospect is what we find most anxiety producing about it and what we try to compensate for through the wholeness of speech. Here death, like the rightful father, had insinuated itself into the mother/son dyad and robbed Keats of a primary love relation, revealing his own "lack," which he projects onto the Psyche figure:

> Fairer than these though Temple thou hadst none,
> Nor Altar heaped with flowers;
> Nor virgin choir to make delicious moan
> Upon the midnight hours;
> No voice, no lute, no pipe, no incense sweet . . .
> No shrine, no grove, no Oracle, no heat
> Of pale-mouth'd Prophet dreaming.

In order not to fail Psyche, as he might have felt he had failed the mother who returned home to the son's "protection" only to succumb to tuberculosis, Keats will internalize her through the expressive mode of language itself. Only in the eternal sanctuary of art does Psyche receive her highest praise making. The ego of the child defends against the pain of separation or object loss by introjecting the missing parent into his own psyche and identifying with that parent. By adopting characteristics of the missing person, that person becomes a part of one's personality.[23] Hence, the child symbolically repossesses the absent object and gains independence from it. Keats acknowledges his brooding over two luxuries: the hour of his death along with the loveliness of Fanny Browne.

Keats offers himself to Psyche as the substitute for her contemporary devotional and replaces all of the machinery of worship she had "lacked":

> So let me be thy Choir and make a moan
> Upon the midnight hours;
> Thy voice, thy lute, thy pipe, thy incense sweet . . .
> Thy shrine, thy Grove, thy Oracle, thy heat
> Of pale-mouthed Prophet dreaming

He will then build within himself a "fane" within some untrodden region of the mind, which rivals temporal nature, but in the end is superior to it because it will not fade. Harkening back to archaic imagery of nesting and nurturing, Keats's repeats himself. The word *dressing* ("a rosy Sanctuary I will dress / With the wreathed trellis of a working brain") suggests a masculine surrogate for gestation or pregnancy, denoting circularity, insulation, protection, and what is inviolable—like the sheltered fetus itself. Keats's use of natural imagery of sustenance the creation of life accomplished by maternal nourishment. Perhaps Keats is, on some deeper level, attempting to compensate for the early deprivation he experienced with his own mother, and in doing so, he has usurped the activity of mothering to grant a long-standing wish to be mothered.

In the final lines, Keats refers to Apuleius's treatment of the myth and brings back the figure of Cupid, who had been temporarily suspended from the action of the poem:

> A bright torch, and a casement open at night,
> To let the warm Love in—

Cupid, in the protective custody of his mother's house, escapes through the window in pursuit of Psyche. Thus the reference is to Cupid's visits by night in the legend. Now that Psyche knows the true identity of her husband and has been deified, there is no need for them to meet only at night. Also, the request, on Keats's part, to let the love *in*, may be inseparable from the fact that Fanny Brawne's window was within view of his room, and he could keep an eye on the open casement. Perhaps, this is a way in which Keats is opening himself up to the possibilities of personal, romantic love, and in doing so, he is memorializing the maternal figure represented by Psyche.

8

GOD DON'T LIKE UGLY
Michael S. Harper's Soul-Making Music

Michael S. Harper's poetry is about witness; about testimony, a precipitous dialectic of seeing and not seeing; of guilt and expiation, terror and beneficence. His poetry takes pain by the throat and does not yield. There is no passive resignation to the history of slavery in Harper's lexicon; that history is always present as nightmare, demanding that we as readers recognize our complicity in the human ordeal of suffering, and ultimately, our responsibility. Perhaps no other poet in recent years shows as clearly the mutual implication of private and public outrage. What America has cost black people, America must in the end condemn only itself. On the other hand, from Harper's social purview, there is an equally fervent need for compassionate understanding. Forgiveness follows atonement. If Ellison understood the invisibility of the black man, and Fanon, his ontological insecurity, and Hayden, his sainted martyrdom, Harper understands that the body—especially the obliterated body of the slave or victim of racial violence—is an apt and searing metaphor for America's amnesia about its past.

For Harper, America's forgetfulness is a learned principle; it is not natural to the intelligence or the heart. Both the intelligence and the heart crave evidence—when things are left over. As Freud knew, our history is implicit and determining of many aspects of the future. We are right to build memorials, compose elegies, to turn back to the Oedipal center of the crossroads to learn that the first sin, even in ignorance, was our own. Facts cannot be unwritten or undone. Poetry is not fact; however, it is archival in the strong poet's consciousness. In "Healing Song" Harper recounts the process of fixing the historical image in an intermediate realm in which the boundaries of history and the flesh have been obscured; their marks of differentiation have blurred their edges into a "love filled shadow, congealed and clarified."[1] In other poems, he uses the photographic negative as a metaphor, reversing positive and negative space, black and white, to decode the language of history and renew its message. In the darkroom negative, lines come to light as manmade inventions, nonexistent in the natural world; they describe differences occuring in texture, light intensity, or

153

depth of space. Images are born in the developing room, seen for the first time. By extension, the black man's chronicle is irremovable from the white man's; the clash between black and white, visibility and invisibility is always just a way of making the picture clearer, the angles congruent, the boundaries more distinct. Transcending the limit, the line, the flesh, is a matter of the soul's propulsion through the atmosphere—and its inevitable labor to suffer and make love come out like a "heartblow."

This is also the nature of the jazz melody from which Harper takes his blues influence; the interval where things become improvisational and time stretches into the eternal now. "History is your own heartbeat." Grief is the embattled world, where private agonies are stitched into the social and political fabric of our nation's history. Harper's private agonies are stitched into the social and political fabric of our nation's history. In *Nightmare Begins Responsibility*, Harper writes: "the responsibility to nightmare is to wake up."[2] With Keatsian intensity and Whitmanesque range, he shows the importance of knowledge as self-demonstration. Who can suffer adequately for another person; how do we ever draw those psychological lines of latitude and longitude, mapping our losses in respect to someone else's? When private pain and social pain are experienced at the same level, autobiography is a grave but essential tool for civic trust and healing. For Harper, the Civil War was about reopening the wound, about human potential, self-emancipation, and biblical prophecy all at the same time. Haunted by ghosts of the past, Harper knows the African-American poet must unsettle history to remake it. The melody must not cease, but exhilarate itself. However, the lessons of history were lost on the generations that followed. Black men were continually sacrificed in spite of the fact that the country depended on them to prosper and flower. Although they are reminders of what America wants to forget, what America has exploited as material and labor for its own health; black men are sloughed off from the capital they created. In "Debridement" Harper does not so much blame white America as much as he tries to remind them of what has been splintered in memory, erased:

> Black men are oaks cut down. . . .
>
> Debridement: the cutting away of dead
> Or contaminated tissue from a wound
> In order to prevent infection.
>
> America: love it or give it back.[3]

Here the warning is clear: America has a wound; the wound is self-inflicted. A sutured wound will heal but may leave a scar. The black man who is subjected to humiliation and servility is another refrain in the long epic of a country's progress bridled by prejudice and oppression. One cannot wash one's hands of it or make it clean by liberal mind-set or proxy. The infection must be gradually cut back, defiled. And so it is true with the legacy of segregation that continues to plague democratic ideals and fills urban ghettos. Indeed, America needs a witness. Sorrow is not borne alone, but is toiled through, creeping its way into sound.

Like Walcott, Harper is aware of the racial contest that divides the world into black and white, colonizer and colonized. In homage to Robert Hayden, he writes, "Dee-troit born and half-blind / in diction of arena and paradise / his ambient night-dreams streak his tongue; / mementos of his mother, of Erma, he image-makes / peopling the human family of God's mirror, mingling realities, this creature of transcendence / a love-filled shadow, congealed and clarified."[4] God's mirror can behold no face but its own inferior incarnation; yet God's mirror seeks, impossibly, an ideal image of itself. Certainly, there are the pious and the virtuous, like Erma, who mirror God's laws. But the face in God's mirror is every human, however wretched or cruel. What separates the divine and the mortal is merely the error of flesh, the ugliness of sin, or the wounded hide of the beast. In some of Hayden's best poems, the representation of God's face as an amalgamation of binary oppositions including good and evil, and black and white is transformed into a grayed, neutral space where the poem is able to project alternate realities. God's mirror is always impenetrable; God's image is never distinguishable from the human face we project there, a Blakean vortex of competing values and meanings.

Throughout Harper's poetry references to just this illegible face of God are found, as historical fact after fact exposes the slaughter of innocent children—who are better "not seen" than "seen" by white Americans who refuse to take responsibility for them. In "American History," Harper takes on the simultaneous roles of witness, journalist, and objective observer of historical fact:

> Those four black girls blown up
> In that Alabama church
> Remind me of five hundred
> Middle passage blacks, . . .
> Can't find what you can't see
> Can you?[5]

The girls did not know who their enemy was. The poem's surprising turn comes with the observer's realization that the middle-passage blacks "under water" are simply in the middle of things, that this is not their war, any more than it is the black girls' war in the Alabama church. They are just finding "harbor" as they did each Sunday, as a steady ritual of religious obedience. When the narrator observes, "Can't find what you can't see," the reader realizes that the girls have been obliterated beyond recovery; that they are, as they have always been, in the gaze of the white master race, invisible. The girls have been dismembered, eviscerated, scattered in pieces. Paradoxically, like the "middle-passage blacks" fleeing the "redcoats" they have, in their deaths, hidden themselves "in a net" away from their pursuers. They leave no trace.

Yet, for Harper, trace is everything because it is what is left of personal sacrifice. It is a visible mark or sign of the former passage or presence of some person, thing, or event. It is a line drawn by a recording instrument, such as the poet's, photographer's or historian's. Trace is like the mark of original sin in the puritanic mind—what we attribute the existence of something to be is always in its antecedent, what came before it, and what damned it to hell. Even with that said, there is no eradicating the sign of what these girls meant, or why they were sacrificed. Blood, from a black slave or a British "redcoat," is the same color regardless which body bleeds.

Private pain and public awareness is also the theme of "A Mother Speaks: The Algiers Motel Incident, Detroit." This poem, which takes the voice of a mother whose son was killed by gunfire, is powerful demonstration of the victimization of victims, even after they have been savagely slaughtered. The poem opens in the obscurity of a blackness that cannot be distinguished from other shades of black; the color of mourning is a random sign in an overall darkness, but cannot be narrowed to this single context. In the poem, a boy is sacrificed to social and political ills that dim even the pallor of a night sky. Overlooking the corpse that has been "prettified" to conceal the disgrace of its ugly disfigurement, the mother is overcome by the fact that her son is no longer recognizable. This son is not a "mirror of God" but has been put in a man's clothing and has been reconstructed to look "human." To the Detroit mother, this is *not* her son, but an imposter. Retouched in a way that will erase the traces of what has been done to him, the son's carcass is cut up and stitched back together as if it were an animal's hide. His flesh has become a symbol of the sacred body to be imbibed and absorbed by the witness, a part of ritual communion.

> They tied the eye
> torn out
> by shotgun
> into place
> and his shattered
> arm cut away
> with his buttocks
> That remained.
> My son's gone
> by white hands

though he said
to his last word—
"Oh I'm so sorry,
officer, I broke your gun."[6]

The martyred son absorbs the guilt of his murderer and in excruciating humility, apologizes to the officer who shot him. What is missing in
this son's speech is justified anger and outrage; anger is reserved for the
reader, who recognizes the irony of the son's innocence. Instead of feeling
anger, the boy blames himself for the oncoming catastrophe. His crime was
his body—that got in the way. "I" (the outlaw, the body) provided the
resistance necessary to break the gun, to make the gun necessary and then
unnecessary again. The boy has paid the price of peace with his humanity,
taking the bullet that will finally silence oppression. The poem ends with
his "last word," as "American History" ends, with the dissolution of the
martyrs' bodies who leave bloodstains on the American conscience.

In Harper's poems, private pain is indistinguishable from political
pain, and the only recourse for that pain is in the music of the line, along
with the various influences he takes on in his own poetic odyssey. Edwin
Fussell has suggested that "American poets have the handicap of writing in
a language imported and modified from Great Britain, suffering many disasters in passage, and subsequently worked over again by the 'euphemism'
. . . of American history."[7] This problem is exacerbated for African-
American poets whose sense of phraseology and rhythm differs from that
found in mainstream American poetry, just as the phraseology and rhythm
of American poetry differs from that found in English poetry.[8] To clear a
creative space that commemorates their shared history and unique experience of language, black poets have long invoked their musical progenitors.

As scholars have noted, Langston Hughes, Robert Hayden, and
Gwendolyn Brooks modified and amalgamated jazz and blues elements
into their liberatory art, simultaneously preserving their historical, artistic, and cultural roots. Although jazz was not the only musical modality
to infuse black poetry with its characteristic rhythm and tone, it was one
that continually challenged white preconceptions about poetry produced
in the black community. Jazz, with its improvisational nature and soar-
ing, sonorous sounds, evoked the soulfulness of black ascendancy in otherwise oppressive or suppressive political conditions. Always on the verge
of continual resurrection, jazz resisted predictability and genericism,
uniting mind and spirit.

Harper has referenced his own history as an unflinching record of
the soul's making—a process still going on. Although he must be located
within his cultural context and that context is as a member of a minority
that has been overlooked in the American canon, one can argue that

Harper has derived his influences from an array of sources, including the British Romantics. At the same time, Harper has never forgotten that he, as an African-American poet, must defend against the prejudices and projections that would obscure his visibility in a long lineage of European-American poetry. More than most contemporary poets, Harper, Fussell observes, has a "weapon to fight back with—music, blues, and jazz."[9] Whereas Fussell is correct in according Harper a weapon, I would add to Harper's metaphoric arms a more subtle power: a Keatsian "negative capability" that allows him to absorb the conditions of black identity and black history into the universal corpus of his work—to live inside and outside his skin. In fact, Harper draws an analogy between the generative and regenerative powers of his art and those of the human body. As Raffa writes:

> An analogy to the human body will help us understand Harper's poetry. Significant historical events (such as the raid at Harper's Ferry) form the skeleton of Harper's art. We may view Harper's imagery as the muscle of his meaning, and his historical view as the brain or nervous system with music as the heart. The rhythm of jazz and the blues are the pulse of Harper's poetry. . . . [10]

For Harper, the African-American continuum fleshes out the skeleton, but he has adopted kin from different racial origins. Along the trajectory, Harper has also, perhaps, adopted his ancestral ghosts, particularly Keats's ghost, a background not only for understanding Harper's poetic ontologism but also for his use of jazz as the "breath" that invigorates his language. Central to the Keats–Harper connection is Keats's metaphor of the "Vale of Soul-Making," in which bodily or earthly pain is ventilated and converted into the utterance and rhythm of the spirit. For Harper, poetry is a pilgrimage for the soul's composing itself through what is suffered in life.[11]

The soul is to Keats as jazz is to Harper. The soul is a moving design originating with pain and is what makes pain inevitable. The artist should absorb, not merely observe important cultural traditions to feel his heartbeat in history or his poems will be ineffective.[12] History is the lesson book, and in Harper's view, music is the most important cultural tradition to be imbibed by the heart in its creation of a soul. Thus, Harper's first book reveals the redemptive power that has always been an important part of the music created in the black experience. He draws on a musical tradition arising from suffering, yet one that transcends historical circumstances.[13] Personal triumph over pain is an emblem of historical and cultural process, making "singing a blessing of hatred."[14]

Indeed, memory and pain are at the heart of Harper's poetry whether writing from personal experience or from collective experience. In

the celebrated collection *Dear John, Dear Coltrane*, the poet points to
music as a language for emotions that cannot be easily translated into
words. In "Maine Landing," for example, the poet's sense of self-desertion
is summed up in these lines: "Though it is mid-March / The snow has
receded / And come again; / And there is nothing in the wind; no music."[15]
Echoing Stevens, Harper contends that the human voice fills its barren
world; however, there are extremes of grief in which the poet is left to the
"oblivion" of a music that is as "punctual and sonorous" as anger.
Following this hollowing of breath, there are echoes. Moreover, in "Three
O'Clock Love Song"[16] addressed to his wife, Harper reenergizes his plaintive tune of musical elegizing. Here, music is reduced to the elemental. It is
everything, and no less than, the air which sustains the body. Air, like
music, and like language, is meant to pump oxygen into the lungs:
"Language is no obstacle / There is none. / I look at your pumped flesh /
and scream / into the form for life / I put there."[17] The soul is awakened by
pain. Language plays a subordinate role to the heart's intuitions; the vernacular of love is soundlessness. Like the jazz musician, the poet shapes a
soul from the pains of the body united with the beats of the heart: a synthesis of breath and prayer to the living, "a love supreme."

Harper pays homage to Keats's "Vale of Soul-Making," an allegory that appears in Keats's letter concerning an alternative to Christian salvation.[18] In Harper's poem, "The Ghost of Soul-Making," however, orthodox religious symbols of collective suffering, persecution, and atonement
are not limited to Christianity, but expand to embrace the agonizing legacy of European Jewry and its continual cycle of oppression, wandering, and
return. The poem begins with an epigraph from a Yom Kippur prayer that
confirms God's ultimate dominion over mortal lives: "On that day it was
decreed who shall live and who shall die" followed by another quote, "Art
in its ultimate always celebrates the victory."[19] Hence Harper is consciously evoking the claims for soul-making in the poetic process by adjudicating
the equal value of art and life. Harper insists that we are all mutually
dependent on one another for the bearing of another's life, or sorrow, into
that which our lives are carefully woven.

Soul-making puts the world to use as a means of making divinity
personal, an acquisition of individual existence. Hence, while discussing
soul-making in the same period as composing the "Ode to Psyche," Keats
forms an analogy between the human heart and the painful lessons of the
world imprinted on that heart. This is a universal, political, and private
heartache that is inextricable from life's progress. The world achieves its
own melody as earthly attachments are suffered and given up. As Keats
wrote in one of his letters, "I will call the human heart the horn Book used
in that School—and I will call the child able to read the Soul made from

that school and its hornbook. . . . Do you not see how necessary a world
of Pains and Troubles is to school an intelligence and make it a soul?"[20] The
heart reads the world, learns its lessons, and acquires a soul. But how can
it be that one can simultaneously lose and acquire something of value?

In Harper's poem, the Ghost of Soul-Making is an eyewitness to
innumerable sorrows. Always summoned to look on persecution and
slaughter, the Ghost is burdened by a human knowledge: "loyalty learned
in the lost records of intricate relations."[21] Continually in mutation, the
Ghost is never identifiable as one thing, but always in the process of
becoming something else. It changes as history changes, continually transforming its being from within to absorb the external circumstances that
permit human suffering on a massive scale. Consistent with its nonessen-
tialist plasticity, the Ghost is both female and male, both inside and outside, both flesh and spirit. But more significant than its dualistic nature, or
its "non-identity," is how the Ghost conducts itself "in the service of others." His martyred song to sainthood makes, in Harper's words, "the
palate sing." This Ghost is omnipresent, both a reaper and a harvester.
Furthermore, the Ghost's very appearance on the verge of human history is
a sign of cycles that are continuous and synthesizing of greater power
struggles. At the close of the poem, Harper's Ghost is a consoling presence
that reminds us of a dialectical process that transforms the body through
the aperture of an enduring sorrow. Harper's timeless acquiescence to the
soul's overcoming of the temporary body is about being liberated from the
body's "delicate bottle":

> . . . She reaps
> the great reward of praise, where answers
> do not answer, when the self, unleashed from the delicate bottle,
> wafts over the trees at sunrise and forgives the dusk.[22]

What interested Keats, and what interests Harper, is the individuation of a soul as a particular entity of a single person. Keats saw this as a
revisionist view of Christianity. Rather than relying on Christ's intervention
in human affairs, Keats prefers a schooling of the heart in which the mind
is enlightened by earthly sorrows.[23] Instead of viewing the world as "a vale
of tears" both Keats and Harper view life through a veil that allows them
to see life as a shadow—a simultaneous process of loving and mourning.

The nature of mourning is always paradoxical. Our most profound identifications seem to be in response to this experience. As Freud
proposed, we are "unwilling to abandon" the lost object that remains present in our imaginations, and we persist in our attachment to it.[24] Mourning
demands not simply a perception that another person is gone, but a realization that a vacancy now exists within the self. The work of mourning

progresses in proportion to a mourner's willingness to suffer grief and maintain the memory of a loved one. Such labor is absorbing and difficult, as Harper writes: "to love is to memorize the one loved / to hold in fear the moment / of that memory, to forget / nothing of that / whose details are lost."[25]

The matrix for making a soul is grief, as Harper writes, "our finger, paining love."[26] Soul-making informs not only the emptiness of the things we imagine to be lost but also gives substance to those things we imagine to be persistently present in the imagination.

Harper's poetry moves between spells of bereavement and life's implausible reclamations, all of which end with his life. This is especially apparent in poems that memorialize Harper's children who did not survive their infancy. Each poem to the lost child consecrates a name—such as in "Reuben, Reuben." Death reveals the power of the name to the very extent that the name continues to elegize its bearer, who can no longer reply to or answer for his name. Although the mourner may consciously concede the loved one's passing, he or she may unconsciously desire the loved one's return, although that desire is futile. As the poet knows, the labor of mourning, like the labor of writing poems, requires a withdrawal from each intact memory image restored for writing or representation. Language itself is a means of deferring loss and termination, by providing substitutions that persist in marking the memory of the lost object as a present reference. However, because the substitute objects (language, name, image, poem) both recover the original object in one sense and do not recover in another, the original object, the painful process of mourning is charged with Keatsian paradoxical character.

Significantly, in Harper's "Black Spring," we find an indication of the bequeathal of life and death within the sequel of a name, which is given by parent to child, like a seed from the original tree:

> We gave it life, mahogany hands,
> loose in song;
> we gave it to children
> in paraffin—
> our biology.
> It grew lovely and indecent . . .
> and, of course, produced
> children of its own.
> We took it back again.[27]

The soul is formed by what is given up, lost, mourned, and taken back again, in the form of a word, a note of music. The poems, "We Assume on the Death of Our Son, Reuben Massey Harper," "Reuben, Reuben," "Deathwatch," "Nightmares Again Another Season," that follow in the collection, return to the theme of giving voice to inner and outer dimensions of mourning. But more significantly is the poet's effort to empty his grief, to show the mechanisms we use to face loss and fear. Each memory of the deceased son is invested with need that cannot be withdrawn without the difficult work of recollection. For Harper, mourning is a matter of recovering the total sum of memory's figurations, its plaintive music. Hence the laboring of grief is like the laboring of a soul, requiring an ongoing course of giving up something to bring something back in, a *seasonal* cycle.

In Harper's poem "New Season," for instance, the labor of mourning continues although the speaker has attempted to find a substitute for the lost infant in the birth of a new one: "From my own wooden smell / she has shed her raisin skin / and come back /sweetened into brilliant music; / Her song is our new season."[28] Indeed, "sweetened" flesh becomes a bereaved music spawned from the heart's inner emptiness rather than to any one individual object. Although in another poem, "Nightmares Again Another Season," the child is already gone, the mother's body still readies itself for the nurturing tasks, a painful overflowing of "useless milk." The body can begin to accept the reality of its condition only by slowly weaning itself from the beloved object.

Keats was also preoccupied with the process of death and the encouraging fact of life's perseverance. Harper shares with Keats a striving for transcendence of pain through art and music. Moreover, Keats's definition of the poet as one who synthesizes sensual and spiritual experience, rather than denies the sensual altogether, is particularly compatible with the jazz musician. In the final section of this chapter, I summarize some of Keats's claims in the letters and then apply these ideas to a reading of the poem "Dear John, Dear Coltrane," a living elegy to the great tenor saxophonist.

A response to the world, as empathetic as Harper's or Keats's, would necessarily have to elude personal boundaries. In "Last Affair: Bessie's Blues Song," Harper takes the voice of the blues singer as her body is brought out after a car crash. Once again, it is the body in Harper that is negated, "disarticulated," in its presentation. The accident victim, like the fugitive slave in "American History" and like the desecrated Christ draped slack over the lap of Mary in the *Pieta*, is nakedly exposed in all its woeful, human terror. The black body has always been invisible; a Ghost. But now the song runs like blood from the body, filling itself with soul. And once again, the problem surrounds who is seeing or "not seeing," who is there to witness what will not be forgotten:

> Disarticulated
> Arm torn out,
> Large veins cross

Her shoulder intact,
Her tourniquet
Her blood in all-white big bands:

Can't you see
What love and heartache's done to me
I'm not the same as I used to be
This is my last affair.[29]

Bessie's body has finally become the signifier of its own twisted agony. The songs she sang about hardship and burden, torn about by love and disappointment, desperate for hope have been used up by the white record dealers who "cut the vein in her neck" and made her a fool about money. At last she is in body, what she pleads for—to be recognized for her pain. This is her last "affair." Bessie had a hard life; "a bad mouth", but she just did not make it real for herself, she, like the boy in Detroit, took it in and absorbed it for others.

The influence of blues singers, such as Smith, and jazz, on Harper's poetry has been frequently noted. Harper says common qualities are found in his work and the jazz musicians', but that this comparison should not be followed too closely: "the music of Coltrane is true unto itself and should not be compared to my own poetry."[30] Yet Coltrane, and the blues singers before him, is representative of a black experiential energy that is rooted not only in melancholy and pain, but also in the assertion of a life force that creates art (or rather, the soul's art) from such melancholy and pain. While the blues reflected the black experience (the effects of poverty, the upheavals caused by disputes and migration, the disenfranchisement of an "unwanted" group of people), jazz was more personal, individualistic. Spontaneity is fundamental to what the jazz musician does; he or she creates completely personal, irreproducible shifts of rhythmic accents.

Harper's moving elegy to John Coltrane is a search for a supreme love that will put the player on the right path, the improvisational character of the poet-musician who fuses body and head into one. In Harper's words, history becomes the future. Self-abnegation, in which the ego is dissolved in the larger body of life, as musician disappears in his own music is a state of achieved quiescence, or numbing pleasure, a "love supreme."

Coltrane was internalized by Harper and became a life force, a piece of breath. For Harper, Coltrane not only characterizes an African-American musical tradition, but also extends an aesthetic vision that is spiritual at the core. Acknowledging the importance of Coltrane as an influence in his work, Harper says that Coltrane takes his musical lineage into "a dimension of expression, and into an area of possibility never taken before."[31] Coltrane "goes someplace," taking with him the terrain covered by past musicians and incorporating them into his own idea of the family, into the family of humankind.

In the poem "Dear John, Dear Coltrane," Harper merges the personal and collective, the momentary and the eternal. A level of contemplation exists in which one can admire a work of art as a form in itself, signifying the beauty of its inherent elements. Coltrane's song ends with the emergence of a soul as the body breaks down, and the poem is a metamorphosis of matter becoming the love of the spirit, as Keats's own Psyche restores the ineffable spirit of the deceased:

> Sex, fingers, toes
> in the marketplace
> near your father's church
> in Hamlet, North Carolina— . . .
>
> there is no substitute for pain:
> genitals gone or going,
> seed burned out,
> you tuck the roots in the earth,
> turn back, and move
> by river through the swamps,
> singing: a *love supreme* . . .[32]

Compressed into a lifetime, Coltrane's song carries historical and religious significance, as the beat transcends the failing heart of the musician. While the generative seed burns out, the music is produced by the ashes. Through Harper, we witness the history of slavery and oppression in Coltrane, in whom the pain of origins is inseparable from the ascending "tenor" notes. Inspiration derives from corporeal breath, from a correspondence between human and natural respiration. What Coltrane takes back from the air— into the "thick sin" of his body—he exhausts himself into a melody of love and final purification, a higher, tenor love:

> So sick
> you couldn't play *Naima*
> so flat we ached . . .
> your diseased liver gave
> out its purity,
> the inflated heart
> pumps out, the tenor kiss,
> tenor love:
> *a love supreme* . . .[33]

Coltrane's tenor kiss is like Keats's nightingale's song, something fading and forming itself from the pulse of the body, the heart, emptying itself from grief. Out of pain comes music and flight, realization and faith in the unknown. In another elegy, "Lady's Blues,"[34] Harper persists in making present the lost object that informs absence. Irreducibly, the spirit of the word resists absolute effacement. Looking over the markers of "an unmarked grave," the poet evokes what can only be left of the diminished spirit:

We visit the bark . . .
the grass, the ground
your face,
no stone your voice;
we kiss the air.[35]

Life is restored through imaginative and rhetorical powers that resist death. If there is no body, no definable marker, the air is sufficient to represent the lost loved one. Imagination is a prefiguration of the afterlife, a means of stepping beyond the limitations of reason and mortal consequence. Air, used by both the musician and the poet, is pure potential, or history in the making.

In the end, however, Keats could not be rescued from death any more than Coltrane could: both artists continued to work feverishly until their last breaths; both vanished inside their songs. The nightingale will never exceed the boundaries of time and space because it is perpetually vanishing; never gone completely. The same is true of the call and response refrain in "Dear John, Dear Coltrane," which concludes with a diminished volume of sound and speech:

a love supreme, a love supreme
a love supreme, a love supreme[36]

Harper is particularly attentive to the expressiveness of pain and its locations in language, embracing difficult paradoxes of bodily and spiritual reflection, private and public reckoning. Through Coltrane, Harper crosses cultural, racial, and temporal boundaries, so that the notes of a song, like a few spirits, can liberate and console one another.

9

KENYON'S MELANCHOLIC VISION
IN "LET EVENING COME"

Let the light of late afternoon
shine through the chinks in the barn, moving
up the bales as the sun moves down.

Let the cricket take up chafing
as a woman takes up her needles
and her yarn. Let evening come.

Let the dew collect on the hoe abandoned
in long grass. Let the stars appear
and the moon disclose her silver horn.

Let the fox go back to its sandy den.
Let the wind die down. Let the shed
go black inside. Let evening come.

To the bottle in the ditch, to the scoop
in the oats, to air in the lung
let evening come.

Let it come, as it will, and don't
be afraid. God does not leave us
comfortless, so let evening come.[1]

In the poem "Let Evening Come," Kenyon begins with the motion of sunlight, suggesting a balance of upward and downward, rising and falling:

Let the light of late afternoon
shine through chinks in the barn, moving
up the bales as the sun moves down.

Sunlight is seen so indirectly, as a belated influence on what has already been nourished by it. From the poet's point of view, the bales no longer initiate sunlight, yet sunlight is so resplendent in the barn it pleases the poet's eye, her preexisting need for beauty. Sunlight is therefore worthy of praise. We should bear in mind that in this beginning stanza, we, as readers, are situated very close up, although the agency of light is as distant as it could

167

be. In the next stanza, we find activity, work, and labor that consumes time in the day, as the poet writes:

> Let the cricket take up chafing
> as a woman takes up her needles
> and her yarn. Let evening come.

The cricket chafes as the woman scrapes the needles of her yarn. All is process, and all is interrelated. The poet is compelled by the last remnants of time before its darkening, when it is transfigured into something else, something yet to be named. By resisting the evening's coming, Kenyon warns us against exhausting ourselves on trying to save what cannot be saved because it is already subject to mutability. Although darkness will come and the poet's vision will be eclipsed, the objects themselves remain. There is always something of this world left in any other. Here is the axis of faith:

> Let the dew collect on the hoe abandoned
> in the long grass. Let the stars appear
> and the moon disclose its silver horn.

Each stanza in the poem begins with the verb *let*, as if to convey acceptance of the inevitable or to permit in a specified manner or to release from confinement. But *let* also suggests the idea of leaving something unfinished or undone. The present moment demands the subsequent moment to continue or complete it. With time, Kenyon advises, things (such as the juice of the apple) age and transform into a different form or taste; even the body decays and finds its way into dust. With the next two stanzas, Kenyon makes us even more aware of the lassitude of the day's ebbing energies and the need for rest. Rest is essential even if it will only contribute to more labor. "The dew collect[s] on the hoe," and then everything accounted for is equally at rest or emptied by loss, light, or lack. Yet in Kenyon's accounting for objects that become empty ("the sandy den," the wind that retires, the shed that goes black), she also anticipates that which would fill them:

> Let the fox go back to its sandy den.
> Let the wind die down. Let the shed
> go black inside. Let evening come.
>
> To the bottle in the ditch, to the scoop
> in the oats, to air in the lung
> let evening come.

A significant change in perspective occurs between these two stanzas. From the positioning of the one who yields to something forthcoming, we shift to the object that receives the allotment of some kind of sustenance. The body is filled by the soul as the soul is emptied of the body. In the absence of one, there is the presence of the other. The same is true of the word: it is simultaneously the absence and presence of the thing it signifies. Whether God exists, the need for comfort in approaching death makes God so necessary to the poem, just as the oats are necessary to the scoop, the den to the fox, and air to the lung. The poet's vision is a synthesizer of things, an interpreter of an otherwise incoherent language that marks itself on both the world and the page.

Like the still-life painter, Kenyon persists in finding the rightness of placed things by continuing to arrange and compose objects in space while rendering those objects through the mediation of an art language. Each object defined and sanctified in nature appears to be the manifestation of the poet's thought, and this thought unifies human thought with God's intention. There is a compositional rightness of things placed in the position in which they were intended.

What Kenyon discovers in closer scrutiny of these objects is their aesthetic quality, that which is not subject to mutability or decay. Yet the poet is ambivalent: in pursuit of transcendent beauty that would supersede the sensual, she seems unable or unwilling to sacrifice the sensuality that includes the cost of temporal process. Imagination, as Keats maintained, is a prefiguration of the transcendent realm and our love of sensual beauty in this world is (for the believer) a realm that follows and in which life originates. Evening is always another sudden afterlife, comprised of all the light and darkness that has come before and after it.

"Let Evening Come" is formed by the language of imperative, demand, a poem that urges the reader to pay attention. The speaker is telling herself what she has to do, which is to do nothing, to give up all resistance to what one cannot control in language or process. The same is true of the reader who yields to what the writer has placed before her. At a certain point, the poem is a fate that encloses the participant within. Indeed, we are watching and listening to Kenyon watching and listening, but to what? It is both her voice, and not her voice. It is the comfort we give ourselves in believing that there is a voice we do not yet know, which nevertheless speaks as God does and reaches deep from within us.

Kenyon's powers of incantation were a combined achievement of poetry and prayer. In fact, one of the marked features of her work is the ordering power of incantation, or repetition, in which details are perfectly noticed. There is survival power in the ability to repeat one's self, a formal power in incantation that sets itself against enormous resistance. The poetic self becomes permeable and is able to pass into the world that might otherwise destroy it.

A poem of unusual reverence, "Let Evening Come" is written in the manner of the psalm, which praises God. In fact, the text resembles the Old Testament psalm "Lord of the World." Both praise God's omniscience in the world as a comfort in distressful times; God is important not only to the soul but to the suffering body that, in soul making, creates the soul: "My soul I give unto his care / Asleep, awake, for He is near, / And with my soul, my body too / God is with me, I have no fear." Compare these with the closing lines of "Let Evening Come":

> Let it come as it will, and don't
> be afraid. God does not leave us
> comfortless, so let evening come.

The adjective *so* works here to amplify the factual nature of the assertions made in previous stanzas. Because of the reasons given earlier, (the ordering of apparently arbitrary or disconnected phenomena), the speaker contends sufficient proof exists that God does not leave us without a purpose supportive of our living or our dying. The evening, like the morning, has its own kind of naturalization, its own means of individuation. The same is true of the poet's language now invested in the things of which it is conscious. Attention turns to intention. Language not only acknowledges, but illuminates the mysterious object, Kenyon seems to say, *let evening come*, by fully accepting what will be handed over to it. Objects of the world, first owned and then dispossessed, are sloughed off, as the body is sloughed off, by the soul that has been incarnated by it. Out of a life of pain and sorrows, one makes a soul. The soul does not so much bear one's sorrow or grief, as it is born from sorrow and grief. The soul is what slips through the felt experience of pain or anguish. It accrues value as the person who suffers begins to give up, piece by piece, attachments to temporal things.

We can assume that Kenyon was familiar with Keats's axiom of "Soul-Making." Her writing is full of references to both the letters and the poetry. According to Donald Hall in a letter, Kenyon's study of Keats was painstaking and perennial. He recalls that Kenyon spent two years absorbed in her study of Keats's—poems, letters, and biographies.

As is true of Keats's "To Autumn," Kenyon's sense of natural order in "Let Evening Come" quickens the pace of the drowsed poet who, like Keats's gleaner (the personified Autumn in the ode),[2] reminds us we must gather what has just ripened on the vine. Sometimes the beauty of natural process overcomes and oversaturates our senses so much so that we embrace beauty even in the shadow of approaching death. As Kenyon often said, perhaps aligning herself with modernists such as Frost, the "natural object is always the adequate symbol."[3] For Kenyon, this perception of beauty sensed in the physical world was both ideal and eternal. Although the poem itself embodies natural process and growth, it also uses its praise of things in language as a means of preserving reverence and meaning.

Within the framework of "Let Evening Come," the poet's attention is drawn by the things of this world; but it is equally drawn by the nouns that name them. Words will eventually outlast things, merely in the act of the poet's saying them. Only the word, or the name, survives natural process and decay. The poet's word, properly handled, is a ghostly presence that eternally returns after it has expired, something that mortal bodies cannot do.

Like Keats, Kenyon was well aware of the stages one goes through in leaving earthly attachments behind. This was the use of the world, as Keats saw it, building a soul out of deep and incomprehensible sorrow. In mourning, Freud reminds us that we must relinguish connections to lost objects and accept substitutes in their place. The only substitute available to the poet, as to the mourner, is more often than not language itself into which the poet takes refuge. In bereavement, especially, poetic language signifies loss as well as suffers for it. Words are always without the things they stand for. Appropriately, Hall's long elegy to Kenyon is entitled *Without*. These poems, for and to Kenyon, become a realm where the fading is still present and yet at the same time, these fading presences are pieces of evidence of what is always missing, what we are always "without."

When characterizing Kenyon's poetry, readers and critics often point to the quality of her poetic voice as uniquely spare, visual, and powerful. Objects of the world gradually sifted through her consciousness, and she seemed to take nothing for granted. On the page, one senses that Kenyon was experiencing a voice that was other than her customary self-identity; the voice seems to come from a source other than the familiar, everyday personality. In fact, this duality of voice gives Kenyon's work its private and public quality. Masterful at creating perceptual distances that reflect back on one another, from close-up to far, in focus and out of focus, she showed the intersections of larger and smaller perspectives on the same phenomena. With the rare quality of her voice, Kenyon was able to confide in the reader and in herself at the same time. She was a poet who paradoxically carved her voice out of sorrow and joy simultaneously.

Voice, in the contemporary sense, is often synonymous with a recognizable tone or style. But that has not always been the case. In fact, critics and poets have been unable to settle on a persistent terminology for this poetic device. For Pound, voice was another name for persona; for Eliot, it was temperament; for Browning, mask; for St. John, perceiver; for others, it is a presence, an ego, a being in the process of becoming itself. Still we cannot say that voice is merely language or signification because we are always aware of how language is manipulated by an individual. Language is always a means of explaining to others one's desire to be.

Alternating between the level of emergent ideas and the stepping back to observe the effect of those ideas, Kenyon, like all poets, was self-characterizing. She not only felt and expressed what she felt, but she also watched herself feeling. Perhaps no writer can both participate in and interpret an experience simultaneously. Language is a belated conveyer of vision and a mysterious entity alien to typical self-consciousness. In both cases, however, there is a sense in which a poet talks to herself, and in in so doing, talks a self into being. Words, so identical to the things they represent, are both temporal and eternal, for a word bears not one life or context, but returns again and again in different contexts. Hence the recuperative power of the word (like the return of the song of Keats's nightingale) is something that is both identical and continuous, transcending fragmented events, human time.

But in the poem "Let Evening Come," poetic identity and self-division are not the issue—faith is. Faith in something solidly beyond the pained self that can in fact support it. "Let Evening Come" is a companion to Keats's "To Autumn," an ode about acquiescence to and acceptance of death. Both poems bring together oppositional states of fertility and decay. Both poems are about lingering at the last "oozings" of the cider press, hours by hours. But Kenyon's voice helps her to listen to the words that console her, the words that persuade her of God's nearness even in moments of self-desertion. Keats's consolation was not part of the immediate drama of the poem, but rather underneath the scenic display of autumnal activities.

Kenyon's cyclical return to the essence of the word "evening" as something that will come not once but for eternity, enclosing within itself all of the evenings that have come and gone, at last gives her a sense of rightness and equilibrium. All things will come in time, the fruit falls propitiously, when it ripens. This is ultimately the rightness of placed things, when the poet knows nothing is to be gained from moving them into yet another position. No one will miss the simple but profound meaning of this psalmlike poem; no one will fail to miss the message of comfort Kenyon so eloquently insprited within it.

For consolation, Kenyon sought in the origins of language itself the possibility of God's support. This is no more evident than in the poem "Let Evening Come." In Kenyon's work, we can and do hope for something more than a physical existence in the world. "God *does* not leave us comfortless" writes Kenyon, not God *would* not or *will* not leave us comfortless. This simple verb, the "non-conditional," may well persuade us that Kenyon herself was eventually consoled by her voice and her vision.

Her belief was almost opaque, serving as a counterpoint to her incertitude. Indeed, poetry helped Kenyon to understand the ordering powers of language and its representations of inner and outer states. She would have to align herself, as she saw Keats did, with those powers through which she affirmed her life as part of an ongoing process of soul-making.

PART III

HEALING PAIN

Acts of Theraputic Writing

10

USING THE PSYCHOANALYTIC PROCESS
IN CREATIVE WRITING CLASSES

Part of the appeal of the creative writing course may be that it offers students opportunities to explore their identities through writing. In the poetry course I teach, writing definitely becomes an absorbing process of self-examination with ethical as well as psychological dimensions. In my class as in most other classes, students are trained in a wide variety of literary genres from the sonnet to the elegy. Whatever particular poetic form they may imitate in both poetry and fiction, however, students write about themselves. In fact, workshop leaders' exploratory approaches to writing are often similar to and to some extent derived from psychoanalytic techniques—techniques that have become progressively integrated into our culture and into our culture of teaching.

Behn and Twitchell's *The Practice of Poetry* is one of many currently popular textbooks that argue that the unconscious can be and should be used by aspiring writers. The text offers writing formulas for evoking the unconscious and making use of its contents for the writing of poetry. Students are exhorted by the text to "mine the unconscious."[1] Sections are headed by titles such as, "Ladders to the Dark: The Unconscious as Gold Mine," "The Self and Its Subjects," and "Accidents, Chance, and the Nonrational." The book's concern for the unconscious is not mere metaphor and word play. The text attempts to examine seriously psychic processes, and each chapter of the book is thematically tied to the discovery of some layer or dimension of the unconscious.

In an opening exercise titled "Translations of Word to Image," students are directed to associate an abstract concept with a concrete image through free association. For example, the student writes the concept the "self" and then, by a process of association, links the word "freedom" to an image of a brussels sprout.[2] After some delay and reflection, the student is then asked to reconstruct the unconscious process that might have brought the terms together. The more recondite the association, the wider the gap between the concept and self-representation, and the more unique to the writer's imagination. In this man-

177

ner, the contents of the unconscious are retrieved as essential artifacts for constructing poems.

The Practice of Poetry seeks to teach students to write poems, but the use of the unconscious in poetry workshops often has therapeutic effects as well. In my experience as a teacher of creative writing, students find the process of writing poetry analogous to the process of therapy.

Both going to therapy and writing poetry are forms of confession. Both psychoanalysis and confessional poetry provide a place in which subjects can vent conflictual feelings and ideas in the presence of a reflective and quizzical other. (Whether it be analyst or reader, this other also comes to embody an observing aspect of the self.) Both psychoanalysis and confessional poetry are "talking cures"—as the private content of the dramatic monologue reveals—texts of self-division and self-disclosure. In both processes, the subject, through talking, undergoes revision.

Both poet and patient use language as a mode of revising the self, of vocalizing a new self into being. What does this mean? In writing poetry, the writer, through conscious intention, creates a message. Slowly, however, through a process of revision, the writer discovers in her own message another message and another previously unknown self, one perhaps trapped in the past, one speaking with striking emphasis, but not in the writer's own familiar self-consciousness.

Poets, like patients, learn to accept and at times sacrifice their fantasies to mold or configure better a personal or social message in an aesthetic form. In writing poetry, critical distance from an expressed message allows the writer to become a witness and therefore to confront her own increasingly emotional self-dramatization. Although Freud considered the creative writer to be susceptible to neurotic syndromes, artistic control, as Jeffrey Berman quotes Lionel Trilling as saying, "is antithetical to neurosis."[3] Art allows the artist to recreate distressing experiences to gain control over them.

This process inevitably begins as students start to write. When writing a poem, students do not just tell the story of their lives, they typically confess to a story they do not want to tell. In following an unconscious logic of expression, students become aware of their own matrices of fantasy and recollection, and they expose secrets they had long concealed or repressed. Often they have the courage to "say" these secrets because they, as writers, are in an important sense distant from them, not yet at the center of passion and conflict that the language often reveals (without truly expressing) at the level of personal experience.

One student, increasingly aware of her own tendency to withhold what she did not care to confront, wrote a poem she titled "Pandora's Box":

> I am like Pandora's Box
> Filled with secrets that I don't want to know
> I will live to be one-hundred and twenty years old
> and not be able to taste the salt on my food anymore . . .
> But the secrets will still be there, alive
> Like acid disintegrating a nickel . . .
> like the water draining out
> Why can't I be rid of them
> There is a whole other me that I don't know about.

Through writing, students find that they release imagery and emotions that seem contrary to their life histories. They might find, for example, that they harbor resentments, anger, or attachments that they come to realize have altered their memories and distort their sense of authentic experience. Students learn to understand these secrets in part because of the practice of writing workshops. In workshops, a leader's emphasis is placed less on what students say directly and clearly in their own voice and more on what they say in associative and allusive language. The students must try to express what the poem itself, and not the writer, is trying to say. In this process, students come to pay careful attention to signifiers that they were generally indifferent or inattentive to when they originally wrote them down.

In writing an image, for example, a student may signify an emotion she does not in fact initially feel. As the student is instructed to tell the story behind the image, however, an emerging emotion associated with the image begins to compel the student to explore the image further. A student, Brigette, in search of a verbal portrait of her mother, wrote:

> My mother's dress is like an aquarium,
> a sea of blue and full of life.
> A school of tropical fish—a rainbow of colors
> nipping at their food floating gracefully
> like a ballerina on a stage.
> The prickly coral reaching out its arms to cradle me.

Here, one can trace the links of association as the "theater" of the mother's dress pattern is animated and compared to tropical fish, then a rainbow of colors being "fed," and finally a ballerina. All three images are signifying of the need to be nourished by or (in the case of the ballerina) recognized by the m/other, which, as Lacan has suggested, is the first desire on which all desire is founded. The mother's dress, compared to the nutrients of the sea, wraps around the mother's body, filling it with intermeshing uterine imagery, which is initially gratifying. The "coral" (or "core") of the dress image, reaches out to cradle the daughter who has projected herself as already within. Through a process of revision and reflection, however, the speaker realizes that the coral also threatens as it cradles.

The result is a double consciousness, as the writer splits herself between being inside the mother's dress and therefore on stage, and being outside in the audience watching herself. The student here not only experiences emotions that are synonymous with her desire to be in some way merged with her mother but also watches herself having those emotions (which helps her maintain her distance). Hence, the coral, the final manifestation of life in the mother, is "prickly" to the touch, suggesting ambivalence or rejection. Several associations are now projected on the mother from whom the writer emerges and for whom she performs.

To see, or to love, is often also to *want* to be seen, or loved. As the student revised this poem, she began to analyze her own ambivalent feelings about her mother, with whom she conflictually both overly identified and needed autonomy from. In writing a poem where she can "see" her mother, this student also writes a collection of images that allow her to see herself. Language begins as an attempt to fulfill an assignment in a poetry course, but it soon becomes a platform for expressing or dramatizing conflictual feelings about her mother. The student's original desire thus becomes a "backdrop" or stage for the expression of more authentic desires.

Another student wrote about her mother, using the same theatrical imagery. In "Curtain Call," Allison begins by remembering her own mother's "childhood dream" and appropriating it as her own:

> to float across the stage in a cloudy dress
> on your toes, a twirl, arabesque . . .
> The crowd would sigh in admiration
> as it rose to its feet and nodded . . .
> Even when tears pricked my eyelids
> I danced for you,
> when the velvet curtain rose
> my eyes skimmed the crowd for you.

Allison's poem about her mother's performance reverses itself into a performance for her mother's "admiration," but her mother is nowhere to be found. The child-speaker is aware of other mothers and daughters intersecting with mutual pride. Deprived of an opportunity to mirror or be mirrored favorably, the poet is confronted with a lack she can no longer hide. Without her mother's validation, her integrating gaze, the performance is meaningless, invisible. In fact, it is only through the hope of the mother's presence and confirmation that the speaker "appears." Without that stability, that point of origination, the child is lost. In defense then, or (as Freud might contend) in need of granting her wishes, the writer makes the poem a new kind of performance in which it is the poet who is spotlighted, raising the curtain to chide her mother's absence. Like Brigette's poem, Allison's is a stage for dramatizing a fantasy of being loved and recognized by the m/other.

In writing confessional poetry, students often learn to look on what they did not consciously intend to say when they wrote as something they themselves on an unconscious level did "intend" or "want" to say. Sometimes they openly confess to shocking, childhood experiences, and sometimes they adopt masks or dramatic personas to distance themselves from an event that they are nevertheless drawn to dramatize in a manner whereby they can both attain and avoid certain kinds of self-understanding. Both Plath and Sexton, for example, preferred confessing through dramatic monologues such as "Lady Lazarus" or "Cinderella" to telling the truth about themselves directly. Through the distance of poetic dramas they are better able to separate themselves from the very raw and intimate material being confessed in the poem.

Ann Sexton referred to her *Transformations* of the Brothers Grimm's fairy tales as "wholly personal":

> I feel my *Transformations* needs an introduction telling of the value of my rape of them. . . . I do something modern to them. I don't know if you know of my other work . . . terror, deformity, madness, and torture were my bag. But this little universe of Grimm is not that far away. I think they end up being as wholly personal as my most intimate poems, but in a different language, and a different rhythm, but coming strangely, for all their story sound, from as deep a place.[4]

Similar to a patient in analysis who overhears herself, sometimes as a kind of imagined and fictional persona, telling the secrets of her own personality, Sexton endows the script of the fables with her own affect, allowing a character to speak for her. While one kind of confession results in literature and another in truth and self-rehabilitation, both seem to confess the "self to the self" through an "imaginative" act of distancing and revision. After sometimes painful disclosure, the writer restores to consciousness a conflict if only for a fleeting moment. It is then up to her to discharge the pain encountered through the displacements of language that tell a story that can be communicated to an audience.

To heal, the poet or patient must learn to be present to the painful material she would ordinarily avoid. Often, what is crippling is not so much what happened but how one accepts the public admonishment not to recount what happened.[5] In keeping the secret, one is forced to construct a hidden identity that insulates one's self from hidden pain.[6] Creative writing classrooms are often unique in their ability to develop into an empathic space where the courage and imagination needed to confront unpleasant truths are supported rather than forbidden.

In barring one's self from the secret, one rejects the possibility of healing, preferring to stay away from dangerous images (such as secrets in Pandora's Box). Dissociation, which leads to the repression of memories, arises from the inability of the individual to assimilate contradictory experience. More so than remembering, poetry begins as disconnected unconscious signifiers, but through a process of revision it ends as a tapestry of powerfully connected meanings. The power of poetry, in fact, often derives from the tensions and dramas of conflicted, repressed meanings.

Otto Fenichel's description of free association as a technique is useful here for understanding both therapy and poetry writing. The dialectical nature of free association operates as the ego is split into observer and participant, so that the former can judge the "irrational" character of the latter. While the "irrational" part has been set free to peruse the unconscious, the other part draws on the resources of logic cast off by the "irrational" or experiencing part.[7] In the analytic hour, delicate changes in consciousness take place. What is revealed is only important insofar as it can be reconsidered and /or revised.

A similar condition is established for the student in the writing workshop where an emotionally powerful immediacy of self-dramatization can be balanced by a distancing self-judgment. Revision in this manner becomes a means of gaining perspective and working through absorbing material. Only by achieving an awareness of patterns that began in childhood and are being self-destructively perpetuated in adulthood, can the poet come to terms with painful memories and begin the therapeutic process of synthesis. A poet who is writing to "confess" something traumatic over which she feels guilt or shame is particularly susceptible to disassociation, secrecy, and denial. The writing workshop, however, provides a social context that encourages a writer to dig deeper. The writing workshop, and the teacher also, reward speech and give students the courage to face inner pain.

In confessional poems, particularly, the symptoms that poems speak can lead, paradoxically, to speechlessness. A writer is split in two: on the one hand there is a perceiving consciousness, but on the other hand there are memories that cannot be spoken. The process of revision, however, shifts this split structure into something more manageable. The writer experiences her own doubleness as a possibility for speech. She is divided into a past participant and present observer. And as the poem takes shape, the writer finds herself simultaneously a talker and a listener. She talks, but as she talks she also finds in her speech material she did not "know" until she spoke.

This is how the patient in therapy uncovers the anguish of her psyche—by digging down and trying to simulate within the mirror of her own thoughts and associations secrets that not only recover the past but also have halted her from fully experiencing the present. Once the spoken discourse of confession becomes the discourse of art, another kind of specter arises: the poem, the ghost of an unspoken past, requires revision. If the aims in the clinical situation are to raise to the surface the tensions beneath illness, what better means than when one's self is brought to bear witness and to assimilate painful experience through the mediation of a critical distance?

To revise a poem is to rewrite a self, refining the errors and vicissitudes of rude chance in rough drafts that can be compared to memory and the past. "Revision," then, in the psychoanalytic context—reintegration, reunification—becomes analogous with revision in poetic composition. The writing of poems sets in motion a process whereby accidental and inchoate signification begins to tell a story through a process of continual revision. "Revision," Galway Kinnell says, "is a moral activity."[8] We alter things for the better; we attempt to improve the substance of the work and bring disparate elements into greater unity.

Over my years of teaching, I have seen many students benefit from self-examination in poetry writing. Teachers can provide necessary support by guiding students through psychoanalytic techniques. What I do is try to literalize the search for key memories through an action. I ask my students to visualize walking home from school, swinging on a swing, looking inside locked or secret drawers, spying on a parent, first becoming aware of death, inspecting an old photograph. I am asking them to envision themselves in a scene in which the past returns but in forms that the mind cannot yet formulate or predict. Hence, the language is always a surprise, an otherness, a "Pandora's box."

Indeed, figurative language helps liberate the unconscious because it is its own kind of censor. Because primary memories are so often forgotten or repressed, the emergence of the contents of the unconscious into the signifying chain of language involves a number of interesting slippages, repetitions, condensations, and metaphorical and metonymical displacements that more properly belong to the tradition of stream-of-consciousness writing, which is also hypnogenic and dreamlike.

Last semester, one of my students wrote a poem about a family boat ride out into the harbor to watch the Fourth of July fireworks. A somber contemplation of something unfinished opens the poem, "The Fourth of July":

> lives in my mind like a freshly
> painted portrait that has yet to dry.
>
> the wet colors have bled into my skin
> like black ink sinks into the pocket of
> my father's white collared shirt.

The speaker's sense of "black ink" being absorbed into the white collar of the father's shirt refers to the act of writing itself. At eight years old, Evan was excited about seeing the fireworks display projected against the flat plane of the dark sky: "an explosive pastel painting." One also intuits that the boy is pleased that he has met the challenge of his own anticipated fear of seeing something so overwhelming. But the poem turns suddenly, and sharply, from the subject of fireworks, and the family picnic, to the nightmarish accidental drowning of the uncle while Evan's father was piloting the boat: "But after seeing the monster my father had become, / the fireworks seemed no brighter than a match."

At this point, a catastrophe has happened offstage, and the next stanza begins with what is already its aftermath: "After the blast and when the water settled, / the bow was empty. Emptiness is much scarier / when you expect something to be there." Whatever the boy had expected remains unmarked, and that fatal blankness, like the blankness of the page, is much scarier when one expects something already to be occupying or written on that space. As the poem progresses, the reader is clued into the fact that the uncle has fallen off the boat due to the rough turbulence of so many boats leaving the harbor at once. For the boy, the freshly painted memory of the fireworks has been blocked out by the greater distraction. The speaker registers his father's presence at the bow, stricken by grief and anguish:

> My father cursed the boat, he cursed the reflections
> in the water, he cursed what he could . . .
> a statue of my father stood alone on the bow
> his proud moustache was limp.

In the distance, the speaker can hear voices yelling, "We got your man!" and the "along side a canoe, girdled by white haze, dangled the nothingness of my uncle." The poem ends with an empty space. The last line is about the speaker missing the fireworks: "I don't remember seeing fireworks that night."

When Evan brought the poem into workshop, the students were struck with the apparent incongruity of the recreational boat ride, the sudden awareness of a terrible tragedy, and then the calm, and rather deflated, return to the subject of fireworks. The poem ends with the speaker's regret over not being able to recall them from that night. The poem was masterfully constructed, the imagery precise and evocative, but there was a gap, or lacuna at the center of action. Yet, for Evan, communicating that blankness was precisely the point of writing the poem—to present the emptiness of the flat plane as something more threatening or "scary" because it should not be blank, like the emptiness left by his uncle who vanished into the river. Listening to the workshop's commentary, Evan became impatient. He seemed to sense that the members wanted the literal event of his uncle's drowning drawn more explicitly into the poem. He had wanted to re-create, as Elizabeth Bishop does in "The Waiting Room," an accurate rerendering of his own thoughts *at the time* he was composing the poem. The child's screen memory (he did not see the fireworks or cannot remember them because he was so distracted by the accident) helps to protect the realization of the danger and its horrible outcome. The history of the event—his uncle falling off the boat and drowning in the river during a fireworks display—is traumatic, and therefore when Evan thought about the scene, he felt blank, numb. However, in conference, Evan told me that *writing the poem was therapeutic*. He was able, perhaps the first time, to relive the boating accident and to confront the last image he had of his uncle, which was, paradoxically, an image of absolute darkness and dreadful vacancy. Evan felt he had blocked the event from his consciousness but that repressing it had not been healthy. Once the words were committed to the page, they were outside him, and he said he could look at them objectively as a writer rather than a child. He understood he felt guilty about being disappointed that he had missed the fireworks when there was such commotion over his uncle's falling out of the boat. Both the fireworks and the drowning had been moored in time. Release could happen only with the inauguration of the writing process.

In the case of repressed memories especially, the patient or poet cannot accept or acknowledge the "true" signified (that is why it is repressed), and a substitute signified is sought to replace it.[9] Hence there is always a means of distancing the phenomenon or true signified from that which will represent and "unmask" it. For example, in Brigette's poem, the mother's dress is signified as an aquarium, then a stage on which the speaker performs. The point is that the "dangerous" signified—anxiety in relation to the mother—is always already present because it is also being worked with and "talked" away.

Let us then establish a clear pattern: first is the intrapsychic material that is communicated from the unconscious to the conscious level in the cloaking of language and then there is the raw data of the poem that communicates with the teacher and other members of the writing workshop. From that point on, emphasis is turned away from the emotional genesis of the poem (as a fossil imprint on the unconscious) and turned toward developing a poem that will speak to the group. Poetry devices provide a kind of shelter from painful awareness by asking students to concentrate less on themselves and more on crafting material language stanzas, lines, and symbols.

This ordering of language in the second, or revisionary, phase of aesthetic arrangement on the page helps the poet-patient both to distance and to dramatize the self. Poetic language offers a tangible substitute for pain, especially the pain of loss or abandonment. The manipulation of language on the page helps students to transform pain by making it something other than it is. The split between poet and talk, ego and imagistic representation, can open the possibility of remedial vision. Here the writer is able to integrate divided aspects of the self, especially those involving the division between past and present. Through distancing, the speaker can be removed from the "I" in the poem, and yet also identified with that figure in the poem. Conversely, through dramatization the speaker and the poet can dig into the emotional center of a poem and give it life. As the poet bears down into utterance, the poem itself moves as a body and begins to breathe.

The confessional poem is a final product of a process of poetic composition whereby the writer can recover and in some measure rewrite her own history. The secret of past affect comes to expression in various related images, as we saw in the case of Brigette's poem about her mother. By releasing the secret, the prohibition against feeling is lifted. Speaking the truth can be liberating after years of avoidance and resistance, and it can implement change.

As Snodgrass has suggested, the value of therapy is in its trying to get energy loosened from certain forms and flowing again.[10] These forms are the patterns of one's life that, once dramatized, need revision and change. In the workshop, students come to release freely that which is present in language but not yet present in self-concept. As a teacher, I find that when students confront what their poem says and then accept their negative feelings, they feel the relief that accompanies therapy. How does this happen? In my own view, this happens through an attentiveness to unconscious "cues" that surface in the imagery or wording of the poem.

A section in *The Practice of Poetry* is called "A Poem that Scares You." Students are asked to find something "scary" in their past and try to relive it in the poem as if it were happening to them now. Typically students begin with a text over which they feel comfortable self-control. In revision, however, students learn to mine their figurative language for what it signifies.

A model for this kind of exercise is Dorianne Laux's poem, "What My Father Told Me." This poem documents the poet's early sexual abuse by her father. Here the adult poet confides in the reader that as a child, dominated by her father, she did what she was told to do, including the chores:

> The iron resting in its frame, hot
> in the shallow pan of summer
> as the basins of his hands push
> aside the book I am reading
> I do as I am told, hold his penis
> like the garden hose, in this bedroom[11]

This is a shocking confession, one to which students respond with both empathy and outrage. What is interesting is that students diffuse the central issue of incest into the larger theme of betrayals at the familial and institutional levels. They are curious about the speaker's numbness, her ability to detach herself from her own actions in the poem, and how her listing of events seems so natural, so much like an everyday occurrence. Often, students are impressed by the speaker's self-composure as she moves from one kind of dangerous affect to another. Her world is morally inverted, having accepted violation as a substitute for love. The mind is betrayed, deeply ashamed for having failed to resist the encounter.[12]

After the initial confession about her father's kind of instruction, the poem shifts to a child's schoolroom and to another kind of instruction: "Summer ends. Schoolwork doesn't suit me. / My fingers unaccustomed to the slimness of a pen / the delicate touch it takes / to uncoil the mind."[13] The narrator then recalls:

> History. A dateline pinned to the wall
> Beneath each president's face, a quotation.[14]

In an oblique manner, the poet is rewriting her life and her history by scrutinizing and by distancing herself from the child she once was and reporting what happened. Unconsciously she points to the absence of a "whole" parent by physically cropping father and presidents into pieces and parts. The lack of a parent in whom she can trust repeats the action from home to school, as she merges bad father with good. Moreover, summer is compared to a "pan" as her father's hands are compared to "basins." Both are containers; but when the scene shifts to the schoolroom, hands are no longer empty, but filled, with the medium of the pen. The pen, like the unconscious, is the instrument that speaks, but speaks silently. It does not accuse.

Viewing each president's face, along with his quotation, the speaker is circumspect about accepting the public lessons of the fathers of her country. Presidents leave legacies, but the legacy of her own father differs so sharply, so acutely. Included in "History" are pictures of "wheat fields, buffalo, a circled wagon train."[15] The poet studies them and concludes with this poignant question, which is also on the mind of the speaker:

> Where do the children sleep?[16]

Through the self-dramatization of the adult poet, the child as speaker is able to exchange her father's lessons for the schoolroom's lessons—her private, agonized, and shameful history, for a public and more dignified history. In this way, she can rewrite her own experience by seeing herself as an ordinary citizen, just another child in the classroom. One can detect a stream-of-consciousness effect in the speaker's recounting thought and feeling by the way in which she twice recalls the same gesture of grasping and "uncoiling." Each thing held has the power to "uncoil the mind." The pen is an instrument for both child and poet; it enables her to reveal what she would ordinarily conceal.

The memory of a powerful and terrifying childhood event does not replace adult experience, but instead makes visible the intensities of childhood as they survive in current life. Key terms in the poem are thus inverted: protection is terrible endangerment; compliance is transgression. From the perspective of the mature poet, both family and government have failed her. Although the actions of the father cannot be erased from memory, the speaker can revise her unconscious guilt surrounding her role in the household as one (like a good citizen) who was just doing "what she was told" to do.

History, *a poet's* history, is "pinned to the wall with dates," and each date is overshadowed by the leverage of the father. Yet the terms of the poem subvert the father's power. With her pen, child and poet speak the "unspeakable" by simply exposing a truth, or being "quotable." Through the narrative of her own life, Laux brings together the consciousness of the wounded, remembered child with the interpretative and remembering self.

Not just Laux, but all of us who read the poem are called to judge yet again the father's immoral act. One of the deepest ironies of the poem is the fact that both the presidents' quotations and the poem itself are appeals to the public to moral action. The poet, like the patient, thus finds power and release in the purging of this material. The poet herself gains power as she challenges the reader to condemn what she herself, as a dependent child, did not have the autonomous power to condemn.

As readers we must deplore the treatment of the child especially in the context of a president's call to moral or public action. But we must also go one step further in dismantling the hegemonic fixity that subordinates victim to perpetrator. Through its implicit accusation, and its wishful transference of power, Laux's poem does precisely that, but only after careful attention and analysis. The poet creates the poem in the first place as a means of venting emotions associated with the trauma to confess her own pain and to survive it. Her ability to survive is supported by the presence of an empathetic analyst or reader who listens to what is being "said" and vindicates the victim by seeing her side of "the truth."

This poem and the responses it calls for are not an easy exercise in imagination. They are a painful exploration of the limits of imagination, an encounter with experiences that shock and repulse us. Imagination, like therapy, is painful because of what is, rather than what is not, exposed. As the child in Laux's poem tries to conceal her "history" of violation and abuse from her classmates, she sees violation everywhere and can find no safety. The wagons can only circle or "coil" around her in defense. How else does one resist self-attack but through repressing the memory and restricting the imagination? But by keeping things out, the child locks things within. Escape can only come later, through the voice of the poet, through self-dramatization and an imaginative revisionary reshaping of the narrative. Through the poem, the poet now knows an implicit judgment that comes to bear on the child from an adult perspective, a judgment that is both psychological and ethical.

This kind of poem, which demands a writer's willingness to "drift over memories" that are "scary," perhaps even traumatic and horrible, in search of something arresting is therapeutic. Such a poem helps a writer to come to terms with divided aspects of herself. In poetry, figurative devices work by means of which one thing is said while something else is meant. Laux's poem is not a simple allegory, but a kind of mirroring of child and adult perspectives rebounding off one another and bridging the distance. If Freud intended "cure" as a purging or catharsis to alleviate symptoms, then this kind of poetry is curative. The patient who has undergone traumatic experience understands that to be a victim is to be separate selves: the one who has been victimized and the one who has survived. The patient's revisionary thinking reveals this and begins to rebuild the riven self. The same is true of a poet's reintegrating of disparate material in an effort to unify a poem into a whole entity.

All poems are personal; even dramatic monologues have autobiographical roots. And students, no matter what form they are working with, will strive to construct some version of the self through the encoded message of the poem. Imagery is what conveys that message, and imagery is what is communicated through their associative deployment of language. Through the ritual of dramatization, students are able to get past certain blockages by which they would otherwise be stopped because, through the veiled indirection of the poem and its passage. Self-drama is a step in the process, for as the student comes to recognize her *self* in the figurations derived from the unconscious, she sees what she in fact kept hidden from herself. Only by allowing this kind of material to surface, however painful it may be, can the poet begin the process of self-healing and positive growth.

11

REWRITING THE SUBJECT

Psychoanalytic Approaches to Creative Writing and Composition Pedagogy

Although a hidden alliance may exist between creative writing and composition factions within English departments, that alliance has been hard won and remains both tentative and discontented. There is more tension between the two groups than camaraderie, and even more tension between creative writing faculty and literary critics. As Eve Shellnut observes from within her "cell" in creative writing, there is growing concern about a climate of anti-intellectualism among creative writing students, who have felt "rebuffed, intimidated, or baffled" as a result of their attempts to reach out into a theory-laden field of professional study.[1] Nancy Welch points out in "No Apology: Challenging the Uselessness of Creative Writing" that the New Critical notion that an artful text does nothing, but simply *is*, has cast doubt on the political efficacy of creative writing and has led to a prejudicial stance against it within the academy.[2] Creative writing, in a sublime sense, suffers from its own aesthetic attribute, rendering it "useless" to composition teachers whose goal is to raise students' class consciousness. Hence, in these redactors' views, students should be first trained to decipher the tropes and conventions of "discourse communities" and only subsequently be allowed to write creatively. Creative writing pedagogy should have no place in composition praxis.

Such pejorative attitudes toward one group or another in English departments only serve to intensify animosities over the worth of what each group is doing with literature and writing. Joseph Moxley suggests that "the general segregation of creative writing from literature and composition corrodes the development of a literary culture."[3] And Wendy Bishop agrees: "We need to be crossing the line between composition and creative writing far more often than we do."[4] Bishop attempts to sample, firsthand, the differentiation between creative writing and composition writing in college classrooms and to assess how those differences affect even her own writing process. Although Bishop is willing to confide that she believes writing in several genres is more similar than it is dissimilar, she concedes that she remains a product of her own literary education, which tends to set them apart.

Because standardization is rarely imposed on most creative writing and composition syllabi, the institutional demarcations of what, in fact, constitutes a creative writing workshop, as opposed to a composition classroom, are defined by territorial considerations. Handbooks describe the nature and kind of skills each writing course offers and delineate its boundaries. Although it is generally assumed that self-exploration is a staple of creative writing workshops, which "mine the unconscious,"[5] writing of this sort also goes on in the composition classroom. Many composition teachers have designed syllabi around the autobiographical, or introspective, and many have conceptualized classes that would mix personal testimony, or firsthand experience, with larger social ramifications in research projects. As Moxley suggests, our passion for specialization within writing departments has caused us to divide and subdivide a (potentially) consolidating process of discovering and shaping meaning.[6]

My sense is that our students view the partitions between compositional and creative writing as being more mirages than real walls they could bump into. Still, it remains true that students inevitably fix certain values on one and then the other: "Creative writing is fun, free-form; composition is hard, limiting, but real work." As with all first impressions, these might in fact end up to be true assessments of what these classes offer and the differences between them. They might even end up being that way because the students themselves have carved out of them self-fulfilling prophecies. As Bishop observes, "Many teachers don't write; those who do write, specialize. Creative writers compose primarily creative work and composition instructors excel at the academic essay, or more likely, the memo, or class handout."[7]

In fact, the boundaries between "creative" or expressivist writing and socioepistemic writing may not always be distinct when we look at creative writing *as* composition. Daniel Halpern's *The American Poetry Anthology* (1975), for example, shows how young poets, deeply introspective and personal, are actually writing under the sway of political consciousness. Influenced by Confessionalism (the most prevalent trend of the 1950s and 1960s), these poets embody the most elementary form of singular linguistic expression—soliloquy—a speech genre that is least obviously influenced by formal requirements and is, among rhetorical forms, most spontaneous and apparently uncontrolled. Although it may seem to be an especially personal or private phenomenon, soliloquy has a social dimension, often internalizing a dialogue with others—especially the audience. A self-ironical approach to the treatment of content distinguishes these new poets. The poem materializes along with the possibility of free play. The self-confidence of the earlier poets who were assured of their own virtuoso powers of expression has faded here into a more

comic, self-derisive pose of the poet's doubting his or her capacity to
make anything happen.

Reflecting the needs of the individual who must reach out, in some
fashion, to a public world, these poets appear, in contrast to their prede-
cessors, sometimes shockingly mundane, poised between isolated expression and social determinism. Let us begin, for the sake of discussion, with
Larry Levis's "The Poem You Asked For":

> My poem would eat nothing.
> I tried giving it water
> but it said no,
> worrying me.
> Day after day,
> I held it up to the light,
>
> turning it over,
> but it only pressed its lips
> more tightly together.
>
> It grew sullen, like a toad . . .
> I offered it all my money . . .
>
> wondering how
> to end things between us.
> For now it had begun breathing,
> putting on more and more
>
> hard rings of flesh.
> And the poem demanded the food . . .
> beat me and took my money,
>
> said Shit,
> and walked slowly away
> slicking its hair down.
>
> Said it was going
> over to your place.[8]

The poem's ironical turnaround is fascinating: writer and text are
reversed as nurturers. The naïve, gullible poet, still thinking that language
is his own invention, his own Frankenstein infant, is stunned by the realization that the poem itself is a selfish parasite, that it is no more than the
dumb signifiers it appears to be on the page. Like all infants, the poem
begins with a symbiotic attachment to the poet as a mother who can best
satisfy its needs. But once autonomous, the poem exercises its own free
will. It no longer belongs solely to the poet who cannot logically possess it;
instead, it circulates its own desire with the desires of the larger reading
public: "Said it was going / over to your place." No longer dependent on
the idiosyncratic poet, the poem has come up with a plan for satisfying its

own needs (which it models on the needs of other people). It then begins to think of itself as an object *of* desire rather than simply *being* the one who is doing the desir*ing*.

In the early 1970s, Levis was considering a change in thinking not only about the object status of the poem but also the speaking subject. Here, both are produced, rather than conceived. To what extent is the poet an agent of free will or linguistic determinism? Is the poem a true progeny of the poet's expression, or is it a replica of the social world that expression inhabits?

Obviously, the narrator of this poem must believe he can begin the sequence of the poem's life, and he has enough free will to "end it." The author intends the poem to be a constrained, aesthetic object. But language has its own idea, and the poem *itself* regards its life as a commodity to be tossed to the best buyer—a matter of supply and demand. This raises an interesting question about writing in general and one that is not exclusive to writing poetry: Do subjects control or choose the language they want, or are subjects driven and determined by language processes that operate them?

Poststructuralist theory has modified and refined our ideas about the relationship between writing and subjectivity. The unrestrained and autonomous subject so admired by liberal humanist theory has been subtly replaced by a conception of the subject as socially circumscribed by the language and the culture it represents.[9] We are often surprised by the irrational turn language makes, changing the subject. As is true of Levis's poem, some aspect of the text always seems to slip beyond conscious control. We point to words, images, or sentences that are simply there and for which we have no explanation of how they got there. Why should that word have led on to the next? In my teaching, I have often observed the way that writing students make mechanical errors in punctuation or syntax to reveal what they could not reveal through words. Is it because they lack the skills to put things right? Or is it something more subtle, a Freudian slip of the tongue, an insistence, or anxiety, a symptom that recurs and brings attention to itself?

All writing is, arguably, an indeterminate process. Language proliferation requires the interplay of cognitive and emotional actions simultaneously. Teachers should help students to locate a voice that is not merely a collection of language bits and pieces, but an agency, one that brings language to harmonized articulation—so that within the manifold order of words, a particular ethos, signature, or even writing "melody" can be heard. A student evolves through "voice" into an instrument that can be trusted to play a variety of sounds and melodies. Voice is not synonymous with "sound," but with the power to produce sound, without which a text would be mute. One is reminded here of Coleridge's famous conversation poem "The Eolian Harp," where the air lute is suspended in the window, leaving to nature's capriciousness the correspondent breeze that will unite all living things. To Coleridge, the voice was a synthesizer of all contributing nuances that comprise the "one life that is with us, and abroad." Indeed, there is something (perhaps mysterious or recondite) that initiates a writer's sound, as well as a desire to make sounds, rather than to be carved into a hard instrument.

Conflicts within composition studies reflect larger cultural conflicts about the nature of the subject and how to regard it. Whereas a writing subject is a product of ideology and socialization, it is also a product of its unique psychology. As Paul Smith has shown in *Discerning the Subject*, the Western philosophical heritage in which the "subject" is construed as a unified bearer of consciousness may well exceed the boundaries by which poststructuralist theory has constructed and delimited that subject.[10] Indeed, the enlightenment idealization of the rational autonomous subject gave way to a more restrained view of subjectivity that was more embedded in social processes. More composition theory began to consider the subject as a social entity who works in a community and understands the socially constructed nature of knowledge. As writing teachers responded to this model of subjectivity, they began working with students in small groups. Such a technique is indebted to creative writing pedagogy, which has always used the exclusive model of writers working together in a community workshop.

"To write," is an intransitive verb. A writer must give utterance to any kind of surplus language—language that is beyond what is self-defining at any present moment. If the disciplines of writing instruction fail to understand that writing is always on one level unpredictable, writing instructors will never grasp how writing, like speaking, is an extension of a language process that must allow for its own errors and vicissitudes. One might say that we are always what we are in language before we have any conscious thought about language. Our acts of writing are often as enigmatic and unconsciously elusive as we are as human beings.

Composition courses should provide students with opportunities to gain more critical competence in handling topics. Composition teachers may disagree about how writing should be represented to students, whether writing be a means of personal expression, political activism, or free-form experimentation in language. English departments have segregated writing courses according to perceptions about writing products (expository, technical, cultural studies, creative writing), rather than considering writing subjects, meaning the students who generate, or produce, writing. Writing courses should ideally work together in a more integrative and comprehensive process of developing ideas about the self (or the subject) and the social world that are always in dialectical formation.

The writing subject is best conceptualized as a dynamic and evolving entity that is shaped by internal and external circumstances that influence behavior. Psychoanalysis sheds light on intrapsychic and interpsychic processes that are always implicated in writing. Writing is a symbolic act inextricable from a person's desire, an act that is sometimes in conflict with the language that cannot adequately express that desire, leading to paroxysms and "blocks." Psychoanalysis helps us to see that unconscious factors are always perambulating just under the surface of a writer's discourse and that we are all vulnerable to them: they are our Achilles' heel or Delilah with a pair of scissors. Most important, psychoanalytic pedagogy supports the idea that writing can be therapeutic and, therefore, more meaningful for the student in the long term than other socioepistemic pedagogies developed for undergraduate writing courses. Psychoanalytic pedagogy shows the benefits of personal writing as linked to improvements in both writing and social consciousness.

Admittedly, in most academic departments, as elsewhere, there is resistance to psychoanalysis—as both a theory and a practice. Many suspect that psychoanalysis has contributed to an increasingly self-indulgent popular culture and has only served to heighten narcissistic and egotistical behaviors, leading to a variety of distortions. Psychoanalysis can be viewed as a cold, forbidding affair or a contested pseudo-science, flawed by misogyny and Victorian austerity. Even the terms *psychoanalysis*, *therapy*, and *personalism* are so fraught with academic stereotyping, speaking about them in everyday vernaculars, vernaculars that might, in fact, help to clarify and de-mystify the meanings of these terms is difficult.

James Moffet states that there are mutually complementary aspects of writing and psychotherapy: "Both require synthesizing of firsthand and secondhand knowledge into a full and harmonious expression of individual experience."[11] Indeed, psychoanalysis, or "the talking cure," can be a valuable resource for teachers to understand the human subject and how the human subject is overburdened by past patterns and habits that will eventually surface in his or her written utterance. Contrary to some preconceptions, psychoanalysis is not limited to the interpretation or analysis of an individual person, but is a mode of critical understanding, which attempts to interpret covert patterns of human behavior influencing larger systems of culture and society.

Considering the constituents of writing behavior to originate in the unconscious, psychoanalysts view the organization of the psyche as split, conflicted, or divided between conscious and unconscious material, order and chaos. Like creative writers, they would consider the stream of language, in any writing trajectory, to be what is simultaneously uncovering, and covering, the human subject in the process of its becoming itself more fully. What can be learned from combining a creative writing with a composition paradigm and allowing students to use writing as a means of self-exploration as well as self-expression?

Psychoanalysis is not new to creative writing teachers; in fact, "it is very old news." Freud emphasized the importance of the writer's unconscious and considered personality to be largely below present awareness. He resolved that we are not the masters of our own minds, but that we are driven by many unconscious processes (wishes, beliefs, conflicts, emotions, memories). Freud's goal in psychoanalysis was to encourage patients to air mental distress. Therapeutic procedures such as free association helped patients to tear down defenses and censors that had supported repressive conditions.[12] Although Freud recognized that repression eliminates threatening material from awareness, he also knew that repression weakens a person's ability to deal with reality. Constructing narratives about painful past experiences enabled patients to acknowledge that a former danger has disappeared and that one is now equipped to deal with it adequately.

Freud was fascinated by creative writers and by their fantasies, and he wrote prodigiously about them. In his essay "Creative Writers and Day-Dreaming," Freud tried to explain why poets and novelists use writing to rid themselves of intimate fantasies they might otherwise be too ashamed to share.[13] Like children, creative writers create worlds of their own, or rather, rearrange things in their world in a way that pleases them. As children grow into adults, however, their outlet of "play" is replaced by a surrogate activity that yields pleasures similar to fantasy or daydream. Key to Freud's theory on creative writing is the quality of shame attributed to the writer whose fantasy must be "concealed" from one part of herself, while "revealed" to another part, to be satisfied. Freud went on to generalize that "a happy person never fantasizes, only an unsatisfied one."[14] Creative writing can reveal fantasies a writer is suppressing. With more work and effort, those fantasies, once discharged and objectified, can become the material of poetry or fiction.

According to Freud, art sublimates essentially forbidden urges within the psyche and redirects and relocates them into a socially acceptable activity. Despite his admiration of artists, Freud viewed art as a substitute form of gratification. He saw artists as neurotic and highly narcissistic, devoted to the pleasure principle and expressing secret mental impulses that are hidden from rational understanding. From Freudian theory, we can learn that writers, like all people, disguise and conceal the very issues they are trying to confront for a variety of reasons. Repression is never absolute; it always bares signs or symptoms of its presence. This is as true of human behavior as it is in writing behavior. In creative writing and personal writing courses, "opening up" to material in the unconscious is often an explicit goal. Creative writing teachers actually use exercises to help students get in touch with, or reveal to themselves, symbols and associations they would otherwise withhold or keep repressed.

All writing pedagogy can make use of the unconscious and can actually help students to improve their writing while still broadening their social and political awareness. A writing teacher, reinforced by the lessons of psychoanalytic theory and creative writing pedagogy, considers the writing student as a whole person and that the most beneficial teaching of writing never loses sight of the rich and complex personhood that underwrites every student text.

When students write from their own experiences (positive and negative) to find something out about themselves, they develop a more confident sense of a fluid writing style and narrative voice. Recently, Lad Tobin and Jeffrey Berman have explored the unconscious origins of the writing process. They have also considered the potentially therapeutic aspects of the teacher/student dyad.[16] Robert Brooke and Mark Bracher rely on Lacanian theory to suggest that students in response classrooms of this type improve their writing because they identify with and want to please the teacher. They argue that a student projects or transfers emotions and associations from his own early-life relationships, especially those of his parents, onto his teacher, just as a patient projects or transfers emotions on to the analyst.[16] Ann Murphy, influenced by Freudian theory, extends Brooke's argument by demonstrating how transference can also account for students' resistance to us, to writing and to self-knowledge.

Teachers of both creative and expository writing, who are interested in furthering a student's progress, can use Freud's theories to enhance their own writing and teaching methods. Writing is a process of finding out what is already, on some level, known, but can also be a means of creating an identity. Words are always self-designating. Thus, a teacher's changing the syntax or order of a student writer's words ultimately expands or changes her identity. This has crucial therapeutic as well as aesthetic implications. A student widens her living perspective through the widening of her language perspective. Revision is not only a writing process; it is also a psychological process of gaining insight into one's own life experience.

Because psychoanalysis is itself such a broad and various field, both theoretically and clinically, I begin here by defining more narrowly the major terms of engagement within this discussion. There is a need to broaden the concept of the writing act so that it will include not only the writing product, but also the human being who is endeavoring to write.

Recommendations for classroom teaching might enjoin personal writing with the more powerful social discourses. How can psychoanalysis shed light on both scenes of instruction?

Using psychoanalytic theory in the writing classroom is a matter of revealing some of the material that students are already contending with, although they might not be consciously aware of that material or how it is affecting their writing behavior. By focusing on what in writing is still subject to interpretation, we move into the inferences of that which is written. This is not to argue that all teachers become quasi-therapists in the classroom or that by encouraging students to write about personal or even painful experiences (even as extensions of more neutral topics that are more socially or politically oriented) teachers will be turned, reluctantly, into therapists. Indeed, ethical and moral problems surround self-disclosure in writing classrooms, a subject fully explored by critical theorists and practitioners who have been commenting on what Jeffrey Berman called "risky writing."[17]

Berman's writing method helps students familiarize themselves with material that has been problematically repressed. However, a student's awareness of unconscious conflict, resistance, or self-defeating behavior is usually not sufficient to produce change. Students must share their personal experiences through writing so that genuine learning can occur. Berman hopes that students will empathize with one another and expand their understanding. By revealing secrets in a public forum, students are better able to integrate the negative or unacknowledged aspects of their pasts into current ego concepts.

Working from the assumptions of psychologist Erik Erikson's ego psychology, Berman's goal is to enable students to reassert a stable sense of identity by recontaining the disruptions of the therapeutic encounter. Unlike theorists who have borrowed their methods from Freudian id psychology (where writing actively resists and escapes ego and superego control), Berman is more interested in how the ego is fortified through social interactions.[18] The proper development of the ego essentially spells healthy growth; the ego permits awareness of self as an autonomous unit in circumscribed areas of life and the integration of the experience. Erikson's concept of the integrated ego has at least three distinct aspects: individuality (a conscious sense of uniqueness and distinctiveness, separate from others and from environment), wholeness (a sense of inner cohesion), and continuity (a feeling one's far past is linked to present identity).[19] Ego identity is essential in protecting against role confusion and for providing the individual with a sense of solidarity within a social group. Yet Berman's teaching incorporates more than ego psychology, as he states:

I would say that there are aspects of ego psychology, object relations, self psychology, and interpersonal psychology that are involved in the process. In addition, students are motivated to produce their best writing because they want to share their feelings and experiences with others. My approach combines elements of psychoanalysis and cognitive psychology: students reach their own interpretations, and they often achieve real breakthroughs. I hope that people read *Risky Writing* and experiment on their own with personal writing.

Indeed, personal and cathartic writing puts more weight on the writing teacher's availability to respond to that student. Barring practical considerations that would make such singular attention to a composition student's work impractical, psychoanalytic theory can be a function of writing that gets to the heart of a student's writing and the compositional problems with which he may be struggling. James Pennebaker's scientific research has proven what most writers have always suspected: that writing about painful or emotional experiences actually reduces physical stress and promotes healing. Jane Gallop has contemplated the interpsychic dynamics within the student/teacher dyad, comparing that relationship to the Oedipal complex, where forbidden desires circulate around and permeate the teacher/student climate. Gallop's view that the teacher/student dyad is already charged with sexual and power issues may have validity; however, her idea of *acting on such feelings* (as a means of dissolving idealizations that are not beneficial to the student) can only subvert the educational process and may have disastrous consequences for both the student and the teacher.

Writing venues of all kinds can help students to assume more responsibility for themselves and for their world. More writing teachers are interested in not only facilitating a student's competent writing but also encouraging healthy ego development. My contribution to the dialogue about the need for crossing the lines of creative and compositional writing, as Bishop has established, can be narrowly defined as an inquiry, which includes a psychoanalytic approach: Does personal or creative writing, with its therapeutic effects, help students to be better writers in other venues? Although obvious discriminations attributed to each field of specialization must be clarified, what is the literal difference between writing that is personal and writing that is socially opinionated; can one type of writing inform the other? How do the pedagogical assumptions of a talking cure that becomes a writing cure[20] intersect with other socially powerful discourses if at all?

With its emphasis on the unconscious and on what one does not yet know about one's self until it is uttered, written down, or "caught" within the repetitions of one's behavior, psychoanalysis offers a view of the writing subject in process. Rather than seeing the potential writer as someone who is chameleonlike and changing with each protean discourse he adopts, the more holistic approach psychoanalysis enables us to view the individual as a core being whose identity is fluid, mercurial, but self-constant. The writer reveals or discloses identity through the drama of writing, whether that writing is overtly "imaginative" or personally reflective, or socially and politically directed to a premeditated audience. Material raised from the unconscious can be useful to the student writer for more prudent self-comprehension, allowing her to view one text from several perspectives.

Understandably, many composition teachers worry that they are not trained to deal with students' emotional lives and do not like the prospect of students' opening up their personal problems along with the writing process. They believe that emotions belong in personal writing, or "creative writing" classrooms. Having taught creative writing for more than a decade both within the university and in the community, I am often asked by colleagues how I "deal with" such emotional outpourings that are inevitably raised in the workshop setting. I agree that emotions (how a student "feels" about writing or about the event disclosed in the writing) are openly discussed in creative writing as the rudiments of authorship and that emotions are borne also through the drafts of poems and stories that a writer is working through.

Yet it would seem disingenuous of my colleagues to assume that emotions or feeling states are magically set aside simply because students have walked into a composition class, rather than creative writing class. A dancer may refrain from dancing in a mathematics class, but that does not mean she will not be back at the bar by midafternoon. Does her dancing affect her perception of mathematical problems, her sense of spatial divisions, her ability to concentrate? Students bring their whole selves into the writing activity. They begin to think comprehensively, rather than partially, about what might offer insights into teaching in either discipline. Creative writing teachers deal with narrative structure and aesthetic form. Opening up the creative process means opening up one's self to the potential of the unconscious and what is stored there, even before there is discussion about how structure is developed, narrative focus maintained, or the power of a particular image. Creative writers are free to impart their knowledge of how to write poetry or fiction in the manner in which they have been taught or have developed exercises and provocative methods for motivating their students to write.

Creative writing is a place where students feel more safety in exposing their personal experiences, even traumatic ones. But suggesting that airing intense or difficult emotions is the only thing that happens in creative writing would be an oversimplification. As Freud poignantly stated while considering the shattering of a psychic structure: "If we throw a crystal to the floor, it breaks, but not in haphazard pieces. It comes apart along its lines of cleavage into fragments whose boundaries, though they were invisible, were predetermined by the crystal's structure."[21] Indeed, whatever rhetorical container a writer chooses to express herself, that product will be shaped by the psychic structure that created it. Some poetry instructors approach writing through the use of traditional forms, but what fills these forms is always a personal matter. Personal writing, distinct from creative writing, can be cathartic—but that is not to say it is dangerous or taboo. Phyllis Mentzell Ryder argues that personal experiences are never separable from rhetorical performances: "In early taxonomies of rhetoric that have been picked up by Berlin and Barthomae, personal or expressivist writing is seen as genre that sets itself outside of, or beyond, in denial of social-epistemic rhetoric. In those arguments, personal writing is delineated as an attempt to place a writer outside ideological frameworks as a creator whose reflections on his or her life are set forth as truths, finalities."[22]

Although many professionals think personal writing is too insular and too "risky" for an academic course, they need only to look in the direction of what is being done in the field. Tobin points out that students frequently feel that the translation from their own mode of expression to the academic language required in a course actually dislodges cohesive identity. Expectations about academic discourse cause students to posture themselves in ways that actually enforce the ideological premises and pretensions that socioepistemic teachers wish to decode. Students can be encouraged to be more effective communicators when imparting their genuine experiences rather than being forced to write in a form that actually guarantees detachment and confusion.

Abraham Maslow and Ira Progoff studied the creative processes of exceptionally gifted people and initiated a particular mode of personal writing that was designed to be therapeutic. "The Intensive Journal" was the result: a complex structured sequence of writing exercises involving recall of imagery and dreams, reflection on life event and a form of self-inquiry.[23] Part of "The Intensive Journal" was what Progoff called "Dialogue Dimensions," where relationships, events and inner conflicts were explored through written conversations. The influence of Progoff's teacher, Jung, is evident in the emphasis on life perspective and symbol.

The personal writer is deliberately disclosing content, making the text a replication of a mind as it encounters itself. This is where many writing students begin, but may not be where they end, in producing a poem or a story or a composition. They begin by "listening to themselves." This is the reflective period in which language—meant to mirror and extend the definition of who one is in the act of writing—discloses to the student her own experiences, through writing. This process is invaluable for students who have never even written autobiographically or self-expressively. They may find that their motivations change when they are telling their own story to themselves. Similarly, they may find that their audience becomes a factor insofar as it can reject or accept the writer because of, or even in spite of, what he or she has disclosed about herself.

When personal expression becomes formalized, it becomes a method of writing. Berman has demonstrated that personal testimony has no real currency without a public stage. Berman's students use their diaries to share their experiences, which also helps them to name and contain them better. When students can fairly empathize with and mirror for each other the feelings that accompany past ordeals, stigmas are erased. Students begin to feel these experiences no longer isolated them and a supportive community is formed, even within the classroom. The personal method of writing in college classrooms is not without risk, but can be highly effective in both airing students' problems and giving them a social context in which they can view those problems and set aside feelings of guilt or shame.

The personal is not public until the enclosed circuit of mind pressing on paper and work pressing on mind is opened up to include an audience. We can see this through the analogy of the strictly classical psychoanalytic encounter. In that scenario, the analyst does not intrude on the patient's free association; rather, the analyst presents himself as a blank screen, and therefore does not empathize with, react to, or respond to what is being disclosed. The patient must be "alone" with his own words, so that they can resonate with associations, before the analyst begins to interpret them. Writing that practices this kind of self-exploration and self-recognition, in both the creative writing and composition course, must be considered personal writing. Personal writing seems to get to the real matters students want to write about—even when those experiences are painful or traumatizing. Writing is not just therapy for the mind; studies show that it has a healing effect on the body as well. The question is: can we bring that kind of writing experience into composition classrooms without compromising serious goals for academic writing?

Empirical evidence behind the therapeutic effects of personal writing, both for mind and body, has been flourishing. In April 1999, *The Journal of the American Medical Association* published the study "Effects of Writing about Stressful Experiences on Symptom Reduction in Patients with Asthma or Rheumatoid Arthritis."[24] In the study, patients were randomly assigned either to a control group or to an experimental group. The control group was asked to write on three successive days for twenty minutes about a neutral subject, whereas the experimental group wrote on the most stressful event of their lives. Physicians examined the study group for symptoms of disease. They found that writing about stressful events exhibited significant improvement whereas the control group saw no changes.

James Pennebaker has been examining the health benefits of personal writing for many years. He conducted experiments in which a variety of people (college students, unemployed, prison inmates) were asked to use writing as a means of ventilating emotions linked to events. Pennebaker came to believe that writing serves to reduce the stressful effects of "thought suppression," the process of emotional inhibition that occurs when someone fails to confide, through talking, then writing, a traumatic experience. He cites studies that show how the lack of acknowledgement of significant experiences can be associated with increased health problems.

The act of verbalizing emotions, or emotional states, on paper offers student writers the opportunity to discharge emotions associated with a particular topic.[25] Writing about stressful experiences can actually alleviate the symptoms of asthma or rheumatoid arthritis.[26] As Pennebaker explains:

> Writing is beneficial, in part, because it converts the experience from images and feelings into language. The birth of the cathartic method came about as Breuer and Freud discovered that their patients benefited from talking in detail about the thoughts and feelings they harbored about the upsetting emotions. Talking, even in the stream of consciousness mode, crystallized forgotten and important thoughts, thus simplifying the process of connecting traumatic ideation and emotion.[27]

When writing is used as a way of exploring emotions and thoughts about stressful events, both emotional and physical health are often improved. According to Pennebaker, "writing about traumatic experiences produces improvements in immune function and translating experiences into words forces some kind of structure onto the experiences themselves."[28] Through personal writing, individuals are better able to organize, structure, and ultimately assimilate both their emotional experiences and events that may have provoked the emotions.

Personal writing need not always be about pain or trauma, but clearly writing can be a means of overcoming doubt and mistrust and acquiring the basis for personal initiative in the social realm. Personal writing can lead to more extended social efforts, which include civil or political advocacy: intervention, and the rights of victims to pursue their claims in court. Berman's recent book *Surviving Literary Suicide* successfully brings personal account into a larger social code of ethics. Students are encouraged to share and reflect on their personal experiences with suicide

and then to explore the cultural myths and misconceptions that make suicide appear, on the surface, romantic or heroic. By becoming informed
about the actual circumstances of suicidal deaths among young people, students in the workshop began to think of preventative measures for stopping the statistical climb in young people taking their own lives.

Psychoanalytic insights may enable us to change the definition not
only of the writing student but also of the writing teacher. Transforming
the individual would require a broader view of the student's potential to
use language in relation to the student's reality or context rather than to
view writing as a practical means of fulfilling a course requirement. Writing
instruction should encourage and support students' self-knowledge as a
preliminary stage for world-knowledge. Teachers are always implicated in
that process. As Tobin proposes:

> My own suggestion—and one that is not popular or politically correct—
> is that we pay more careful attention to the research and experience of
> psychotherapists. I am not equating composition and therapy nor am I
> suggesting that psychotherapeutic relationships are free from the power
> politics and self-deceptions I am criticizing in the writing class. I am sim
> ply saying that it makes no sense to ignore lessons from the field in which
> the workings of the unconscious and the subtle dynamics of the dyad rela
> tionships have been carefully and systematically analyzed.[29]

Both creative writing and composition pedagogy should be allied in
their concern for the positive effects that personal expression (which is also,
emphatically, connected to a social context) can have and in acknowledging
psychoanalytic theory's usefulness in understanding student writing.
Introspective writing, in fact, helps students to be more self-critical and therefore more tolerant of others within a social context such as the classroom.
Tolerance comes from firsthand experience in writing: one must tolerate one's
own mistakes while correcting them. In the last part of the chapter, I offer
some ideas for using therapy in the writing classroom, which may help students not only deal with personal problems, but also improve their writing
skills. Creative writing, although itself a shifting paradigm, anticipates many
of the psychoanalytic insights into writing in general. The following section
details the comprehensive theories of Mark Bracher and Jeffrey Berman and
shows how significant their findings are when applied to a writing class.

Although the Freudian term *talking cure* is now more than a century old, the idea of a *writing cure* is newer and boldly postulated in
Bracher's *The Writing Cure*. As he asserts at the beginning of his project:
"the instruction of writing constitutes what is perhaps the most favorable
venue outside of individual psychoanalytic treatment for pursuing psychoanalytic research and practice."[30] One might well pause here to ask the
questions: does this approach have advantages; and what kinds of delin

eations need to be made between students who might benefit from such an approach? Is a psychoanalytic *writing cure* appropriate for all students or only for those students who are already at risk, showing symptoms of mental illness? Should a teacher, as a "lay psychoanalyst," dare to make those kind of judgments within the teaching field?

In *The Writing Cure*, Bracher argues that intrapsychic conflict is often at the root of conflicts in the ego that result in writing difficulties. From a psychoanalytic perspective, a writing subject is always in conflict between the id (unchecked desire for gratification) and the superego that censors it. Alienated desire, or "the Other," may represent the one who oversees or tries to subvert a subject's progress; "the Other" may be alternatively supportive or condemning of its own existence. In exploring that Lacanian model, with its registers of the Real, Imaginary, and Symbolic, Bracher shows how a writer's conscious intentions and unconscious impulses are in discord. One drafts a piece of writing to find out what it has to say or what it dramatizes, which is often at odds with what one intended to say. The writer must try to help the writing, the words on the page, say what it intends to say. Taking the Other in also requires pushing the Other out, to maintain the boundaries between a stable self-concept and bodily flux. Language is always darting between positions of self-avowal and self-doubt; it is a stage on which both creative writing teacher and composition teacher hope to see their students perform.

In Lacanian terms, the ego is always involved in contesting what would undermine its solidarity, always finding out its own fictiveness. Hence a writer is continually unsettled by the expectance that there is no access to the Real, but rather a continual questioning of one's own adequacy and authenticity through language. Whereas Freud encouraged people to trust the salutary ego as something that was so armor plated it could do battle with external norms and find satisfactory security and be understood, Lacan is more skeptical. As Welch states, "Lacan's tale emphasizes a permanent post-mirror stage of alienation and self-division,"[31] and this has significant implications for the teaching of both creative and expository writing.

All human beings have endured experiences that they have repressed or concealed from themselves, that are too difficult to express. This extreme dichotomy between what a patient, or potential writer, has concealed from herself, and what words reveal, is more obvious in creative writing practice, but would enhance composition teaching as well. As Bracher has demonstrated, composition teachers should know what the components of intrapsychic conflict are, or potentially could be, and how these dynamics influence fluidity, grammar, and syntax. Forces such as enjoyment, desire, fantasy, and anxiety are often unconscious, autonomous entities within the psyche at odds with each other. The slippage of unconscious signifiers into a writer's text, as in "a slip of the tongue," clearly demonstrates that human subjects are filled with conflicts. Speculation about how certain drives, fantasies, rebellions, and resistances are constantly affecting or effacing student writing is at the heart of psychoanalysis and may provide insights into writing pedagogy.

Although creative writing and personal writing groups rarely become group therapy, instructors must be supportive and particularly responsive to emotional expectations on the parts of even their most fragile students. Students need to be ensured that there is safety in exposing what they did not know was on their minds until it was revealed in the writing session. Similarly, Berman notes in his prefatory remarks about self-disclosing writing, "This was the key safeguard: empathy, the ability to understand another person's feelings and thoughts without judgment or criticism."[32] Empathy is not to be taken lightly as a protection against endangering students who have disclosed intimate details about their lives in narratives that are sometimes shockingly straightforward. In the exposing of themselves *to themselves*, whether through a symbolic or literal narrative of a life history, students eventually will discover the dualistic nature of their own psyches. All approaches to writing can make use of unconscious material, determining it as one path to self-comprehension and the comprehension of others.

One could predict that theorists such as Berman and Bracher, who are most interested in the forces and drives underlying a student's writing, would not see a distinction between the "creative" process and its extension into composition writing, and compositional writing and its extension into other forms of writing. What interests psychoanalytic theorists is the possibility of using writing as a mode of personal and social change where change is needed. Addressing the freedom and limits of expression in the composing classroom, creative writing teachers can actually help composition teachers view the writer not only as a writer who produces creative texts, but also as a writer engaged in a human activity of truly being present to one's self and others. What I would add here is the prospect of allowing composition students to experiment with writing that appears visually uncharacteristic on the page (with staggering lines or inclusions of stanzalike paragraphs) as a means of self-analysis. Free associative writing may have its own structuring logic and therefore offer itself to further examination. The writing student reveals himself in not one but manifold ways that would never be disclosed if the writing had not yet commenced. Why not try to expand the margins of what is taught in one writing context over another, because writing is a fluid and ubiquitous process? Creative writing, with its emphasis on "exploring the unconscious," can encourage composition students' fluency in language as language seeks to reveal and conceal itself.

With more awareness of the writing subject as complex and involved in a process of "uncovering" and "recovering" material below the surface of the standard academic essay, teachers can be more sensitive to the writing problems they detect in their students. Berman's work continues to be groundbreaking, allowing, in many instances, the students to speak for themselves through journal and diary entries. When a poem or a journal entry self-consciously addresses its own inner tensions and tentative self-resolution, the effect is confessional. A desire for self-integration is openly articulated, but only, paradoxically, through its own dissociative strategy. As Bracher demonstrates in his scrutiny of intrapsychic conflict and accordant writing problems, the writer is always vulnerable to the inner antagonisms of the "me" and "not me," to the ego and internal otherness of a largely ego-alien unconscious desire and enjoyment. Certain habits, which are unconsciously gratifying, are rarely admitted to. Self-difference lies at the heart of the divided subject and its split intentions and qualities. In some pedagogical situations, a teacher can use the obstinacy of "difference" to invite students to reflect more intensely on themselves.

When a writing student is free to express the unacknowledged, he or she may confront internal censors that would threaten to judge, stifle, or nullify material that is not easily accepted by the ego. We have then a situation in which writing is jeopardized by intrapsychic conflict. But herein lies also the *curative* aspect of writing. A student can construct an independent identity stable enough to confront her errors, and she can begin to revise them. Excavation is only one stage in the process; the other stage is building and rebuilding from the material that has been unearthed. Indeed, composition theory can learn much from creative writing's insistence on spontaneity, change, and resurgence. And it can learn even more from the internal dynamics that are dramatized by the writer who writes about the *difficulty* of writing.

Revision or "remaking" the self through writing has obvious parallels in rehabilitating and healing the injured psyche. Creative writers often refer to their writings as extensions of themselves, even as surrogate bodies through which they have sought to transmute their own suffering into an art that can communicate a "common" experience. More than most writers, creative writers have used personal writing as a therapeutic outlet for releasing volatile emotions from the unconscious, and then "composing" them to bring them under better conscious control. Observing this "symbiosis" between creative writers and psychoanalysis, Berman has used student diary writing as a way of opening up trust and conviction in the writing process. His findings are startling: a textual body such as the psyche can and will heal itself when its wound is exposed to a sympathetic audience.

Led by the unconscious, personal writing, such as the kind Berman encourages in his students, causes a writer to confront a version of the self and subsequently to revise it so that it will fit more comfortably into an identity theme. In McCarriston's poem "Revision," the writer purposely divides herself into two minds, two bodies:

Revision

Absorbed in the work, final touches
to a poem that rings true, she is stopped.
She lifts her head but does not turn to see
whose eyes are in locking beam, the eyes of a tiger.
She knows. It is herself . . .
the writer faces a window,
and from outside, snow and light on it,
backlight her shape . . .
making a woman typing
a page, a faceless mythic figure.
Then she was the two of them, as she is now . . .
And she leans unsteady in the door frame
appraising the woman at abysmal distance . . .
as a longing streams between them across
the room of years, a tenderness exchanged
in the common body.[33]

In "Revision" the writer dramatizes the divided self, a trauma that results, and is to some extent mitigated, by an imaginary unification of those selves. Here "longing" or desire crosses the room of years, suggesting that there is a "common" body that desire shares. Writing a poem is a performance that enables the writer to heal herself. In this already extraordinary self-confrontation, we perceive something even more astonishing: there is always an invisible "third" party in the room, observing the tensions between the writer and the woman being written about—two versions of the same self. This is the speculative Lacanian Other, or superego, canceling out rough "drafts" or former incarnations of the self that prove unsatisfactory. The Other intrudes on the writer's process: observing, chastising, even threatening to silence.

What most fascinates the narrator of the poem is seeing herself through a series of "prior" selves, each one recognized as a possible "true" self, each one promising a more satisfying existence. There is simply no outer drama here, no other motive at hand, than the drama of a writer/speaker who struggles to maintain self-continuity, or at least the *mirage* of identity, through constructing various versions of the same self/text. The discourse of the unconscious has entered our consciousness and altered the way we think about the past. Writing and revision secure for the writer a sense of self, a matrix for integrating all previous identifications in one coherent identification with the text.

With the insights gained from this kind of analysis, which is not a critique of language structure, organization, or theme, but of a writer's *intention* as a subject in the process of realization, teachers guide students to reflect on themselves. In the revising process, the writer negotiates a distance between herself and the "word" that embodies her. Writing is a technique; teaching or responding to writing is also a technique and both need practice. A teacher who is insightful about a student's evolving need to synthesize his writing self with self-identity can encourage a student to write analytically about these very insights. A teacher's response is crucial to a student's advancement and development as a writer whose interest in writing will go beyond the limits of an introductory writing course.

Bracher clearly aligns the teacher with the psychoanalyst in very constructive and productive ways. Drawing from the traditional model of the psychoanalyst as the "blank screen" that "fills in" certain gaps in the patient's speech, Bracher advocates a method that would help students explore their ego-alien fantasies by pursuing their unconscious desires to "know" what language exposes. This is the fundamental desire behind all textual self-representation: to become evident as a whole and speaking subject. The teacher must not assume an authoritative role that will establish an imbalance between student (trying to please the teacher) and all-knowing authority. This is precisely what the creative writing teacher does by rote. The psychoanalytic teacher's response should be to request more writing—to ask the questions that will not serve to silence the unconscious, such as: What do you mean by this? What does this mean to you? What comes to mind when you think about this? Do you have any other thoughts, feelings, or memories related to this?[34]

Bracher's positioning of the teacher as a reflector of the student's unconscious desire "to know" causes him to step aside from being the sole object of that desire. Still, Bracher is wary of empathetic mirroring, convinced that such mirroring may encourage dependency in students who want to avoid confronting personal problems. A teacher, oriented by psychoanalytic markers, must reexamine her own desires and countertransferences, to help a student develop a "need" in writing that is not only self-reliant but also self-initiating. But this becomes appreciably more difficult and complex when a teacher is responding, as Berman does, to self-disclosing writings in diaries or journals. Similarly, creative writing teachers who provoke student "testimonies" or confessionals, particularly by asking students to relive a painful or traumatic experience in childhood (or to think about being a child again), are put in a precarious position. They must weigh the benefits of uninformed commentary against an already informed silence.

Writing is not a simple or random process, but a task that requires a writer to mitigate internal conflicts, a task that is often overburdened by the past and by personal disposition. The teacher's job, potentially, is to recognize that psychic conflict and inner turmoil in the student writer do exist and to be alert to the triggers producing ghostly lacunas that haunt a student's writing. A writer's ghosts may simply be related to old patterns and practices of writing instilled in the writer from his earliest schooling, strategies he has relied on to "hoodwink" the teacher. Or the ghosts may be actual fears and images embroiled in the writing process itself, resisting expression or overcompensating for a number of inconstancies through verbal and written insistence.

To illustrate, I offer here some examples of student poems that suggest that writing can be not only therapeutic, but it can also lead to a better understanding of one's self and one's life. In a composition class, I ask students to write about an experience that they consider to be life altering. Students often write about suffering the loss of a loved one. Although they choose to write about loss or grief, the writing itself clearly becomes an exercise in wishful replacement, which is cathartic. In denying the empty space of the lost object, which is brought to bear in the life of the poem, students who are still grieving the death of a parent, use language to bring that parent back to life. While writing, students are of course not conscious of their competing psychological and writing aims—divesting life while reviving it through textual reification. We might ask here: what is the lost object within whom is mourned and mourned again through the evocation of these word images? What *cannot* be represented in language? Is there a hollowness that is *not* anticipating that which will fill it?

In Eileen's poem "The Snapshot," she restores to her memory a painful absence of her father, who can only be made *present* through an unconscious wish. Thus she must work the poem, as one works a machine that simulates one's action, to restore him through the subtending image:

Six years old when the picture was snapped
Tiny, tanned arms and legs wrapped
Around my dad
Our smiles match
In my childhood room . . .
The quilt on the tiny bed
is a light one, that means summer
My Birthday month
The helium balloon floats
Like a reminder above our heads
With the colorful words
"Bronx Zoo" printed on its shiny coat
The picture preserves the scene
I preserve the memory

In this poem, Eileen grieves for her father while looking at a snapshot of him and her together, posed. A balloon floats over her, suggestive of the contents of life and death: a container of air. A snapshot, her writing of the poem, is preserved like the memory that sustains it, also a container. While the balloon rises in the unconscious, the poet pours her thoughts into it as one would pour hot metal into a mold or exhaled air into a balloon. The poem becomes its own elegy, a grave in which the secret of the father is demarcated by a name, a spirit of place: "Bronx Zoo." The balloon that floats like a reminder of the poet's birthday is a breakable skin or "coat" that is protecting the absent father from disappearing again. Who does not think of a balloon without anticipating it popping into pieces, shreds? The poem itself is upholding, however tentatively, the integrity of the whole, and repressing the actuality of its pieces (the words). As is true of the Lacanian mirror stage, Eileen's gaze is interlocking with the gaze of her former self now looking back at her, assuring her of her own presence by confirming that she has extracted herself from the past. "Am I she, or me?" Both the poet and the remembered child identity serve as camera lenses, preserving the memory of a memory, as word hinges on yet another word to progress, and yet defer, its own meaning.

Significantly, the poem ends with an assertion: "I preserve the memory," suggesting that the writer is reminding herself that she will not renounce the lost internalized object she still grieves. The picture is just a "scene" until thought erects its memorial to it. Feelings are displaced onto the lost loved one and then recaptured in an experience of identification. Hence, in her identification with her "lost" father, Eileen asserts *his* wish in her own to maintain his place in her memory along with *his* wish not to be lost by *her*. In this way, Eileen can obviate the verdict of reality that the memory cannot be preserved because the object no longer exists in or out of time.

In another student's poem, Brenda surprises herself by remembering more than she would have about her response to her father's death had she not begun or sought to "finish" the poem. Here again is a kind of overspilling or surplus of information that has found its way from unconscious sign to verbal signifier:

When I was Seven
Small glimmers of gold
flicker in fishy water
like the color of mac-n-cheese
on a glossy cardboard box . . .

Saturday afternoon and
it's almost time for lunch.
"Mom, Dad's sleeping on the mower!"
screams my brother. . . .
Fish flash golden smirks . . .

In the driveway,
Mom performs C.P.R.
On a lifeless man
I call "Daddy."

Crying,
she cradles his head
until medics
confirm her failure

Inside,
forgotten noodles float
like dead fish

The imagery of the dead fish painfully and poignantly reveals
Brenda's wish for a reversal of fortune. In a reaction formation, her symbolism of the fish floating up to the surface replicates her mother's efforts
to pump oxygen into her father's lungs. When the hope is gone, death
becomes "real"; it is born for the first time. Brenda reported feeling a sense
of "relief" in writing the poem, a pleasurable exhaustion like the one associated with crying until one goes numb or falls asleep. Student writers who
have found that writing can reduce painful feelings while being meaningful
and moving to others often note this kind of sensation of relief, expendi-
ture, and genuine "good feeling."

In both of these cases, I responded to the students with enthusiasm
and showed them the far-reaching curative aspects of these works.
Although these were poems written in a composition class, I assured both
Eileen and Brenda that their grieving would help others to understand their
own mourning process better. The poem gave them an opportunity to come
to terms with the dead father and with the affect-laden signifiers associated with him in the unconscious. From this juncture, Eileen and Brenda
could pursue related topics in other writing genres such as research projects, journalism, and prose memoir having to do with father/daughter relationships, separation and mourning, the long-term effects of losing a parent at a young age. Creative writing and composition praxis can work in
tandem to clarify and reconcile inner divisions that may be haunting students or even hurting them by retrieving material that is crucial to their life
experience. Emotions cannot be simply "cut away" from the larger context
of a social or political person. Being a social or political person should, in
fact, provoke personal passions. Composition teachers should do more
one-on-one interpretive work with their students to help them gain a fuller
appreciation of what they have written.

Childhood repressions persist into adulthood where they prevent
true self-knowledge and may even lead to neurosis. Reaction formations such
as displacement, projection, and denial impede psychological and writing

development. During periods when free association is not impeded, a patient relives childhood experience. Behaviors and emotions are unconsciously displaced from the past to the present and from important people in the patient's life to the therapist. This process is called *transference*, and it provides the analyst with evidence about the patient's problems and usually involves some childhood love for the parents; this transferred attachment makes the patient receptive to the analyst's influence. The analyst tries to intensify this process to make the transference, rather than the original symptoms, the main focus of treatment (in other words to move from a discussion of sadness or anger to the sadness or anger directed at the therapist).

Within the teacher/student dyad, a degree of transference always occurs. As Bracher remarks, "free writing, as advocated by Elbow and others, functions much like free association in analysis: it helps students discover their ideas, their true interests or desires. Any kind of direction from the analyst or teacher risks inhibiting or derailing this process by imposing the Other's desire. . . . "[35] Bracher's point is well taken because the diversion of seeking the Other's approval in the writing contributes to writing incoherence and poor development of thoughts. In free writing, the audience must be a skilled and sympathetic observer. This is the healing effect that underlies Berman's theory in *Risky Writing*. But *Risky Writing* is also (as its title suggests) an examination of the ethics of response to students writing about "risky" experiences. Creative writing teachers most often encounter such "risky" writings and encourage students to write them. Few worry about the relationship between the evaluation of writing and the student's desire to know the teacher's desire, or how their students frame and respond to the writing situation in terms of transference and countertransference. Yet writing teachers of both schools clearly should be concerned with these peripheral issues, because they eventually go to the heart of teaching success or failure.

What kinds of responses should teachers offer to students who are undergoing the labor of revealing things that they would not know how to reveal if the writing had not offered them up to consciousness? Should a teacher respond without comment, withholding praise, identification, acknowledgment, or sympathy? Or should a teacher actively encourage and commend a student's efforts? Should a teacher correct a personal writer's grammatical errors or remain neutral to the standards, or lack thereof, in a composition?

In my own courses, I use a method of "soft grading" (checks and check minuses) along with a running written commentary along the margins of their papers. Sometimes, I include miniature pictorial symbols such as of a traffic light or a racing horse when I want a student to pause or slow down and reconsider some aspect of the text. Of course, these pictures are crudely drawn, but they help to soften the imposition of editorial interruptions. Grading is always an imperfect system and should be reinforced by a teacher's continued prodding of the student's intention—either in conference or along the borders of the paper itself. Maintaining a give-and-take dialogue and using a student's willingness to work through the issues brought up in this dialogue as an indication of progress in the course is important.

Questions surrounding the realities of teaching through a psychoanalytic method have caused several instructors to equivocate about the wisdom of such an approach. Countertransference can prevent the analyst from responding accurately. Issues in the analyst's own psyche may come to bear on how he perceives the patient and how he reacts to the patient. Bracher's motives for pursuing psychoanalytic research in *The Writing Cure* have met with concern from some critics, such as Ann Murphy, who wonder if such a method could actually destabilize a student who is already at risk, rather than help that student to confront her problems, especially because Bracher discourages teachers from offering empathetic responses to students who are struggling with inner conflicts. Bracher insists that students recognize their unconscious desires rather than try to evade them. Yet, he also assures us that he "takes care that a student's level of anxiety never becomes overwhelming."[36] As one of my colleagues, Pam Presser, reasoned in her dissertation chapter on overdetermining student writing in the composition classroom, Bracher himself has created a fantasy in which a teacher has the capacity to control a student's level of anxiety, and he fails to acknowledge the ways in which students (discerning his psychoanalytic approach) might well produce narratives that would facilitate his goals, leading to a flawed, if not ambiguous, study.[37]

These issues are not easily resolved in writing evaluation or in the clinical session. Creative writing teachers may unconsciously praise "suffering" as it is transmuted into an art language. Teachers may even encourage an "aesthetics" of sorrow, realizing its power to rescind pain in an expression of beauty. Yet teachers must always burden the responsibility for eliciting a student's pain, fear, or anger. Teachers are not psychiatrists, but fires do not start without flint. Although teachers are not qualified to diagnose mental illness, they need not try to escape awareness of it when they do detect it. They should be aware of the clinical services available to students and should, without hesitation, offer to guide students to those resources. Risk, as Berman has made abundantly clear, is not an action taken only by students, but also by teachers. At the risk of encouraging student dependency, or reinstating student's parental idealizations, or even "unresolved transferences" in the teacher/student dyad, a teacher should assume that these kinds of "risks" are inherent in our profession and should be responded to with compassion.[38] To abandon a student whose risk-taking has jeopardized her self-control may have devastating consequences.

Self-disclosure, when properly responded to uncritically and compassionately, can actually help a student expunge experiences that were disfiguring of the self in the past. But self-disclosure is not an activity that happens in isolation. Virtually all writing involves some kind of self-disclosure, and students can make use of that in pursuing writing as a means of knowing not only one's self, but also the relationship between self and others. By drawing up the past specter through word signs, one version of the self is brought to bear on another and becomes equal to itself, a student diarist's double in language and flesh. Bee, a student in one of Berman's workshops, realizing the value of her self-disclosure about domestic abuse, concludes she is a part of a "common" body" the messenger and the message. Most important, she realizes that her classmates have not abandoned her as a result of her "telling" any more than she would abandon the prior self she has conjured up in the writing of her narrative. The telling and hearing of a story is never a simple act but is something that finds inroads into the deeper meaning and significance of collateral events. An individual's suffering is always placed in a larger stream of human suffering and reveals a larger context by which all life continues.

We begin and end here with the concept of the writer writing, not with the result of the text. What remains is a page of writing, a room, and the language that gives meaning to its presence and without which there would be no presence at all. Such an internal dialectic demands a "figure be cut out" (as in a Matisse cutout) from that, rather than the writing be cut out from the figure. The teacher's role, whether creative or compositional, in the process of a writer's writing is of "absolute difference,"[39] a background from which the subject distinguishes herself as positive, rather than negative. It is only through a transposition of background and foreground that content can fully emerge.

Self-exploration can be an active tool in composition, as it is in the more "artful" forms of creative and personal writing. By using access to the unconscious, a writer can discover a fund of material of which she would not have ordinarily been aware. Creative writing as a model for composition relies a great deal on the phenomenon of memory, emotion, free-association, self-dramatization, and self-description. The composition teacher's primary response to student writing thus will be to encourage more writing to help a student to know what she would not have known without beginning to write. Like the leader of a creative writing workshop, the composition teacher can learn neither to validate nor to criticize either the ego or the unconscious desire of the student. The instructor can ask for more. Emphasis then is placed on a powerful delivery of these personal events so that the student focuses on the persuasive means rather than the "ends" of the work, what is integral to self-expression and self-presentation.

We need to think more flexibly and contextually about writing perspectives, especially those circulating through the assumptions of psychoanalysis. A psychoanalytic framework for understanding and responding to self-revelatory writing that is, to one degree or another, descriptive of all genres of writing, is an important topic for writing teachers, whether they seek to elicit such writing in their teaching. In fact, teaching composition and creative writing would benefit both from focusing less exclusively on the writing process and products and more on the writing subject.

More specifically, focusing on the writing subject through the lens of psychoanalysis provides several potential benefits. It reveals a broader and deeper mutual ground for composition and creative writing than teachers are presently aware of, and this common ground will eventually open up interesting possibilities for sharing pedagogical techniques and greater unity in the English curriculum between composition and creative writing courses. This perspective reveals that personal writing and socially engaged writing are not mutually incompatible or in competition with each other, as often assumed. Rather, these modes of writing are implicated at the deepest level, the level at which the writing subject, or student, is struggling with conflict between the idiosyncratic and collective parts of the self.

Both Bracher and Berman have developed theoretical markers that are as illuminating as they are instructive to teachers and other professionals. Psychoanalysis can be a filtrate for the creative writing or composition teacher, encouraging empathetic awareness of what might be underlying student performance in writing situations. If creative writing is included in the general concept of compositional writing, as simply a higher chord played on the same melody, a psychoanalytic approach seems not only natural, but the most helpful to individuals who want to use writing as a liberating tool. Poetry and expressive writing evoke responses from students that are unintentional, and therefore revealing of opposing impulses. Similar insights can be gained through composition studies. A piece of writing is not only a reflector of a given subject but also of a writer's need to *confront* a particular subject. And that need is conveyed through thoughts and symptoms that show themselves most vividly at the moment they are being talked or "written" away.

12

"TO BEDLAM AND ALMOST ALL THE WAY BACK"

The Image and Function of the Institution in Confessional Poetry

In *Ecrits* Lacan presents the mirror stage as a platform for the subject to establish an organic relation with reality. Part of securing a relation to reality is the process of filtering out, or rejecting, images that do not fit into the organized concept of the self.[1] At the same time, this structured identity (the "je"), is never identical to the subject's felt experience. We cannot grasp our own "true" structure from within; we must grasp it from an authoritative perspective, or gaze, outside of ourselves. In some ways, we are always confined by "seeing" boundaries that are drawn by others. As the Gilman story showed, walls may support us, but they can also imprison us. In psychiatric hospitals, especially, patients instinctually adapt to certain behavior patterns that the institution has mandated. They seek to fill in the spaces that have been designated by the doctors or therapists as normalized spaces. If these patterns are properly imitated or assimilated, a patient may be considered cured and released. But this is not an easy task, especially when an authorized view of reality is not consistent with a patient's or poet's reality. When the poet feels that she is being pulled by invisible strings or that there is a true disjunction between the reality of her mind and the reality of her body, she may well assume that the institution has turned her into a mechanical doll:

> That night, I was a mechanical doll,
> And I turned round and round, to the right and the left,
> And I fell on my face and broke in half,
> And they tried to fix me with all their skill
> So I was a proper doll once again,
> After that, my manner was poised and polite,
> But I was already a different kind:
> An injured twig hanging by a thread.[2]

These stanzas from Dahlia Ravikovitch's "Mechanical Doll" describe the responses some patients have in the wards, numb, broken, and mended together again, but with all of the cracks still showing. "Humpty Dumpty" is the perfect nursery rhyme analogy for a mind that has been irrevocably shattered. Renovation and rehabilitation can make a new person out of the old one. But repairing, or restoring, the old one is never truly possible. On another level, the mechanical doll who has been "straightened out" ("Though my steps were measured and rhythmical / And I had blue eyes and golden hair / . . . And a trimming of cherries on my straw hat") has now self/divided. Although the mechanical doll performs instinctively according to someone else's rules, the omniscient voice of the poem is contrary to the image she is forced to project. Conformity, especially for the domestic doll who has been infantilized, is not merely an asset, but a condition for staying unbroken.

Poet Anne Sexton knowingly confronted her readers with material that made them uncomfortable. For some, her poetry was too subversive, too brutal and confrontational for a woman to write, and for anyone, regardless of gender or class, to read. For others, Sexton was able to embody a tragic truth that was incontestable for women of her generation and background who did not fit into the conventional mold, and yet she would triumph, through verse, in a way no ordinary woman could. As Diane Wood Middlebrook writes in her biography of Sexton:

> Sexton's work offered the mental hospital as a metaphorical space in which to articulate the crazy-making pressures of middle-class life, particularly for women. The home, the mental hospital, the body; these are women's places in the social order that apportion different roles to the sexes. . . . Sexton's poetry in forcing discipline upon madness, fed opposite types of cultural appetite: for truth about the feel of illness. . . . [3]

In her own generation, Sexton articulated the "feel of illness" in a way that only her fellow confessional poets—Plath, Bishop, Berryman, Roethke, and Lowell—could articulate in their own poems. She was extraordinary in her ability to exact the conditions of her own terror. She let her reader know that dark, impenetrable sides of the human psyche exist that are too awful, too treacherous to approach, yet there is no turning back. Early in 1957, Sexton began writing poetry at the request of her psychiatrist, Dr. Martin Orne, for whom she wrote one of her most powerful poems. As Colin Clarke writes, "as Sexton began to write and to see her writings as poetry, rather than the expressions of a mentally ill patient, she also began to see that the mental ward was not the only metaphorical space in which she was confined."[4] Her body and her gender role, both of which signified submission and the need for approval from masculine authorities also confined her. Sexton's biographers detail a childhood that was riddled with neglect and abuse, her mother was emotionally detached and icily sarcastic, contributing to Sexton's troubles with her own role as a mother. Her father was particularly abusive when he was drunk and berated his daughters for their lack of femininity.[5] Sexton went to boarding school, then finishing school in Boston and, in an apparent act of parental defiance, she eloped with Kayo Sexton in 1948. After giving birth to her second child, she began to seek treatment for depression and morbidity. This led to Sexton's first hospitalization at Westwood Lodge where she seemed to be suffering from suicidal urges and an uncontrollable anger toward her children. She was treated with psychoactive medications and released. After her release, she began to see Dr. Martin Orne, and after overdosing on a barbiturate, she was admitted to Glenside Hospital, "a grim institution for mental patients, where she stayed for two or three weeks."[6] She avoided electroshock therapy, but the psychiatrists clearly did not have a comprehensive understanding of her illness.

During this very chaotic and turbulent period, Sexton began to write serious poetry. She enrolled in Lowell's poetry seminar in 1958 at Boston University and began to publish. In 1960, fewer than four years after she had just begun to write poetry, Sexton's first book was published. *To Bedlam and Part Way Back*[7] is devoted to Sexton's experiences as a mental patient.

As the title of the book suggests, the poem is only a partial recovery from the original madness of Bedlam. A book of poetry, in its representative spirit, is always on some basic level metonymy: a part for the whole and is itself only the sum of its separate parts. Sexton's poems helped her to partially achieve an active control over the excesses of emotions to which she was prone, and her idiosyncratic style, which tends to involve the compartmentalization of images. These images, often from wildly different categories, were conceived as metaphysical conceits, but work together as a confederated whole. Poetry then, at least for Sexton, was always a self-portraiture, in which she could make the different parts of her intimate life work in a unified totality, and she could see herself doing that. Poetry, rather than prose, could impose rules, structures, and margins that helped her to better contain herself, as the institution had managed to put her back together again.

In the hospital, Sexton began writing about the other patients whom she considered to be her community. However, apparently she saw herself as distinctive and in a different class. Because of the stigma surrounding mental illness, she preferred to speak of the institution euphemistically, as a "summer hotel" such as, for example, in "You, Doctor Martin" with a reference to herself in the second stanza: "I am queen of this summer hotel / or the laughing bee on a stalk / of death." Of course, the summer hotel is thick with honey, a hive of swarming, buzzing bees, not a place in which one feels comfortable. The hive simulates the buzz of the brain when it is at its height of manic frenzy, and yet all of the

bees, like all of the patients, in their droning hums or miseries, sound the
same. Little differentiates them with respect to their various mental disorders. Dr. Martin Orne's clinical observation of them tends to blend them
together, rather than set them apart. They are all locked up specimens of
their species. Lowell, too, declares that he is "cock of the walk" in his
ward. The animal imagery points to the high degree of self-derogation the
patients experienced through their being classified by mental health offi-
cials who constantly monitored them in the wards.

The poem "You, Doctor Martin" consists of seven lines with the
first stanza rhymes in an abcabca pattern, while each following stanza
rhymes a little differently: abacabacb. The irregular meter contributes the
often halting or fractured syntax of the poem. Despite some of the characteristics of regular form and spacing, "You, Doctor Martin" is a poem that
defies its own initial terms of containment. Sexton begins by defying Dr.
Orne's authority by addressing him as "Martin."

> You, Doctor Martin, walk
> from breakfast to madness. Late August,
> I speed through the antiseptic tunnel
> where the moving dead still talk of
> pushing their bones against the thrust
> of cure. And I am queen of this summer hotel
> Or the laughing bee on a stalk
> of death.[8]

Although the format of the poem remains consistent, the flexibility of the
meter allows Sexton the freedom to break with rigidity and to enjamb the
lines at the heart of the poem. There is formal spillage here as perception
overcrowds its normal allotment. As Sexton said about her own prolific
nature, she was a person of excess on all fronts.

Indeed, Doctor Martin Orne walks from breakfast to madness, as
if it were usual. His routine is normal; and yet the patients he consults with
are abnormal and delusional. His ability to demonstrate control over his own
life is what his patients are unable to do. They can, in such extreme conditions, only obey the residential rules that will standardize their lives and
make them routine, normal. The second stanza begins with Sexton reporting
on the routines patients follow as if they were convicts or schoolchildren.
They wait in line "at the frozen gates" for dinner. They speak their shibbo-
leth and mechanically "move to gravy in [their] smock of smiles." Obviously
the patients will need smocks, because, from the point of view of normal
society they are out of control, and therefore best confined to a hospital.
Additionally, from Dr. Martin's point of view, these mad patients are unable
to control their mind or their bodies because their brains have been unwired
and need to be set right again. To overcompensate for the expectation that

the mentally ill patients can only cause mayhem in the dining room, "[they] chew in rows, our plates / scratch and whine like chalk. . . . "

Like some boarding or reform schools, mental institutions overlook the individual and become programmatic and dehumanizing. Ironically, mentally ill inpatients must look to the institution to help them regain their independence and self-confidence. Order in each institution is accentuated so that the members will all be accounted for. In part, rehabilitation is effected through various activities that will keep the patients busy and help them to synthesize mental and physical tasks better. In the mid-1950s, occupational therapy and recreational therapy were incorporated into the patients' daily routines. Patients were encouraged to work productively with their hands, although they were not allowed sharp instruments. Such activities were distracting and challenged patients to work cooperatively and toward an end product they could actually see finished and used. But when Sexton is first put to work making moccasins, she is unsure that her work will stay undamaged by her own hand. Her hands disobey her. Still she strives to create, even if the product is meaningless; it is the work that matters. She believes that the repetition and discipline of institutional life will help her in the long run. The poem continues with the image of the chalk:

> In school. There are no knives
> for cutting your throat. I make
> moccasins all morning. At first, my hands
> kept empty, unraveled for the lives
> they used to work. Now I learn to take
> them back, each angry finger that demands
> I mend what another will break
>
> tomorrow.[9]

It is interesting to compare this stanza, which deals with the stitching together of the soles of moccasins, with the activity of creating a poem, stitching together stanzas and words. Both activities are sublimating of more dangerous impulses of self-aggression and self-desire. Although the poem making is a healing process, a mending together of the two sides of the self, the "good" and the "bad" as seen through the indoctrinating powers of the institution and its rewards and punishments, it is always temporary and fragile. One cannot count on consistency tomorrow. Because confessional poetry is an outpouring of the mind's immediate perceptions—a very extemporaneous poetry—there is no telling what will come of the poem "tomorrow" if the mind has altered its plan. The mad cannot depend on being rational. Sexton's writing about empty shoes emphasizes the necessary application of "feet," which is the proper unit, or measure, of the "walk" of the line. Like Dr. Martin, Sexton must balance technical precision with the spontaneous emotions that might turn the meter from regular to irregular, or topple the form. He walks "from breakfast to madness," and she speeds through "the antiseptic tunnel" of the hospital ward. Although her pace is faster, she is still bound by regulation and confinement.

Returning to the original subject of Doctor Martin, in the poem, Sexton sees him as a "god," an omniscient presence in the wards or "blocks" who has a "third eye" and moves among the "separate boxes / Where [the patients] sleep or cry":

> Of course, I love you;
> you lean above the plastic sky,
> God of our block, prince of all the foxes...
> Your third eye
> moves among us and lights our separate boxes
> where we sleep or cry.

Sexton uses the obvious Freudian dimension of transference in her relationship to Dr. Martin. She has, "of course," fallen in love with her father substitute who is naturally related to God, the primordial Father. Her world is a doll's world, where everything is unbreakable plastic—rather than glass. Plath's metaphor for the institution was the glass bell jar, Roethke's the glass greenhouse. Yet for Sexton, the walls of the institution are not to be trusted to the patient; everything is a possible weapon to be used against the self. Dr. Martin, aloof to the inmates' suffering, is both enviable and despised. Sexton's use of the noun *boxes* suggests a camp bunk that is being policed by flashlights. Confinement of any sort, even prisons, is designed to keep a constant watch on the prisoners. But the boxes in which the patients sleep also imply a clinical system of classification that goes on in the hospital, which Sexton finds as demeaning as it is infantilizing:

> What large children we are
> here. All over I grow most tall
> in the best ward. Your business is people
> you call at the madhouse . . . Out in the hall
> the intercom pages you. You twist in the pull
> of the foxy children who fall
> like floods of life in frost.[10]

Here Sexton has made a definitive discovery: her doctor has his own life, and she cannot delude herself into believing that he exists only for her, as she does for him. Nevertheless, in "You, Doctor Martin," Sexton struggles to find a practical way to meet the institutional requirements that she be herself again, which to her means being self-recognizable or whole. She ends the poem with the realization of herself as she is now:

> Now I am myself,
> counting this row and that row of moccasins
> waiting on the silent shelf.

The container for the self has changed from a box to a shelf, from something to be looked "into" to something that is kept, as in "put away" or displayed for consumption. Like the patients themselves, the moccasins are there to be inventoried (as in diagnosed and treated), so they can either be worn (as in released) or put back in storage. Sexton takes some pride in the fact that she has managed to produce a product—in the fullest sense. Dr. Martin's occupation, which is "therapy," has resulted in her being able to walk out of the madhouse on her own two feet.

In another poem that bears a similarity, or may even be an homage to Elizabeth Bishop's 1950 poem "Visits to St. Elizabeths" (a poem about visiting Ezra Pound during his long institutionalization) Sexton spends more time observing her fellow patients. In "Ringing the Bells," she describes a ward of patients so used to confinement that their responses are instinctual. Psychiatry was to help the individual to better adapt to the social environment. The individual is no longer an entity by or through which the environment is measured or conformed to. The patient must adapt to the simulated normalcy of the institution itself. As Sexton reveals:

> And this is the way they ring
> the bells in Bedlam
> and this is the bell-lady
> who comes each Tuesday morning
> to give us a music lesson . . .
> we are the circle of crazy ladies . . .
> and smile at the smiling woman
> who passes us each a bell,
> who points at my hand
> that holds my bell, E-flat . . .
> and this is the small hunched squirrel girl
> on the other side of me
> who picks the hairs over her lip,
> who picks the hair over her lip all day,
> and this is how the bells really sound . . .
> and although we are no better for it,
> they tell you to go. And you do.[11]

Indeed, it is a tragic but comic view of the mentally disturbed patients trying to orchestrate a little harmony among the noisiness of their instruments, something like being buzzing bees, that cannot help themselves. The speaker's bell is "E-flat", which she rings automatically, and with the sterility of a mechanical doll. Although the music teacher is not a doctor, the patient is trying to be compliant and to please her, to meet her gaze with the proper image she imagines the teacher desires. The music teacher represents the authoritative gaze that is ever present in the ward and by which the subject tries to recognize herself being seen and sanctioned. "Fitting in" for the mental patient is a matter of synchronizing her thoughts and reproducing obedient patterns that have already been established to guide her as a responsible person. As Lacan writes, the authoritative gaze is ever-present in the ward, just as it is in normal society. Of all the objects in which the subject may recognize his dependence in the registrar of desire, the gaze is specified as inapprehensible. That is why the gaze is so misunderstood because the subject manages 'to symbolize his own vanishing in the illusion of the consciousness of *seeing oneself see oneself*, in which the gaze is elided.'"[12] Hence, the poet's task is precisely this: to envision herself as an object outside of herself (one that can be normative) and to appraise herself favorably, or unfavorably, according to that perspective.

In the case of "Ringing the Bells," Sexton has responded to the hand that responds to the lady who points at her and tells her what she should be, what sound she should make, what part she should play. Although this is not a particularly sonorous note, or even an unusual one, Sexton manages to let the music teacher (the "bell" or "hell" lady) manipulate her. In keeping with the institutional mentality, she is nothing but what she does in accordance to the rules: she is E-flat, "untroubled and clean / as a workable kitchen." Being E-flat, neutralized and functional, her "bells" (the singing in her head) have been properly tamed and can be used as utensils. She is now the facilitator of her own life, a sign that she is getting "well" and can return to her proper position in the household.

Poems about confinement in mental hospitals are talking poems. They are often odysseys of self-reflection as well as of self-refraction. And they invite the reader to enter into the world of the patient and to share his image of reality. Poets such as Lowell, Sexton, and Plath often use the image of the glass, greenhouse, the mirror, or the bell jar to express their ongoing confusions about the poem as a reflector of self-identity, yet a problem to be overcome. What happens in the mirror of the poem, as well as the image of the mirror in the poem, helps the patient to see herself as a coherent entity rather than an arbitrary mass of disconnected fragments and bodily movements. Although the structuring of identity in a personal poem is far from being "real," it supports and solidifies a poet's difference from the self she has just purported to be real on the page. If the poet can eliminate the possibility of that self being authentic, he or she gains more credibility as a self by slipping through it.

For example, at the end of Sexton's treatment, or in the second half of the book *To Bedlam and Part Way Back*, Sexton begins her trip back into the outside world with a poem about a mirror. In "For John, Who Begs

Me Not to Enquire Further,"¹³ Sexton addresses John Holmes, a friend and poet who begged her to not go further in using her own pain and personal material for making poetry. But Sexton was set on using her private experience as a content for her formal excursions. She had an understanding that she could not give her reader anything outside of herself as content; that she would be a human demonstration of an "accident of hope." Poetry could not tell the tragic story without one's tapping one's own head, and feeling its fragility: "it is a small thing / to rage in your own bowl."¹⁴

The bowl, of course, is the poem, a private space in which one sees one's self. In the same poem, she uses another glass to say something about her confinement and the uses of psychotherapy. Being in the institution gave her a sense of order, "something worth learning / in that narrow diary of my mind, in the commonplaces of the asylum / here the cracked mirror /or my own selfish death / outstared me."¹⁵ Being "outstared" by the death that is selfish to claim her life as something for itself, Sexton has learned that it will always be a part of her and that it will outlast her trying to understand herself. Still, it is the poet's job to peer into it, even to make peace with its ferocity.

Elizabeth Bishop's "Visits to St. Elizabeths,"¹⁶ surveys the interior grounds of the hospital, through the nursery rhyme meter of "This Is the House that Jack Built," which is reminiscent of Sexton's "Ringing the Bells" (again a pun on the name or signature of the poet: for a sexton rings the church bells proficiently). It is no accident that *Elizabeth* is both the name of the poet and the name of the saint presiding over the insane patients who have become accustomed to their confinement. This is the house that Jack built and that got away from Jack. While visiting Ezra Pound, she tours the sanitarium's residents, but she cannot accurately make out their meanings and certainly cannot detach one patient's story from another's because they all seem to share a common thread: one is a sailor, another a Jew, another a cranky man, all are constantly migrating from place to place because they are locked within their own minds that, from the point of view of the institution, are minds "unlocked." The central metaphor is the "watch," which is a pun on the idea of *being watched* by the speaker and by the supervisors who are watching the speaker watch the patients.

In Bedlam and in St. Elizabeths, patients live in time suspended; there is no going backward or forward completely; instead medication makes them frozen, terrifyingly dulled and inert. These are minds, like the "stuffed loon" in Bishop's "First Death in Nova Scotia," which have taken "the bullet" and have been comatose for years—like the loon, they "hadn't said a word."¹⁷ The loon (here, the pun is explicit), keeps council on its white, frozen lake, a metaphor for the marble-topped table. Like the lobotomized, or cataleptic patient, the loon's insides have been removed so that it can remain on proper display, petrified, and tame. It has been a trophy for Uncle who snatched it from its ordinary habitat to make it a part of his own. For Bishop and for Sexton, the doctors snatch their patients and put them inside confines where they can control them and fill them with ideas about what is normal or abnormal. Indeed, the taxidermy analogy holds: the loon has taken a "bullet" just as a patient takes a pill or a treatment that renders him catatonic and yet his crazy, frantic, or erratic thoughts fly elsewhere.

In Bishop's depiction of Bedlam, the patients are "wound up" like watches and then let loose to spin out. They only simulate the normal or the sane; narcotics have "flattened" their moods, made them shapeless and contingent on one another for their own definitions and diagnoses. One fantasy world merges into another; and the visitor begins to construct her own reality, her own poem, out of the various realities and delusions of the residents. Like "Jack's house," the madhouse is built, incrementally, board by board, nail by nail. To create it, there must be an inside and an outside, the one looking from within his cage, and the one looking at him "within" from the outside. Repetition is key in sestinas (one of Bishop's favorite forms to work in), but things get confused and reused as they do with the constructing of any poem, particularly one that uses the refrain as a kind of step in the process. In "Visits to St. Elizabeths" Bishop mocks the idea of order or continuity in a place that has purposely deprived its patients of any sensation or novelty in life. The poem recycles its own history, just as the patients are locked, obsessively, into the grooves of their own thoughts that are now as anachronistic and absurdly displaced as they themselves are. It is always the same pattern, the same level of doom.

This is the house that Jack built. The stanzas, like levels of stairs, seem not to be able to bear the human weight that they must be strong enough to stable; and the house is in danger of catastrophic collapse. As Bishop writes:

> This is a world of books gone flat.
> This is a Jew in a newspaper hat
> that dances weeping down the ward
> under the creaking sea of board . . . [18]

The "Jew in a newspaper hat" is a compelling image because the poem is written in 1950, concurrent with the discovery of the concentration camps. The Jew's hat is worn like a "lampshade" on his head, only it is constructed from the news. Bishop's indictment of the "sane" is implicit in the incongruity of a Jew in a newspaper hat and the discovered actualities of Nazi Germany's barbarians in the years immediately after the liberation.

Sylvia Plath's portrait of "Miss Drake" is also about how patients try to preserve their cohesive identities even in their deluded state. The poem is representative of the hospital poem, which allows the speaker-observer to separate herself from competing realities that are either too threatening or too alien to the fragile ego. The poem about the institution is often a poem about looking and seeing *what is being looked at* in ways that will reveal for the patient her own sense of the "real" through the discerning of comparative boundaries. One sees one's self as through the bars of one's cage or through the barred windows of the hospital room; through what one is not, as much as what one is.

"Miss Drake Proceeds to Supper"[19] was written in 1956 during Plath's first hospital stay after her suicide attempt. The poem is a sardonic example of a male literary tradition, particularly, Pound's "Portrait of a Lady." Miss Drake seems genuinely affected as a woman of means for whom appearances signify success. Although she is obviously mobbed by delusions that torture and demean her every move, she upholds, for the sake of being seen, her dignified stance. To the observer, she is not where she appears to be; she has, or rather her mind has, migrated elsewhere.

Plath takes particular notice of this "new woman in the ward" whose

> footing sallow as a mouse
> Between the cabbage-roses
> Which are slowly opening furred petals
> To devour and drag her down
> Into the carpet's design.[20]

Miss Drake gives Plath, as a patient speaking from within the asylum, the luxury of looking out at the "insideness" of Miss Drake's psychosis which has made the immediate world a danger for both women. Miss Drake's mind has been shattered beyond repair; she is only "adazzle with bright shards / of broken glass," and testing the air is excruciatingly painful. Miss Drake is a good example of a fragile mind that has been caught by the inverted glass container of Plath's bell jar. Like a butterfly or an insect, Miss Drake is a specimen that will be seen through the distorted lens of those who view her from the outside—her doctors, her relatives, and fellow inmates. They will see her trapped there going about her business just as she would if she had not been caught by the glass jar.

In such a context, Miss Drake will be expected to accept her contrived routines as if they were natural to her, that this really is not a "loony bin," but a villa or a hotel. She proceeds to supper as if it is an occasion, or even an ordination. One cannot dismiss the possibility that Plath is playing with the Last Supper motif to suggest Miss Drake's exemplary martyrdom. She seems pierced by sharp objects that assail her

from everywhere: "She can see in the nick of time / How perilous needles grain the floorboards / and outwit their brambled plan. . . ."[21] Miss
Drake feels that some plot is being planned against her and overesti-
mates her importance.

Yet, Miss Drake—with "webbed foot" alights into the patients'
dining room as if she were a drake among ducks. Although Miss Drake's
paranoia, her wary breath, makes her hallucinate, she is dignified in her
attempt to comply with the rules of her supervision, her outer cage. The
poem's elevated diction conjures up both the frailness and peril that per-
vades the mental institution, its bizarre accompaniment of delusions and
nightmares on each ward. However, the iambic meter of the poem is exact,
ordered, tedious in its attention to craft. Where order is exact and routines
methodically followed, the patients seem robotic and desensitized. They are
not so much "fixed" as they are pieced together.

In "Evening in the Sanitarium"[22] Louise Bogan adopts a long lop-
ing line, reminiscent of the quiet incidence of Eliot's "The Love Song of J.
Alfred Prufrock" or "Preludes" when the evening is drawn out and the
mentally ill negotiate who they are as patients and residents in the sanitarium with whom they were on the outside and how much of the former
identity can be preserved in a context in which psychiatry is trying to alter
them in ways that will help them to rehabilitate their injuries and reenter a
normal society. On the other hand, the mental institution is simply an
extension of the sane world in its superficial elements. Rewards are given
to the patients who comply with the rules of conduct, who use their time
productively by engaging in tedious games that distract them from painful
afflictions or delusions:

> The free evening sky fades, outside the windows fastened with
>   decorative iron grilles.
> The lamps are lighted; the shades drawn, the nurses are
>   Watching a little.
> It is the hour of the complicated knitting on the safe bone
>   needles . . .
> The deadly game of chess; the book held up like a mask.[23]

The poem is from the perspective of the observer, the one who is
transparent to the reader, who leads the reader on a tour of the mad and
brings no attention to herself. The occupants are frozen poses of diagnosis:
"the manic-depressive girl / Now leveling off, one paranoiac afflicted with
jealousy, / Another with persecution. Some alleviation has been possible."
The speaker then turns to address the patients directly. "O lucky older wife,
who has been cured of feeling unwanted." She will return to her hollow
and unfulfilling routine of being a normal housewife: "To the suburban
railway station you will return, return, / To meet forever Jim home on the
5:35. / You will be normal and selfish and heartless as anybody else."[24]

Inside the languid sanitarium, things will be ordered in ways that will help them to maintain themselves as if by remote control. Everything is predictable and on schedule. Rehabilitation will be slow, but will end successfully with the patient's return to a world that is ambiguous and ever waiting like death. "Mrs. C. again feels the shadow of the obsessive idea. / Miss R. looks at the mantel-piece, which must mean / something."[25] Like Plath's speaker, this speaker is unobtrusive; and yet, she has a clear inkling that behind the masks of lobotomized placidity (some of them induced by narcotics or electroshock therapy) there lurks a human mystery that cannot be solved. Madness in Bogan's purview, is not so different from creativity and from the process of writing a poem. We look for symbols everywhere. On the mantle, we assume there is a figurine or a clock; a symbolic object that signifies something more than it is. It too, has its own hidden reality, which is not the spectator's, but is contingent on the spectator's ability to interpret its meaning. The poem then ends with a metaphor for psychiatry as a discipline and treatment for what ails these patients, but what may, in fact, ail all of us to one degree or another.

Lowell's *Life Studies* assays the effects of confinement in a variety of ways, including his imprisonment as a conscientious objector to World War II, but foregrounds his hospital poems. In Lowell's poem "Waking in the Blue,"[26] which is about literal confinement in a mental institution, Lowell graphically describes the hospital experience beginning with the night attendant, a "B.U. sophomore, whose mind is doubly removed" from the reality of the place as he absorbs himself in the philosophical text, '*The Meaning of Meaning*.'" For the depressed Lowell, the "Azure day / makes [his] agonized blue window bleaker." The only thing he can see is through the window, and the withstanding affability of the day makes a rude comparison with his own mood. "This is the house for the 'mentally ill.' Where is my sense of humor?"

To distract himself, Lowell becomes his own observer. Art provides him an alternative to loneliness—because he can entertain himself with the other patients and their apparent psychoses. And similar to Bishop and Plath, he observes a gallery of deluded patient-actors who masquerade as "victorious figures of bravado ossified young." They are playing at life as a kind of beaux tableau within the institution, but they are *not* carefree imposters. This is no game. They are indigenous to the place that has isolated them as social outcasts. Once divided into old-timers and new colonizers, the hospital population understands this is purgatory, an outer office to hell. "We are old-timers, / each of us holds a locked razor."[27]

The poem ends with the speaker before the "metal shaving mirrors," where he sees

> . . . the shaky future grow familiar
> in the pinched, indigenous faces
> of these thoroughbred mental cases,
> twice my age and half my weight. . . .

What he sees is the future of his own regression, increase in years, decrease in mass; the men who inhabit the asylum are "thoroughbred mental cases"; they have become the pure form of the disease. They present with symptoms with which the doctors are well acquainted, but they do not know how to treat except to keep them confined and out of reach of the blade with which they could cut their own throats. Each patient is depressed enough to be suicidal, although he may not be existentially motivated. He has been locked into the mortifying existence of waiting for his life to be over, and yet locked out of the chance of liberating himself from it.

Lowell's earlier poem "In the Cage" is concerned with the perspective of the observer from within, rather than the outsider who is initiated into "the box" or the prison. Inside the prison, "The lifers file into the hall / According to their houses—two / of laundered denim.[28] The dehumanizing aspect of the lifers is in how they are contained by visible and invisible boundaries: the hall, the houses, the garb; the walls that inscribe him and do not let him out. "Life" is an existential labor for the "lifer" who does time as something distinct from life, the way the canary sings, distinct from any pleasure of meaning.

The poem's form replicates a sense of framing: strict rhythmic order; there are eight syllables per line and a consistent meter. Yet, there is chaos within this order, as the inmates' regimen is continually interrupted by the sounds of prison life that escape the metrical "bars" of the poem, shattering the poem's metrical hold over its own anarchy of content:

> . . . On the wall
> a colored fairy tinkles blues,
> and twitters by the balustrade,
> Canaries beat their bars and scream.[29]

The second part of the poem refers to the prisoners who rise up from "tunnels with spades / In mud and insulation." Their work is upward from the depths; a vision of hell. Here, the pacifists must suffer martyrdom for their resistance; they must suffer for Adam's sin: "the night blackens the heart of Adam. Fear, the yellow chirper, beaks its cage." Fear makes the canary "beak" or gnaw at its own cage, as if fear is something that announces its perimeters but cannot manage to escape them; fear is something that is locked within and cannot escape itself. What blackens the heart of Adam is pressing in, the bars of the cage, or the space infiltrating the bars that promise by contrast another kind of illusionary freedom.

Which is the real prison? The mind or the institution: the bars of the cage or the space infiltrating the bars?

Lowell's view of confinement in an early manuscript poem shows confinement through a different perspective. Instead of looking out, the prisoner is looking in; he is approaching the prison. On the bus, "Puerto Ricans scratched their crotches / with handcuffed hands."[30] Yet the surroundings of the prison imitate pastoral confections: "some artificial lakes / a scarlet canoe." Although Danbury is an imposing structure, it is somehow welcoming: "the country club / our model prison." The cement building was as "functional / as my fishing tackle box."

The comparison of the institution (both the jailhouse and mental hospital) with a fishing tackle box hints at the implements of the masculine enterprise; the mind is tricking itself; the poet is intent on seeing himself *see himself* through a gaze that will allow him to function within the novel environment. He fantasizes encountering a "hospitable" country club rather than an "inhospitable" prison. The tackle box, like the prison cell, the metered poem, has everything one needs to perform a task within a contained structure. The task is to view the implements of one's mind as that which can be reassembled through rehabilitation, then put back in the box in orderly parts or pieces.

Like psychoanalysis, confessional poetry involves a complicated interplay of subject interpositions. The poet's search for himself within the poem, similar to the patient's talk in therapy, is often a regressive and self-perpetuating *mirage*, always contingent on the gaze that sees it from the outside, the silent interlocutor who hears the poet's or patient's confession. As subjects, we are always voices within voices, boxes within boxes, cages within cages. In Lowell's poem "Thanksgiving's Over," Lowell's narrator, feeling guilt at having his wife committed, recognizes that he is not only complicit in her imprisonment, but also that it is his as well. He cannot escape her purview from which he ultimately judges himself:

"Thanksgiving's Over" begins with an epigraph:

> Thanksgiving night, 1942: a room on Third Avenue.
> Michael dreams of his wife, a German-American Catholic,
> who leapt from a window before she died in a sanatorium.[31]

As the poem proceeds, we learn that the first voice in the poem belongs to the dead wife, returning to her husband in a dream. In the wife's narration, Lowell uses some of the same symbols for the confinement experience as he had already employed in "In the Cage":

> I heard
> the birds inside me, for I knew the Third

> Person possessed me, for I was the bird
> Of Paradise, the parrot whose absurd
> Garblings are glory.[32]

The wife's chaos is compelled by her confinement in a mental world and exacerbated by her physical confinement, which does not allow her to do anything but parrot the voices of inner and outer authorities. Lowell then layers the confinement in this poem with the wife possessed or contained by a "third person," a reference to the Holy Spirit and a pun for Lowell himself as the actual voice behind the speech. Moreover, the wife's voice is an inner occupant within the larger structure of the voice that is related to us by her husband who is dreaming the voice. Her voice is compelling because it speaks a language separate from the narrator's; rather, *it is an expression of the narrator's subconscious*, a garbling of bird sounds, lower and more immediate than signifying speech.

In a complex layering of confining images, Lowell, as poet, is responsible for the sanity of the narrator and his relation to his wife's madness. The only references to bars in this poem come from the narrator's voice, a porous boundary between the confined and the madness of voices that cannot be confined:

> And the bars
> Still caged her window—half a foot from mine,
> It mirrored mine:
> My window's window.[33]

The window only gains its definition, as a window, through the consciousness of the artist who designates it a window, a view; otherwise it is merely an opening through the wall. For the poet, it is always a question of the view of the viewer: the difference between seeing and looking. Consciousness has to pierce through the obdurate surface to begin to organize chaos into a totality that means something; and yet, this too, is an illusion that belies the garble of bodily experience. The narrator's view never opens without being mirrored back and inward; and yet it is not a static view, but part of the flowing dynamic of all synchronistic views together from which it, like the signifier that comes forward from all language possibilities, distinguishes itself.

In this poem, Lowell uses a reflection in a window or mirror, to reveal the truth of the narrator's situation. Only the caging of the bird necessitates the release of the voices, otherwise they have no active need to escape. The subconscious that is now identified with the wife (the Otherness within), hears the voices of those birds pent up within her and can do nothing to restrain them: "Bars / Shielded her vigil-candle," "The bars / Crashed with her"; "her eyeballs—like a lion at the bars."

The caged predatory animal is a metaphor for the wife's vigilant stare outward, her anger at her guards. Her leaping is like the voices that refuse to be constrained, the surplus of feeling that demands the narrator's putting up the bars. While the subconscious voice of the wife is in constant need of releasing the voices, the narrator is constantly aware of the bars that will mollify them. The poem ends with the narrator sitting with his rosary beads, grinding them to nothingness. The voices are now silent on the point of forgiveness, a hollowness more unshakable than silence itself.

"Thanksgiving's Over" is a dark poem and, in some ways, it reflects the erosion and interminable flux that troubled Lowell throughout his life and career. *Life Studies* was centered on Lowell's autobiographical experiences and memories. In "For the Union Dead"[34] Lowell's sardonic, comedic point of view assails the dignity of the static war monuments by juxtaposing it with the city's panting overconstruction and maniacal fatigue. Old tourist sites such as the city have been replaced by the building of a labyrinth of "underworld" parking garages. The poem begins he imagines "Behind their cage / yellow dinosaur" steamshovels "grunting / as they cropped up tons of mush and grass / to gouge their underworld garage."

To live in such a context is to be hollow, burned, and stale, to be part of the ash heap, or the ditch. Lowell animates the memorial statues to see them for what they are—excuses for a public dedication in which William James is present. Yet the symbolic meanings of their sacrifice of life has come to a dead standstill in policy: static reform, hollow gestures. "Their monument sticks like a fishbone / in the city's throat. / Its Colonel is as a lean / as a compass-needle," we may assume, pointing the way. In Lowell's view, the Colonel chooses life and dies, leading his black soldiers to death; he is inflexible ("he cannot bend his back").

As the poem continues, Lowell makes clear the juxtaposition between a city's war memorial and the meaning of the soldiers' fixity in stone—with the aging of the observer, they become younger "each year" and they no longer battle with their muskets, but "doze" and "muse." It is a matter of interpretation: now the poet sees their presence as fraudulent history; they are cast in the realm of aesthetic apprehension and meaningless. The object is not merely what the viewer sees and discerns, but the object is what stares back at the viewer, and turns all inquisition about one's world back on one's self. Speculation ends with images of confinement: receptacles of servitude—the slaves that have never been freed from their bronze stones, the ditch that the father of Colonel Shaw prefers as a monument to his son who was "lost with his niggers." Lowell's derisive use of the noun *niggers* emphasizes the absurdity of the situation: Colonel Shaw's father cannot see the travesty in using that word. In a surreal moment, the television set that contains the drained faces of the Negro schoolchildren who "rise like balloons" with their faces unanchored, are the bubbles that contain Colonel Shaw. History will not allow "the blessed break" that would cease to perpetuate him as a martyr.

From Lowell's perspective, the urns or vessels are constant reminders of crypts and graves. The aquarium, now a grave for the fish, embanked in a "Sahara of snow", neither being inhabitable; the fish once compliant, but active, now only ghosts, phantoms, unrealizable. From the rectangle of the building to the antiquated tanks, which are "airy dry," the speaker rotates his gaze to reflect on the rectangular fence of the Commons. Watching the steamshovels as prehistoric animals that emerged from the sea, Lowell knows that civilization's progress is really regressive— that the honor and monuments are not really about perpetuating life but about life's leveling extinction. It is a bleak moment that he shares with the "Union Dead."

Finally, in the late poem "Shoes," from Lowell's "Hospital" series in *The Dolphin*, the poet returns to the function and meaning of the institution as a metaphorical framework for exploring human existence and its endless paradoxes. The mental institution forces the patient to regard life from the perspective of its being worth living or not. In these moments, the patient is not unlike the philosopher; neither one is more mad than the other in expressing the futility of living with pain and without a meaning for why pain should be endured. But of course, Lowell is a Catholic; his suffering is significant and universal, although he cowers at the thought that this is all there is to redeem us.

In the poem, Lowell depicts an overpopulated ward where the confined are limited in their options. "Too many go express to the house of rest / buffooning to-froing on the fringe of being, / one foot in life and little right to that [. . .]."[35] After more than twenty years of regular attacks of mania that could only be controlled by straightjackets, Lowell seems not to be taking this confinement too seriously. He is used to the routine: from crack up to the supervisor's "crack down" on those who would ignore the rules. He now finds that being thrown together with fellow patients is an absurd equation that only the doctors could think up in their overpracticality. His fellow patients are crazy like he is, and require the same kind of treatment, and yet they are absolutely distinct in their reasons for being there. To be lumped together in a ward is always to beg the question, "why? why have we been brought here together?" A few lines later, Lowell observes, "'Where I am not', we chime, 'is where I am.'" The lunatic has "lost his mind." It is not there, or wherever it is, it is not where it should be. The patients know the ward's routines, they say the same things, and they all have a sense of reality that does not correspond to reality. Although the patients are present in body, they are not really present at

all. They have escaped, just as if they had walked out on their own voli-
tion. As Lowell maintains:

> My shoes? Did they walk out on me last night
> And streak into the glitter of the blear?
> I see two dirty white punctured tennis shoes,
> Empty and planted on the one-man path.
> I have no doubt where they will go. They walk
> The one life offered from the many chosen.[36]

Lowell's shoes have walked out on him; they have in fact escaped,
or they have leapt to their standstill end, suicidal and punctured. The final
line reminds the reader that the main function of the mental hospital is to
preserve order by limiting options, to delineate and order time and space
as a means of controlling and instructing patients about conforming to
social norms. Lowell's shoes will be "planted on the one-man path" having
found freedom, but their fall from the window of the hospital room suggests that the leap toward freedom is an option that may also result in stale-
mate or death. Within the hospital ward, constraint is a concept that necessitates transgression. Suicide becomes a possibility that is offered as a way
"out" rather than chosen as an option for going someplace else. The entire
concept of confinement is to maintain control over the inmates. It is very
much like Beckett's *Waiting for Godot*, where the suicidal characters say
they will go, but do not move. And perhaps this is the confounding truth
that the mental patient confronts when looking at the barred windows that
keep him from leaping; suicide is not chosen; it is merely a way of undoing, of stalling where one already is.

13

ASYLUM
A Personal Essay

Treatments for mental illness during the twentieth century included psychotherapy in conjunction with hydrotherapy, vitamins, physical restraint, insulin therapy, and electroshock therapy. Hospitals modeled on McLean (where Lowell and Sexton were treated) were overcrowded and bureaucratic. Patients agreed to go into the hospitals for extensive diagnostic tests or sought a safe haven that would help them avoid their destructive or self-destructive behaviors. Writing about being inside the mental institution has the potential for metaphorically releasing locked wards within the mind of the patient or former patient, even retrospectively.

With my chapter on Bedlam in the background, what follows is a memoir about my struggle with depressive anxiety in the early 1970s. My goal in writing this piece was to try to demonstrate how a narrative could offer its own absolution. Perhaps Freud himself knew best of the power of revived narratives as a means of relieving symptoms displaced to the "somas." As Alan Stone writes:

> In some sense, what all schools of psychoanalytic therapy have in common is a developmental, historical account of the individual. We may disagree about which events are critical, but we agree that the individual's narrative is important in treating the individual's psychopathology.[1]

Stone goes on to suggest that Freud's theories helped to give people convincing "self-descriptions" so that they could comprehend better their personal histories from the perspective of their present suffering. The construction and ordering of those painful narratives are what much of psychoanalysis is about. Telling stories about ourselves and about others, to ourselves and to others, is the most natural and earliest way in which we organize our experience and our knowledge. It is not surprising that psychoanalysts now recognize that identity implicates narrative, "neurosis" being a reflection of either an insufficient, incomplete, or inappropriate story about one's self.

In writing this memoir, I wanted to reconcile my history as a former patient with my work as a reader of Freud. I hope this will not be considered a confessional piece, but rather a work that frankly discusses depressive anxiety when it becomes most unmanageable. Even years after a patient recovers, he has difficulty in removing, even anatomically, the symptom from the treatment, the Jekyll from the Hyde.[2] As Judith Herman has revealed in *Trauma and Recovery* and Kay Jamison has so eloquently expressed in *An Unquiet Mind*, symptoms of mental illness are often half-wishes and half-denials of the afflicted body, symptoms that call attention to and deflect away from themselves.

(Narratives, like elegies, open wounds to the air and begin the healing process. They help to negotiate the space between feeling and naming; they help people who have undergone painful experiences to warm themselves back into existence.)As I have tried to show in the essay on Gilman, Freud intended it to be this way when he remarked, "What we have to do is . . . to lead the patient's attention back from his symptom to the scene in which and through which that symptom arose; and, having thus located the scene, we remove the symptom by bringing about, during the reproduction of the tramatic scene, a subsequent correction of the psychical course of events which took place at the time."[3]

June 1971
Dear Freud: My head aches with all the bullies of words. We say things more than once to keep them alive.

While I was growing up in that split-level house with the pink gingham curtains and the tar-sputtered driveway that always looked like a Rorschach test, Friday was my father's payday. So we would clamber into the ice-black Plymouth with the slashed-up upholstery and go to a restaurant. My mother, always tired, appreciated the time off. Aware of the formality of going out, she would take out her lipstick, smack her lips together, a waxy, tomato red, the safe signal for my father to back out of the driveway. Regardless of weather, my father rolled the window down and shoved out his elbow into the mulberry-scented breeze. *From the back seat, I watch the trees along the street undulate, reminding me of hula girls in an airline advertisement I'd seen once in a magazine.*

Those should have been good times for my family. But something was amiss, something that crouched in the ambiguity of our desperate feelings toward one another. My mother's social affect never matched her innermost pain and deprivation. So, when I saw her talking to neighbors on the porch, it always struck me that there was an odd incongruity between my mother's public face and her private one. I was thrown off balance by observing this; it gave me the same uncomfortable feeling that Italian movies dubbed into English did. *You know what they're saying, but it doesn't help. The words come out but the mouth never rests; never stops moving. It's like a puppet being jiggled by unseen strings. Mental illness hurts all the time. I am thinking again of my mother. My mother never drove and never learned to drive because she was afraid of hitting small children.*

We often drove to the Anchor Inn restaurant, built in the squashed-down shape of a lighthouse, where live lobsters were plunged into the sunny, gurgling tank next to the hostess stand. The hostess was Vivian. The tank was ostentatiously lit by light bulbs, where the lobsters floated so slowly they looked like undetonated orange bombs or missiles. Sometimes, in a lighter mood, I imagined they were languid water ballerinas with antennas. When I got older, Vivian told me the truth about the lobsters and what would eventually happen to them.

The truth was, she said, that the lobsters were displayed there so that the customers could pick out the ones they wanted to eat. Was it privilege or a delicacy; I could not decide which. On what basis would one choose? Such clumsy creatures—pushing their catatonic red-ant faces up to the glass, distorting my vision with their one-eyed fatal view—their jumbled claws and heavy roseate armors. Vivian, with her half-flip schizoid hairdo, sweeping a family of four to an open booth, assured me that boiling lobsters alive stunned them immediately. Because their backbones were somehow detached and exposed, they died in less than a minute. *When the time came around they'd feel no pain. Not feeling pain is always a comfort, I thought.*

Once, years earlier, after a period of depression, I took a kitchen knife from the silverware drawer and slit both wrists, but only superficially. Against the shadowy blue veins, the horizontal cut appeared white as a scrape. I could just make out the serrated edge of the knife as it imprinted the skin. When the blood came, I watched it spurt like ink out of a fountain pen. Then I recalled the time we went to Yellowstone Park and waited for Old Faithful to spout as she was expected to, like clockwork. That was 1970, a trip across country. We saw Navajo Indians there; we rode donkeys on a safe tourist path around the edge of the Grand Canyon and dared each other to look down. My mother bought a ceramic ashtray from a ninety-six-year-old potter who scratched her name on the clay bottom of each piece: Maria. My parents never suspected I wore long-sleeve shirts to hide the bandages I had put on.

At college, I began to have trouble sleeping, and my mind was reeling with unquiet thoughts; lights were always too bright, voices sounded like waves crashing. I began going weekly to the psychologist on staff at the college, Dr. Cimmeneti. I will never forget his stuttery name, *it sounded like cinnamon.* I told Dr. Cimmeneti that I was depressed and anxious. He was seated in a big black leather chair. He saw no reason to panic. But one day, I was riding up the escalator in Filenes's Basement, watching the people riding down, slower than we were. I saw a woman with an oversized hat, a teenager in a T-shirt, a couple riding two-astride the step in order to embrace. Then I saw a face that was not human. When we got to the bottom of the escalator, I could hear the bells of registers ringing, my sister mumbling something, but I kept saying, "There is a wolf on the escalator. I saw a wolf!" People kept swishing their shopping bags while my sister froze like a statue in the middle of the crowd, her mouth wide, as if she were playing freeze tag. How could you see a wolf? *What's the matter with you?* To my sister's horror, I sat down in front of everyone on one of the mannequin's stands and began to cry very publicly and very loudly. I still remember how dazed, indifferently aghast, the mannequin seemed to be in her premature spring outfit and bake-away flesh. I must have said to my sister something so cliché ridden, like "they're going to take me away."

Authorities alerted my parents later that day and things moved fast. I was sixteen years old, having skipped my senior year of high school. Skipping wasn't difficult to do in the moratorium years after Woodstock and Kent State when flower children recited fatigued ideology or just got stoned. My parents appeared at the hospital, always clumsier than other parents with my father's extra-large shoulders amplified by a coat and my mother's fussy stoutness. My father was unsure how to act; he just stooped with the humility of not being able to repair technical things. He was also angry, enraged, at me. *How could you do this, why are you trying to punish me? Why can't you be normal; we don't deserve this.* My sister, always called on to be more proper than the rest of us, put her elbows on her knees in one of the waiting room chairs and held her hands up to her ears as if she were shutting out the cold. My mother stayed bewildered and looked to my father to tell her how to feel.

At the hospital, we drifted with the same suspended animation as Vivian's lobsters did, waiting for some invisible net or hand to scoop us up. Psychiatric inpatients occupied the eighth floor, free to roam as far as the elevators and nurses' station. For the first few days, I stayed awake, afraid so I felt I had to keep watch. I was always afraid of prowlers as a child, but my mother said that there was always somebody on guard. *By the time the firemen go to sleep, she says, the milkman is up, delivering.* For years, I thought of the milkman like that—a knight or savior toting his bottles from one silver milk box to another, taking away the glass deposits.

Our wing had twelve patients. Maybe the pain at its worst is really a miracle in disguise because you know you are one of the fortunate ones who can still feel the difference. The body, like a cutting from a plant, has begun to seek survival from some foreign, but healthier soil. Having the sickness "out" means it has gone too far; you are held together the way a ceramic pot is held together once the wet clay is set. The way back to recovery is full of antipathy and concentration, and as I learned, for some, could be fatal.

I told my mother I was not crazy; she patted my hand, said I was just sick, there's nothing to be ashamed of in being sick; it's not like being crazy. My mother thought that craziness was mind over matter.

We did what we could, played cards, waited for the side effects of medications to wear off. Those days, there were lounges full of trembling or pacing patients in blue jeans or bathrobes, chain smoking; smoking was acceptable, so we smoked and smoked, extinguishing our cigarette butts in Styrofoam cups. Why were we here? The nurses seemed not to know. We monitored those same nurses behind the bulletproof glass, thinking we were the ones who were deaf because we could not hear them speaking to each other in their frigid Morse code.

The doctors tried out sample drugs such as Stellazine or Serax, drugs they give to 200-pound prisoners just to keep them in line. The drugs buffered the sharpness, but took away taste. Everything tasted like pennies. The doctors were detached, even harassed. We would go to our private appointments in their offices with the cockeyed Monet prints and myriad diplomas on the walls. The clock kept hammering down each hour in which sometimes we spoke, and sometimes we said nothing, but we were forced to sit there, being watched.

Back and forth we paced between two congregation rooms: one with plastic patio chairs and a couch shaped like a flamingo in which we sat heavily and watched television. Into the group therapy room in which we gathered at ten o'clock every morning, the doctor brought a video camera to tape our sessions and play them back to us.

To keep sane, I took notice of things, particularly outside the window, the way plants stalled and withered on the window ledge. I tried to reach out to the other patients who seemed to share some interest with me or who had been in psychiatric treatment before and seemed to know the ropes.

There was Sue, sixteen years old, who seemed, at least on the surface, more normal than anyone. She talked admirably, had Pollyanna stick-straight hair, and was extremely supportive of others. She was good at technical things; her father had showed her how to string boats in a bottle and she carried one or two in with her. I remember being transfixed by the idea of someone being able to do that, having such steady hands. What an odd thing: a boat that was captured in a bottle, that lay on one side, fitfully replicated and embalmed, a boat made of wood and straws and bits of authentic metal from real boats. On the bottle, an illegible note. We were all like that: delicately hinged on a skeletal thread, built back together a piece at a time, bottled up and corked full of transparent air, or thrown back in the fog waiting for rescue.

There was Alan, also sixteen, who had to see the psychiatrists privately and who had a kind of palsy that made him shake all the time, especially his hands. He had cut his wrists twice, burned his arms with a match. *Maybe the body is yourself until you hurt it. Then it becomes something else, entirely.* I do not remember how he came into the group. He spent a long time refusing to talk; he would just say his name. But after a week or two, the doctors pulled out of him a terrible rage toward his father, whom he blamed for his mother's barbiturate overdose. His father was his jailer, he said; but now he had waged war on the doctors. Once I saw Alan flip a heavy glass coffee table in therapy because the woman psychiatrist had snickered at him when he said, "Fuck you." She could not resist coming back with a sassy blow, so she said, "I'd like to see you try." *Very unprofessional, I would now judge. Why did she do that?* Forcibly put out, Alan disappeared down the long corridor. Alan felt he was justified in hating those who tortured him, and he was tortured, growing ghostlike and distant. One Saturday afternoon, he took a belt and hanged himself from a heating pipe that meandered over the plaster-skinned walls and ceiling. The hanging is not what killed him; he did not break his neck. He had taken a stash of his ten o'clock quaaludes just like his mother did. *Her name was something like "Happy" or "Sunny"; imagine that.*

Mickey had the bad secret. The doctors kept alluding to it: "the thing" that Mickey could not easily talk about. On one cool October day, a day when other high school seniors were horsing around the flagpole before the first bell of school, fifteen-year-old Mickey was telling the story yet again. She had tried to drown her baby brother in the toilet by stuffing his head down in the bowl until he choked. Now she heard voices; they told her she would burn for that. *She had read Joan of Arc; she had rehearsed the last soliloquy in her bedroom imagining the fires, lapping up from the wood. She believed in hell and Hail Marys. She was a Catholic girl who had been taught right from wrong.*

Each group therapy session was aimed at unearthing the unearthable. We all had sins; we all had to account for them. And so we talked and talked, sometimes in front of the video camera. Later, our confessions would then be played back to us. Sometimes the psychiatrist who led the group made a false start and played back the prior session in reverse; then we could see ourselves in the strangest light of a fast-forward recovery. We continued the histrionic replays that brandished the encouragement and approvals of the doctors. And when one of us flatly caved in on the industrial rug, we would all absurdly huddle over the fallen comrade, trying to cradle him in the numbness of our own zombielike pain.

Maybe we thought we had been caught in some horrible dream; the outside world became more distant and motionless like a watercolor of lilac and oak trees, confetti winks of blue-golden sky. From therapy session to therapy session, we went on monotonously, sedated or cranked up, emotionally flamboyant or locked-jawed, like grandfather clocks all chiming at different settings. The sleep-depressives mingled with the manics, the borderlines with the schizophrenics. I learned how to be the kind of sickness I was. *"What could I do, do, do?" My mother is saying this, but the words keep running after her lips, can't keep up (the needle is stuck on the arm of the phonograph). Every second is a second past, you can't hold what's already gone. She thinks I want to die; she doesn't know it's the world in my mind, not me, that feels like it's dying.*

In 1971 there were many diagnostic labels, but not so many that various patients could not be clumped together. We knew each other's classification, but did not mind mixing. The psychiatrists, bifocals dangling on chains, warned us that the line between psychosis and neurosis was the line between distinguishing "reality" from "delusions." For the psychotics, the way back would be longer and more onerous. The doctors vacillated between anger and pity. *Privilege or delicacy? The lady or the tiger?* The doctors' two emotions kept getting mixed up, and I never knew what to expect.

My doctor, Dr. Panicky, believed in hypnosis, which he explained as the purging of the original trauma through regression techniques. I would lie down on the cabbage-green couch, and he would swing a pocket watch over my head while I counted down from twenty and hyperventilated. Then he would take my hand and move it with his hand in some peculiar parody of an exorcism. I would wake up screaming in a fetal position. This would happen rhythmically and punctually three times a week. I still cannot read Kafka. I now understand that this technique is a distant descendent of Charcot's first experiments on hysterics. I was merely a casualty of some misreading of an old classical text handed down from some magistrate of the psychoanalytic establishment to this third-generation doctor, who was fond of cigars, sadistic puns, and marble paperweights. The doctor was board certified; my parents scraped together every dollar they could to pay for these treatments. *In the very, very far distance of a corner of the soundproof room, I still imagine I can feel the weight of his body, see myself wrestling off the bulk of this man with his red beard, chain watch, vest, and notepad.*

Twenty or thirty years ago, even the idea of seeing a psychiatrist, of being a "mental case" was a stigma, a repellent; it brought shame on the family, it was held hostage to the secrecy of relatives who did not want to intrude too much. After a series of visits to new psychiatrists, I found one whom I liked because she was a woman. She was a pale, lion-maned, portly woman who had wanted to be a surgeon, but women were not taken seriously as surgeons in the 1950s. She would hold her steady, crotchet-addicted fingers up to the light, and sigh longingly, "I would have made an excellent surgeon." Instead, she took up piano and went to concerts. Her third choice was to become a psychiatrist.

It may be surprising for some to hear that mental illness, like all biological phenomena, often comes in cycles such as the blooming of trop-ical plants. My doctor told me I could go back to school because there was nothing wrong with my brain. In graduate school, I became interested in reading psychoanalytic theory. I read Freud diligently and felt superior to my own condition. It was like having a new passport, a new allegiance, a new erudition. But only six years later, Freud has been discredited; the Library of Congress hesitates about putting up an exhibition of his work. The veracity of recovered memory has come under scrutiny of chemists and right-wing conservatives. Yet today I continue to be fascinated by the word *psychoanalysis*, as a theory, a treatment. Against my better reason, I still attend expert lectures on psychoanalysis. Watching diagrams go up on the blackboard, I think along the margins of my notes how shocked my psy-chiatrists would be to see me here, doctors who are by now old or dis-gruntled or dead. *But I am thinking again of the complexity of the wormy, spongelike brain, how once Descartes thought that the pineal gland was where the soul and body met (we gasped at the sight of it in seventh grade biology), how someone once held a plastic model of the brain up in front of me to show me precisely how fragile it was.*

We, who teach literature and psychoanalysis, are not sensitive enough to the kinds of assumptions our students make about the field. We should probably approach theory with the same sanguine humility Arctic explorers approach uncharted territories, realizing that our ownership claims are vast, but largely symbolic. For most patients suffering symp-toms, theory is simply beside the point. Perhaps we do not always want to have access to how cures work because somehow the mysticism surround-ing the cure is a comfort. Cures should be stronger than we are.

Psychoanalysis, as Freud conceived it, will never be divorced from the spoken narrative. What cannot be remembered will come back to us as a myth of the past, a cosmic pattern in the brain with its fatal imprint of the mad or sad gene, an inheritance of darkness. Once I believed that I could read the constellations of the stars by simply lying flat on the grass and looking up, drawing imaginary lines like the spokes of atomic mole-cules. I knew making them touch was impossible—miles separating what had now broken, silently and inexplicably, apart.

I hold in my hands the standard edition of Freud's works with Freud's 1921 photograph on the cover. Freud's eyes have the studious look that eyes do when the left does not precisely match the right; dark eyes, arched eyebrows, a receding hairline, an exquisitely shaped head. He is wearing a white shirt and overcoat, and I imagine he is uncomfortable, a little too replete in formal attire. His lapels are so very wide, fashionable. In another, more detailed photograph, on the cover of *Harvard Magazine*, Freud's features are more pronounced. He has at least two wavering worry lines on his forehead and a deep furrow as he concentrates. Again the dark eyes, unequivocally black, differ from one another. The right eye is winsome, imperious, unfazed. The left eye is terrorized, afflicted, astonished at what it sees.

In this photograph he has posed with a cigar between his pointer and middle fingers as if it were a smoldering pen. On the second button of his worsted wool vest, I see a gold watch chain that probably slips into an undisclosed pocket. The lead article asks: "Freud's Vision: Psychoanalysis failed as science. Will it survive as art?" My eyes keep moving over the words: psychoanalysis *failed*. Freud's birthplace: Frieberg in Moravia, a place that changed allegiances during and after the war. My father was born in Hungary.

Shift to a memory: I am riding again in the back of my father's black Plymouth, listening to the radio crackling a Broadway tune. It's payday again. My mother is in the front seat, with her new bouffant hairdo looking out the window and reading signs off gas stations or new shopping center stores. She is aimless, withdrawn. My father is talking about head shrinkers, and he is laughing, mocking. His Hungarian accent is pronounced. He says he has never heard of such crap; "head shrinkers," they're all quacks. I am imagining a laboratory of heads shrinking. I am imagining the doctors now cradling them in the palms of their hands.

14

SIGNIFYING PAIN

Recovery and Beyond

In Hall's poem "Affirmation," the poet avers the pure and simple fact that "to grow old is to lose everything." Although we do not choose to look at the inevitability of loss, we glimpse it somehow, in the everydayness in which things move away or sink beyond rescue:

> To grow old is to lose everything.
> Aging, everybody knows it.
> Even when we are young,
> we glimpse it sometimes, and nod our heads
> when a grandfather dies. . . .
> Then we row for years on the midsummer
> pond, ignorant and content. But a marriage,
> that began without harm, scatters
> into debris on the shore. . .
> Let us stifle under mud at the pond's edge
> And affirm that it is fitting
> and sweet to lose everything.[1]

Such a sentiment prompts a rereading of Thomas Hardy's "Transformations"[2] where the truth of loss—of what surrenders or dies—is resurrected in another form: "A ruddy human life / Now turned to a green shoot." In Hall's poem, mud is the constituent of water and earth, dissolving and eradicating the differences between what something is made up of and what is made up from something. What we hold most dear to us is impermanent. This is the normal flow of life. Still, what is lost to us will not fail to fill a void, although it may be unrecognizable at first. In "Transformations," Hardy meditates on the long blossoming of the spirit into earth and earth back into spirit: the beloved "fair girl" has entered "this rose" and so, Hardy consoles himself, the dead are not "underground" but are apt to "feel the sun and rain, / And the energy again / That make them what they were!"

But such fantasies cannot completely eradicate our human fears about mutability. As Olds writes, "I don't want things to be lost. In the poems that I have written about the dead, I just want them to come back. With love poems, I want them to live."[3] In the works of the writers I have discussed, signifying pain is the mortal dilemma, an admixture of the extremes of human pain and joy, the one ushering in the other. For the students in my creative writing classes, even at nineteen or twenty years old, writing becomes a "Pandora's box" in which the unconscious is made accessible, surprising them with the untold story of their own lives, helping them to cross the threshold of years.

Indeed, one of the points I have tried to emphasize is that psychoanalysis has given us a lantern with which we may delve into the darkness of our psyches and examine the artifacts of our past history to make sense of the influence it has had on our present lives. Psychoanalysis, even in its determinism, rests in the belief that ancient wounds can be healed if we choose not to hide from ourselves. When psychoanalysis is paired with writing, certain universal truths become evident—such as the human need to be recognized and held in esteem, and the need to accuse when wronged. I have compared the reader to one who hears and absolves confession, and the writer to a confessor of guilt and shame. Shame is different from guilt. Shame, as Young-Bruehl proposes, is the effect of thwarted expectations we all have from birth for being loved, to be cherished.[4] Self-esteem unfolds in a person's image of herself, which extends out and into the world but is never fixed or finished. In its nostalgia for a perfect union of infant and caretaker, "to be sweetly and indulgently loved,"[5] the ego casts itself in the light of the Other, but is sometimes disappointed, flung down into the darker shapes of shadow. Love that is rejected can rebound into the mooring of self-absorption and withdrawal, an inwardness and paralysis.

Writing becomes a way out, a path that may not just be the writer's way out, but may be the path for others. Although it disturbs us to hear about things that break, what Olds calls "the human agreement," things that are appalling, we perhaps empathize more profoundly with others' grief and sadness as we would want others to empathize with our own.

If shame is an effect of our perceived failure to be loved in the way we hoped to be, then guilt arises from the harm we do to others; or as Des Pres has argued, the guilt of simply being present to a crime and doing nothing to stop it. "Metaphysical guilt" is the lack of absolute fellowship with the human being as such, resulting from a witness' simply being present to an occurrence that, from all moral perspectives, should have been prevented. We are rarely guilty about doing harm to ourselves; but depression and guilt *are* harmful, especially when they are bottled up. Writing can help to ease tensions through the mediation of language, the converting of emotions into words and imagery. Confessional writing, personal writing and expressive writing, are not forums for self-pity or self-indulgence as some critics have charged; they are forums for appeal and absolution. Through personal writing, we give birth to ourselves.

Yet writing is inherently a social act; we have learned from psychoanalysis, particularly from Fanon, that there is no difference between the individual and the social world to which he relates. Rich has argued a similar parable concerning women subjected to the desires of men and patriarchy. Self-esteem begins in the pupil of the eye of the other in whom we seek a perfect mirror of ourselves. Fear and hatred are convoluted forms of desire that negatively influence our social and political world, negative projection that can be so detrimental to group solidarity begins with individual character. Hatred is, in many instances, a species of self-loathing, directed on a target rather than expending it on one's self. As Young-Bruehl characterizes the psychic causes or ideologies of desire cordoned off and circulating around racism and homophobia in *The Anatomy of Prejudices:* ". . . different prejudices are characteristic of different psychic or character types and different social conditions promote different character types and their corresponding prejudices. . . ."[6]

We are not only our own keepers, but each other's. When we write, we signify not only for ourselves, but also *for the other*. Language belongs to no one person, but to a social world; it is representative of we who seek to represent ourselves. Olds speaks for us all when she says, "We come from the wilderness of our selves. We are humans crying out, crying out to one another."[7] *Compassion* means "to suffer with" and requires an imaginative entry into the world of another's pain, closing the distance between solitariness and communion. Poetry must mediate our culture through the best examples of personal strength and weakness and, even in the bleakest circumstances, embrace life without reserve. As Octavio Paz comments, "Facing death the spirit is life, and facing the latter, death."[8] Writers speak so others should speak.

Although psychoanalysis began as a therapy for the individual whose intensity of suffering warranted medical intervention, and although it made some errors along the way, it has also opened a dialogue for examining cultural and political issues, which are necessary to change. Social problems have psychological roots and all intervention begins with examining those roots. The domicile is a unit of the larger political structure, a cell in the body politic. Writing about domestic abuse, Olds and McCarriston have exposed the deepest betrayals done to human innocence. Implicated in the abuses of the individual is psychoanalysis itself—a male-dominated institution that, in Gilman's time, fortified the myth of female hysteria, originating in the womb, as the sole cause of women's uncontrollability and discontent. Gilman wrote in despair about the kinds of abuses she detected in the male psychoanalytic enterprise. But that was more than 100 years ago. With the advent of psychoanalytic schools pioneered by Anna Freud, Melanie Klein, and their clinical granddaughters, Young-Bruehl and Jamison, to name just a few of grand stature, psychoanalysis is no longer strictly the province of medicine, but also of narrative and personal testimony.

(Through these writers, it becomes clear that the act of writing is both a means of resistance and defense; that writing harbors the most excruciating memories, or traumas, long enough to exorcise them through the word.)The "word" is both a sword and a shield: it can both inflict and protect against the pain of a wounding. Freud believed resolutely that it was the edification of the word that would discharge painful or volatile emotions. Yet sometimes writing is compelled by forces that have less to do with reducing symptoms, but by the need to record a history of agony so that history will not repeat itself. Again and again, writers who have in one way or another felt oppressed or stigmatized have used the written word to regain equilibrium and to renounce the powers that would stifle or subjugate them. In seemingly intolerable situations, such as the Holocaust, the drive to write down one's memoirs is powerful, a way of bearing witness is the goal of the struggle. As Wiesel writes:

> Rejected by mankind, the condemned do not go so far as to reject it in turn. Their faith in history remains unshaken, and one may well wonder why. They do not despair. The proof: they persist in surviving—not only to survive, but to testify. The victims elect to become witnesses.[9]

Some of the writers I have discussed here have been victims and survivors. Others would not describe themselves as such, having passed through stages of decline and renewal just as we all do. But I am not certain that each human being has not, in his or her own manner, proved that enduring psychic pain is concomitant with the need for a language that can survive it. The art of the lyric is the morality of its music, the structuring of narrative bodies in language has movement and shape. As the writer gives herself over to the "dancing in language,"[10] some genuflection away from the pain is already achieved. If there has been any guiding principle behind my collecting these essays it has been, admittedly, not theoretical, but personal. Through my reading, I have sought to discover the human, what bridges my own isolated experience with that of others. I have learned that anguish is sometimes too unremitting, too excruciating, that the most profound human truths can only reach out of the chasm of the blackest mood. Yet the story itself becomes a redemptive one as the writer tries to meditate on the objects that metaphorically represent states of mind.(Given the opportunity to articulate a reason for suffering and for writing about it, these writers share a belief in love as a resilient feature of the afflicted psyche, which, like the weight of a drooping sunflower, struggles to prop its head up incrementally toward sunlight, filament by filament, taking it a day at a time.)

AFTERWORD

On the day that I completed the first draft of this book, it was prematurely warm for March. I went to the post office to mail the manuscript, and then to teach my lackadaisical honors class. When an evangelical student from Cedar Rapids, Iowa, ignored my question about Byron, pointing out, instead, that my blouse clashed with my slacks, I knew it to be an ominous sign. I wanted to glower at him, but just bowed to the inevitable. That was not like me—and it was not like me to slip the piece of chalk I had been writing with into my pocket, as if it were a souvenir.

That evening I went to Catholic University to meet Don Hall who was reading a poem in honor of the late James Wright. It was good to see him. We sat on the stone bench appraising the moon, and I asked more questions about Jane Kenyon. Don still smoked cigarettes, but was not wearing the suit he wore when he married Jane or when he buried her or when we gathered in Louisville under tumultuous clouds to exchange conference papers about her work. Don reminisced about Jane's love for Keats and said he was still changing his mind about a word in a line for his new collection. I accompanied him to his hotel by taxi, and, as he stepped out onto the curb, I rolled down the window, and told him I had mailed the book. "It's about pain," I said. "Whose pain?" he asked, not turning around. Drawing the line between writing poems and scholarship, I said "This time, I hope it is about somebody else's."

Don disappeared into the festooned gold lobby and the black cab took off with me looking out at the Washington Capitol and a few visible stars glimmering over the skyline like fireflies switching on and off. When I got home, I discovered the lump in my left breast. It was like feeling my body speaking in a foreign language, trying to signify something too horrible to comprehend. For the first time I was alone in the deepest, literal sense—I could feel the chill of the grass growing up all around me and night sunk into its own crib with the kind of weight that mimics the dead.

I was diagnosed with early stage one breast cancer and went through the most harrowing months of treatment. Spring became more mobile and inaccessible, as if it were nothing but a spectacle of heat and blazing color. It was difficult not to think about death, as if I had been given a glimpse of the intractable, like the overripe peach atrophied in soft places, bruising over.

Still, I found writing to be a necessity. When I was too sick to sit upright in a chair, I lay down on the floor like my daughter used to sprawl out with her messy set of crayons. I worked on my articles or stories for editors who became my friends through their supportive e-mails—Jeanne Gunner, Denise Knight, Kate Sontag, Martin Gliserman—and reread Mark Bracher's *Writing Cure*. At Jeff Berman's urging, I started to write about what I was going through. I needed to demonstrate on myself the healing powers of narrative. When I was hit with yet another of the plagues I thought merited Pharaoh status, I found that the writing not only distracted me from thinking about cancer, but also afforded me some humor. I began to think of the words as being mortal, that they, too, needed to be spared and restored.

This puts me in mind of a friend of mine, Toby Quitslund, who was preparing to move out of the house where she lived for twenty-five years with her husband, Jon, a Spenserian scholar and jazz enthusiast, and her two sons. That dusky, dignified townhouse with its chestnut woodwork and squeaky parquet floors was her refuge during two dire illnesses, including a bone-marrow transplant. She had filled it with books, a turn-legged dining room table, and a hodgepodge of Victorian relics and antiques. That was the house where she had lost her hair and grown it back again, and welcomed the change of season with the relief of simply being there to greet it. In the weeks that she was preparing for leaving, I watched her shed tears as she climbed back up the narrow basement stairs, having had to go down at least twenty times a day to retrieve her mother's family heirlooms, which she had packed away decades ago before her mother's death.

Now, it seemed too painful to dislodge the dust-covered stuff and to find and rediscover her mother's eccentric dynasty of Tiffany dishes and sterling flatware, all in some state of disuse or disrepair. She said, "This is just like my mother; she didn't know how to take care of anything." The objects themselves were not what hurt her; they were elegant things that could be easily revived with a little polish or sandalwood. What injured her was her mother's neglect and abuse of the things people should cherish. Instead, she found moth holes in the taffeta evening dress, chips on the demitasse cups, cracks in the crystal, and rust on the plated silver.

So, after so many years, my friend was handling the bits and pieces of her mother's estate as they fell open to her from a heap of bashed-in cartons. Running her fingers through the torn fabrics, counting out the mismatched silverware and never finding a single set that made sense or was complete, she was reliving the grief of being separated from her mother all over again just as she was leaving the house she had lived through to middle age. In each of the teacups, dessert spoons, candlesticks, which I helped her to bind or protect in bubble wrap, she lost and recovered the dim face of her mother in blurring reflection. For her, it was another period of descent into pain and mourning from which she would reemerge with the words to tell about, half-broken but renewed.

(No pain is "somebody else's." I was wrong about that. Pain is as inevitable as love and dying and the somber weather that catches up with itself. Now healthy, I can look out at the same trees I observed last summer) I have come full circle. The leaves have redoubled themselves; they never get so caught in the synapses of wind or rain that they fail to avail themselves to hope. Hope is a brutal part of them; deep in the sap of the wood. This is what we, as writers and teachers, seek to capture and recapture: that nascent alphabet, that cryptic riddle of words that renders us human all over again when the moment is ripe, when we can shore up courage and replace fear with reverence. That search is the first and last thing we do. My hope is that this book will end not at the ending, but with the beginning—that it offers optimism to readers who are already part of a community that acknowledges and abets a writer's struggle to fill the emptiness, which is at the root of every word.

NOTES

Preface

1. Jamison, *An Unquiet Mind*, 214.

2. Anderson and MacCurdy, eds., *Writing and Healing toward an Informed Practice*, 2.

3. Lacan, *Four Fundamental Concepts*, 73–73. In his chapter "The Eye and the Gaze," Lacan follows Merleau-Ponty's idea that the gaze is presented to us in the form of a strange contingency, but adds that what we find on the horizon of our experience is namely the lack that constitutes castration anxiety.

4. Lowell, *Lord Weary's Castle*, 100–112.

5. Ibid., 111.

Introduction

1. Hoffman, "Sustained by Fiction."

2. Ibid.

3. Ibid.

4. Ibid.

5. Ibid., 111.

6. C. Frost, "Self-Pity," 162–175.

7. C. Frost, "Self-Pity," 173.

8. Bracher, *Lacan, Discourse, and Social Change*, 172.

9. C. Frost, "Self-Pity," 173.

10. Ibid., as quoted by Frost, 167–169.

11. C. Frost, 174.

12. Keats, "*Letters*, in Gittings, 37.

13. Ibid., "Ode to a Nightingale," Perkins, 1184.

14. Hoffman, "Sustained by Fiction."

15. Keats, "Ode to a Nightingale," 1184.

16. Cited in Mayer, "Scribbling My Way," 29.

17. As quoted by Orr, "Our Lady of Sorrows," 34.

18. Ibid., 36.

19. Alcorn, *Changing the Subject*. Alcorn's groundbreaking work on psycho-analysis, discourse, and literary and cultural criticism has had far-reaching influence on contemporary commentary about pedagogy and its social ramifications and potential for change. See bibliographical information on Alcorn's other works, such as *Narcissism and the Literary Libido* and "Changing the Subject of Postmodern Theory" in *Rhetoric Review*.

20. *The Letters of John Keats*, 61.

21. DeSalvo, *Writing as a Way of Healing*, 5.

22. Ibid., 3.

23. Anderson and MacCurdy, eds. *Writing and Healing*, 7.

24. Des Pres, *The Survivor*, 41. Des Pres explores the individual and univer-sal consequences of political terror in which victims who survive are compelled to give testimony to what they witnessed. Des Pres, like Wiesel, is concerned with the moral question of what we can learn from a history of atrocity and what can be done to make certain that collective crimes of such magnitude in a civilized world will not happen again.

25. Ibid.

Chapter 1. The Healing Effects of Writing about Pain

1. Jamison, *Touched with Fire*, 121. Precise reference: Leon Edel, "The Madness of Art," *American Journal of Psychiatry*, 132 (1975):1005–1012, quote on p.1008.

2. Bracher, *The Writing Cure*, 213–214.

3. Herman, *Trauma and Recovery*, p.1. Herman's book is the groundbreak-ing study, a classic in the field of psychology, bridging the traumatic effects suf-fered by war veterans and victims of sexual abuse. Herman's book is meticulous-ly documented in clinical experience, but also shows rare and luminous insights into the parallel worlds of politics and the domicile, maintaining a feminist per-spective on what should be done in the aftermath of trauma for victims who have undergone severe harm brought on by terror and what can be done to help them to recover. Herman's use of narrative as a therapeutic strategy for coping with patient's self-blame and self-recrimination is essential to my bringing together writ-ing as a "curative" form of retrieving and reconciling the past.

4. Kenyon, *Otherwise*, 188. Although I do not go in depth into the subject, Kenyon's courageous struggle with manic depressive illness is the focus of many of her most celebrated poems. It forms the trajectory of her life of self-examination, and her scrutiny of the suffering that so many have identified with, for whom her writing has made it, in that camaraderie, easier to bear.

5. Bogan, *Journey around My Room*, 70.

6. Ibid.

7. Ibid.

8. Berman, introduction to Marshall Alcorn's *Narcissism and the Literary Libido*, ii.

9. Berman's *The Talking Cure* is crucial to this study not only for its contribution to literary representations but its careful analysis of how psychoanalysis can help students in the writing classroom: to improve their writing while gaining valuable insights into their experience, past and present. He has pioneered the therapeutic use of "diary" writing in composition classrooms and, to much acclaim, has furthered our understanding of how suicide has been so romanticized in literature and culture that it poses a danger to impressionable students, and therefore must be demythologized as a grandiose act to prevent idealizations of suicides that may prove both catastrophic and irreversible.

10. Clarke, *In the Ward*, 37.

11. Ibid.

12. Lowell, *Life Studies*, 89.

13. Frost, "The Oven Bird," 197.

14. Lowell, quoted by Ellman and O'Clair, 939, #3

15. Rosenthal, *The Poet's Art*, 25.

16. Phillips, *The Confessional Poets*, 13.

17. Lowell, *Life Studies*, 88.

18. Ibid.

19. Lowell, *Life Studies,* 23.

20. Plath, *The Collected Poems*, 257.

21. Ibid.

22. Freud and Breuer, "Mechanism of Hysterical Phenomena," 37.

23. Caruth, *Unclaimed Experience*, 2–17. From the Introduction, "The Wound and the Voice." Cathy Caruth's writing is not only elegant but also profound in its capturing of the literary appeal myth held for Freud. In vivid language,

Caruth unweaves the tale of Tancred and its parable of suffering, but adds her own interpretation to Freud's, offering another layer of meaning. Caruth's writing is, in many ways, more astonishing than Freud's in its attempt to bring the trauma and its repetition into the fold of a signifying language.

24. Young-Bruehl and Bethelard, *Cherishment*, book flap cover.

25. Des Pres, *The Survivor*, 47.

26. Hall, *Without*, book flap cover.

27. Braham, *Dürer*, 20. Every object in the picture probably has some significance contributing to the theme of melancholy. Interpreted as the futility of secular study as contrasted with the happy orderliness of the Christian contemplative *St. Jerome in His Study*, a part of the three part series showing Dürer's confidence in Christian progressiveness.

28. Jamison, *An Unquiet Mind*, 214.

29. Kenyon, *Otherwise*, 189–193.

30. Ibid., 193.

31. Jamison, *An Unquiet Mind*, 220.

32. L. G. Sexton, and Ames, *Anne Sexton*, 335.

33. A. Sexton, "The Fury of Rainstorms," in *The Death Notebooks*, 43.

Chapter 2. Violating the Sanctuary/Asylum

1. Poirer, "Mitchell's Rest Cure," as quoted on p. 17. Also see *Norton Anthology of Literature*, 648.

2. Ibid. Also see Berman's definitive chapter on Gilman "The Unrestful Cure: Charlotte Perkins Gilman" and "The Yellow Wallpaper" in *The Talking Cure*, pp. 33–59. Berman goes into depth concerning Gilman's unsuccessful attempts to be treated for severe depressive illness.

3. Ibid.

4. Berman, in *The Talking Cure*, 36.

5. Freud, "Therapy and Technique," in Ewen, 147.

6. Freud and Breuer, "Mechanism of Hysterical Phenomena," "Preliminary Communications (1893)," in *Studies on Hysteria*, 44.

7. Freud and Breuer, in *Studies on Hysteria*, 42.

8. Herman, *Trauma and Recovery*, 10.

9. Guillain, *J. M. Charcot*, 44.

10. Herman, *Trauma and Recovery*, 10.

11. Guillain, *J. M. Charcot*, 145,

12. Herman, *Trauma and Recovery*, 11.

13. Guillain, J. M. Charcot, 176.

14. Herman, *Trauma and Recovery*, 11. In praise of Charcot, Freud eulogized: "No credence was given to the hysteric about anything. The thing that Charcot's work did was to restore its dignity to the topic. Little by little, people gave up the scornful smile with which the patient could at that time feel certain of being met."

15. As quoted by Herman, *Trauma and Recovery*, p.13. Herman's argument is supportive of Masson's hypothesis about Freud's suppression of the seduction theory. It is important to note, however, that Anna Freud renounced this theory, suggesting it constituted a slander of Freud's reputation and was founded in "nonsense." More recently Freud's critics have been more judicious to Freud and his motives for doubting his patients' stories about abuse and molestation, giving little or no credence to the idea that he was shielding Fleiss.

16. Malcolm, *Psychoanalysis: The Impossible Profession*, 94. Malcolm's book is an elegant and precise summary of the history and development of Freud's ideas, and at the same time, a significant criticism of Freud's condescending attitude toward woman, an attitude that has been perpetuated by the profession. She is particularly suspicious of Freud's treatment of Dora, as can be seen in the fine pages she devotes to the topic.

17. Freud, "Fragment of an Analysis," 173.

18. Malcolm, *Psychoanalysis: The Impossible Profession*, 96.

19. Freud, "Fragment of an Analysis," 193.

20. Guillain, J. M. Charcot, 142.

21. Freud, "Fragment of an Analysis," 183.

22. Ibid., 189.

23. Freud, "Preliminary Communications," 42.

24. Ibid.

25. Ibid., 43.

26. Ibid.

27. Freud, "Fragment of an Analysis," 215.

28. Ibid., 176.

29. Ibid., 177.

30. Chesler, *Women and Madness*, 60. Feminist and writer Phyllis Chesler takes a direct look at women's madness and institutionalization and researches the many documented cases that were mishandled or misdiagnosed by physicians who were acting on the dubious methods of a medical enterprise that had no tolerance for women's uncontrolled temperaments. In the worst case scenarios, these women's psychoses were indifferently treated if not taken advantage of by the patriarchal system that was prejudiced against them.

31. Freud, "Preliminary Communications," 41.

32. Ibid.

33. Malcolm, *Psychoanalysis: The Impossible Profession*, 96.

34. Ibid.

35. Freud, "Fragment of an Analysis," 173.

36. As quoted by Berman in *The Talking Cure*, 51.

37. Gilman, "The Yellow Wallpaper," 661.

38. Freud, "Fragment of an Analysis," 215.

39. Ibid.

40. Ibid., 189.

41. Ibid., 183.

42. Gilman, "The Yellow Wallpaper," 660.

43. Freud, "Preliminary Communications," 43.

44. Gilman, "The Yellow Wallpaper," 663.

45. As quoted by Berman in *The Talking Cure*, 65.

46. Ibid., 37.

47. Ibid.

48. Ibid.

49. Ibid., 42.

50. Gilman, "The Yellow Wallpaper," 652.

51. Ibid., 651.

52. Ibid., 659.

53. Rejection of a sexual origin for traumatic symptoms always met with Freud's condemnation. Dora challenged Freud's interpretation of the dream symbol of a jewelry box as female genitals, with "I knew you would say that." Freud dismisses the obvious conclusion that Dora has begun to anticipate his thinking—it has become as predictable as her resisting the implications of any interpretation. A century later, critics would fault Freud for his overattribution of symptoms to sexual motifs.

54. Malcolm, *Psychoanalysis: The Impossible Profession*, 96.

55. Gilman, "The Yellow Wallpaper," 653.

Chapter 3. Breaking the Code of Silence

1. Herman, *Trauma and Recovery*, 6.

2. Ibid., 32.

3. Cited by DeSalvo in *Writing as a Way of Healing*, p.35. The reference is from David Aberbach's *Surviving Trauma, Loss, Literature and Psychology.*

4. Glück, "The Forbidden," 56. Reprinted in *After Confession*, 244–253.

5. Ibid.

6. Glück, *Ararat*, 27.

7. McCarriston, *Eva-Mary*, 69.

8. Ibid.

9. Ibid.

10. Des Pres, *The Survivor*, 47.

11. Plath, *The Collected Poems*, 222–224.

12. See Berel Lang's *Act and Idea in the Nazi Genocide*. Lang provides a rich and fascinating discussion of the motivations and beliefs underlying the idea of genocide in the psychology of Nazism, as well as the difficulty philosophical inquiry posed for him as a second-generation Jew writing about the comprehensibility (on any rational scale) of such irrational barbarianism.

13. Plath, *The Collected Poems*, 223.

14. Butscher, *Sylvia Plath: Method and Madness*, 327.

15. Olds, *Satan Says*, 3.

16. Ibid., 6.

17. Ibid.

18. Ibid., 14.

19. Cummings, "The Refrain of the Repressed," 21–27.

20. Ibid.

21. Herman, *Trauma and Recovery*, 43. Herman categorizes the symptoms of posttraumatic stress disorder into three main categories: hyperarousal, intrusion, and constriction. Hyperarousal reflects the persistent expectation of danger, intrusion, the indelible imprint of the traumatic moment; constriction, the numbing response. "Traumatized people feel and act as though their nervous systems have been disconnected from the present." p. 35.

22. Panken, "Incest Rediscovered," 548.

23. Herman and Hirschman, *Father-Daughter Incest*, 22.

24. McCarriston, *Eva-Mary*, 14.

25. Ibid., 13.

26. Ibid., 24–25.

Chapter 4. Fathering Daughters

1. Rich, "When We Dead Awaken," 603.

2. Berman, "One's Effort," 610.

3. Stone, "Freud's Vision, 39.

4. Ibid., 87.

5. Rich, "When We Dead Awaken," 605.

6. See Gilbert and Gubar, *The Madwoman in the Attic*. The text explores the distinctly female tensions in literary production by women in the Victorian age and, specifically, the bifurcated view of women as both producers and representations in texts. The woman writer experiences her own gender in a patriarchal culture, as an obstacle to originality and voice. The authors show how a gynocentric reading of texts show prevailing egotistical ambition on the part of women and the many strategies women used to circumvent suppressive patriarchal constraint.

7. Cited by Berman in *The Talking Cure*, 132.

8. Ibid.

9. Ibid.

10. Freud, *Gradiva*, vol xxi in Strachey.

11. Ibid., 27.

12. Freud, "Civilization and Its Discontents," 742.

13. Cited by Berman in *The Talking Cure*, 123.

14. Plath, *The Collected Poems*, 129.

15. Ibid., 130.

16. Cited by Berman in *The Talking Cure*, 124.

17. Plath, *The Collected Poems*, 129.

18. Ibid.

19. It is worth mentioning again Lacan's theory that the origin of signifiers that populate the unconscious is heard speech, chiefly from a time that the child was unable to understand what was said in its hearing even though they may have been and remain laden with affect, especially if the source was parental. This is consistent with the speaker's sense of colossus as a mouthpiece full of primitive babbles that she unable to decipher.

20. Plath, *The Collected Poems*, 129.

21. From Ted Hughes introduction to Plath's *The Collected Poems*.

22. Plath, *The Collected Poems*, 124.

23. Young-Bruehl and Bethelard, *Cherishment*, 167.

24. Ibid.

25. Plath, *The Collected Poems*, 131.

26. Ibid., 222-224.

27. Gilman, "The Yellow Wallpaper," 660.

28. Freud, "Creative Writers and Day-Dreaming," 438.

29. Shelley, *Frankenstein or the Modern Prometheus*, 19-20.

30. Ibid., 111.

31. Ibid., 112.

32. The text of *Frankenstein* was apparently inspired by several incidents that stirred Shelley's associations that she conveys as the circumstances surrounding the origins of *Frankenstein*. Due to inclement weather, the collected party had gathered inside, conversing about ghost stories, and Shelley was particularly struck by the *History of the Inconstant Lover*. This was a lover who, "when he thought to clasp the bride to whom he had pledged his vows, found himself in the arms of the pale ghost of her whom he had deserted" (p.7). From then on, the lover was imbued with the kiss of death; everyone he touched withered "like flowers snapped upon the stalk" (p.8). Shelley was evidently fascinated by the ghostly prospect of premature aging and death, as this tale describes, and has Victor explain that he had worked for two years to infuse life into an inanimate being but now the "beauty" of a dream is denigrated to "horror and disgust." Because of her mother's fatal infection, Shelley would see herself as the one who had the kiss of death and might weigh her own guilt through the moral dilemma that faces Victor: is he a murderer by deed or effect? The jealous monster destroys all of the people for whom Victor feels affection as potential rivals for Victor's love, especially Elizabeth. Fated to kill (infect) all others with his kiss, the unfaithful lover rejects (murder being the ultimate rejection) loved ones before they can reject him, saving himself from the pain of risk and losing again. Frankenstein shares the dilemma of the "lover" who did not intend the death or maligning of his beloved. Instead, it is the guilty effect of the deed that has come back to haunt him. For something done in the past, his betrayal of a woman, the lover is punished by having his loved ones taken from him, one by one, a punishment that keeps him eternally alone and in sorrow.

33. Plath, *The Collected Poems*, 223.

34. Shelley, *Frankenstein*, 142.

35. Ai, *Cruelty*, 10.

36. Ibid., 38.

37. Ibid., 22.

38. Ibid., 13.

39. Olds, *The Gold Cell*, 26.

40. Ibid.

41. Sexton, *The Death Notebooks*, 37–38.

42. Ibid.

43. Ibid.

44. Ostriker, *Stealing the Language*.

Chapter 5. Carving the Mask of Language

1. Freud, "Creative Writers and Day-Dreaming," 437.

2. Stevens, p. 229.

3. Behn and Twitchell, *The Practice of Poetry,* 63.

4. Masters, *Spoon River Anthology,* 387.

5. See Holland, *The I.*

6. As quoted by Berman in *The Talking Cure*, 4.

7. Browning, *Robert Browning's Poetry*, 94.

8. Merleau-Ponty, "The Child's Relations with Others," 127 in Rzepka, 17.

9. Rzepka, *The Self as Mind*, 18.

10. Ibid.

11. Browning, 18.

12. Plath, *The Collected Poems*, 244.

13. Ibid.

14. Ibid.

15. Berman, *The Talking Cure*, 122.

16. Snodgrass in "Interview with Elizabeth Spires," 42-43. Preceded Lowell in establishing confessionalism as a school and contends that Freudian transference in which archaic feelings of love are projected onto the therapist, happens not only in therapy, but also in poetry. The poet can do this through the direct evocation of real people in autobiographical poems or through the substitute metaphor or analogy that stands for these people. By playing out the old patterns through the poem, the poet can put them to rest. Snodgrass relates an interesting story about transference: he had sought help from a psychiatrist to explore "writer's block." "I never saw my therapist. He was behind a mirror, a voice that said 'Good morning.'" The point of this therapy was to be nondirective and to eliminate the possibility of transference. Snodgrass came to learn that the therapy was unsuccessful because there was no possibility for transference. His second therapist could not understand why the

transferal had been avoided when the goal of analysis is to make transferal and analyze what happened in it.

17. Snodgrass, "Interview with Elizabeth Spires," 42.

18. Eliot, "Tradition and the Individual Talent," 37–44. Here, Eliot argues for
a dissociation of emotions, where the poet projects emotions onto an object,
expressing the nature of the object to convey the emotion. According to Eliot, no
emotion should be expressed in the poem without its objective correlative.

19. Ibid.

20. Eliot, "The Love Song of J. Alfred Prufrock," 449.

21. St. John, *No Heaven*, 42-49.

22. Ibid., 43

23. Ibid.

24. Ibid., 47.

Chapter 6. Giotto's Invisible Sheep

1. Walcott, *Dream on Monkey Mountain*, 269.

2. Baugh, *Derek Walcott*, 81.

3. Walcott, *Another Life*, 41.

4. Quoted in Rei Terada, *Derek Walcott's Poetry*, 24.

5. Ibid., 1.

6. Walcott, *Another Life*, 1.

7. Lee, *Jacques Lacan*, 18.

8. Alcorn, *Narcissism and the Literary Libido*, 16.

9. Balakian, "The Poetry of Derek Walcott," 70.

10. Walcott, *Another Life*, 47.

11. Ibid., 59.

12. Ibid.

13. Ibid., 60.

14. Ibid., 61.

15. Ibid., 64.

16. Ibid., 59.

17. Ibid., 61.

18. Ibid., 59.

19. Ibid., 61.

20. Ibid., 58–59.

21. Ibid., 152.

22. Vendler, "Poet of Two Worlds," as cited in Mason, "Derek Walcott," 269.

23. Fanon, *Black Skin, White Masks*, 110.

24. Walcott, *Another Life*, 3.

25. Fanon, *Black Skin, White Masks*, 17.

26. Walcott, *Collected Poems*, 17.

27. Walcott, *Another Life*, 77.

28. Balakian, "The Poetry of Derek Walcott," 175.

29. Walcott, "Gros-Ilet," 256.

30. Walcott, *Another Life*, 60.

31. Ibid., 22.

32. Baugh, *Derek Walcott*, 80.

33. Walcott, *Another Life*, 3.

34. Walcott, as cited by Balakian, 175.

35. Walcott, *Another Life*, 4.

36. Ibid.

37. Benson, "The Painter as Poet," 266.

38. Walcott, *Another Life*, 3.

39. Ibid., 44.

40. Ibid.

41. Ibid., 10.

42. Ibid., 6.

43. Ibid., 4–5.

44. Lee, on desire in *Jacques Lacan*, 67.

45. Fanon, *Black Skin, White Masks*, 110.

46. Walcott, *Another Life*, 9.

47. Ibid., 7.

48. Ibid.

49. Ibid.

50. Lee, *Jacques Lacan,* 136.

51. Baugh, *Derek Walcott,* 86.

52. Walcott, *Another Life,* 42–43.

53. Terada, *Derek Walcott's Poetry: American Mimicry,* 2.

54. Ibid., 22.

55. Walcott, as cited by Terada, 22.

56. Baugh, *Derek Walcott,* 67.

57. Walcott, as cited by Terada, 43.

58. Walcott, *Another Life,* 152.

59. Ibid., 15.

60. Ibid., 55.

Chapter 7. Rescuing Psyche

1. See Ward, *John Keats.*

2. In Perkins, *English Romantic Writers,* 1114.

3. Ibid.

4. Gittings, *The Letters of John Keats,* 253. Quotations from the "Ode to Psyche" are from this edition of the *Letters.* Also consulted is Forman's more complete edition of *Letters.*

5. Gittings, *The Letters of John Keats,* 394.

6. This letter is from Keats, *Complete Letters of John Keats,* Letter 239, p. 522. When letter is numbered, it is from Complete Letters.

7. Keats, *Letters,* 358-359. The dream story is a derivative of the "Third Calendar's Story" or "A Thousand and One Nights."

8. See Apuleius, *The Golden Ass.*

9. Keats, *Letters,* Letter 186, p. 468.

10. Keats, *Letters,* Letter 137, p. 357.

11. Hillman, *The Myth of Analysis,* 27.

12. Keats, *Letters,* 251, in Gittings, 250.

13. Jack, *Keats and the Mirror of Art,* 205.

14. Waldroff, "The Theme of Mutability," 410–419.

15. Refer to Bowlby, *Attachment and Loss.*

16. Jones, *Adam's Dream*, 48. Jones sees the impetus of Keats's evocation of Psyche to be part of a psychic revival of mythic consciousness of the inner Self or Soul.

17. Jack, *Keats and the Mirror of Art,* 2.

18. Keats, *Letters,* Letter 79, p. 191.

19. See Plato's *Symposium* and *Phaedrus.* Both dialogues include originating myths of the soul that are influential on Apuleius's adaptation of the myth for he was an "excellent follower of Plato" and expresses the tangled web of human desire caught between erotic passion and spiritual passion. For a discussion of what Plato means by love as related to the soul's progress from sexual passion to spiritual passion, see Rist, *Eros and Psyche.*

20. Ward, *John Keats,* 15.

21. Gittings, 167.

22. Caron, 16.

23. Hall, *A Primer of Freudian Psychology,* 77–78.

Chapter 8. God Don't Like Ugly

1. Harper, *Images of Kin,* 38.

2. Ibid.

3. Ibid., 98.

4. Ibid., 14.

5. Ibid., 196.

6. Ibid., 205.

7. Raffa, *Nightmare Begins Responsibility,* p. 115. The actual quote by Fussell is Edwin Fussell, "Double Consciousness: Poet in the Veil (for Michael S. Harper)" in *Parnassus: Poetry in Review* (Fall/Winter 1975), p. 7.

8. Ibid.

9. In Raffa, *Nightmare Begins Responsibility,* 115.

10. Ibid., 114.

11. Psyche (or "soul") was particularly entwined with the emotional value of consoling, nurturing, and grief, on which Keats placed an emphasis in his development of a myth of poetics. The figure of Psyche resurfaces through Keats's poetry and letters. Keats suggested that psyche was the secret principle of all life: anima, spiritus, pneuma. This is the breath of divine suspiration into the life of the mortal. But Keats, unlike Plato, locates divinity within, and through, the bodily senses. To

understand the life of the soul (or psyche) Keats insisted on examining the life of the senses in human nature. In search of such a total synthesis of body, mind, and heart, Keats dramatizes the Psyche myth as a shifting metaphor for what is immortal about earthly beauty, countering time's devastation and decay.

Yet, while nearing the end of his life, Keats was drawn to Psyche for personal rather than strictly philosophical reasons: Psyche becomes the Keatsian muse, an aid to his pursuit of questions of imagination, aesthetics, and faith. The poet called Psyche "the loveliest vision," far lovelier than the Moon or Venus because she was a goddess with an acquired knowledge of painful human experience. In Psyche, Keats came to see the personification of mystery, melancholy, and the inevitable process of growth and decay, a figure who ratified the human venture of "soul-making."

12. Raffa, *Nightmare Begins Responsibility*, 116.

13. Ibid.

14. Harper, *Dear John, Dear Coltrane*, 63.

15. Ibid., 23.

16. Ibid., 32.

17. Ibid.

18. Keats's discussion of "Soul-Making" is included in the letters to the George Keats's February 14–May 3, 1819. Encompassed in these letters are some of Keats's major themes and ideas concerning the nature of the imagination, the example of Wordsworth, disinterestedness, theories of salvation, and the meaning of suffering in relation to the soul. It is probable that Harper was, indeed, had that letter in mind—he was certainly familiar with it—but I have no evidence that this was a deliberate allusion.

19. Harper, *Honorable Amendments*, 88–89.

20. Gittings, *The Letters of John Keats*, 249.

21. Harper, *Honorable Amendments*, 88.

22. Ibid.

23. Gittings, 279.

24. See Freud's "Mourning and Melancholia,"584–589.

25. Harper, *Dear John, Dear Coltrane*, 24.

26. Ibid., 23.

27. Ibid., 58.

28. Ibid., 69.

29. Ibid., 128–129.

30. Raffa, *Nightmare Begins Responsibility*, 117.

31. Ibid., 131.

32. Harper, *Dear John, Dear Coltrane*, 74.

33. Ibid., 75.

34. Ibid., 7.

35. Ibid.

36. Ibid., 75.

Chapter 9. Kenyon's Melancholic Vision in "Let Evening Come"

1. Kenyon, *Otherwise*, 176.

2. Keats, *Selected Poems*, 197–198.

3. As quoted by Donald Hall in a letter to the author, dated April 28, 1998.

Chapter 10. Using the Psychoanalytic Process in Creative Writing Class

1. Behn and Twitchell, *The Practice of Poetry*, 6.

2. Ibid., 9.

3. Berman, *The Talking Cure*, 285.

4. Anne Sexton as quoted by L. Sexton and Ames, 133.

5. Wallen, "Memory Politics," 39.

6. Ibid., 38.

7. Meredith Skura as quoted by Wallingford, *Robert Lowell's Language*, 14.

8. Galway Kinnell, as quoted by Olds, in *SFPR* vol. 10. #1–2 [1992] 86.

9. Peter Caws, lecture notes, 11 Nov. 1990.

10. Snodgrass, "Interview with Elizabeth Spires," 38–46.

11. Laux in Behn and Twitchell, *The Practice of Poetry*, 105.

12 Wallen, "Memory Politics," 38.

13. Laux in Behn and Twitchell, *The Practice of Poetry*, 105.

14. Ibid.

15. Ibid., 106.

16. Ibid.

Chapter 11. Rewriting the Subject

1. Shellnut, "Notes from a Cell," 11.

2. Welch, "No Apology," 117–134.

3. Moxley, *Creative Writing in America*, 25.

4. Bishop, "Crossing the Lines," 181.

5. Behn and Twitchell, *The Practice of Poetry*. The first section of the handbook is subtitled "Mining the Unconscious." Louise DeSalvo writes in *Writing as a Way of Healing* that such unraveling of the unsteady stream of repressed emotion surrounding memories can be curative for the writer. When traumatic symptoms become fixed in the subconscious, they are often replaced by neurotic symptoms.

6. Moxley, *Creative Writing in America*, 25.

7. Bishop, "Crossing the Lines," 185.

8. Levis, "The Poem You Asked For," 236.

9. Alcorn, *Changing the Subject*.

10. Smith, *Discerning the Subject*, xxx.

11. Moffet, "Writing, Inner Speech, and Meditation, 133–81.

12. In Freudian analysis, the patient reclines on a couch so that she might devote more energy to the demanding mental tasks that are required. The patient is required to say whatever comes to mind through free association. As Freud wrote:

> Your talk with me must differ in one respect from ordinary conversation. Whereas usually you try to keep the threads of your story together and to exclude all intruding association, here you proceed differently. You will notice that you relate things various ideas will come . . . and you feel inclined to put aside certain criticisms and objections. You will be tempted to say to yourself: This or that has no connection here, or is unimportant, or nonsensical, so it cannot be necessary to mention it, but mention it nonetheless, even if you feel a disinclination against it, or indeed just because of this. Never forget that you have promised absolute honesty and never leave anything unsaid because for any reason it is unpleasant to say it.

See Ewen, Robert B., 56.

13. Freud, "Creative Writing and Day-Dreaming," 436.

14. Ibid.

15. See Tobin's *Writing Relationships* and "Reading Students, Reading Ourselves."

16. Transference can be fully negative such as when powerful distrust or anger is displaced from the target of a parent to the target of the analyst. In fact, cases exist in which the analyst cannot master the unleashed transference and the analysis has to be ended. The analyst must not provoke love or hate, which would give the patient an excuse for refusing to recognize and learn from transferential love and hate. Managing the transference is the most important aspect of psychoanalysis.

17. Berman's book is titled *Risky Writing: Self-Disclosure and Self-Transformation in the Classroom*. His other books that treat self-disclosure and self-transformation in the classroom include *Diaries to an English Professor* and *Surviving Literary Suicide*.

18. Young-Bruehl also takes issue with the drive instincts in Freudian id psychology. In her book *Cherishment* she argues that the baby's orality is both affectional and erotic and that the ego's drive is expressed through affectional relatedness with its mother. Hence, the ego instincts have a growth principle, just as the libidinal instincts do. Satisfying the ego's interests allows the ego to develop and influence the sexual or erotic desires and the aggression they involve. The caretaker acts as an auxiliary ego to the emerging ego. The ego models its self-cherishment on its having been cherished. There is a process of identification with the cherisher that is central to the ego's development. Ego development begins with the presence, rather than the absence of the affirmative, with what must be a natural predisposition toward cherishment in the mother/infant dyad, rather than the anxiety or defense against not having it.

19. See Ewen, *Theories of Personality*.

20. I am referring here to Berman's *The Talking Cure* and Bracher's *The Writing Cure*.

21. Ewen, 859.

22. Ryder, in her paper " Disturbing Personal Boundaries." Also, as Lad Tobin writes in *Writing Relationships*: Perhaps as an overreaction to decades of microanalysis of the individual writer (Don Murray's conferences and Linda Flower's protocol analysis are prototypes here), we have leapt over relationships to macrotheories about social construction, discourse communities, women's ways of knowing, sociocognitive theory, and cultural critique.

23. See Progoff, *At a Journal Workshop*.

24. Smyth et al., "Effects of Writing," 1305–1309.

25. Bracher, *The Writing Cure*, 147.

26. Smyth et al., "Effects of Writing."

27. Pennebaker, "Self-Expressive Writing," 166.

28. Ibid.

29. Tobin, "Reading Students, Reading Ourselves," 77–91

30. Bracher, *The Writing Cure*, 147.

31. Welch, "Playing with Reality," 51–96

32. Berman, *Risky Writing*, 67.

33. McCarriston, *Eva-Mary*, 72.

34. Bracher, *The Writing Cure*, 167.

35. Ibid., 169.

36. Ibid., 6.

37. See Presser, "Golem as Metaphor."

38. See Bracher's comment in *The Writing Cure* on "Countertransference and the Ethics of Confessional Writing," section that illuminates the complexities of transference and countertransference in the student/teacher dyad. Although I certainly support Bracher's claim that the teacher's empathetic identification and mirroring of a student's desire to be seen and accepted in the light of praise, affection, and acknowledgement can lead to problems concerning boundaries, unexpressed expectations on the part of either teacher or student, I am wary of Bracher's suggestion that the problem originates in the student: "This is especially true of students who are insecure or needy." Just how does a teacher know a student is insecure or needy if he or she has not already initiated a dynamic in which those rather unattractive qualities have pronounced themselves? This issue of transference and countertransference has sparked a great deal of debate, particularly surrounding Gallop's controversial book, *Feminist Accused of Sexual Harassment*. Freud gives this topic attention in his article "Observations on Transference-Love," 378–384.

39. Ibid., 167.

Chapter 12. "To Bedlam and Almost All the Way Back"

1. Lacan, *Ecrits*, 6

2. Ravikovitch, *A Dress of Fire*, 15.

3. Middlebrook, *Anne Sexton*, 98.

4. Clarke, *In the Ward*. I am indebted to Clarke's study of Sexton and Lowell; he gives a thorough treatment of the subject of confinement in confessional poetry, offering us a revisionary history of the term *confessional* as based not on a literary form or modality but on the actual circumstances of institutionalization in the lives of key poets of the period.

5. Middlebrook, *Anne Sexton*, 13. Apparently Sexton's father found fault with his daughters' bad table manners and bad complexions.

6. Ibid., 34.

7. A. Sexton, *The Complete Poems*.

8. A. Sexton, *To Bedlam and Part Way Back* in *The Complete Poems*, 3.

9. Ibid.

10. Ibid.

11. Ibid., 28.

12. As cited by Clarke, *In the Ward*, 155. The quote comes from Lacan, *Four Fundamental Concepts*, 83.

13. A. Sexton, *The Complete Poems*, 34.

14. Ibid.

15. Ibid.

16. E. Bishop, *Questions of Travel*, 92.

17. Ibid., 82.

18. Ibid., 93.

19. Plath, *The Collected Poems*, 41.

20. Ibid.

21. Ibid.

22. Bogan, *Journey around My Room*, 84–85.

23. Ibid.

24. Ibid.

25. Ibid.

26. Lowell, *Life Studies*, 75.

27. Ibid., 76.

28. Lowell, *Lord Weary's Castle*, 53.

29. Ibid.

30. Hamilton, 93. Cited by Clarke, 25.

31. Lowell, *Lord Weary's Castle*, 110.

32. Ibid., 111.

33. Ibid.

34. Lowell, "For the Union Dead" in *The Norton Anthology of Poetry*, 580–582.

35. Lowell, *The Dolphin*, 1–3.

36. Ibid.

Chapter 13. Asylum

1. Stone, "Freud's Vision," 36.

2. See Amy Ellis Nutts' memoir "Asylum" in *The Gettysburg Review*, Spring 1997, 57-65.

3. Freud, "The Aetiology of Hysteria," 98.

Chapter 14. Signifying Pain

1. Hall, "Affirmation," 48.

2. Hardy, "Transformations," 63.

3. Singer, "An Interview with Sharon Olds," in *SFPR*, 88. cf. p.380.

4. Young-Bruehl, from a keynote address to *The New York Freudian Society*, January 15, 2000. Young-Bruehl's new book publication, *Cherishment*, was the occasion for her address.

5. Ibid.

6. Young-Bruehl, *The Anatomy of Prejudices*, 30.

7. Olds, *SFPR*, 83.

8. Cited by Des Pres, *The Survivor*, 147.

9. Ibid., 19.

10. Olds, *SFPR*, 91.

BIBLIOGRAPHY

Aberbach, David. *Surviving Trauma, Loss, Literature and Psychology*. New Haven, Conn.: Yale University Press, 1989.

Ai. *Cruelty*. Boston: Houghton Mifflin, 1973.

Alcorn, Marshall W., Jr. *Changing the Subject in English Class: Discourse and the Constructions of Desire*. Carbondale: Southern Illinois University Press, 2002.

———. "Changing the Subject of Postmodernism's Theory: Discourse, Ideology and Therapy in the Classroom." *Rhetoric Review* 13, no. 2 (1995): 331–49.

———. *Narcissism and the Literary Libido: Rhetoric, Text, and Subjectivity*. New York: New York University. Press, 1994.

Alvarez, A. *The Savage God*. New York: Random House, 1972.

Anderson, Charles, and Marian MacCurdy. *Writing and Healing toward an Informed Practice*. Urbana, Ill.: National Council of Teachers of English, 2000.

Apuleius. *The Golden Ass Being the Metamorphoses of Lucius Apuleius*. Translated by Richard Aldington, 1566. London: Harvard University Press, 1965.

Balakian, Peter. "The Poetry of Derek Walcott." *Poetry* 147 (1986): 169–77; quotation from 170.

Baugh, Edward. *Derek Walcott: Memory as Vision*. London: Longman, 1978.

Behn, Robin, and Chase Twitchell, eds. *The Practice of Poetry: Exercises from Poets Who Teach*. New York: Harper Collins, 1992.

Benson, Robert. "The Painter as Poet: Derek Walcott's 'Midsummer.'" *Literary Review* 29 (1986): 257–268.

Berman, Jeffrey. *Diaries to an English Professor: Pain and Growth in the Classroom*. Amherst: University of Massachusetts Press, 1994.

———. Introduction to *Narcissism and the Literary Libido: Rhetoric, Text, and Subjectivity*, by Marshall W. Alcorn Jr. New York: New York University Press, 1994.

———. *Narcissism and the Novel*. New York: New York University Press, 1990.

———. "One's Effort to Find a Little Truth: Ethel Schwabacher's Artistic and Psychoanalytic Odyssey." *Psychoanalytic Review* 78, no. 4 (Winter 1991): 607–628.

———. "Psychoanalytic Diary Writing and the Transformation of Self and Society." *Journal for the Psychoanalysis of Culture and Society* 1, no. 1 (Spring 1996): 123–126.

———. *Risky Writing: Self-Disclosure and Self-Transformation in the Classroom.* Amherst: University of Massachusetts Press, 2002.

———. *Surviving Literary Suicide.* Amherst: University of Massachusetts Press, 1999.

———. *The Talking Cure: Literary Representations of Psychoanalysis.* New York: New York University Press, 1985.

Berman, Jeffrey, and Alina M. Luna: "Suicide Diaries and the Therapeutics of Anonymous Self-Disclosure." *Journal for the Psychoanalysis of Culture and Society* 1 (1996): 63–75.

Bishop, Elizabeth. *Questions of Travel.* New York: Farrar, Straus, and Giroux, 1965.

Bishop, Wendy, and Hans Ostrom. *Colors of a Different Horse: Creative Writing Theory and Pedagogy.* Urbana, Ill.: National Council of Teachers of English, 1994.

Bogan, Louise. *Journey around My Room: The Autobiography of Louise Bogan: A Mosaic by Ruth Limmer.* New York: Viking, 1980.

Bowlby, John. *Attachment and Loss.* London: Penguin Books, 1971.

Bracher, Mark. *Lacan, Discourse, and Social Change: A Psychoanalytic Cultural Criticism.* Ithaca, N.Y.: Cornell University Press, 1993.

———. *Lacanian Theory of Discourse.* New York: New York University Press, 1994.

———. *The Writing Cure.* Carbondale: Southern Illinois University Press, 1999.

Braham, Alan. *Dürer.* London: Spring Books, 1967.

Browning, Robert. *Robert Browning's Poetry: A Norton Critical Edition:* New York: Norton, 1979.

———. *Robert Browning's Poetry: Authoritative Texts, Criticism.* Selected and edited by James F. Loucks. New York: Norton, 1979

Butscher, Edward. *Sylvia Plath: Method and Madness.* New York: Seabury Press, 1976.

Caruth, Cathy. *Unclaimed Experience: Trauma, History, and Narrative.* Baltimore, Johns Hopkins University Press, 1996.

Carson, Ann. *Eros: The Bittersweet: An Essay.* Princeton: Princeton University Press, 1986.

Caws, Peter. Lecture Noted, 11 Nov. 1990.

Chesler, Phyllis. *Women and Madness*. New York: Harcourt Brace, 1989.

Clarke, Colin. "In the Ward: Issues of Confinement in Mid-Twentieth Century American Poetry." Ph.D. diss. George Washington University, 2001.

Cummings, Allison M. "The Refrain of the Repressed: Incest Poetry in a Culture of Victimization." *AWP Chronicle* (December 1994): 21–27.

DeSalvo, Louise. *Writing as a Way of Healing: How Telling Our Stories Transforms Our Lives*. Boston: Beacon Press, 1999.

Des Pres, Terrence. *The Survivor*. Oxford: Oxford University Press, 1976.

Eagleton, Terry. *Literary Theory: An Introduction*. Minneapolis: University of Minnesota Press, 1963.

Eliot, T. S. "The Love Song of J. Alfred Prufrock." In *The Norton Anthology of Modern Poetry*, ed. Ellman and O'Clair. New York: Norton, 1973.

———. *On Poetry and Poets*. New York: Farrar, Straus and Cudahy, 1957.

———. *Selected Essays*. London: Faber and Faber, 1966.

———. "Tradition and the Individual Talent." In *Selected Prose of T. S. Eliot*, edited by Frank Kermode. New York: Harcourt Brace and Farrar Straus, 1973.

Ellman, Richard, and Robert O'Clair, eds. *Norton Anthology of Modern Poetry*. New York: Norton, 1973.

Ewen, Robert B. *Theories of Personality*. 5th ed. London: Earlbaum, 1998.

Fanon, Frantz. *Black Skin, White Masks*. Translated by Charles Larn Markmann. New York: Grove Press, 1991.

Felman, Shoshana, ed. *Literature and Psychoanalysis: The Question of Reading: Otherwise*. Baltimore, Md.: Johns Hopkins University Press, 1982.

Freud, Sigmund. "The Aetiology of Hysteria." In *The Freud Reader*, edited by Peter Gay. New York: Norton, 1989.

———. "Civilization and Its Discontents." In *The Freud Reader*, edited by Peter Gay. New York: Norton 1989.

———. "Creative Writers and Day-Dreaming." In *The Freud Reader*, edited by Peter Gay. New York: Norton, 1989.

———. "Delusions and Dreams in Jensen's *Gradiva*." In *The Standard Edition of the Complete Psychological Works of Sigmund Freud*, edited by James Strachey. London: Hogarth Press, 1956–1966.

———. "Fragment of an Analysis of a Case of Hysteria ('Dora')." In *The Freud Reader*, edited by Peter Gay. New York: Norton, 1989.

————. "Mourning and Melancholia." In *The Freud Reader,* edited by Peter Gay. New York: Norton, 1989.

————. *The Standard Edition of the Complete Psychological Works of Sigmund Freud,* edited by James Strachey. London: Hogarth Press, 1956–1966.

Freud, Sigmund, and Josef Breuer, "On the Psychical Mechanism of Hysterical Phenomena." In *Studies on Hysteria.* New York: Avon Books, 1966.

Frost, Carol. "Self-Pity." In *After Confession: Poetry as Autobiography,* edited by Katherine Sontag and David Graham. Minneapolis, Minn.: Graywolf, 2001.

Fussell, Edwin. "Double Consciousness: Poet in the Veil (for Michael S. Harper)," in *Parnassus: Poetry in Review* (Fall/Winter 1975), p. 7.

Gallop, Jane. *Feminist Accused of Sexual Harassment.* Durham, N.C.: Duke University Press, 1997.

Gilbert, Sandra, and Susan Gubar. *Madwoman in the Attic: The Woman Writer and the Nineteenth-Century Literary Imagination.* New Haven, Conn.: Yale University Press, 1984.

Gilman, Charlotte Perkins. "The Yellow Wallpaper." In *The Norton Anthology of American Literature,* 3rd ed. vol.2. New York: Norton, 1989.

Gittings, Robert, ed. *The Letters of John Keats.* Oxford: Oxford University Press, 1988.

Glück, Louise. *Ararat.* New York: Echo Press, 1991.

————. "The Forbidden." In *Proofs and Theories: Essays on Poetry.* New York: Harper Collins, 1994.

Guillain, Georges. *J. M. Charcot: 1825–1893 His Life His Work,* edited by Paul B. Hoeber. New York: Harper and Brothers, 1959.

Hall, Calvin. *A Primer of Freudian Psychology.* New York: Mentor, 1953.

Hall, Donald. "Affirmation." *New Yorker,* May 21, 2001, 46.

————. *Without.* New York: Houghton Mifflin, 1998.

Halpern, Daniel, ed. *The American Poetry Anthology.* New York: Avon Books, 1975.

Hamilton, Ian. *Robert Lowell: A Biography.* New York: Random House, 1982.

Hardy, Thomas. "Transformations." In *The Norton Anthology of Modern Poetry,* edited by Ellman and O'Clair. New York: Norton, 1973.

Harper, Michael S. *Dear John, Dear Coltrane.* Urbana: University of Illinois Press, 1985.

————. *Honorable Amendments.* Urbana: University of Illinois Press, 1995.

————. *Images of Kin: New and Selected Poems.* Urbana: University of Illinois Press, 1977.

Herman, Judith Lewis. *Trauma and Recovery: The Aftermath of Violence from Domestic Abuse to Political Terror*. New York: Basic Books, 1992.

Herman, Judith Lewis and Lisa Hirschman. *Father-Daughter Incest*. Cambridge, Mass.: Harvard University Press, 1981.

Hillman, James. *The Myth of Analysis: Three Essays in Archetypal Psychology*. Evanston, Ill.: Northwestern University Press, 1972.

Hoffman, Alice. "Sustained by Fiction while Facing Life's Crises." *New York Times*, August 14, 2000, sec. E–D1.

Holland, Norman. *The Dynamics of Literary Response*. New York: Oxford University Press, 1968.

———. *The I*. New Haven, Conn.: Yale University Press, 1985.

Jack, Ian. *Keats and the Mirror of Art*. Oxford: Clarendon Press, 1967.

Jamison, Kay Redfield. *Touched with Fire: Manic-Depressive Illness and the Artistic Temperament*. New York: Simon and Schuster, 1993.

———. *An Unquiet Mind*. New York: Knopf, 1995.

Jones, James Land. *Adam's Dream: Mythic Consciousness in Yeats and Keats*. Athens: University of Georgia Press, 1975.

Keats, John. *The Complete Letters of John Keats*, edited by Maurice Burton Forum. London: Toronto-Oxford University Press, 1952.

———. *The Letters of John Keats*, edited by Robert Gittings. Oxford: Oxford University Press, 1988.

———. "Ode to a Nightingale." In *English Romantic Writers* by David Perkins. San Diego, Calif.: Harcourt Brace, 1967.

———. *Selected Poems*. New York: Penguin, 1988.

Kenyon, Jane. *Otherwise: New and Selected Poems*. Minneapolis: Graywolf Press, 1997.

Lacan, Jacques. *Ecrits: A Selection*. New York: Norton, 1977.

———. *The Four Fundamental Concepts of Psychoanalysis*, edited by Jacques Alain Miller. New York: Norton, 1973.

Lang, Berel. *Act and Idea in the Nazi Genocide*. Chicago: University of Chicago Press, 1990.

Laub, Dori. "Bearing Witness on the Vicissitudes of Listening." In *Testimony: Crisis of Witnessing in Literature, Psychoanalysis, and History*, edited by Shoshana Felman and Dori Laub. New York: Routledge, 1992.

Lee, Jonathan Scott. *Jacques Lacan*. Boston: Twayne Publishers, 1990.

Levis, Larry. "The Poem You Asked For." In *The American Poetry Anthology*, edited by Daniel Halpern. New York: Avon Books, 1975.

Lowell, Robert. *Collected Poems*. New York: Farrar, Straus and Giroux, 1997.

———. *The Dolphin*. New York: Farrar, Straus and Giroux, 1973.

———. *Life Studies*. New York: Farrar, Straus and Giroux, 1997.

———. *Lord Weary's Castle and the Mills of the Kavanaughs*. New York: Meridian Books, 1961.

Malcolm, Janet. *Psychoanalysis: The Impossible Profession*. New York: Vintage Books, 1981.

Mason, David. "Derek Walcott, Poet of the New World." *Literary Review* 29 (1986): 269–275.

Masson, J. M. *The Assault on the Truth: Freud's Suppression of the Seduction Theory*. New York: Farrar, Straus and Giroux, 1984.

Masters, Edgar. *Spoon River Anthology*. In *The Norton Anthology of American Literature,* edited by Baym, Fanklin, Gottesman et al. New York: Norton, 1988.

Mayer, Musa. "Scribbling My Way to Spiritual Well-Being." *MAMM Magazine* (April 2000): 28–30.

McCarriston, Linda. *Eva-Mary,* edited by Julia M. Walker. Chicago: Triquarterly Press, 1993.

McColley, Diane. "Eve and the Arts of Eden." In *Milton and the Idea of Women*. Urbana: University of Illinois Press, 1988.

Merleau-Ponty. "The Child's Relations with Others." Translated by W. Cobb. In *The Primacy of Perception,* edited by J. M. Edie. Evanston, Ill.: Northwestern University Press, 1964.

Middlebrook, Diane Wood. *Anne Sexton: A Biography*. Boston: Houghton Mifflin, 1991.

Moffet, James. "Writing, Inner Speech, and Meditation." In *Coming on Center: Essays in English Education*. 2nd ed. Portsmouth, N.H.: Heinemann, 1988.

Moxley, Joseph M., ed. *Creative Writing in America: Theory and Pedagogy*. Urbana, Ill.: National Council of Teachers of English, 1989.

Myers, Nancy, Edward P. J. Corbett, and Gary Tate. *The Writing Teacher's Sourcebook*. New York: Oxford University Press, 1994.

Nutt, Emily. "Asylum" in *The Gettysburg Review*, Spring 1997, 57-65.

Olds, Sharon. *The Gold Cell*. New York: Knopf, 1992.

———. Interview with Frieda Singer. In the *South Florida Poetry Review* 10, no. 1–2 (1992): 85–93.

———. *Satan Says*. Pittsburgh, Pa.: University of Pittsburgh Press, 1980.

Orr, Gregory. "Our Lady of Sorrows." In *Bright Unequivocal Eye: Poems, Papers and Remembrances* from the first Jane Kenyon Conference, edited by Bert Hornback and Donald Hall. New York: Peter Lang Publishers, 2000.

Ostriker, Alicia. *Stealing the Language.* Boston: Beacon Press, 1997.

Panken, Shirley. "Incest Rediscovered." *Psychoanalytic Review* 78, no. 4 (Winter 1991) pp. 547–567.

Pennebaker, James, W. *Opening Up: The Healing Power of Expressing Emotions.* Rev. ed. New York: Guilford, 1997.

———. "Self-Expressive Writing: Implications for Health, Education, and Welfare." In *Nothing begins with N: New Investigations of Free Writing,* edited by Pat Belanoff, Peter Elbow, Sheryl Fontaine. Carbondale: Southern Illinois University Press, 1991.

Perkins, David. *English Romantic Writers.* San Diego, Calif.: Harcourt Brace, 1967.

Phillips, Robert. *The Confessional Poets.* Carbondale: Southern Illinois University Press, 1973.

Plath, Sylvia. *The Bell Jar.* New York: Harper and Row, 1971.

———. *The Collected Poems,* edited by Ted Hughes. New York: Harper and Row, 1981, and New York: Harper Perennial, 1992.

———. *Journals of Sylvia Plath.* New York: Dial Press, 1982.

Plato. *The Works of Plato.* Selected and edited by Irwin Edman. New York: Random House, 1928.

Poirer, Suzanne. "The Weir Mitchell Rest Cure: Doctor and Patients." In *Women's Studies* 10 (1983): 15–40.

Presser, Pam. "Golem as Metaphor: Symbolic Struggle and the Artificial Anthropoid." Ph.D. diss., George Washington University, 1999.

Progoff, Ira. *At a Journal Workshop: Writing to Access the Power of the Unconscious and Evoke Creative Ability.* New York: Putnam, 1992.

Raffa, Joseph. *Nightmare Begins Responsibility: The Poetry of Michael S. Harper.* New York: John Brown Press, 1990.

Ravikovitch, Dahlia. *A Dress of Fire.* Translated by Chana Bloch. New York: Sheep Meadow Press, 1978.

Rich, Adrienne. "When We Dead Awaken: Writing as Re-Vision." From *On Lies, Secrets, and Silences.* In *Ways of Reading: An Anthology for Writers,* edited by David Bartholomae and Anthony Petrosky. 5th ed. Boston: Bedford/St. Martin's, 1999.

Rist, J. M. *Eros and Psyche: Studies in Plato, Plotinus and Origen.* Toronto: University of Toronto Press, 1964.

Robinson, Paul. *Freud and His Critics*. Berkeley: University of California Press, 1993.

Rosenthal, M. L. *The Poet's Art*. New York: Norton, 1987.

Rothenberg, Albert. *Creativity and Madness*. Baltimore, Md.: Johns Hopkins University Press, 1990.

Ryan, Robert. "Keats and the Truth of Imagination." In *Wordsworth Circle*. Vol. IV, 4 (259–270).

Ryder, Phyllis Mentzell. "Disturbing Personal Boundaries." Unpublished paper.

Rzepka, Charles. *The Self as Mind: Vision and Identity in Wordsworth, Coleridge, and Keats*. Cambridge, Mass.: Harvard University Press, 1986.

St. John, David. *No Heaven*. Boston: Houghton Mifflin, 1985.

Scott Lee, Jonathan. *Jacques Lacan*. Boston: 1990.

Sexton, Anne. *The Complete Poems*. Boston: Houghton Mifflin, 1981.

———. *The Death Notebooks*. Boston: Houghton Mifflin, 1974.

Sexton, Linda Gray, and Lois Ames, eds. *Ann Sexton: A Self-Portrait in Letters*. Boston: Houghton Mifflin, 1977.

Shelley, Mary. *Frankenstein or the Modern Prometheus*, edited by Johanna M. Smith. New York: St. Martin's Press, 1992.

Shellnut, Eve. "Notes from a Cell." In *Creative Writing in America: Theory and Pedagogy*, edited by Joseph M. Moxley. Urbana, Ill.: National Council of Teachers of English.

Skura, Meredith Anne. *The Literary Use of the Psychoanalytic Process*. New Haven, Conn.: Yale University Press, 1981.

Smith, Paul. *Discerning the Subject: Theory and History of Literature*. Foreword by John Mowit. Vol. 55. Minneapolis: University of Minnesota Press, 1988.

Smyth, Joshua, Arthur Stone, and Adam Hurewitz. "Effects of Writing about Stressful Experiences on Symptom Reduction in Patients with Asthma or Rheumatoid Arthritis: A Randomized Trial." *Journal of the American Medical Association* 281, no. 2 (April 14, 1999): 1305–1309.

Snodgrass, W. D. "Interview with Elizabeth Spires." *American Poetry Review* 19, no. 4 (July 1990): 38–46.

Stevens, Wallace. "Palm at the End of the Mind." In *Selected Poems and a Play*, edited by Holly Stevens. New York: Random House, Vantage Books, 1972 w. ca.

Stone, Alan. "Freud's Vision." *Harvard Magazine* (Jan./Feb.1977): 39–42.

Terada, Rei. *Derek Walcott's Poetry: American Mimicry*. Boston: Northeastern University Press, 1992.

Tobin, Lad. "Reading Students, Reading Ourselves: Revising the Teacher's Role in the Writing Class." In *The Writing Teacher Sourcebook*, edited by Nancy Myers, Edward P. J. Corbett, and Gary Tate. New York: Oxford University Press, 1994.

———. *Writing Relationships*. Portsmouth, N. H.: Heinemann, Boynton, Cook, 1999.

Vendler, Helen. "Poet of Two Worlds." *New York Times Review of Books*, March 4, 1982: 23–27.

Walcott, Derek. *Another Life*. New York: Farrar, Straus and Giroux, 1973.

———. *Collected Poems 1948–1984*. New York: Noonday Press, Farrar, Straus and Giroux, 1988.

_____. *Dream on Monkey Mountain and Other Plays*. New York: Farrar, Straus and Giroux, 1970.

———. "Gros-Ilet." *Literary Review*, 29 (1985): 256.

Waldroff, Leon. "The Theme of Mutability in the 'Ode to Psyche.'" *PMLA* (1977): 410–419.

(Wallen, Ruth. "Memory Politics: The Implications of Healing from Sexual Abuse." *Tikkun* (Nov./Dec. 1994).)

Ward, Aileen. *John Keats: The Making of a Poet*. New York: Viking, 1963.

Wallingford, Katherine. *Robert Lowell's Language of the Self*. Chapel Hill: University of North Carolina Press, 1988.

Welch, Nancy. "No Apology: Challenging the Uselessness of Creative Writing." *Journal of Composition Theory* 19 no. 1 (1999): 117–134.

———. "Playing with Reality: Writing Centers after the Mirror Stage." CCC 51, no. 1 (1999): 51–69.

Young-Bruehl, Elisabeth. *The Anatomy of Prejudices*. Cambridge, Mass.: Harvard University Press, 1996.

———. *Anna Freud: A Biography*. New York: Norton, 1988.

Young-Bruehl, Elisabeth, with Faith Bethelard. *Cherishment: A Psychology of the Heart*. New York: Free Press, 2000.

INDEX

Aberbach, David, 60
Abuse: childhood, 75; collusion of society in, 75; domestic, 31, 59, 73-74, 77; family, 76-77; law and, 78; masochism and, 75; parental, 100, 102; physical, 13; reaction to, 75; revenge and, 102; sexual, 13, 59, 75, 88, 260n3; symptoms of, 75
Aetiology of Hysteria, The (Freud), 43
"Affirmation" (Hall), 249
Aggression: theories of, 87
Ai, 100, 101, 102
Alcorn, Marshall, 260n19
Alienation: post-mirror stage of, 205, 206; of self, 26; source of, 123
Ambivalence, 180; in fetish, 86
"American History" (Harper), 155, 156
American Poetry Anthology, The (Halpern), 192
Anatomy of Prejudices, The (Young-Bruehl), 251
Anderson, Charles, 12, 56
Another Life (Walcott), xiii, 120-133
Anti-intellectualism, 191
An Unquiet Mind (Jamison), xii, 240
Anxiety, 96, 240; castration, 90, 259n3; confessional writing and, 69; control of, 53; defense, 44; memory and, 31; as repetition of old childhood injuries, 82; separation, 143
Apuleius, 141, 143, 147, 151
Ariel (Plath), 71
Art: allusions to political realities, 129; discourse of, 182; of dying, 70; exorcism of pain through, 31; healing powers of, 35-36; language of, 123, 169; pain as catalyst for, 19; power to rename colonial world and, 132; re-creation of distressing experiences in, 178; as substitute form of gratification,

197; transcendence of life by, 3; unconscious expression in, 11
Attachment and Loss (Bowlby), 143
Axelrod, Steven, 24

"Beekeeper's Daughter, The" (Plath), 85
Bell Jar, The (Plath), 115
Berlin, James, 9, 10
Berman, Jeffrey, 8, 10, 33, 38, 52, 177, 198, 205, 217, 256; on empathy, 199, 207; personal testimony and, 203; on risk, 215; *Risky Writing,* 214; on self-disclosure in writing, 207; *Surviving Literary Suicide,* 203, 204; on Sylvia Plath, 85; *Talking Cure, The,* 261n9; use of student diary writing, 208, 261n9; writing method of, 199
Bethelard, Faith, 33
Bettleheim, Bruno, 135, 142
Beuscher, Ruth, 85
"Billy" (McCarriston), 76-77
Bishop, Elizabeth, 184-185, 225, 226-227, 228
Bishop, Wendy, 191, 192
"Black Spring" (Harper), 161
Blame: indeterminacy of, 71
Blood: as women's curse, 102
Bogan, Louise, 22, 230, 231
Boundaries: drawn by others, 219; ego, 116; personal, 38, 40, 162; psychiatric violation of, 38, 40, 41, 52; transgression of, 81-82; traversing, xii
Bowlby, John, 143
Bracher, Mark, 4, 19, 198, 205, 206, 217, 256; on role of teacher, 210; on transference, 214; *Writing Cure, The,* 215
Brawne, Fanny, 135, 137, 138, 139, 140, 142, 148, 149, 151

recourse for, 157; revenge as remedy for, 102; of separation, 150-151; as signification, 147; signification of, xi, 7, 20, 32, 36, 249-253; social, 154; social/political dimension of, 15; soul awakened by, 159; transcendence through art, 162; transformation, 185; triumph over, 158; validation of, 6; writing through, xi

Pappenheim, Bertha, 24

"Parisitism and Civilised Vice" (Gilman), 53

Patriarchy, 48, 56, 81; anger at, 83; assumptions of, 82; circumventing, 266n6; fixation with father and, 82; language of, xiii; rhetorical codes in, 82; stereotypes of women in, 101; structures of culture in, 82

Paz, Octavio, 251

Pennebaker, James, 12, 200, 204

Persecution: absorbing the truth of other's, 14

"Pippa's Passes" (Browning), 114

Plath, Otto, 88, 90

Plath, Sylvia, xi, 7, 27, 31, 220; anger toward father in works, 85, 87, 92, 93; on anguish, 34; *Ariel,* 71; "Beekeeper's Daughter, The," 85; bellicosity of, 83; *Bell Jar, The,* 115; castration fear and, 90; "Colossus, The," 85, 86, 87, 94; confessional writing of, 61, 68; "Daddy," 11, 28, 70, 71, 89, 92, 93, 94, 99, 100; death of father, 86, 88, 90; disappointment in relationships with men, 86, 92; dramatic monologues and, 181; Electra complex and, 88, 89, 92; "Electra in Black," 85; fears of inadequacy, 92; flawed relationship with father, 87, 88; grief of, 89; on history, 25; hospitalization, 224, 229; images of men by, 84; interest in cruelty, 28; "Lady Lazarus," 114-115, 117; language of patriarchy and, xiii; "Mary's Song," 28-29, 30; "Miss Drake Proceeds to Supper," 229, 230; resentment of male power in writing, 91; shifting blame for suffering by, 30; suicidal urges of, 114, 115, 229; technical achievements, 91; use of analysis, 85; use of Jewish survivor as analogy of oppression, 70

Plato, 146

"Poem You Asked For, The" (Levis), 193

"Poet of Two Worlds" (Vendler), 126

Poetry: African-American, 157; amalgamation of jazz/blues into, 157-165; anguish as central force of, 68; autobiographical, 116, 154; confessional, 61; conflict resolution and, 7; conversation, 194-195; dissociating from emotion, 116; as dramatic monologue, 110; empathy and, 22; as escape from emotion, 116; as expression of personality, 116; as force, 106; forgiveness and, 77; healing power of, 35-36; incest, 75; meaning of, 5; as mode of self-dramatization, 30; as outgrowth of emotion, 11; personal tragedy in, 135; politicism of, 68; power of, 182; religious, 67; revision in, 182-183; self-dramatization in, 30; as self-portraiture, 221; student, 211-214; therapeutic use of, 22; of witness, 153

Poovey, Mary, 83

"Porphyria's Lover" (Browning), 113, 114

"Portrait of a Lady" (Pound), 229

Postmodernism, 7; challenges to meaning and, xiii; dramatic monologue in, 117; emergent self in, 33; emphasis on language as constructive of self, 118; mimicry and, 131; views of self in, 117

Poststructuralism: boundaries in, 195; writing and subjectivity in, 194

Post-traumatic stress syndrome, 59, 265n21

Pound, Ezra, 171, 225, 227

power of poetry: as disconnected unconscious signifiers, 182

Practice of Poetry, The (Behn and Twitchell), 177, 178, 186

Prejudices, 251

Preliminary Communication (Freud), 32, 46

Prelude, The (Wordsworth), 63

"Preludes" (Eliot), 230

Presser, Pam, 215

Progoff, Ira, 202

"Prostitute" (Ai), 101

Psychoanalysis: assuaging painful symptoms in, 23, 24; bringing disorder into order in, 31; confessional writing and, 11-12, 19-36; criticism of, 82; exploitation of patients in, 42-43; fantasy in, 53; as form of confession, 177; free association in, 39-40, 49, 197; goals of, 40, 81; hypnosis in, 40, 42, 44, 47; insights into behavior in, xiii; interpretation in, 40; isolation of traumatic events in, 44; language and, 11-12; listening to one's self in, 92; literature and, 86; narrative

identification and, 10; prohibitions and,
10; redemptive quality of, 1; risk in, 203;
as testimonial, 1; therapeutic, 202
Writing, women's: aggression and, 81-106;
aggressive fantasies directed at men in,
106; articulation of male body in, 84;
challenge to gender ideology in, 83;
consistency in, 84; double vision in, 84;
expression of emotion in, 83; literary
criticism and, 83; man as "law" and, 81;
misogyny and, 81; rage at oedipal father
and, 81-106; representations of men in,
84; reversion of gender roles in, 84;
thetorical strategies in, 83; unconscious
patterns in, 96
*Writing and Healing toward an Informed
Practice* (Anderson and MacCurdy), 12, 13

Writing as a Way of Healing (DeSalvo), 12
Writing Cure, The (Bracher), 205, 206,
215, 256
"Writing the Wounded Psyche" (DeSalvo), 37

"Yellow Wallpaper, The" (Gilman), 8, 9,
15, 31, 37-38, 48-57, 99; as case study,
56; denial of outlet for fantasy in, 53;
depiction of mental illness in, 48;
exploitation of wife's illness in, 48; fantasy of control of male figure in, 95; free
association in, 49, 54; language use in,
51; patient's reclining position in, 51;
scene as place of secrecy and, 54; self-
projection in, 49
Young-Bruehl, Elisabeth, 33, 91, 92, 250,
251, 252